Contents*

*   The contents listed correspond to the Eduqas Full A Level
    Specification which matches equivalent WJEC A2 Specification as follows:

    Eduqas Theme 1: D,E,F = WJEC Theme 1: A,B,C

    Eduqas Theme 3: A,B,C = WJEC Theme 2: A,B, and Theme 3: A

    Eduqas Theme 3: D,E,F = WJEC Theme 3: B,C and Theme 2: C

    Eduqas Theme 4: D,E,F = WJEC Th

About this book

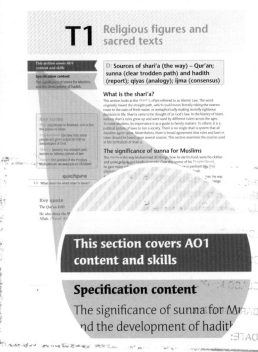

With the new A Level in Religious Studies, there is a lot to cover and a lot to do in preparation for the examinations at A Level. The aim of these books is to provide enough support for you to achieve success at A Level, whether as a teacher or a learner, and build upon the success of the Year 1 and AS series.

Once again, the Year 2 and A2 series of books is skills-based in its approach to learning, which means it aims to continue combining coverage of the Specification content with examination preparation. In other words, it aims to help you get through the second half of the course whilst at the same time developing some more advanced skills needed for the examinations.

To help you study, there are clearly defined sections for each of the AO1 and AO2 areas of the Specification. These are arranged according to the Specification Themes and use, as far as is possible, Specification headings to help you see that the content has been covered for A Level.

The AO1 content is detailed but precise, with the benefit of providing you with references to both religious/philosophical works and to the views of scholars. The AO2 responds to the issues raised in the Specification and provides you with ideas for further debate, to help you develop your own critical analysis and evaluation skills.

Ways to use this book

In considering the different ways in which you may teach or learn, it was decided that the books needed to have an inbuilt flexibility to adapt. As a result, they can be used for classroom learning, for independent work by individuals, as homework, and they are even suitable for the purposes of 'flipped learning' if your school or college does this.

You may be well aware that learning time is so valuable at A Level and so we have also taken this into consideration by creating flexible features and activities, again to save you the time of painstaking research and preparation, either as teacher or learner.

Features of the books

The books all contain the following features that appear in the margins, or are highlighted in the main body of the text, in order to support teaching and learning.

Key terms of technical, religious and philosophical words or phrases

> ### Key terms
> Hajj: pilgrimage to Makkah, one of the five pillars of Islam

Quickfire questions simple, straightforward questions to help consolidate key facts about what is being digested in reading through the information

> ### quickfire
> 1.1 What does the word shari'a mean?

Key quotes either from religious and philosophical works and/or the works of scholars

> ### Key quote
> My ummah will never agree upon an error.
> (Hadith of Prophet Muhammad)

WJEC/Eduqas

Religious Studies
for A Level Year 2 & A2

Islam

Idris Morar

Edited by Richard Gray

Illuminate
Publishing

Published in 2017 by Illuminate Publishing Ltd, PO Box 1160, Cheltenham, Gloucestershire GL50 9RW

Orders: Please visit www.illuminatepublishing.com
or email sales@illuminatepublishing.com

© Idris Morar

The moral rights of the author have been asserted.

All rights reserved. No part of this book may be reprinted, reproduced or utilised in any form or by any electronic, mechanical, or other means, now known or hereafter invented, including photocopying and recording, or in any information storage and retrieval system, without permission in writing from the publishers.

British Library Cataloguing-in-Publication Data

A catalogue record for this book is available from the British Library

ISBN 978-1-911208-37-2

Printed by Barley Press, Cuffley, Herts

11.17

The publisher's policy is to use papers that are natural, renewable and recyclable products made from wood grown in sustainable forests. The logging and manufacturing processes are expected to conform to the environmental regulations of the country of origin.

Every effort has been made to contact copyright holders of material reproduced in this book. If notified, the publishers will be pleased to rectify any errors or omissions at the earliest opportunity.

This material has been endorsed by WJEC/Eduqas and offers high quality support for the delivery of WJEC/Eduqas qualifications. While this material has been through a WJEC/Eduqas quality assurance process, all responsibility for the content remains with the publisher.

WJEC/Eduqas examination questions are reproduced by permission from WJEC/Eduqas

Series editor: Richard Gray
Editor: Geoff Tuttle
Design and Layout: EMC Design Ltd, Bedford

Acknowledgements

Cover Image: © weerasak saeku / Shutterstock

Image credits:

p. 1 © weersak saeku / Shutterstock; **p. 7** Brent Hofacker; **p. 9** Yulia_B; **p. 10** Alexander Snahovskyy; **p. 11** Jasminko Ibrakovic; **p. 12** NAPI WAN ALI; **p. 13** ESB Professional; **p. 15** Creative commons; **p. 16** Kolliadzynska Iryna; **p. 22** ZouZou; **p. 23** Leonid Andronov; **p. 24** Public domain; **p. 25** Simon Veit-Wilson, Creative commons; **p. 27** VFXArabia; **p. 29** Paul Fearn / Alamy Stock Photo; **p. 30** Jeff Morgan 16 / Alamy Stock Photo; **p. 39** Paul Fearn / Alamy Stock Photo; **p. 40** (top) ZouZou; **p. 40** (bottom) FS Stock; **p. 41** Paul Fearn / Alamy Stock Photo; **p. 42** Illustrator; **p. 44** (top) ServingIslam / Creative commons; **p. 44** (bottom) Frankie Fouganthin / Creative commons; **p. 45** Public domain; **p. 48** Leonid Andronov; **p. 50** Orlok / Shutterstock.com; **p. 54** hikrcn; **p. 55** Public domain; **p. 56** (top) muhammad afzan bin awing; **p. 56** (bottom) Public domain; **p. 57** Quick Shot; **p. 58** Creative commons; **p. 60** (top) dpa picture archive / Alamy Stock Photo; **p. 60** (bottom) Jyrl Engestrom; **p. 61** Kzenon; **p. 69** (top) Public domain; **p. 69** (bottom) Koca Vehbi; **p. 70** Dudarev Mikhail; **p. 71** kossarev56; **p. 72** (top) Anton Jankovoy; **p. 72** (bottom) Orren Jack Turner, Public domain; **p. 72** emc; **p. 73** Creative commons; **p. 74** Aisylu Ahmadieva; **p. 75** Public domain; **p. 82** Sonia Halliday Photo Library / Alamy Stock Photo; **p. 81** Belish / Shutterstock.com; **p. 84** Courtesy of the Imam; **p. 88** (top) Lmspencer; **p. 88** (bottom) Creative commons; **p. 93** Creative commons; **p. 103** michaeljung; **p. 104** (top) a katz / Shutterstock.com; **p. 104** (bottom) AHMAD FAIZAL YAHYA; **p. 105** Zurijeta; **p. 107** manzrussali; **p. 109** Photos RM / Alamy Stock Photo; **p. 114** oneinchpunch; **p. 116** Gage Skidmore / Creative commons; **p. 118** (top) Public domain; **p. 118** (bottom) BasPhoto; **p. 122** ChameleonsEye / Shutterstock.com; **p. 123** Zurijeta; **p. 124** Tupungato; **p. 126** Yusnizam Yusof / Shutterstock.com; **p. 128** Brian Minkoff / Shutterstock.com; **p. 130** Ayoub Khiari – Kayor; **p. 131** veroxdale / Shutterstock.com; **p. 136** Anthony Ricci / Shutterstock.com; **p. 137** Ministry of Justice, Open Government Licence; **p. 138** (top) JStone / Shutterstock.com; **p. 138** (bottom) ZoneCreative; **p. 140** lev radin / Shutterstock.com; **p. 141** GraphicsRF; **p. 142** Robert Fowler; **p. 146** Rena Schild / Shutterstock.com; **p. 150** Zurijeta; **p. 151** thomas koch / Shutterstock.com; **p. 154** imeduard / Shutterstock.com; **p. 155** thomas koch / Shutterstock.com; **p. 156** Prometheus72 / Shutterstock.com; **p. 158** BalkansCat / Shutterstock.com; **p. 162** Fotokon; **p. 164** Leonid Andronov; **p. 167** klenger; **p. 168** (top) Martchan / Shutterstock.com; **p. 168** (bottom) mdsharma / Shutterstock.com; **p. 169** Martchan / Shutterstock.com; **p. 171** hikrcn; **p. 172** (top) Lenar Musin; **p. 172** (bottom) Kevin Eaves; **p. 173** Martchan / Shutterstock.com; **p. 174** evantravels / Shutterstock.com; **p. 176** Saida Shigapova; **p. 179** Turkey Photo / Shutterstock.com; **p. 181** thomas koch / Shutterstock.com; **p. 182** (top) Tannison Pachtanom; **p. 182** (bottom) Public domain; **p. 184** Lipik; **p. 185** Joshua Sherurcij; **p. 186** CRSS PHOTO / Shutterstock.com; **p. 190** Klemen Misic / Shutterstock.com; **p. 192** meunierd / Shutterstock.com

Study tips advice on how to study, prepare for the examination and answer questions

Study tip

It is vital for AO2 that you actually discuss arguments and not just explain what someone may have stated. Try to ask yourself, 'was this a fair point to make?', 'is the evidence sound enough?', 'is there anything to challenge this argument?', 'is this a strong or weak argument?' Such critical analysis will help you develop your evaluation skills.

AO1 Activities that serve the purpose of focusing on identification, presentation and explanation, and developing the skills of knowledge and understanding required for the examination

AO1 Activity

After reading the sections above on what is shari'a and the significance of the sunna for Muslims, make definitions of sunna and shari'a. What are the similarities and differences between them? Try to think of three similarities and three differences.

AO2 Activities that serve the purpose of focusing on conclusions, as a basis for thinking about the issues, developing critical analysis and the evaluation skills required for the examination

AO2 Activity

As you read through this section try to do the following:

1. Pick out the different lines of argument that are presented in the text and identify any evidence given in support.

Glossary of all the key terms for quick reference.

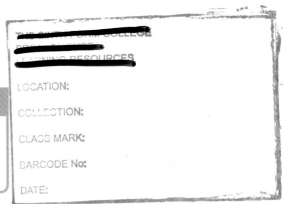

Specific feature: Developing skills

This section is very much a focus on 'what to do' with the content and the issues that are raised. They occur at the end of each section, giving 12 AO1 and 12 AO2 activities that aim to develop particular skills that are required for more advanced study at Year 2 and A2 stage.

The Developing skills for Year 2 and A2 are grouped so that each Theme has a specific focus to develop and perfect gradually throughout that Theme.

AO1 and AO2 answers and commentaries

The final section has a selection of answers and commentaries as a framework for judging what an effective and ineffective response may be. The comments highlight some common mistakes and also examples of good practice so that all involved in teaching and learning can reflect upon how to approach examination answers.

Richard Gray
Series Editor
2017

AO1 Developing skills

It is now important to consider section; however, the informati be processed in order to meet be done by practising more ˙at run throughout this ' ˙nation. For as˙

T1 Religious figures and sacred texts

This section covers AO1 content and skills

Specification content

The significance of sunna for Muslims and the development of hadith.

D: Sources of shari'a (the way) – Qur'an; sunna (clear trodden path) and hadith (report); qiyas (analogy); ijma (consensus)

What is the shari'a?

This section looks at the **shari'a**, often referred to as Islamic Law. The word originally meant the straight path, which could mean literally taking the nearest route to the oasis of fresh water, or metaphorically making morally righteous decisions in life. Shari'a came to be thought of as God's law. In the history of Islam, various shari'a rules grew up and were used by different rulers across the ages. To some Muslims, its importance is as a guide to family matters. To others, it is a political system of laws to run a society. There is no single shari'a system that all Muslims agree upon. Nevertheless, there is broad agreement that rules and laws in Islam should be based upon several sources. This section examines the sources used in the formation of shari'a.

The significance of sunna for Muslims

The **sunna** is the way Muhammad did things: how he ate his food, wore his clothes and spoke politely and kindly to people. Over the course of his **Prophethood**, he gave many other examples including how to pray, how to perform the **Hajj** pilgrimage, and how to set up an organised community in Madinah.

Muhammad is not seen as a divine figure, yet he was not any ordinary man. He was the last and final messenger from Allah, which meant that he had Allah's blessings. He is thought of as a perfect person, providing a perfect example for Muslims to follow. Not just his message, but also his sayings and actions, are a template to copy.

The Qur'an is the direct word of God, however, the Qur'an does not contain any of the details that Muslims use to carry out their day-to-day practice. The methods of prayer, fasting and dealing with family relations, marriage and divorce, are all spelled out in the examples of Muhammad. The Qur'an itself tells Muslims to obey Muhammad, the messenger, thereby justifying the sunna.

The Qur'an is the unquestionable word of God according to Muslim scholars, important for finding out the answers to everything. The translator Abdel Haleem in his introduction to the Qur'an describes its importance as 'fundamental and paramount'.

Key quote

The Qur'an is the supreme authority in Islam. It is the fundamental and paramount source of the creed, rituals, ethics, and laws of the Islamic religion. It is the hook that 'differentiates' between right and wrong, so that nowadays, when the Muslim world is dealing with such universal issues as globalisation, the environment, combating terrorism and drugs, issues of medical ethics and feminism, evidence to support the various arguments is sought in the Qur'an. This supreme status stems from the belief that the Qur'an is the word of God,

Key terms

Hajj: pilgrimage to Makkah, one of the five pillars of Islam

Prophethood: the idea that some people are given a special role as messengers of God

Shari'a: literally, the straight path; known as Islamic system of law

Sunna: the actions of the Prophet Muhammad, an example for Muslims

quickfire

1.1 What does the word shari'a mean?

Key quote

The Qur'an 4:80

He who obeys the Messenger, obeys Allah. **(Yusuf Ali)**

revealed to the Prophet Muhammad via the archangel Gabriel, and intended for all times and all places. (Haleem)

Some scholars have questioned the origins of the Qur'an, the way of reciting it, and alternative versions which existed in the early days of Islam under Caliph Uthman. Alfred Guillaume suggests Muslims need to face up to the problems of understanding the origin of the Qur'an, just as the Christian West did with the Bible at the time of the Reformation.

The vast majority of Muslims accept the Qur'an unconditionally and look to it as the ultimate source of knowledge. The interpretations of other topics which follow are based on this assumption.

AO1 Activity

After reading the sections above on what is shari'a and the significance of the sunna for Muslims, make definitions of sunna and shari'a. What are the similarities and differences between them? Try to think of three similarities and three differences.

The development of hadith

Key quote

One day I came to meet Imam Bukhari and asked him: 'Are you the person who has memorised seventy thousand hadith?' Imam Bukhari replied: 'I have learned more than this off by heart! I even

Muslims eat dates to open their Ramadan fast

know the place of birth, death and residence of most of those companions from whom the hadith are narrated.' (Sulayman ibn Mujahid)

The Qur'an itself is God's words and instructions to the Prophet, but it does not tell us very much about the Prophet himself. For that, Muslims need to turn to another source, the hadith. Unlike the Qur'an, the hadith is not a holy book and is not the word of Allah.

During the lifetime of Muhammad, the people closest to him were known as his sahaba, the companions. After his death, they often related stories and sayings from the Prophet. Over time these were passed on by word of mouth to others. It is thought that some sayings may have begun to be written down under the third Caliph or ruler of Muslims after Muhammad, Caliph Uthman. Written down copies from this period do not survive today.

Two hundred years after Muhammad's death, arguments flared up about the sayings of the Prophet. Thousands of hadith were talked about. There was a fear that some hadith were forged or inaccurate, based on someone's opinion and not on what the Prophet had said. To clear up the confusion, several scholars set out to compile what they saw were the authentic or real hadith.

Key quote

Uthman's edition to this day remains the authoritative word of God to Muslims. Nevertheless, even now variant readings, involving not only different reading of the vowels but also occasionally a different consonantal text, are recognised as of equal authority one with another. The old Kufic script in which the Quran was originally written contained no indication of vowels, and so the consonants of verbs could be read as actives or passives, and, worse still, many of the consonants themselves could not be distinguished without the diacritical dots which were afterwards added, when and by whom we do not know. … Originally considerable freedom prevailed, until a later generation insisted on uniformity but never entirely achieved it … The Muslim world has not yet come to grips with the problem which Christian Europe faced after the Renaissance. (Guillaume)

Key terms

Hadith: a saying of the Prophet Muhammad

Sahaba: those who lived around Muhammad and witnessed his actions

quickfire

1.2   Where did Bukhari travel to?

Key terms

Bukhari: a collection of hadith named after the most famous collector Bukhari from Uzbekistan, who lived from 810 to 870

Qur'anism: to follow the teachings of the Qur'an but reject the hadith as a source of authority

Hadith collections

Imam **Bukhari** was one of the most famous collectors of hadith. Bukhari was born in Uzbekistan. His father had been a scholar who studied Muhammad's sayings, but died when Bukhari was still young. Despite this, his mother arranged the Hajj pilgrimage when Bukhari reached the age of 16. Bukhari had a passion for scholarship and set out after Hajj to travel the Middle East in search of hadith. He went to Makkah, Madinah, Baghdad, Jerusalem, Damascus and Egypt. His tour took him 16 years. He brought what he found back to Samarkand where he compiled his collection of hadith.

Muslim ibn al-Hajjaj became a student of Imam Bukhari and produced his own collection of hadith, drawing on the work of his master. Others made further collections. One such collection was made by Abu Dawood, who spent 20 years travelling the Middle East collecting vast numbers of hadith then reducing them to what he thought were the most reliable. Sunni Muslims regard six major collections of hadith to be the most reliable.

Shi'a Muslims have different collections of hadith, though the content is similar. Shi'a Muslims' collections do not include hadith that have been passed on by those who opposed Caliph Ali. Shi'a regard Caliph Ali as the first legitimate ruler after Muhammad, and his descendants thereafter. Any hadith narrated by enemies of the party of Ali, the Shi'a, could not be accepted.

All of this means that unlike the Qur'an, there is no single version of hadith that all Muslims agree on. This has led some Muslims to follow **Qur'anism**. Qur'anists do not accept any hadith at all. Qur'anist Muslims claim that only the Qur'an, the word of God, should be used as guidance. The traditional Sunni Muslim scholar Khaled Abou el Fadl refutes the ideas of Qur'anist Rashad Khalifa by saying that the hadith are essential for understanding the context of the revelations of the Qur'an.

Key quotes

The religion of Islam (Submission to God alone) has been severely corrupted. More than 200 years after Prophet Muhammad's death, the human being started to innovate some man-made doctrines and lies and falsely attributed them to the prophet and to this great religion. Over the years, these innovations (Hadith and Sunna) have become an official source of laws and Sharia besides the Quran in most of the so-called Islamic countries. It has been proclaimed that Quran alone is not enough as a source of law. **(Khalifa)**

Many of the narratives that contextualise the revelations of the Qur'an and that set out the broad historical experiences in Mecca and Medina and record testimonials about how the early generations of Muslims understood and practised their faith are part of the hadith and sunna that the Qur'anists wish to excise and abolish. But doing so will solve little, if anything, because it will leave the text of the Qur'an standing alone without its history, the circumstances that motivated it, and the challenges that inspired it, and questions relating to intentionality, purposefulness, and objective will become far more difficult to resolve. **(Abou el Fadl)**

Since the hadith are so wide ranging, it is possible for Muslims to follow the hadith but make quite different selections that they refer to, and different interpretations as a result. Here, we will focus on the main categories of hadith and how they became judged reliable within the mainstream body of Muslim opinion in the ninth and tenth centuries, the period during which the main collections were formed.

The different categories of hadith

Key quote

My servant draws near to me until I love him. And when I love him, I am his hearing with which he hears and his sight with which he sees. (Hadith qudsi of Prophet Muhammad)

There are different ways of categorising the hadith. If you were to pick up a copy of a hadith collection, you might find that within it there are divisions into various chapters based on themes or topics: prayer, good manners, marriage and so on. This helps the user to look up topics but is not the way the hadith are actually categorised. For centuries, hadith have been divided according to how reliable Muslim scholars believe they are.

The most reliable hadith are called sahih hadith. They have been verified by scholars as being said by Muhammad and accurately repeated by word of mouth from person to person to the point at which they were written down. Hasan hadith are good hadith which are generally reliable except for a minor question mark here and there. Daif hadith are weak hadith, which scholars had doubts about. There are other hadith thought to be fabricated.

Some of the hadith narrated by Muhammad have special status because he was directly inspired by Allah at the time. These are known as hadith qudsi. They are said to be Muhammad's words on Allah's direct inspiration, but not the words of God which form the Qur'an. The word wahy in Arabic is used for both revelation and inspiration. The Qur'an is seen as the directly revealed word of Allah. Allah can also give messengers good thoughts, or inspiration, about what to say. They put the thoughts in their own words, but the ideas or inspiration originated with God.

There are some traditions of sayings from other Prophets, including a small collection of hadith of Prophet Isa, Jesus. Other traditions are available of the companions of Muhammad, who as people closest to him left valuable stories about their lives and interaction with the Prophet. Neither of these form part of the literature that formulate the shari'a. It is the reliability of Muhammad's sayings that is important, and is determined by an examination of the content of the text and by the reliability of the people who heard and passed on each message.

The overall reliability of text

By reading any book, how would you know it is true? You might research the subject and find other sources, and cross reference them. You might look for factual accuracy, to see if any of the details are wrong. You could see if any of the details are out of place, belong to a different time, or might be biased. In the modern world, academic research has developed historical critical methods of analysing text. These are not the same as the methods applied by Muslims to the hadith. Islamic scholars around 1100 years ago lived in a very different age and applied the best methods of their time to determine the accuracy of hadith texts. The text of a hadith was known as the matn, and particular methods were used to check its reliability.

Hadith scholars regarded the Qur'an, without question, as the most reliable reference point. First and foremost, the details of any hadith were compared to the teachings in the Qur'an. No hadith could be allowed which contradicted the Qur'an, since this would be going against the word of God.

Specification content
The different categories of hadith in relation to the overall reliability of text and chain of transmission.

Memorial to Bukhari, Samarkand, Uzbekistan

Key terms

Bias: the idea that a person might be unfair or one-sided, and reflect this in what they say

Daif: a weak hadith, thought of as unreliable because of questions about the chain of transmitters

Hadith qudsi: sayings of Muhammad that are thought to have been directly inspired by Allah

Hasan: hadith which have been collected and are thought of as good with the exception of one or two minor questions about their authenticity

Historical critical: modern methods of understanding sources by analysing context, bias and cross referencing

Isa: the Arabic word for Jesus, who is regarded as a Prophet in Islam

Matn: the body of text within a hadith

Sahih: the best and most reliable hadith, which have been collected with a reliable chain of transmitters

Wahy: revelation, also inspiration to Prophets

quickfire

1.3 Why might the content of a hadith be rejected?

The reliability of the text of the hadith

As hadith collections formed which had been established as reliable, newly found hadith could not be accepted if they contradicted established hadith. Hadith were rejected if they appeared to support a particular tribe or family, since they were biased. Hadith which appeared to refer to later events or were more extreme than the Qur'an in any matter were also rejected.

People who lived in Arabia at the time of Muhammad and the early Muslims lived largely in tribes. They were expected to follow a man, as head of the tribe; to believe in the religion and customs of the tribe; and to be loyal to it. It was expected to promote the tribe and hide any misdemeanour that someone in your tribe committed. That made it harder for hadith collectors to sort out the truth, but all the more remarkable that they actively looked to disengage Muhammad's comments from corruption by tribal loyalty.

Hadith collectors were applying rational thought during the Islamic Golden Age, when Muslims were translating texts from the ancient world. However, this was not truly logical. Sayings of the Prophet appeared over 23 years in response to a variety of different times and circumstances. In vast collections of hadith, many do not appear to agree with others, despite the best efforts of the collectors. Commentaries have been produced to help understand the context of hadiths and make sense of the collections.

The chain of transmission

Just as important as the text of any hadith is who passed it on, the narrator. Since it was over two hundred years from the first sayings to the hadith collections, this meant that several people passed it on. These form the chain of narrators or isnad. To establish the chain of narrators was just as important for verifying the reliability of the hadith as the subject matter.

To pass the checks, each hadith should have been heard by a companion of the Prophet, a trusted person who lived with him and knew exactly what he said. There should be an unbroken list of names of who told who the saying. If there was a gap, then the hadith would be rejected. Furthermore, each person in the chain should be regarded as honest. Those known to lie or spread rumours were rejected. Pious and honest Muslims were seen as the most reliable. Forgetful people, even if honest, were not trusted.

It is possible for the same saying of the Prophet to be narrated in several different hadiths. Muhammad was surrounded by many companions, who told their stories to their own followers, passing it down through different people. This would add to the probability of the hadith being reliable.

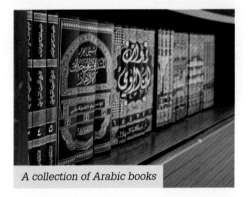
A collection of Arabic books

Key term

Isnad: the chain of transmitters, who passed on the hadith to who, all the way from the first person to hear Muhammad until the time the hadith was written down

quickfire

1.4 Give two reasons why narrators of a hadith might be accepted and two reasons why they might be rejected.

AO1 Activity

Draw a flow chart to show how the sayings of Muhammad ended up in the hadith collections. Include in the chart all the stages of checking that might be done by the hadith collector.

From a modern perspective, it could be questioned how reliable a chain of narrators could possibly be over such a long time span. Nevertheless, hadith collectors took their work seriously. When Bukhari travelled to Baghdad, a crowd gathered round and decided to test him. They mixed up hadith and hadith narrators to see if they could catch Bukhari out. He spotted every single error. Bukhari was reputed to have a photographic memory and lived in an age of oral tradition where it was common for people to memorise sayings off by heart.

Here is an example of a chain of narrators, known as an isnad, from the first hadith of Bukhari:

We have heard from Al-Humaydi Abdallah ibn al-Zubayr who said that he heard from Sufyan, who said he heard from Yahya ibn Sa'eed al-Ansari who said he was informed by Muhammad ibn Ibrahim al-Taymi that he heard 'Alqama ibn Waqqas al-Laythi say that he heard 'Umar ibn al-Khattab say on the sermon pulpit that he heard the Prophet Muhammad say: 'Actions are only by intentions...'

The hadith about Umm Warraqh

An example of debate over hadith and their authenticity can be seen from the following hadith. **Umm Warraqh** was a woman appointed to lead prayers over her ahl dariha. This could have meant her neighbourhood of hundreds of men and women, or perhaps her household of men and women, or perhaps just women. This might contradict with other hadith which suggest that only men should lead prayers. Yet men leading was part of the male-dominated tribal society at the time, so it could be argued that the hadith may be authentic because it cannot be taken from any tribal code of society. Some regard it as a hasan or good hadith because there is a chain of narrators with only a minor query; others that the query is that narrator Abdur Rahman is unknown so could be unreliable.

> Example of a debated hadith: hadith of Abu Dawud no. 592
>
> Al-Walid bin Jumaih reported from Abdur Rahman bin Khallad, reported from Umm Waraqah:

The Messenger of Allah used to visit Umm Warraqh at her house. He appointed a muzzein to call adhan for her; and he commanded her to lead ahl dariha in prayer.

This hadith is one controversial example. Of course, it could always be argued that faith and practice today need not literally follow the practice of 1400 years ago. Historical critical methods might interpret this tradition differently. However, for many Muslims, the example of the Prophet is so precious that they spend a great amount of time and energy trying to verify the authenticity of the hadith, so that they can best follow the perfect and final example: Muhammad.

Key details of Islamic faith and practice have their origin, in principle, in the Qur'an, and their detail in the hadith, as shown in the table.

Islamic teaching	Qur'an	Hadith
Daily Prayer	Tells Muslims to obey Allah and follow the Prophet. Stand devoutly before Allah at the beginning and end of the day.	Encourage Muslims to pray five times a day in the set sequence of standing, bowing and sitting, in the same way as the Prophet Muhammad prayed.
Fasting and Ramadan	States that fasting is advised for you to gain a sense of Allah and to remember the Night of Power, the first revelation of the Qur'an.	Muslims learn to fast from first light until sunset by not eating, drinking, telling lies or cheating. The ill do not need to fast.
Food and eating	Tells Muslims to eat meat slaughtered in a halal way, giving details mentioning the name of Allah and using a sharp blade.	Add details about how the Prophet ate using his right hand, beginning meals by saying Bismillah and eating calmly and respectfully, not over indulging.

Despite the vast collections of hadith, not all issues that Muslims face today are answered. Over time, Muslim scholars developed two further methods of establishing what Muslims should do in given situations which needed addressing. These were the methods of ijma and qiyas.

Key person

Umm Warraqh: a woman appointed to lead prayers by Muhammad in Madinah over her household or community, possibly including men and women.

Key term

Ahl dariha: home, or household, or community

A Muslim prostrating in prayer

Specification content

The development of qiyas and ijma.

Key terms

Fatwa: the opinion of an Islamic scholar on a matter, binding only on themselves and those who pledge allegiance

Ijma: agreeing a teaching by consensus of scholars or even the whole community

Qiyas: comparison to a similar situation to arrive at a teaching

Ulema: Islamic scholars

Key quote

My ummah will never agree upon an error. (Hadith of Prophet Muhammad)

quickfire

1.5 How was a successor appointed to Muhammad?

Key person

Abu Bakr: a companion of Muhammad and the first Caliph or leader of the Muslims after Muhammad, according to Sunni Muslims.

The development of ijma

The Qur'an and hadith are based on the revelations of Allah and the sayings of Muhammad between the years 610 and 633. So how did Muslims deal with issues that arose later, or with issues that did not appear to be clearly answered by the above sources? When the Prophet died, there was no agreed upon successor, so the companions of Muhammad met and eventually agreed between themselves on who should succeed. They chose **Abu Bakr**, according to Sunni Muslims. This coming together and agreeing an answer to a problem is called ijma.

The concept of voting for representatives or even directly to decide a matter, in a referendum, is something we are used to nowadays. Ijma is not the same as democracy, although some Muslims regard ijma as justification for asking the opinion of the whole Muslim community about an issue. However, Muslims are not completely free to decide the answer. They must choose according to what is allowed within the boundaries of the Qur'an and sunna.

The Qur'an and hadith are the primary sources for shari'a, and can never be over-ruled by secondary sources ijma and qiyas. This is because the first two sources originate with Allah and His messenger. Human beings can make mistakes and are not directly in contact with Allah, so they cannot overrule what has been revealed.

Different views about ijma

Some Muslims regard ijma as valid only to the first few generations of Muslims and the companions of the Prophet. This is because they either personally knew or knew people who were close to Muhammad, so could be trusted to decide matters in line with what he taught. There were various matters of religious practice which needed to be defined. All of the main details about how to pray the main five daily prayers were already determined by the Prophet. But the exact details about the Ramadan Taraweeh prayers and the Call to Prayer before the Friday prayers were defined by the ijma of the companions.

Other Muslims regard ijma as relating not just to matters of religious practice but also to social issues. Questions were asked about who it was permissible to marry. It was clear from the Qur'an that a Muslim man was not allowed to marry his daughters, mother or sisters, but what about the next generation? It was decided by ijma that it was also prohibited to marry grandmothers and granddaughters.

Ijma is often taken to mean the agreement of scholars. In modern times Islamic scholars, called Ulema, sometimes meet together and issue rulings called fatwas. However, it is disputed whether ijma can apply in the modern world and if so, if agreement between all scholars is needed or all Muslims in the entire world. Some Muslims regard the agreements of modern scholars on modern-day issues such as abortion and euthanasia as worthy of the status of ijma; others that they are just personal opinions with no status other than with the person who made them.

Shi'a Muslims give special status to the person of the Imam, who follows in the tradition of the family of the Prophet and is regarded as having the status to explain the meaning of the Qur'an without error. Interpretation should be carried out by leaders within this tradition for the Shi'a.

A meeting of Imams in Malaysia

The development of qiyas

A hadith in the collection of Imam Tirmidhi gives Muslims guidance on how to find the answer to questions. The Prophet spoke to his companion Mu'adh ibn Jabal to prepare him for his work as a governor of a province. He needed to know that Mu'adh would be able to decide matters sensibly when he did not have the Prophet around him to ask for help, since the province was far away. The Prophet asked Mu'adh how he would judge matters.

Mu'adh said: 'I will judge matters by what is in the Book of Allah, the Qur'an.'

The Prophet asked: 'But what if you do not find the answer in the Book of Allah?'

Mu'adh said: 'Then I will judge by the example of Allah's messenger, the sunna.'

The Prophet replied: 'But what if you do not find an answer in either the Qur'an or the sunna?'

Mu'adh said: 'Then I will decide according to my opinion.'

The Prophet was delighted and thanked Allah for giving him such a good governor in Mu'adh.

Qiyas is not just an opinion based on thought, but taken from an original teaching in the Qur'an or hadith and applied to a new situation. A woman called Al-Khath 'amiyyah came to Muhammad after her father had died. He had not had the opportunity to perform the Hajj pilgrimage. Al-Khath asked Muhammad if it would benefit him if she performed the Hajj for him. The Prophet replied by saying that it would benefit him if she paid off his debts in money, by comparison, Hajj is like a debt of devotion to God, so yes it would benefit him. Qiyas, then, involves comparison and reasoning to apply a teaching to a new situation.

Qiyas could be used to form your own opinions. Shi'a Muslims prefer to use the reasoned consensus of those in the family line of Muhammad whom they trust to make the best reasoned judgements. Not everyone can make interpretations. Shi'a follow the guidance of their appointed Imams who take qiyas one step further with logical reasoning.

Muslim women students

AO1 Activity

Make a summary of different interpretations of ijma and qiyas.

Refer to:

(1) consensus   (3) later scholars   (5) comparisons

(2) companions   (4) all Muslims   (6) reasoning.

What is fiqh?

If shari'a is Islamic Law, then **fiqh** is the way this law is interpreted. Shari'a law is God's law, which Muslims do not fully understand. Fiqh is a way of understanding it in detail and with depth. It is the nearest human beings can get to understanding God's laws. There are many books published entitled Islamic fiqh. They are different people's interpretation of Islamic Law, using the Qur'an, sunna and opinions of scholars. After the Prophet's death the early communities of Muslims established and expanded their communities. The companions of Muhammad decided what the key teachings meant in everyday application. Fiqh only really developed later on.

Specification content

The work of Al-Shafi in devising a methodology for fiqh (deep understanding) of shari'a.

Key term

Fiqh: interpretation or deeper understanding of Islamic Law

quickfire

1.6   Name the main four schools of Sunni Islamic fiqh.

Key terms

Abbasid: family who ruled the Islamic Empire during the eighth and ninth centuries when the schools of thought were founded

Hanbali: Sunni Islamic school of thought originating from the scholar Ahmad ibn Hanbal, 780–855

Hanifi: Sunni Islamic school of thought originating from the scholar Abu Hanifa, 702–772

Ibadi: an Islamic school of thought which is neither Shi'a nor Sunni but has elements of both

Ismaili: Shi'a Islamic school of thought originating from the scholar Al-Qadi al-Nu'man d. 974

Jafari: Shi'a Islamic school of thought originating from Imam Jafar al-Sadiq, c 700–765

Madhab: the name for a school of Islamic Law

Maliki: Sunni Islamic school of thought originating from the scholar Malik ibn Anas, 711–795

Shafi'i: Sunni Islamic school of thought originating from the scholar Al-Shafi, 767–820

Zaidiyyah: Shi'a Islamic school of thought originating from Zayd ibn Ali, 695–740

quickfire

1.7   In what ways did Al-Shafi influence the development of fiqh?

Around 150 years after Muhammad died, the Islamic empire became more settled after a period of expansion. Scholars had more time to think about and work out rulings, and these rulings became known as books of fiqh. Although there are some differences between the scholars' opinions, there are also many similarities. Both their teachings and their methods of using the Qur'an and sunna were important. As also was whether they took either a Shi'a or Sunni Muslim perspective.

There are four main schools of thought in Sunni Islam named after the four men who developed them. They were Abu Hanifa, Al-Shafi, Malik ibn Anas and Ahmad ibn Hanbal. The schools of fiqh named after them are known as the **Hanifi**, **Shafi'i**, **Maliki** and **Hanbali madhabs**. There are different schools of fiqh in Shi'a Islam. The main branches include the **Jafari**, the **Zaidiyyah**, and the **Ismaili**. A further school of thought called the **Ibadi** is distinct from both Shi'a and Sunni.

Al-Shafi's contribution to fiqh methodology

Key quote

True knowledge is not that which is memorised; it is that which benefits. (Al-Shafi)

One of the most influential Sunni Muslim scholars, who developed his own school of fiqh, was called Al-Shafi. Al-Shafi lived from 767 to 820. Al-Shafi was born in Gaza to a Yemeni mother. His father died when he was aged two, so his mother moved to Makkah to be nearer other members of her family. He was related to the family of the **Abbasid** rulers at the time, so well connected, but despite this he grew up in poverty. Al-Shafi was a brilliant student and was said to have learned the whole Qur'an off by heart by the age of seven. He became a student of Imam Malik, one of the four main scholars of Sunni fiqh. Al-Shafi studied for years under Imam Malik in Madinah. It was said that Al-Shafi had a photographic memory. He was a sharp marksman at archery and a skilled master at chess.

He then travelled to Baghdad where he discussed with scholars of the Hanifi school of thought in the medieval equivalent of the coffee shops of a bustling capital city. When the arguments got too much Shafi returned to Makkah where he gave talks about Islam at the great mosque around the Ka'aba. The scholar Ahmad ibn Hanbal listened to him there. In his travels and in his discussions with the founders of the other Sunni schools of thought, Al-Shafi greatly influenced the development of fiqh.

AO1 Activity

Imagine you were in a medieval coffee shop (or equivalent) in Baghdad, listening to one of Al-Shafi's arguments. Write an account of how Al-Shafi and another scholar argued. You may need to read down to the next page to understand the position of the other scholar you choose.

Al-Shafi defined sources of authority to be used in fiqh in order of priority. He said that the Qur'an, the word of God, must always come first. Second was the sunna of Muhammad. As the messenger of Allah and a final and perfect example for Muslims to follow, everything he did and said was regarded as a source of authority second only to the words of Allah. Thirdly, Al-Shafi accepted the ijma or agreement of the companions of Muhammad as an authority on issues. He also accepted the opinions of the companions of Muhammad, because they knew best the Prophet's teachings. He did not accept any traditions or customs of the companions; only those of Muhammad were used. He rejected local customs and traditions as they might draw a Muslim away from the practice of Muhammad. Lastly, Al-Shafi defined logical comparison, qiyas, as the next source to be used.

Al-Shafi lived at a time when the Abbasids ruled the Islamic world. People were interested in science and learning. He provided a step-by-step way of making sense of the teachings of Islam that could be formed into a fiqh or deeper understanding. This was a great step forward which ensured standardisation of shari'a which until his time had not been so developed. There were many areas in which Al-Shafi did not leave guidance. He did not work out the different teachings about how to conduct interfaith dialogue. His use of reasoned discussion was limited. No one could openly discuss with him whether or not God exists, or the Qur'an was really the word of God, because he lived in a religious age when these things could not be questioned. Therefore, his influence on the development of shari'a at the time was more than anyone else. He left behind him a fiqh which could be used in an organised way as a system of law.

The tomb of Imam Al-Shafi in Cairo, Egypt

The major law schools in applying fiqh within Islam

The Qur'an is based on revelation, not reasoning. Muslims accept it whether they think it makes sense or not. Some Islamic scholars also accept a form of reasoning to work things out. Reasoning does not always sit easily alongside revelation. Although, some argued, if there is one truth, then this can be found through both reasoning and revelation, and the answer will be the same. The use of reasoning and logical argument has been a point of contention between different Islamic thinkers through the ages. In the golden age of Islam under the Abbasids, reasoning was prized. Scholars met in the tea houses of Baghdad to discuss and work out the answers to theological questions. The prevailing ideas of the time were those of the Mutazilah, who believed that everything could be worked out through logic. Although they eventually fell out of favour, reasoning was still prevalent amongst the Muslim thinkers in Spain in the twelfth century. The scholar Al-Ghazali criticised it in his book, *The Incoherence of the Philosophers*. Interaction with them caused Al-Ghazali a crisis of faith, after which he threw away many of his collection of books and ushered in a new era in which reasoning was frowned upon in Sunni Islam.

You may have heard about the inquisition in the Christian Church, but there was also an inquisition in the Islamic world under Caliph Al-Mamun in the ninth century. He tried to order everyone to agree with the belief that the Qur'an was written by humans, not God, and put people who disagreed with him on trial. Today, in the Western world there is freedom of belief, so people can freely decide their own religious position, but for much of Islamic history this was not the case. During the Islamic inquisition, called the Mihna, some scholars such as Ahmad ibn Hanbal asked for the freedom to believe in traditional Islam. Yet today, followers of the Hanbali school of thought in countries such as Saudi Arabia, are not often associated with religious freedom.

Abu Hanifa lived in Iraq and spent his time discussing Islam with descendants of the companions who moved there. Similar to Al-Shafi, he defined the Qur'an as the most important source of shari'a since it was the word of Allah. Next came the hadith, followed by ijma and qiyas. Unlike Al-Shafi, Abu Hanifa thought it reasonable to allow differences in shari'a to take account of local traditions and customs. He also allowed for variation in the rules of the scholars according to their discretion.

Specification content

The establishments of the major law schools in applying fiqh within Islam.

Key terms

Mihna: the Islamic inquisition when the Caliph or ruler decided to tell the Muslims what they should believe and set up trials and punishments for those who refused to agree with him

Mutazilah: Islamic belief that God is totally separate from creation, so did not make the Qur'an

quickfire

1.8 What did the Mutazilah believe?

Key terms

Allawi: a Shi'a Islamic sect largely in
Syria and Turkey

Aql: reasoning used particularly by
Shi'a scholars in working out Islamic
teachings where the Qur'an and hadith
are unclear

quickfire

1.9 What is the difference between qiyas
and aql?

Key quotes

Either he is from the Ahl-ul-
Hadeeth [Salafi Muslims], or
Hanafi, or Shafi'i, or Maliki, or
Hanbali [Sunni Muslims]. He
who ascribes to the four Madhabs
ascribes to people who are without
doubt not infallible.

As for the one who ascribes to the
Salaf as-Salih [Salafi Muslims],
then he ascribes to that which is in
general infallible, and indeed the
Prophet mentioned that from the
signs of the saved sect that they
adhere to that which the Messenger
of Allah was upon and what the
Companions were upon, so who
ever adhered to it is with certainty
upon guidance from his Lord.
(**Muhammad al-Albaani**)

The danger of less-qualified
individuals misunderstanding the
sources and hence damaging the
shari'a is a very real one, as was
shown by the discord and strife
which afflicted some early Muslims,
and even some of the Companions
themselves, in the period which
preceded the establishment of the
Orthodox Schools.

In a Western-influenced global
culture in which people are
urged from early childhood
to think for themselves and to
challenge established authority,
it can sometimes be difficult
to muster enough humility to
recognise ones own limitations.
(**Abdul Hakim Murad**)

As a Sunni Muslim, Malik ibn Anas lived in Madinah and was Al-Shafi's teacher.
He placed importance on the traditions of the people of Madinah as he felt these
traditions were directly handed down from the Prophet and likely to be closest to his
practice, the sunna. Malik also allowed scholars to use reasoning and discretion in
their teachings.

The fourth main school of law according to Sunni Muslims is that of Ahmad ibn
Hanbal. During his lifetime the Mihna took place. The ruler of Muslims, the Caliph,
ordered people to accept the Mutazilite position that the Qur'an was created by
human beings. Many Imams refused and said that people should be free to believe
different things, including that the Qur'an was the word of God. Ahmad ibn Hanbal
was put in prison, but later on the Caliph backed down and freedom of belief was
permitted. His experiences influenced Ahmad ibn Hanbal to take a very traditional
approach and he opposed individuals making their own interpretations of shari'a. He
said that shari'a should be interpreted by scholars under strict and limited criteria.

Shi'a law schools

Many Shi'a schools of thought also grew up. All Shi'a scholars must come from the
descendants of the family of the Prophet. Imams within Shi'a Islam are considered
to have powers of interpretation of the Qur'an. Jafar al Sadiq became known as
the founder of a school of thought. Jafar al Sadiq taught thousands of students in
Madinah in the eighth century, including Abu Hanifa and Malik ibn Anas, founders
of the Sunni schools of thought. The educated Imam acts as interpreter of the Qur'an
using reasoning to take account of the circumstances of the time. Whereas Sunnis
considered qiyas, using comparisons to make teachings, the Jafari school used aql or
logical reasoning. They went further than Sunnis in this regard.

Other schools of thought grew up. Zaydi Shi'a agreed similar teachings to the Hanafi
but accepted Shi'a Imams as interpreters. An Ibadi school grew up, independent of
both Shi'a and Sunni schools. If a particular ruler took power, then one school of
thought or another might be favoured, or another might spring up: it became even
more complicated as time went on.

As Islam spread far and wide, so did the different schools of thought. The Hanafi
school became the major school of thought in most of central Asia, Pakistan,
Uzbekistan and Afghanistan. The Shafi school spread to Malaysia, Indonesia and East
Africa. The Maliki school of thought dominates north Africa from Morocco across the
Egypt. Hanbali Muslims are mostly to be found in
Saudi Arabia and the United Arab Emirates. Shi'a
Muslims of the Jafari school are to be found across
Iran and in pockets in northern Pakistan, central
Afghanistan and eastern Iraq. Ismaili Muslims
form minorities in many countries; larger numbers
live in northern Kashmir in Pakistan and India.
Ibadi Muslims are found in Oman. Turkey is a
mixture of Sunni Hanafi and the Shi'a Allawi sect.

Despite over a thousand years of history, if you
were to visit a mosque today, you would find
prayers being carried out almost unchanged from

A Mosque bookshelf

the practice of the Prophet, as interpreted by the founders of the major schools of
fiqh. On the bookshelf you might see books of fiqh of the Islamic shari'a school that
the mosque follows and the Imam was trained in. Later sects and groups have sprung
up, but the importance of the fiqh of the early Muslims remains.

Not everyone accepts the established law schools. Salafi Muslims such as shaykh
Muhammad al-Albaani believe that scholars are not perfect, so Muslims today
should use the original sources to make their own interpretations. The traditional
Sunni scholar Abdul Hakim Murad rejects this, claiming only the scholars of the
Madhabs possess the necessary knowledge and skills to interpret shari'a today.

AO1 Developing skills

It is now important to consider the information that has been covered in this section; however, the information in its raw form is too extensive and so has to be processed in order to meet the requirements of the examination. This can be done by practising more advanced skills associated with AO1. The exercises that run throughout this book will help you to do this and prepare you for the examination. For assessment objective 1 (AO1), which involves demonstrating 'knowledge' and 'understanding' skills, we are going to focus on different ways in which the skills can be demonstrated effectively, and also refer to how the performance of these skills is measured (see generic band descriptors for A2 [WJEC] AO1 or A Level [Eduqas] AO1).

▶ **Your task is this:** Below is a **summary of the main sources for shari'a**. It is 200 words long. You are needed to use this for an answer but could not repeat all of this in an essay under examination conditions so you will have to condense the material. Discuss which points you think are the most important and then re-draft into your own summary of 100 words.

The main sources for shari'a can be divided into primary and secondary. The first source is the Qur'an, the final, unchanging directly revealed word of God which must be considered before all else. No shari'a judgement can contradict the Qur'an; but as a source it leaves Muslims without answers to many practical questions. The sayings of Prophet Muhammad as the last and final messenger from Allah form the second primary source. He exemplifies and adds to many of the teachings in the Qur'an. Of the secondary sources, the first is ijma. This is the agreement of Muslim scholars, where a question is faced that cannot be answered by the primary sources alone. Where they still cannot find an answer, qiyas is used, which involves using an existing teaching for another situation, as an example to follow in a new situation for which there is no source. For Shi'a Imams and scholars, aql may be exercised as a source in place of qiyas. Aql is logical reasoning; Imams are qualified to make rulings because of their status in Shi'a Islam in the line of the family of the Prophet. Shari'a was developed through the fiqh of particular scholars, who themselves are looked to as sources of authority as they have worked out the answers to many questions of shari'a through detailed study.

When you have completed the task, refer to the band descriptors for A2 (WJEC) or A Level (Eduqas) and, in particular, have a look at the demands described in the higher band descriptors towards which you should be aspiring. Ask yourself:

- Does my work demonstrate thorough, accurate and relevant knowledge and understanding of religion and belief?
- Is my work coherent (consistent or make logical sense), clear and well organised? *(WJEC band descriptor only but still important to consider for Eduqas)*
- Will my work, when developed, be an extensive and relevant response which is specific to the focus of the task?
- Does my work have extensive depth and/or suitable breadth and have excellent use of evidence and examples?
- If appropriate to the task, does my response have thorough and accurate reference to sacred texts and sources of wisdom?
- Are there any insightful connections to be made with other elements of my course?
- Will my answer, when developed and extended to match what is expected in an examination answer, have an extensive range of views of scholars/schools of thought?
- When used, is specialist language and vocabulary both thorough and accurate?

Key skills Theme 1

The first Theme has tasks that deal with the basics of AO1 in terms of prioritising and selecting the key relevant information, presenting this and then using evidence and examples to support and expand upon this.

Key skills

Knowledge involves:

Selection of a range of (thorough) accurate and relevant information that is directly related to the specific demands of the question.

This means:

- Selecting relevant material for the question set
- Being focused in explaining and examining the material selected.

Understanding involves:

Explanation that is extensive, demonstrating depth and/or breadth with excellent use of evidence and examples including (where appropriate) thorough and accurate supporting use of sacred texts, sources of wisdom and specialist language.

This means:

- Effective use of examples and supporting evidence to establish the quality of your understanding
- Ownership of your explanation that expresses personal knowledge and understanding and NOT just reproducing a chunk of text from a book that you have rehearsed and memorised.

As you work through each section of the book, the focus will be on a variety of different aspects associated with AO1 so that you can comprehensively perfect the overall skills associated with AO1.

This section covers AO2
content and skills

Specification content

The extent to which the shari'a is
made by God.

Issues for analysis and evaluation

The extent to which the shari'a is made by God

The shari'a is the straight way and it became known as Islamic Law. Muslims
believe it is a set of teachings for Muslims to follow to live their lives in the way
God wanted. That does not necessarily mean it was 'made' by God. Islamic scholars
put together books of fiqh, which form versions of shari'a, over time, using
different sources. The question is to what extent this means that God controlled
this process.

Allah created the world, according to Muslims, and everything in it. He created the
Qur'an as the final holy book as a message to guide human beings. Muslims regard
the Qur'an as the direct word of God, so to the extent that the shari'a is based
upon the Qur'an, it is indeed made by God. The Qur'an is used first and foremost
in the shari'a. All shari'a scholars looked to the Qur'an as the primary source of
knowledge and nothing could be decided that contradicted what God said. That
means that God made the central teachings in the shari'a; however, the Qur'an is
not the only source. It does not give details about how to pray or laws of marriage
and morality in any detail. Scholars had to search further for answers.

Study tip

Consider in your answer how God works in the world. This may not be clear,
because people cannot see God. Muslims believe God can work through
revelation, in the form of holy books, and through inspiring Prophets like
Muhammad. Many Muslims believe in fate, that God decides all actions, so it is
possible that God actually worked through the lives of the scholars who made
shari'a, in an indirect way. The more you can delve in to what it means for God
to work in the creation of shari'a, the better.

AO2 Activity

As you read through this section try to
do the following:

1. Pick out the different lines of
   argument that are presented in
   the text and identify any evidence
   given in support.
2. For each line of argument try to
   evaluate whether or not you think
   this is strong or weak.
3. Think of any questions you may
   wish to raise in response to the
   arguments.

This Activity will help you to start
thinking critically about what you
read and help you to evaluate the
effectiveness of different arguments
and from this develop your own
observations, opinions and points
of view that will help with any
conclusions that you make in your
answers to the AO2 questions
that arise.

Next, scholars turned to the hadith. Muhammad, the last Prophet in Islam, said
that he left behind him the Qur'an and his example to Muslims as guidance. The
sayings of the Prophet record what he did: since he was God's messenger and a
perfect example; following what he did is regarded as God's will. However, his
words are not God's words; he was inspired by God, one step removed. Muslims
take it on trust that the hadith collections accurately record his words. However,
sources for what he said and did were written by humans two hundred years later.
The hadith collectors went to great lengths to check that the sayings agreed with
the Qur'an and were reliably passed on. But the potential for human error remains.
It can be said that Muslims believe the sunna of Muhammad was inspired by God
and that way, through generally accurate reporting, God had inspired shari'a.

Hadith collectors made judgements about which traditions they accepted and
which they rejected. Hadith collectors went to great lengths to choose sayings that
agreed with the Qur'an and were passed on by people they trusted. They were
trying to source the teachings that were really from God, and not made up by
people; however, there was always a possibility of human error.

The Qur'an and the sunna do not answer all questions. Teachings about how to
organise Friday prayers, or who someone can marry, are not fully answered in the
Qur'an. Early Muslims felt they needed answers to these questions. So they met
together to decide by ijma, consensus. They felt it was justified by the traditions
of Muhammad, so was in line with what Allah had intended, although it was a
human decision.

The use of qiyas, or comparison, and the use of further reasoning by Shi'a scholars,
developed the role for humans in applying the shari'a, although they always

prioritised the Qur'an and hadith first, following the principles laid down by Al-Shafi. He influenced many scholars in creating an organised version of shari'a after nearly 200 years of oral tradition. He took his work very seriously and always checked teachings with the Qur'an and sunna. He rejected anything that might have been made up by local people. He was trying to ensure shari'a was rooted in God's teachings. But he did so after human history had moved on from the time of the Prophet.

Divisions grew up over time, as different schools of fiqh arose. God's influence can be seen in that all schools look back to the word of Allah, first and foremost, in making shari'a. The influence of humans can also be seen in the distinctive features of the many different interpretations. The schools of thought were divided as to whether to take account of local traditions or to allow scholars a degree of freedom to make suitable interpretations themselves.

Al-Shafi was one of the scholars who put together his fiqh step by step. He said that the Qur'an and sunna are the primary sources because they are the word of God and the example of God's Prophet, so they must always come first. Next he allowed the ijma or consensus of the companions who knew Muhammad; their judgements; and qiyas or comparison with other similar situations where the answer to a teaching was unknown. Ijma and qiyas were secondary sources. This meant that God's role was central, and human interpretation was limited within what God had defined; however, it did allow for creation of teachings that were not directly revealed from God.

Other Islamic scholars went further. Abu Hanifa allowed for understanding of local traditions. Shi'a scholars used aql, reasoning, to decide on teachings where answers were unknown. In all cases, the scholars kept God in mind. They were trying to define what they thought God wanted. Muslims believe that God can influence or even define all that they do, so in this indirect way, God still had a role in the process. At the same time, no human except the Prophets is perfect. There was a chance that humans had bias, or didn't know, or went astray from what God meant.

Some Muslims did not accept that the Qur'an was God's words. The Mutazilah thought that God was beyond human language and could not have written the Qur'an. Others, called Qur'anists, accept the Qur'an as God's words but reject the hadith as words of a man. But for the vast majority of Muslims today, the Qur'an and hadith are central to their lives. They have faith in them as God's message and they follow what they say in their prayers. They attend mosques which, on the whole, follow a version of shari'a, which they believe is the way God wants them to live.

Some Muslims argue passionately that it is heresy to regard shari'a as anything other than made by God. They believe that Islam is a total system, a complete way of life; God cannot be divorced from any part of it. God's message is timeless, so human morals and standards of well-being should apply for all time. To them, believing in shari'a is an act of faith inextricably linked to belief in the Qur'an. This has implications for their outlook: if shari'a is made by God then they feel they must take steps to implement it, to create shari'a courts where there are none and to encourage Muslims to use them, because that is God's plan.

Study tip

It is vital for AO2 that you actually discuss arguments and not just explain what someone may have stated. Try to ask yourself, 'was this a fair point to make?', 'is the evidence sound enough?', 'is there anything to challenge this argument?', 'is this a strong or weak argument?' Such critical analysis will help you develop your evaluation skills.

Key quotes

Western policymakers, 'Islamic' regimes, and indeed large numbers of individual Muslims have all grossly misinterpreted Islamic law. Sharia is not a rigid and immutable 'law of God' based on unchanging texts written in the Middle Ages. Understood and applied correctly, sharia is an imminently flexible, dynamic jurisprudence that is fully compatible with the modern human rights framework. (Elbayar)

By saying that it was good for the time, you risk leading impressionable and often disenfranchised young Muslims to ask: why isn't it good for our time? Morality, like human well-being, is timeless. (Azzam)

Others take a more nuanced viewpoint. Kareem Elbayar argues that there is much wrong in the way that shari'a has been interpreted by people, but that it retains an important image as divine law by most Muslims. Abolishing shari'a is not the way forward. Elbayar argues that the principles of justice and fairness, human rights and modesty, are created by God, but their application is carried out by humans. This application has been done very badly in the past, but if shari'a is understood properly, then more flexible versions can be made, more in keeping with God's original intention.

Key quote

The derived shari'a law (or Islamic Jurisprudence) should be set aside as the legal system in all Muslim countries. It was a body of law that was derived and put together by men (no female participation) many centuries ago. The agendas of rulers were always on the radar. Originally, the shari'a law might have been helpful for its inclusiveness and tolerance but today Muslim clerics and autocratic rulers use shari'a law as an instrument of control that propagates injustice and deprivation. (Askari)

Hossein Askari argues for a complete reformation in many areas of Islam, including the abolition of shari'a. He argues that it is not God-made at all. Male kings and Caliphs created the law system to entrench their power, which was unfair to women, minorities and the poor. Unlike the Qur'an and sunna, the shari'a is dispensable. Other reformist Muslims on the whole argue that shari'a as we know it was the creation of oppressive regimes of the past and if anything, goes against the spirit of compassion and mercy which God willed for Muslims.

Key questions

What does it mean for God to make something? In what ways can God make something happen, if that is His will?

Do the human contributions to hadith collections, ijma and qiyas or aql, take away from God's role or help explain God's divine law?

Are criticisms of shari'a today evidence that shari'a did not come from God?

AO2 Activity

List some conclusions that could be drawn from the AO2 reasoning from the above text; try to aim for at least three different possible conclusions. Consider each of the conclusions and collect brief evidence to support each conclusion from the AO1 and AO2 material for this topic. Select the conclusion that you think is most convincing and explain why it is so. Try to contrast this with the weakest conclusion in the list, justifying your argument with clear reasoning and evidence.

AO2 Developing skills

It is now important to consider the information that has been covered in this section; however, the information in its raw form is too extensive and so has to be processed in order to meet the requirements of the examination. This can be done by practising more advanced skills associated with AO2. The exercises that run throughout this book will help you to do this and prepare you for the examination. For assessment objective 2 (AO2), which involves 'critical analysis' and 'evaluation' skills, we are going to focus on different ways in which the skills can be demonstrated effectively, and also refer to how the performance of these skills is measured (see generic band descriptors for A2 [WJEC] AO2 or A Level [Eduqas] AO2).

▶ **Your task is this:** Below is a **summary of two different points of view concerning whether the sources used for shari'a are reliable**. It is 150 words long. You want to use these two views and lines of argument for an evaluation; however, to just list them is not really evaluating them. Present these two views in a more evaluative style by firstly condensing each argument and then, secondly, commenting on how effective each one is (weak or strong are good terms to start with). Allow about 200 words in total.

The Qur'an cannot possibly be considered unreliable, because it is the unchanging, directly revealed word of God. The hadith were collected painstakingly by Bukhari and others who went to great lengths to ensure the text and chain of narrators were reliable. Scholars exercised their judgement in carrying out ijma, qiyas or aql, with the greatest of seriousness based on years of training. The founders of the schools of fiqh, the madhabs, discussed at length taking into account local tradition and the habits of the Madinans to accurately record what we know as the shari'a.

God revealed the Qur'an, not the shari'a. The Qur'an was interpreted by people, with the help of hadith passed down over many years, adding a degree of unreliability to the sources. If shari'a was reliable there would be one version: the fact that so many schools grew up suggests that the sources were not reliable enough to agree upon. Islamic scholars rarely reach ijma, and qiyas may be unreliable because there are so many new situations that simply did not exist in the days of Muhammad, that a meaningful comparison cannot be made.

When you have completed the task, refer to the band descriptors for A2 (WJEC) or A Level (Eduqas) and, in particular, have a look at the demands described in the higher band descriptors towards which you should be aspiring. Ask yourself:

- Is my answer a confident critical analysis and perceptive evaluation of the issue?
- Is my answer a response that successfully identifies and thoroughly addresses the issues raised by the question set?
- Does my work show an excellent standard of coherence, clarity and organisation? ***(WJEC band descriptor only but still important to consider for Eduqas)***
- Will my work, when developed, contain thorough, sustained and clear views that are supported by extensive, detailed reasoning and/or evidence?
- Are the views of scholars/schools of thought used extensively, appropriately and in context?
- Does my answer convey a confident and perceptive analysis of the nature of any possible connections with other elements of my course?
- When used, is specialist language and vocabulary both thorough and accurate?

Key skills Theme 1

The first Theme has tasks that deal with the basics of AO2 in terms of developing an evaluative style, building arguments and raising critical questions.

Key skills

Analysis involves:

Identifying issues raised by the materials in the AO1, together with those identified in the AO2 section, and presents sustained and clear views, either of scholars or from a personal perspective ready for evaluation.

This means:

- That your answers are able to identify key areas of debate in relation to a particular issue
- That you can identify, and comment upon, the different lines of argument presented by others
- That your response comments on the overall effectiveness of each of these areas or arguments.

Evaluation involves:

Considering the various implications of the issues raised based upon the evidence gleaned from analysis and provides an extensive detailed argument with a clear conclusion.

This means:

- That your answer weighs up the consequences of accepting or rejecting the various and different lines of argument analysed
- That your answer arrives at a conclusion through a clear process of reasoning.

As you work through each section of the book, the focus will be on a variety of different aspects associated with AO2 so that you can comprehensively perfect the overall skills associated with AO2.

Specification content

Different understandings of the term shari'a: shari'a as civil law; shari'a as religious law and shari'a as a moral guide.

Key terms

Civil: relating to family life or society; personal matters rather than criminal

Mahr: a payment from the groom to the bride to seal the contract of marriage

Nikkah: Islamic marriage contract

Secular: not religious, without reference to religion or God

An Islamic wedding

E: The role of shari'a and its importance for Muslims

Different understandings of the term shari'a

As a religious code, should shari'a be about religious laws, and not matters to do with family or social life? Or should shari'a be a guide for marriage, divorce and family matters? How far should shari'a be a moral law and should it be applied by Islamic governments? There are wide-ranging views on shari'a and it has been interpreted very differently at different times and in different parts of the world.

Shari'a as civil law

In the UK, there is criminal law and **civil** law. If you murdered someone, the police may arrest you and press charges against you in a criminal court. This is an example of criminal law. An example of a civil law case is if someone wrote bad comments about you and published them in a newspaper. You could argue that the comments caused you upset and damaged you, and take the person who made them to court to ask for compensation. This is an example of civil law. In most countries marriage and divorce are matters of civil law. Shari'a regards criminal cases such as murder as a matter that the victim's family should pursue, as a civil case.

Businesses may set up contracts with other businesses about their terms of trade. This is another example of civil law. Nowadays, these are regulated by national governments, although in the past, ordinary families and businesses looked to religion to regulate civil matters. In the Middle East that meant Islam. Shari'a rules grew up concerning marriage and family life. Marriage was defined by a contract in a **Nikkah** ceremony. The Nikkah marriage gave the parties rights. Both man and woman were required to say they agreed and were not supposed to be forced to marry. A **Mahr** or dowry is paid from the man to the woman to seal the contract.

Key quote

Marriage is the basis for blessings and children are an abundance of mercy. (Hadith of Prophet Muhammad)

Marriage law in Islam went further than tribal tradition at the time. In the Mahr, women were allowed to own property. Women and daughters could also receive an inheritance. Shari'a, however, did not guarantee women equality as **secular** law codes do today. Usually women were allotted only half the share of property that male heirs inherited. Despite this, shari'a weddings remain very popular amongst Muslims around the world. Many see marriage as an emotional and spiritual contract and choose to carry out the ceremony within the traditions of Islam, which they also hold dear.

Shari'a courts

Many countries allow Muslims to use shari'a for family matters. In India, where a majority follow the Hindu religion, Muslims may follow shari'a for personal matters and refer disputes to shari'a courts. In Britain, there are several private shari'a courts. These are for members of the Muslim community who voluntarily choose to attend. They are not part of the official UK system of law. In 2008, the Archbishop of Canterbury wrote that Muslim and Jewish civil law courts could be of value in the UK.

Nevertheless, the existence of these courts is controversial. Some people question whether women, in particular, really agree to go to the courts or face family pressure from men to attend. Critics say that women would be treated more equally in a secular law court. Many Muslim scholars interpret shari'a to forbid homosexuality and make other rulings which many find unacceptable.

Modern banking systems work by lending money to someone, who must repay the money and extra as an interest payment, called riba. The lending bank considers this fair: they are taking a risk and have costs to pay. On the other hand, the debtor risks getting into difficulty making repayments if the interest rate goes up. Traditionally, shari'a forbids interest. Instead, a house could be bought through a shared ownership arrangement. The lender buys the house and the debtor pays them an agreed amount, including additional payment for their trouble, to buy the property.

Muslims in the UK struck a first by introducing shari'a-compliant mortgages, the first Western country to do so. Some Muslims regarded taking an interest-bearing loan as acceptable due to necessity, if there was no other practical way to get accommodation. Others worked with banks to create a new product, shari'a-compliant mortgages. These worked in a similar way to other loans except that instead of charging interest, the bank makes a different agreement with the home owners, so payments are instalments or some other arrangement leading to ownership.

Shari'a as religious law

Shari'a originally was thought to mean the straight path, or the best way to live for Muslims. The Qur'an is the first source of shari'a, as the word of Allah. Yet the Qur'an itself suggests that religion should be a matter of choice. People cannot be compelled to believe something. In the early history of Islam, Caliph Al-Mamun tried to force Muslims to accept that the Qur'an was created by people. In the end the Imams were granted freedom to hold traditional beliefs. Yet within the next couple of hundred years, many Imams went on to define beliefs and take away that freedom they had fought for.

Categories of action

Some religious believers emphasise the importance of doing good deeds. Others emphasise belief. You might not be in a position to do good deeds, or you might make mistakes, but believing the right thing is what counts. Intentions are a form of belief. Some hadiths say that reward and punishment is allotted at Judgement according to the intentions rather than the actions themselves. Shari'a cannot judge intentions. It can, nevertheless, make rulings to encourage people to take what scholars think are the right actions. To make that easier for people to understand, different categories of action have been defined.

A wajib action is compulsory, such as prayers, five times a day. Mustahab actions are recommended, such as reciting the Qur'an and caring for friends and neighbours. These actions carry with them blessings from God. Mubah actions are allowed (the term halal is also used); they are usually everyday tasks such as driving a car or choosing what to wear or what to buy. There is no reward and no punishment for these actions as they do not form part of shari'a restrictions. Makruh actions are disapproved of, but not forbidden. Using lots of water whilst washing to prepare for prayer, is disapproved of. Haram actions are forbidden and Muslims should avoid such actions, which may carry with them God's punishment, or punishment through shari'a. It is haram for Muslims to eat pork or drink alcohol.

The categories of actions make shari'a sound unambiguous. However, circumstances can alter shari'a rulings. It is forbidden to eat pork, but if a Muslim was starving and had nothing else to eat, it would then become permissible. If harm or even death might occur, it would become compulsory to avoid this by eating the pork. Rewards takes into account intention, so if a person meant well,

A Muslim bank in Morocco

Key quotes

The Qur'an 30:39

What you paid in interest, so that it may increase people's wealth, does not increase with God. (Yusuf Ali)

The Qur'an 2:256

Let there be no compulsion in religion. (Yusuf Ali)

Key terms

Haram: a forbidden action

Makruh: an action that is disapproved of but which is, nevertheless, permitted

Mubah: an everyday action not covered by shari'a, therefore neither approved nor disapproved (also referred to as halal)

Mustahab: a recommended action

Riba: monetary interest paid in addition to repaying a loan

Wajib: a compulsory action in shari'a

quickfire

1.10 What happened in the Mihna?

Key quote

A person's actions are rewarded according to their intentions.
(Hadith of Prophet Muhammad)

quickfire

1.11 What sorts of cases do shari'a courts deal with?

A medieval Islamic Qazi (judge)

Key terms

Apostasy: leaving a faith, seen by some as a crime

Imaan: literally means faith in Islam; a group which supports gay, lesbian bisexual and transgender Muslims

Ottoman: rulers of Turkey, Saudi Arabia and much of the Middle East from the sixteenth to the nineteenth centuries

Qazi: Islamic judge (sometimes spelled Qadi)

quickfire

1.12 List the options available as the outcome for a case in a shari'a court

but made a mistake and broke a shari'a ruling, they might still be granted reward by God in the afterlife.

Some countries, such as Pakistan and Saudi Arabia, have introduced blasphemy laws to forbid saying anything against God or his Prophet. People have been accused of making derogatory remarks about Muhammad, or of damaging copies of the Qur'an. In some cases the accused have been killed. Despite the Qur'anic teaching that religion should not include compulsion, Muslims who decide to convert to other faiths can face the death penalty for a crime called apostasy. Muslims who enforce this punishment believe it has been ordered by God.

It has been noted earlier that there are many different schools of thought in shari'a. British Muslims for Secular Democracy are a group which argues in favour of human rights. They consider supporting universal human rights to be more in keeping with the spirit of compassion in Islam than rulings from traditional shari'a. People should not face any pressure to follow any one particular faith or belief and if they choose to change religions they should be free to do so. This is enshrined by the United Nations in the Universal Declaration of Human Rights. Many Muslim countries have signed up to the Declaration, believing that it is in the spirit of Islam.

Shari'a as moral guide

A Muslim might decide it is morally right not to lie, backbite or gossip, following the guidance of the sunna of Muhammad through the shari'a. That would be an individual choice. Historically, in some Muslim lands, Islamic scholars set up shari'a courts which dealt with moral cases including adultery, rape and other crimes. Shari'a can be used both as a personal moral guide and as a system of law to enforce a code of morality.

In the early days of Islam, many people lived in fear of their lives from attack, tribal warfare, murder or mistreatment. Islamic shari'a put in place a simple set of rules that demanded Muslims treated others fairly. They were not allowed to cheat when trading. Muslims should not kill or injure others in their daily lives. They became respected for their honesty and assistance in giving alms to the poor and needy.

Shari'a courts gave most weight to Muslim male witnesses, and put less trust in women and non-Muslims. A Qazi or judge presided over the court and made the decision himself. Several options were available to him. In some cases, the family of a victim could simply forgive the guilty person, or grant freedom after the payment of compensation. In other cases a judge might be free to decide whether or not to apply a punishment. In some cases, where the Qur'an appeared to call for a certain punishment for a crime, this had to be applied.

Shari'a courts in the Middle Ages did not apply the same standards of justice as we have today. But they were often not as strict as you might think. In the case of adultery, it was required that four trustworthy, adult male Muslims see a person in a sexual act with another. If only three did, the standard of proof would not have been met.

Some Muslims have criticised medieval shari'a. According to Abu Hanifa, homosexuality was a crime, although it was up to a judge whether or not to apply a punishment. Others said punishment was death. By contrast, the Ottoman Turkish Caliphs led Islam in the nineteenth century when they made homosexuality legal. Some modern-day Muslims set up a group called Imaan which argues that according to the Qur'an there is nothing wrong with being gay and Muslim. The variety of different interpretations of shari'a makes it difficult to agree on a single moral code.

AO1 Activity

Make a list of criticisms of shari'a law that are mentioned in this chapter as bulleted points. How might different Muslims respond to those criticisms? Try to write down two different responses to each criticism that you have listed. Remember that responses can agree, disagree, or take a third, middle position.

Different understandings of shari'a around the world

In the UK and other Western countries, Muslims form a minority group within secular states. They must follow UK laws along with everyone else. This has advantages for them: there are laws against discrimination which benefit Muslims as they help get equal treatment when applying for a job. Where freedom of religion is allowed, it is a duty on Muslims to follow all of the laws of the non-Muslim state. Some scholars argue that the obligations of Muslims, such as to attend Jummah prayers, are not compulsory upon Muslims who do not live in a Muslim country. Others argue that it does not matter where a Muslim lives, the obligations are the same. Many Muslims support charities and local community initiatives to help their neighbours, whoever they are, in their local communities.

The Muslim Law Council UK was set up to organise shari'a for family and personal law in the UK. They provide services and make judgements to support Muslim men and women regarding marriage and family issues. Some people see shari'a as incompatible with the ideals of a secular state. Yasmin Alibhai-Brown is a newspaper columnist and prominent Muslim who believes that Muslims should support secular democracy. She argues that shari'a can be used to oppress women's rights.

Key quote

Who'd be female under Islamic Law? (Yasmin Alibhai-Brown)

Iran and Saudi Arabia

In the Middle East, the Islamic Republic of Iran is thought of as a religious state. Shari'a law as interpreted by Shi'a Imams forms the country's law code. There is a system of elections in Iran, a parliament called a Majlis, and men and women representatives are elected to serve in it. This is different from a Western democracy, because the parliament's laws and its representatives must be approved by Imams as being consistent with the Qur'an and the shari'a. Women are required to wear veils and cover all but their hands and faces. Shari'a is enforced by a religious police force. Nevertheless, shari'a brings certain rights in Iran, including the right of women to education. More than half the students at university in Iran, on both BA and PhD courses, are now women.

Saudi Arabia, by contrast, is ruled by a powerful family called the House of Saud. This family favours a certain strand of Islam known as Salafi, or sometimes called Wahhabi after its founder, **Al-Wahhab**. This school of thought became highly influential as oil revenues paid for Salafi preachers and mosques to be set up in other countries. Salafism is an austere version of Islam. Women are strictly veiled whilst men run almost all of the positions of government. Salafism rejects the traditional schools of shari'a and instead promotes direct interpretation of the companions of Muhammad as those closest to the Prophet and most likely to know what he said. Salafis usually reject the role of the mufti to interpret shari'a teachings, and reject many cultural practices such as the visiting of tombs and Sufi meditations. Despite this apparent austerity, Salafi Muslims are open to reinterpretations of shari'a, as we shall see in the section on ijtihad.

quickfire

1.13 State one advantage for Muslims of secular laws.

Specification content

Different understandings of the term shari'a and the different ways in which it is applied by Muslims throughout the world today.

Yasmin Alibhai-Brown

Key terms

Majlis: parliament in Iran or gathering of Muslims

Mufti: Islamic teacher who may make interpretations of shari'a

Sufi: someone who follows an inward, spiritual version of Islam

Salafism: belief that Muslims should go back to the literal practices of the companions of Muhammad independently of the schools of thought and the interpretations of their scholars

quickfire

1.14 What is a Majlis?

Key person

Al-Wahhab: Muslim who lived from 1703 to 1792 and called for Muslims to return to a pure version of early Islam, removing what he saw as later practices and teachings. Influential in Saudi Arabia.

Pakistan and Turkey

Pakistan was a British colony which retains British law as its main system of law. Parallel to this, shari'a law courts have been set up to adjudicate on religious and family matters. There is sometimes confusion between them. A case can be decided in a shari'a court only to be appealed to a higher secular court. This has led some to call for shari'a courts to be made superior. India is a state which follows secular law but has provision for personal and family law for Muslims to be judged by shari'a.

Turkey used to be ruled by the Ottomans, who paved the way for a modern, secular country. In social policy, homosexuality was made legal, many years before the UK. During the twentieth century, Ataturk became the leader of Turkey which he made into a secular country. In recent years, some Muslims in Turkey have called for a return to shari'a law and a more religious state.

AO1 Activity

Television World News feature on shari'a. Imagine you are in the newsroom and you are switching to reporters in five different countries, each one in turn. Write the script for what you would ask them about Islam and shari'a in each country, and how they might reply.

The role of the mujtahid (jurist)

Specification content

The role of the mujtahid (jurist) and taqlid (imitation).

A **mujtahid** is an Islamic scholar who is knowledgeable about Islam. Traditionally it was a man but there have been women who have exercised this role, especially Shi'a Muslims. The mujtahid has to be able to read the Arabic of the Qur'an fluently and know how to interpret the Qur'an and hadith. They should know the legal theory of fiqh. Lady Amin, who lived from 1886 to 1983, was Iran's most famous female jurist who wrote fifteen books of interpretations.

Mujtahids make opinions called fatwas. Sometimes these are regarded as rules, but they may also be viewed as simply opinions. Fatwas were used by judges in shari'a courts. Together with legal experts and teachers, mujtahids paralleled professors and were free to make their own academic opinions.

For the first two hundred years after Muhammad's death, Sunni Muslims were free to make their own opinions based on the Qur'an and the sayings of Muhammad. As time went on, it was felt that only an experienced mujtahid was qualified enough to make opinions. These mujtahids together agreed teachings by ijma and formed the schools of thought as we know them: Shafi, Maliki, Hanbali and Hanafi. The Sunni mujtahid should understand the principles of Islam, be a pious and trustworthy person, and be able to understand good arguments.

Key terms

Hawza: special schools attended by Shi'a mujtahids

Mujtahid: an Islamic scholar considered qualified to make authoritative teachings

Taqlid: imitation, to follow another Muslim teacher's opinions

Shi'a mujtahids attended special schools called **Hawza**. On the curriculum were detailed studies in the Qur'an and hadith; the Arabic language; the principles of law and justice; the hadith narrators; studies in reasoning and logic; how to reach consensus and how to judge fairly with authority. They became respected for their knowledge and learning throughout the Muslim world.

Key quote

If you are unsure what to do, enquire. (Hadith of Prophet Muhammad)

Taqlid (imitation)

As time went by there were few, if any, scholars who were well qualified enough to take on the role of mujtahid. Instead, scholars decided to follow or imitate the opinions of earlier mujtahids.

Taqlid means to imitate or copy. Sunni law schools decided that shari'a had been settled by the companions and early mujtahids, so it was better to imitate their superior knowledge than debate afresh. A period known as the 'golden age' of Islam, when Muslims had been at the forefront of translating works of science and knowledge, also declined. There was less discussion, reasoning and intellectual debate. Sometimes this is referred to as the closing of the gates of ijtihad.

For Shi'a Muslims, it is essential to follow the teachings of a knowledgeable scholar within the line of the Prophet's family. If a person is not able to find one in person then they may follow taqlid. Unlike Sunni Muslims, Shi'a continued to interpret the Qur'an and hadith, and to form consensus through their Imams who were thought to possess the knowledge to interpret the texts without error. Most Shi'a believe their lead Imam, twelfth Imam in the line of Imams, became hidden. The scholar who is educated to make teachings is in effect speaking in place of the twelfth Imam whom they are not able to contact presently, but who is believed will return in the future.

Ijtihad (intellectual struggle)

Key quote

When a judge uses ijtihad to make judgment and the judge is right, then he will have two rewards. If the judge passes judgement and makes a mistake, then he will have one reward. (Hadith of Prophet Muhammad)

Ijtihad literally means forming a personal opinion. No opinion which contradicts the primary sources of shari'a is accepted by Muslims; however, in many situations the original sources do not provide clear guidance. This led to ijtihad. When Caliph Umar expanded the Muslim Empire, he had to decide what to do with newly taken farming land. Some of Umar's soldiers expected a share in the land that they had fought to gain, but Umar feared that would put local farmers out of work. So Umar made the ijtihad opinion that local farmers should keep their land and pay tax to him instead. Umar did not consult the Qur'an in his judgement and was criticised for not doing so. Then he found a verse in the Qur'an 59.10 (Yusuf Ali): 'The next generation say: "Our Lord! Forgive us, and our brethren who came before us into the Faith, and leave not, in our hearts, any grudge against those who have believed."' Umar reasoned that this meant the land should stay with the farmers as their children might become Muslims. If they were thrown off the land, they might bear a grudge in future. Umar also reasoned that the Qur'an suggested land gained by the Muslims should be used to help the poor, not given to the rich, as this would be divisive.

Key quote

The Qur'an 59:7

What Allah has given to His Messenger and taken from the people of the townships, belongs to Allah, to His Messenger and to kindred and orphans, the needy and the wayfarer; so that it may not make division with the wealthy. (Yusuf Ali)

Caliph Uthman found there were different versions of the Qur'an read by different Arab tribes, which caused confusion. He decided that Zayd bin Thabit should compile a single, authoritative version. The later Muslim scholar **Al-Ghazali** referred to this process as an example of ijtihad. Muslims consider the Qur'an to be the first and foremost authority within shari'a, but if Uthman had not decided upon this act of ijtihad, it might not exist in the form that we have it today.

Some Muslims believe only the early companions of the Prophet could exercise ijtihad, because they knew what Muhammad said and did. Other Muslims believe we should again exercise ijtihad so that new opinions can be made to help answer modern-day situations. Many traditional Muslims believe that the founders of their schools of shari'a law were educated and knowledgeable enough to make opinions,

Key term

Ijtihad: forming a personal opinion

quickfire

1.15 What was special about the 'golden age'?

Specification content

Specific reference to the debates surrounding ijtihad (intellectual struggle) and contrasting views from within Sunni and Shi'a Islam on ijtihad.

Mosque gateway in Damascus

Key person

Al-Ghazali: traditional Sunni Muslim scholar who lived in the Middle East 1058–1111, who discouraged the practice of ijtihad at this time.

quickfire

1.16 What process did Al-Ghazali refer to
as an example of ijtihad?

but within a couple of hundred years, most of the questions had been answered and ijtihad was no longer practised.

Al-Ghazali was an influential Sunni Muslim scholar who lived in the eleventh century. Al-Ghazali's life was topsy-turvy. He engaged in lively debates against philosophers but went through a crisis of faith and took time out, before once again engaging in debate. Al-Ghazali argued that shari'a was there for the public interest, and the teachings of shari'a should take into account human needs. He also suggested that there should be a purpose to the rulings for the good of society. This has been interpreted by some to mean that shari'a should be for the good of human rights and equality for women. However, during his time Al-Ghazali often argued against making rational opinions and in favour of traditional practice of religion. He wrote a book called *The Incoherence of the Philosophers* and was influential in closing the gates of ijtihad for many centuries.

Different views on ijtihad from Shi'a and Sunni perspectives

Aql is similar to qiyas, beginning with comparison to a similar teaching in the Qur'an or hadith, but Shi'a Imams may develop reasoning further than the Sunnis. The Shi'a did not always use the term ijtihad, but practised it by their most educated Imams throughout the times when the Sunnis closed the gates of ijtihad. Shi'a scholars developed judgements in four categories: Qat, opinions over which the Imams were certain; Zann, opinions they thought true with reasoning; Shakk, teachings over which the Imams had doubt; and Wahm, reasoning which had errors in it. These provided a framework for Shi'a mujtahids to develop their judgements.

In modern Iran, a majority Shi'a Muslim country, ijtihad was encouraged. After the Islamic revolution in 1979, the country was led by an Ayatollah, who was a Muslim jurist qualified to give judgements and interpretations for the good of the country. There are other examples of Shi'a ijtihad in the modern day. Shi'a Imam Sayid Hassan Al-Qazwini gave ijtihad that Muslims may take a mortgage with interest if in need of housing. Muslims usually bury the dead very quickly after death, but Imam Al-Qazwini gave ijtihad that is allowable to conduct an autopsy on a dead body, as modern science has made this a safe and helpful procedure to establish cause of death.

Sunni and Salafi views

In the modern world, modernist and Salafi Muslims re-opened the gates of ijtihad and make fresh opinions about issues they needed answering. Sometimes this was done with a focus on returning to the original understanding of the companions of Muhammad, and sometimes with a view to taking a more modern approach. The modernist reformer Dr Muqtedar Khan went much further and published a website entitled ijtihad, in which he suggests Muslims should engage more with the Western world, accept gay marriage and the validity of other faiths.

The liberal, reformist scholar Ziauddin Sardar argues that Muslims should wholeheartedly embrace ijtihad today, but are not doing so.

Key quote

Serious rethinking within Islam is long overdue. Muslims have been comfortably relying, or rather falling back, on age-old interpretations for much too long. This is why we feel so painful in the contemporary world, so uncomfortable with modernity. Yet, ijtihad is one thing Muslim societies have singularly failed to undertake. (Sardar)

Key terms

Qat: opinions over which the Imams were certain

Shakk: teachings over which the Imams had doubt

Wahm: reasoning which had errors in it

Zann: opinions considered true through reasoning

quickfire

1.17 Give two ijtihad opinions from Imam Al-Qazwini.

Salafi scholar Rashid Rida

Rashid Rida was born in Lebanon in 1865. A Sunni, he gradually adopted Salafism. He published an influential magazine. Rida said that Muslims should read the Qur'an and hadith, and the reports from the sahaba, who were the companions who lived alongside Muhammad, and make their own opinions about Islamic teachings. He did not see why Muslims should follow what traditional scholars said without question. He rejected taqlid and thought that the gates of ijtihad should be reopened to make fresh interpretations.

Creation and evolution

Creation is the idea that God, a divine power beyond time, was the first cause and present and at work in the creation of the world and everything in it. Evolution is the scientific theory that plants, animals and humans slowly evolved from one species to the next over time, caused by natural factors such as the environment they lived in.

Like Christians and Jews, Muslims believe in the theory of creation, that one God was the first cause for the world and the creation of human beings. However, there are different interpretations of this. **Charles Darwin** argued that the different species evolved, one from another. Many religious Christians and Muslims at the time rejected Darwin's theory of evolution, because they thought it took away from the idea of God as creator. Rashid Rida thought that Muslims did not have to believe in the story of creation in the way that the Muslim scholars did. It could have been a story with hidden meaning, rather than a literal account.

Ironically, he was not the first Muslim to suggest that the creation might have gradually evolved. Ibn Khaldun lived from 1332 to 1406 in North Africa and Spain at a time when it was ruled by Muslims. He wrote that the creation gradually progressed from plants to animals; to monkeys and finally to humankind.

Ibn Khaldun lived at the time when Muslims did not engage in ijtihad. He was one of the traditional Muslim scholars, like others of whom Rashid was critical.

The debate over evolution continues today. Some Muslims reject the theory out of hand. **Dr Usama Hasan** was an Imam scientist in London. He made comments accepting the theory of evolution in 2008; however, his congregation of followers at the mosque rejected those comments, causing the Imam to stand down. The episode showed that for some Muslims nowadays, ijtihad is a step they are not prepared to accept.

Political Islam

Rida was critical of the political leaders of Muslim countries who had come to power under colonial rule by Britain and France. He thought the British were more advanced and preferred the British rulers, who were Christian, to the Ottoman Muslim Caliphs. Rida thought that Muslims would be better living under an Islamic state, with laws defined by ijtihad. He was criticised by many traditional Sunni Muslims.

Rashid Rida thought that he was encouraging Muslims to return to their roots and follow a more authentic version of Islam. He became popular amongst many younger Muslims. Others criticise him as departing from traditional Islam. Some of Rida's ideas have been used by Muslims who want to develop a political form of Islam and create countries based on extreme versions of the faith. His ijtihad was not liberal: it was a strict and literal interpretation of Islam followed by Muhammad's companions.

Specification content

A comparison of the approaches taken by Salafi scholar Rashid Rida and modernist Islamic scholar Tariq Ramadan.

Key people

Charles Darwin: the scientist that first presented a coherent theory for the process of evolution.

Dr Usama Hasan: scientist and Imam in East London, who supported the theory of evolution as in keeping with the belief in creation.

Rashid Rida: a famous Salafi scholar.

Rashid Rida

Key quotes

Look at the world of creation. It started with minerals and gradually developed plants, animals and many more species. Then came the monkeys and from them humans, with highest intelligence. (Ibn Khaldun)

Many believers in God have no problem with an obvious solution [to the story of creation]: that God created man via evolution. (Hasan)

Tariq Ramadan

Modernist Islamic scholar Tariq Ramadan

Tariq Ramadan is a Swiss Muslim who teaches Theology at Oxford University. He has sometimes called himself a modern reformer of Islam. Tariq Ramadan noticed that many Muslims were reacting against modern society, because they were unhappy at having been ruled by colonial powers. Some thought that anything Western was against Islam. Tariq Ramadan thought that the best way of persuading Muslims to reform their ideas was to persuade them gradually.

Tariq Ramadan said there should be a pause on capital punishment to allow for a debate to take place. He thought that a debate would be the best way to persuade Muslims to change. Corporal punishments, such as flogging, are still carried out in some Muslim countries but are regarded as inhumane and prohibited by the UN Declaration of Human Rights. Some human rights proponents have criticised Tariq Ramadan because they felt he ought to say more clearly that corporal and capital punishments are wrong, and not apologise for Muslim regimes who still uphold them. However, he argues that such a position would simply alienate those regimes who would then refuse to listen to the arguments.

Tariq Ramadan has condemned terrorism. He has also said that people should not be forced to follow Islam and that women should not be made to wear a veil. On the other hand, he does not accept homosexuality as valid within Islam. Tariq Ramadan appears to tread a path between traditionalism and the modern world. He wants Muslims to engage with traditional teachings and discuss them, but to do so in dialogue with modern society, rather than separate from it.

Key quotes

We agree to integrate into the host society … I accept the laws, provided they do not force me to do something that is against my religion. If you must become a bad Muslim in order to be a good Frenchman, we say no … We must reject the [kind of] integration that tells us: 'Be a Muslim, but change your garb.' (Ramadan)

Muslims must speak out and explain who they are, what they believe in, what they stand for, what is the meaning of their life. They must have the courage to denounce what is said and done by certain Muslims in the name of their religion. (Ramadan)

Ramadan condemns those who are opposed to the unique way of dress that distinguishes Muslims from others (such as the veil), describing them as traitors who have surrendered to Western thought. He also condemns those who think that the Qur'an and the sunna cannot be a source of authority for contemporary personal and cultural behaviour, and depicts liberal Muslims who understand liberalism in the Western sense, [i.e. as an outlook which] encourages rationalism and personal individuality, as 'Muslims without Islam'. (Guindy)

AO1 Activity

Venn diagram. Draw 3 overlapping circles, so that each circle overlaps in the middle.

Label the circles: Sunni, Shi'a, Salafi.

Place the following into the diagram, choosing whether to put them into overlapping parts (and so, applicable to both or all three circles) or only with one circle.

Try to add additional points to your diagram, such as examples for each.

What do you think the viewpoint of a secular Muslim would be? Where would you add them to the diagram?

- Qur'an as primary source
- Hadith, sayings of Muhammad
- Use aql, reasoning
- Use qiyas, comparisons
- Use ijma, consensus
- Ijtihad must be carried out by highly trained scholar
- Muslims should read and make their own opinions
- Regard teachings of companions as important
- Imitated earlier teaching
- No new opinions, for most of the Middle Ages
- Encourage ijtihad in the modern world
- May use shari'a together with state law

Tariq Ramadan has been criticised for speaking to different audiences with different messages. He says he accepts the theory of evolution, but also argues that the world is created by God. Whilst arguing for integration, he rejects assimilation of culture. He suggests that Muslims should be proud of their identity. That may mean creating new, European identities for young Muslims, who see the culture of their parents as no longer relevant. In creating this with Islam at the centre, some accuse Tariq Ramadan of seeking to Islamise the young, whereas Tariq Ramadan says it is about gradual, more effective integration which rejects notions of Western cultural superiority.

AO1 Developing skills

It is now important to consider the information that has been covered in this section; however, the information in its raw form is too extensive and so has to be processed in order to meet the requirements of the examination. This can be done by practising more advanced skills associated with AO1. For assessment objective 1 (AO1), which involves demonstrating 'knowledge' and 'understanding' skills, we are going to focus on different ways in which the skills can be demonstrated effectively, and also refer to how the performance of these skills is measured (see generic band descriptors for A2 [WJEC] AO1 or A Level [Eduqas] AO1).

▶ **Your next task is this:** Below is **a summary of the scope of shari'a law**. You want to explain this in an essay but they are your teacher's notes and so to write them out is simply copying them and not demonstrating any understanding. Re-write your teacher's notes but you need to replace the words used (apart from key religious or philosophical terminology) with different words so that you show that you understand what is being written and that you have your own unique version.

Scope means the range; the limits that shari'a applies to. First and foremost as God's law, shari'a informs Muslims of their religious rules. Shari'a provides laws about when prayers must be said, how animals must be slaughtered for food and how zakat be paid. Secondly, shari'a is a civil and family code. Shari'a is the basis for the Nikkah wedding contract and gives the framework for divorce. Thirdly, shari'a is a moral guide. Anything from prohibiting taking interest and outlawing murder is defined by shari'a. This can be interpreted at a personal, family or state level. Religious scholars who define shari'a issue fatwa rulings which apply to themselves and their followers who voluntarily agree to follow them. Some Muslims argue that as actions are judged by intentions, only God can know this, so shari'a is but a guideline for individuals and should not be used to judge Muslims. Others use it for family law and set up shari'a courts to deal with those cases. Some countries have defined the scope of shari'a to include criminal law and enforced strict punishments, including corporal and capital punishment. Reformist Muslims say it is time to update and restrict the scope of shari'a and separate the secular state from religious affairs.

When you have completed the task, refer to the band descriptors for A2 (WJEC) or A Level (Eduqas) and, in particular, have a look at the demands described in the higher band descriptors towards which you should be aspiring. Ask yourself:

- Does my work demonstrate thorough, accurate and relevant knowledge and understanding of religion and belief?
- Is my work coherent (consistent or make logical sense), clear and well organised?
- Will my work, when developed, be an extensive and relevant response which is specific to the focus of the task?
- Does my work have extensive depth and/or suitable breadth and have excellent use of evidence and examples?
- If appropriate to the task, does my response have thorough and accurate reference to sacred texts and sources of wisdom?
- Are there any insightful connections to be made with other elements of my course?
- Will my answer, when developed and extended to match what is expected in an examination answer, have an extensive range of views of scholars/schools of thought?
- When used, is specialist language and vocabulary both thorough and accurate?

Key skills

Knowledge involves:

Selection of a range of (thorough) accurate and relevant information that is directly related to the specific demands of the question.

This means:

- Selecting relevant material for the question set
- Being focused in explaining and examining the material selected.

Understanding involves:

Explanation that is extensive, demonstrating depth and/or breadth with excellent use of evidence and examples including (where appropriate) thorough and accurate supporting use of sacred texts, sources of wisdom and specialist language.

This means:

- Effective use of examples and supporting evidence to establish the quality of your understanding
- Ownership of your explanation that expresses personal knowledge and understanding and NOT just reproducing a chunk of text from a book that you have rehearsed and memorised.

Specification content

The extent to which human
interpretation may impair
understanding of shari'a.

AO2 Activity

As you read through this section try to
do the following:

1. Pick out the different lines of
   argument that are presented in
   the text and identify any evidence
   given in support.

2. For each line of argument try to
   evaluate whether or not you think
   this is strong or weak.

3. Think of any questions you may
   wish to raise in response to the
   arguments.

This Activity will help you to start
thinking critically about what you
read and help you to evaluate the
effectiveness of different arguments
and from this develop your own
observations, opinions and points
of view that will help with any
conclusions that you make in your
answers to the AO2 questions
that arise.

Issues for analysis and evaluation

The extent to which human interpretation may impair understanding of shari'a

Shari'a is considered by Muslims to be law made by God. Allah sent the Qur'an as
the first source of shari'a. Nothing humans could say would be as good as God's
word, but the Qur'an often provides only vague guidance in places, making human
interpretation necessary.

The first human interpreter of shari'a was Prophet Muhammad. He was considered
the perfect example and interpreter to help Muslims understand shari'a. His
companions and the early generations of Muslims knew the Prophet well, so their
interpretations are considered next. Muslims find Muhammad's interpretations
from the hadith, but these were collected around 200 years later. Human collectors
like Bukhari applied their own interpretations in deciding which hadith to accept as
reliable.

In the first few centuries of Islam, the schools of fiqh grew up. Human
interpretations found answers to key questions that arose on all matters from
prayer rituals to food laws to criminal punishment. They used the Qur'an and
hadith as primary sources that no injunction in fiqh could contradict. Traditional
Muslims regard them as the experts in interpretation of shari'a which we can never
surpass. They had better access to the people of the time who understood what the
Prophet passed down.

Key quote

Islamic law is a shorthand expression for an amphorous and formless body of
legal rulings, judgements, and opinions that have been collected over the course
of many centuries. On any point of law, one will find many conflicting opinions
about what the law of God requires or mandates. (Abou El Fadl)

Other Muslims question whether they really did settle matters. Which law school
should a Muslim follow, or can they mix and match? Shi'a Muslims have further
human interpretation through their Imams, whose authority lies in being of the
Prophet's family, so their interpretations cannot be against what God wants.

Any individual Muslim could make their own opinions on shari'a. Many Salafi
and modern reformist Muslims think that is a good thing. Muslims who read
the Qur'an for themselves can decide on the best course of action. Sunni and
Shi'a Muslims disagree. Shi'a Muslims believe that their Imams and particularly
mujtahid scholars should make the interpretations for people to follow. They
are highly educated in fiqh interpretation, Arabic and logic, so they make better
interpretations.

Sunni Muslims also disagree. Most Sunnis believe that Muslims should follow the
schools of law developed in the early days of Islam, and imitate the interpretations
of scholars like Al-Shafi, who founded one of those schools. Sunnis believe they
made the best interpretations of shari'a and later opinions might impair human
understanding, because people do not have such good knowledge as these
early scholars.

Reformist Muslims may say that human interpretation is good and actually helps
to understand shari'a. Humans can reinterpret shari'a for the modern day and
make Islam fit in better with modern concepts, such as the Universal Declaration
of Human Rights. Without interpretation, there are some unacceptable parts of
shari'a, such as the treatment of women as less reliable witnesses than men. Other
Muslims may see it as wrong to change what they believe is a fixed, God-given law,
which should stay the same forever.

Sayyid Qutb was a leading thinker in the Muslim Brotherhood in the 1950s. He argued that the Muslim world had left behind the true teachings of Islam and reverted to a pre-Islamic state of Jahiliyyah. He argued that to obey shari'a is an essential form of worship for Muslims. Muslims should obey the Qur'an rather than use it for discussion. Muslims must struggle to impose the shari'a in all areas and look for differences between themselves and Western society. He felt as God's law it should apply to all areas of life. Qutb thought that socialism and nationalism had failed as ideologies and should be replaced by Islamism. He influenced many radical Muslims who were to follow his ideas of political Islam. Other Muslims criticised him for creating new political constructs. He defined Islam in very similar terms to Marxists and nationalists, in reaction to what he did not like about them.

Key quote

There are people today who think that admitting God's absolute greatness decreases the value and importance of humans in the creation, as if God and mankind are rivals competing in greatness and power. Meanwhile I feel that whenever our perception of God's greatness increases, with it we become greater, because we are the creation of a great God. (Qutb)

Study tip

It is vital for AO2 that you actually discuss arguments and not just explain what someone may have stated. Try to ask yourself, 'was this a fair point to make?', 'is the evidence sound enough?', 'is there anything to challenge this argument?', 'is this a strong or weak argument?' Such critical analysis will help you develop your evaluation skills

Muslim intellectuals and scholars have criticised Qutb for presenting a flawed understanding of shari'a. They feel that Muslims are affected by the times they live in and change their view of shari'a as a result. It is popular to express religious identity, discuss fatwas and define rules about which foods Muslims should eat or clothes Muslims should wear in their daily lives at college and university. The origins of such conversations are sometimes dubious authorities not educated in religious tradition at all.

Khaled Abou El Fadl argues that shari'a has a special place in the hearts of Muslims as something which is morally pure and beyond human corruption. Nevertheless, he distinguishes between Islamic Law and Muslim law. He argues that what we have is Muslim law, made by imperfect humans. Many Muslims today give misleading interpretations of shari'a which have created a crisis of authority. Nevertheless, this does not stop passion and interest from Muslims who want to search for a truth which works for them in the modern world.

Key quotes

Certain people started to base their fatwas too much on their immediate political circumstances or their psychological state and stopped taking the consensus of hundreds of years of cautious scholars into consideration. (Murad)

The crisis of authority plaguing Islamic law today does not affect its relevance or importance. But it does mean that Islamic law does not have the reasonableness of the determinations generated on its behalf or attributed to it. In the contemporary age, many voices speak in the name of Islamic law, and the problem is that some of these voices are quite unreasonable. (Abou El Fadl)

Key term
Jahiliyyah: state of ignorance according to Muslims which pre-dated the coming of Prophet Muhammad

Key questions
What is shari'a? Is it divine law or human interpretation of it?

Who were the human interpreters of shari'a in the first few centuries of Islam and what did they contribute to the understanding of shari'a?

How might some people be influenced by the conditions of the time to give impaired human opinions of shari'a?

AO2 Activity
List some conclusions that could be drawn from the AO2 reasoning from the above text; try to aim for at least three different possible conclusions. Consider each of the conclusions and collect brief evidence to support each conclusion from the AO1 and AO2 material for this topic. Select the conclusion that you think is most convincing and explain why it is so. Try to contrast this with the weakest conclusion in the list, justifying your argument with clear reasoning and evidence.

Specification content

The extent to which a description of shari'a as law is misleading.

The extent to which a description of shari'a as law is misleading

Shari'a can be described as a straight path. In some ways, shari'a is like law, because a system of courts with judges, deciding over rulings made by mujtahid jurists, grew up in the Middle Ages. This was an organised system like law, although not to the same standards as modern law courts.

Shari'a provides guidance for religious practice. It gives Muslims details about how to pray and categorises actions into compulsory, forbidden and others in between; however, the Qur'an says there is 'no compulsion' in religion. Shari'a guidance in religious matters may help a Muslim lead a life according to God's will to get to heaven. It is not the same as law as we know it. In fact, human rights laws in many countries make it illegal to force people to believe a certain religion or belief.

Shari'a mostly covers religious, civic and moral matters. In many cases these are about personal matters of belief which no one can be made to follow. It can be argued that in this way shari'a is not a law, although some Muslims go to shari'a courts to sort out marital affairs, giving shari'a status in family law. Shari'a provides rules about marriage contracts and other civic matters such as trade. Shari'a courts in many countries, including the UK, can help Muslims deal with these matters and provide judgements, like law courts.

Morals are partly about good manners and partly about laws such as do not murder. Shari'a provides guidance on both. Most countries have their own law courts to deal with criminal cases. At some times in history, and in some places such as Iran and Saudi Arabia, shari'a law does provide the basis for criminal law. To some extent Islam provided judges, rules and organisation at a time when there had been few. At this time shari'a did not operate in the same way as modern courts: there were no juries and women witnesses did not carry the same authority as men.

Key quotes

The Islamic society is that which follows Islam in belief and ways of worship, in law and organisation, in morals and manners. **(Qutb)**

Mankind today is on the brink of a precipice. Humanity is threatened not only by nuclear annihilation but by the absence of values. The West has lost its vitality and Marxism has failed. At this crucial and bewildering juncture, the turn of Islam and the Muslim community has arrived. **(Qutb)**

The schools of law in Sunni and Shi'a Islam were set up by individuals who took their work very seriously. Al-Shafi laid out clear principles for interpreting Islamic teachings in order of priority: begin with the Qur'an and hadith, then use ijma of the companions and finally compare to similar teachings where no direct teaching is available. This logical text-based process is similar to a legal process, and a system of mujtahid scholars and qazi judges became established to organise shari'a like a legal system.

Law applies the same to all individuals equally; however, different individuals can have different interpretations of shari'a. There is disagreement about this between different Muslims. Shi'a Muslims believe they must follow the teachings of a jurist. Some Salafi Muslims believe they can read the Qur'an, hadith and interpretations of the companions of Muhammad and make their own opinions. A law has to apply to everyone and cannot be different for different people. Reformist Muslims support secular states and secular laws. They believe it is better to reform shari'a to make it relevant to the modern day. By accepting secular law, they treat shari'a not as a law but as a personal guide to life.

AO2 Activity

As you read through this section try to do the following:

1. Pick out the different lines of argument that are presented in the text and identify any evidence given in support.

2. For each line of argument try to evaluate whether or not you think this is strong or weak.

3. Think of any questions you may wish to raise in response to the arguments.

This Activity will help you to start thinking critically about what you read and help you to evaluate the effectiveness of different arguments and from this develop your own observations, opinions and points of view that will help with any conclusions that you make in your answers to the AO2 questions that arise.

Sayyid Qutb argued that shari'a is all-embracing law and important for Muslims. He thought that some Muslims had sought to explain or even apologise for what Islam taught and change it to fit in with modern Western values. He and other Islamist Muslims thought that shari'a should become an all-embracing law for Muslims, a part of the law system for everything from family law to criminal law to laws of state. He criticised Western laws and thought that they did not answer the need for God to be at the centre of all aspects of life.

Study tip

It is vital for AO2 that you actually discuss arguments and not just explain what someone may have stated. Try to ask yourself, 'was this a fair point to make?', 'is the evidence sound enough?', 'is there anything to challenge this argument?', 'is this a strong or weak argument?' Such critical analysis will help you develop your evaluation skills.

Qutb's simple message was attractive to many but based on a flawed interpretation of shari'a according to others. Khalied Abou El Fadl defines shari'a as a man-made attempt to make sense of God's law, built up ad hoc over hundreds of years. It contains all kinds of opinions, rulings and other bits and pieces of documentation in historical documents. That does not make it a clearly codified system. Describing shari'a as if it was a clear code of law in a single book, like the Qur'an, is misleading, because it is very different. The human interpretations made over the centuries may have been with the aim of helping Muslims, but they are all made by people who inevitably have human failings, just like everyone else, because there are no perfect Muslims except for the Prophets.

Shari'a has been interpreted in so many different ways it is misleading to call it a law. It can form part of an Islamic legal system, or it can be a code for civic, religious or moral life. It is popular as an idea with many Muslims, yet many Muslims make their own differing opinions which cannot work if there is to be a single system of law. Salafi and reformist Muslims take views which are so different that it would be difficult to imagine a single shari'a. If there are many versions of shari'a then it will be difficult to apply. Furthermore, reformists consider it better to follow secular law, and use shari'a as a personal moral code, rather than a law. To think of shari'a as equal to the laws of a country is misleading. Despite this, to many Muslims it is still important as what they see as the blessed law of God.

Key quote

Islamic law refers to the cumulative body of legal determinations and system of jurisprudential thought of numerous interpretive communities and schools of thought, all of which search the divine will and its relation to the public good. The stated objective of Islamic law is to achieve human well-being. Islamic law is thus the fallible and imperfect attempt by Muslims over centuries to understand and implement the divine norms, to explore right and wrong, and to achieve human welfare. (Abou El Fadl)

Key questions

What makes a law and a legal system?

Are God's law and the laws and traditions that Muslims use the same thing?

What areas do Muslims mostly use shari'a for? Are these the same things that you would expect a legal system to cover?

What do you think some people agree with, and others oppose, Qutb's views?

AO2 Activity

List some conclusions that could be drawn from the AO2 reasoning from the above text; try to aim for at least three different possible conclusions. Consider each of the conclusions and collect brief evidence to support each conclusion from the AO1 and AO2 material for this topic. Select the conclusion that you think is most convincing and explain why it is so. Try to contrast this with the weakest conclusion in the list, justifying your argument with clear reasoning and evidence.

Specification content

Whether or not the doors to ijtihad
are closed.

Whether or not the doors to ijtihad are closed

Ijtihad means personal opinion. It was used to interpret the shari'a in situations where traditional teachings were unclear. All Muslims accept that Muhammad helped interpret the Qur'an and accept his teachings. They also accept that the companions of Muhammad, and the early community of Muslims, knew him well and therefore their ijtihad is likely to be accurate. The early Islamic world in which ijtihad was freely practised was an era of comparative openness, inclusivity and success. Harold Rhode describes the exchange of knowledge which helped make the Muslim world a leader in its time in the early days of the Caliphate.

Key quote

During the first four centuries of Islam, Muslim scholars seem to have exercised independent judgment freely, and debated rigorously new issues that arose. Muslim scholars studied Arabic translations of ancient Greek texts which they thought might help them understand the nature of mankind as well as other aspects of life. These texts, though clearly non-Islamic, nevertheless provided scholars with useful insights. There were also intellectual interchanges with Jewish scholars, particularly in the fields of science, medicine, language, and geography. (Rhode)

Most Sunni Muslims believe that the gates of ijtihad closed soon after the four schools of Sunni law were founded. Al-Shafi and others went into great detail to interpret the Qur'an, sunna, ijma or consensus of scholars and use comparisons to other situations to answer all questions that he felt needed answering. Sunnis believe that soon after, scholars did not have sufficient knowledge to reinterpret Islam. So the gates of ijtihad closed and instead scholars followed taqlid, imitation of earlier scholars and their opinions. The medieval Muslim scholar Al-Ghazali is sometimes thought of as having closed the gates. He argued with Islamic philosophers of the time, saying that their approach was incoherent and did not make sense. After going through a crisis of faith himself, Al-Ghazali wrote about the importance of taking a traditional approach to Islam, without the need for further ijtihad.

Shi'a Muslims have their own schools of law and Imams, who are highly trained to interpret shari'a. They did not close the gates of ijtihad, but restricted its interpretation to the most educated of Imams in the line of the Prophet's family. These Imams attended special Hawza schools in which they were specially trained to make judgements. Ordinary Muslims were taught to follow the jurists and forbidden from making their own opinions. Unlike Sunni Muslims, Shi'a Imams used aql, reasoning, to apply shari'a rulings and continued to do so over the centuries. To them, the gates of ijtihad never closed. Harold Rhode notes how modern politics has affected the way different Shi'a Imams have approached ijtihad. In modern Iran, there is much less use of it, whereas historically Shi'a Imams across the world have used reinterpretation much more often.

Key quote

For Shiites, the Gates of ijtihad have never been closed. Shiite religious figures also have the title mujtahid, or 'one who engages in the exercise of independent judgment and critical thinking to try to solve contemporary problems'. ... Most Iranian mullahs rarely use ijtihad. The Iraqi and Lebanese Shiites are more likely to engage in independent judgment than their counterparts in Iran. (Rhode)

Salafi Muslims believe the gates should be open. They base their interpretations on the Qur'an, sunna and teachings of the sahaba (companions). Rashid Rida influenced Salafi Muslims to believe that anyone could read the sources for

AO2 Activity

As you read through this section try to do the following:

1. Pick out the different lines of argument that are presented in the text and identify any evidence given in support.

2. For each line of argument try to evaluate whether or not you think this is strong or weak.

3. Think of any questions you may wish to raise in response to the arguments.

This Activity will help you to start thinking critically about what you read and help you to evaluate the effectiveness of different arguments and from this develop your own observations, opinions and points of view that will help with any conclusions that you make in your answers to the AO2 questions that arise.

themselves and make their own ijtihad opinion. Taqlid, a form of imitating earlier interpretations made by scholars, has been practised over the centuries since the gates of ijtihad closed. This is not quite the same as making an individual opinion afresh, because it is copying the opinion of an earlier scholar. Taqlid and the scholars who made taqlid rulings have been widely criticised. It has been argued that taqlid on the basis of scholars copying scholars is very far removed from the original interpretations of Muhammad and the companions. Better Muslims go back to the primary sources themselves and make original interpretations. Against this view, others argue that the scholars were the experts. Young Muslims today, who have some education in science or engineering, cannot possibly hope to rival the centuries old expertise of Islamic experts. New interpretations fail to acknowledge this expertise.

Study tip

The study of ijtihad raises questions for the Muslim world today. How far should Muslims change their interpretations? A good analysis at Band 5 will recognise the issues involved and their significance for the religion and its followers; refer to views of various scholars and provide a confident and perceptive analysis.

Khaled Abou El Fadl believes that opening the gates of ijtihad has led to chaos. People with a passion for Islam but little knowledge have made all kinds of strange rulings which have led to a crisis of authority in Islam. He argues that the gates of ijtihad never really closed in the Islamic world over the centuries, it is just that we have not researched the vast number of diverse sources to find out the many and varied interpretations which continued to be made. He recommends rooting ijtihad in traditional scholarship rather than taking independent views.

Reformist Muslims also believe the gates of ijtihad should be open, and interpret ijtihad in different ways. They feel that Muslims should accept secular law and modernise shari'a to accept equality of everyone including other faiths, gay Muslims and minorities. Some traditionalist Muslims disagree and think that is a change too far. They fear reformists will interpret away the very basis of Islamic beliefs leaving only a vague set of traditions that are not very different from those held by other religions. Khaled Abou El Fadl criticises the ijtihad interpretations made by amateurs from both the Salafi and reformist approaches as not being grounded in Islamic scholarship.

Different Muslims may give different answers to this question depending on their tradition. To some, ijtihad was closed from the time of the early scholars onwards. To others, it is wide open for reinterpretation in the modern world. Muslims are free to make their own choices about whether they wish to exercise personal opinion, or subscribe to a teaching from the past.

Study tip

It is vital for AO2 that you actually discuss arguments and not just explain what someone may have stated. Try to ask yourself, 'was this a fair point to make?', 'is the evidence sound enough?', 'is there anything to challenge this argument?', 'is this a strong or weak argument?' Such critical analysis will help you develop your evaluation skills

Key quote

Reopening the proverbial doors became the means for licensing a chaotic condition where numerous participants under the slogan of practising ijtihad claimed to be authoritative experts of Islamic law. So, for instance, many of the leaders of Islamic movements were by training engineers or computer scientists, and many of the popular and influential voices of reform were never trained in law, leave alone Islamic law. (Abou El Fadl)

Key questions

What is ijtihad and why might it be seen as controversial amongst Muslims?

Why do you think some Muslims regard ijtihad as only valid in the early days of Islam?

What might a Salafi; a Shi'a; a reformist and a traditional Sunni Muslim think about ijtihad from their differing perspectives?

AO2 Activity

List some conclusions that could be drawn from the AO2 reasoning from the above text; try to aim for at least three different possible conclusions. Consider each of the conclusions and collect brief evidence to support each conclusion from the AO1 and AO2 material for this topic. Select the conclusion that you think is most convincing and explain why it is so. Try to contrast this with the weakest conclusion in the list, justifying your argument with clear reasoning and evidence.

Key skills

Analysis involves:

Identifying issues raised by the materials in the AO1, together with those identified in the AO2 section, and presents sustained and clear views, either of scholars or from a personal perspective ready for evaluation.

This means:

- That your answers are able to identify key areas of debate in relation to a particular issue

- That you can identify, and comment upon, the different lines of argument presented by others

- That your response comments on the overall effectiveness of each of these areas or arguments.

Evaluation involves:

Considering the various implications of the issues raised based upon the evidence gleaned from analysis and provides an extensive detailed argument with a clear conclusion.

This means:

- That your answer weighs up the consequences of accepting or rejecting the various and different lines of argument analysed

- That your answer arrives at a conclusion through a clear process of reasoning.

AO2 Developing skills

It is now important to consider the information that has been covered in this section; however, the information in its raw form is too extensive and so has to be processed in order to meet the requirements of the examination. This can be done by practising more advanced skills associated with AO2. For assessment objective 2 (AO2), which involves 'critical analysis' and 'evaluation' skills, we are going to focus on different ways in which the skills can be demonstrated effectively, and also refer to how the performance of these skills is measured (see generic band descriptors for A2 [WJEC] AO2 or A Level [Eduqas] AO2).

▶ **Your next task is this:** Below is **a brief summary of two different points of view concerning the extent of the similarities and differences between Rashid Rida and Tariq Ramadan**. You want to use these two views and lines of argument for an evaluation; however, they need further reasons and evidence for support to fully develop the argument. Re-present these two views in a fully evaluative style by adding further reasons and evidence that link to their arguments. Aim for a further 100 words.

Tariq Ramadan takes a diametrically opposed view to Rashid Rida. Tariq is a modern Muslim intellectual, who has claimed at times to be a reformist, whereas Rashid was a radical Salafi who supported political change against colonial rulers. He thought it would be better to live in a religious state. Ramadan wants Muslims to take pride in their scholarly heritage and find a balance between that and the modern world within the secular state.

There are many common elements in the approaches of Rashid Rida and Tariq Ramadan. Both saw Muslims were reacting against colonialism and its legacy and both wanted to steer Muslims to reform their own traditions to cope with this. Both refrained from criticising Islam and some breaches of human rights because they recognised the emotional importance of Islamic Law needed to be recognised to get Muslims on side. Both aimed to reinterpret shari'a for the present day and considered it important to include it in some way in future Muslim administrations.

When you have completed the task, refer to the band descriptors for A2 (WJEC) or A Level (Eduqas) and, in particular, have a look at the demands described in the higher band descriptors towards which you should be aspiring. Ask yourself:

- Is my answer a confident critical analysis and perceptive evaluation of the issue?

- Is my answer a response that successfully identifies and thoroughly addresses the issues raised by the question set?

- Does my work show an excellent standard of coherence, clarity and organisation?

- Will my work, when developed, contain thorough, sustained and clear views that are supported by extensive, detailed reasoning and/or evidence?

- Are the views of scholars/schools of thought used extensively, appropriately and in context?

- Does my answer convey a confident and perceptive analysis of the nature of any possible connections with other elements of my course?

- When used, is specialist language and vocabulary both thorough and accurate?

F: Muslim understandings of jihad

The different meanings of jihad (struggle)

Specification content

The different meanings of jihad (struggle) both greater and lesser.

In the past few years jihad has been in the news quite often. There have been images of bloodshed from places such as Afghanistan and Syria, with Muslim fighters called mujahedeen proclaiming it a jihad. They appear to believe that what they are doing is in the cause of religion. Other Muslims denounce such acts and claim that this is nothing to do with jihad. So what does this term mean, and what do different Muslims understand by it?

The Qur'an literally refers to jihad as striving. It is something Muslims do and put effort into, when at times it can be difficult. The purpose is to do the right thing for Allah. **Averroes**, a famous Sunni Muslim scholar from medieval Spain, said that there were four different types of jihad:

- The greater jihad, the jihad of the heart to struggle against the temptations of the devil.
- The jihad of the word, to strive to speak the truth and tell others about Islam.
- The jihad of the hand, through choosing to do the right things and stop wrongdoing.
- Jihad of the sword, holy war.

To struggle in the way of God could involve all kinds of activities. A Muslim might give up buying a new mobile phone and instead give that money to help the poor and needy. A student might stop talking about the latest gossip in their college canteen, and spend a few minutes telling their friends good things about their belief in Islam. In the evening, a Muslim might miss their favourite television programme to go and hear a talk about Islam at their local mosque, so that they can learn more about their faith. In each of these, a Muslim may prefer to do something else but instead takes the more difficult option and does something for the sake of their religion. All of these may be classed as forms of jihad.

Whatever view a Muslim takes on the meaning of it, they agree that jihad is important. Muslim scholars often simplify the different types of jihad into two: the greater jihad, involving a personal struggle, and the lesser jihad, which can involve violent and non-violent action.

Key quote

Somebody asked, 'O Muhammad, who is the best among the people?' Muhammad replied: 'A believer who strives for what Allah wants with his life and his possessions.' The person then asked: 'Who is next?' Muhammad said: 'A believer who retreats to the mountains and spends time in prayer, away from idle people.' (Hadith of Prophet Muhammad)

Greater jihad

The root of the word 'Islam' means peace, and there is a great deal in the Qur'an and the traditions of the Prophet to promote peace rather than war. In the Qur'an 5:48, Muslims are encouraged to acknowledge that Allah made people different. They should not fight against each other, but compete to have the best character and do virtuous actions. This daily struggle for a Muslim is known as 'greater jihad'.

Key quote

The Qur'an 2:256

There shall be no compulsion in religion. (Yusuf Ali)

Key terms

Greater jihad: the inner or inward personal struggle of a Muslim to live the Islamic life

Jihad: striving and struggle in favour of the way of Allah according to Muslims, which can take various different forms

Mujahedeen: the plural of Mujahid, Muslims who take part in jihad

Key person

Averroes: known as **Ibn Rushd** in Arabic, Averroes was one of the leading Muslim intellectuals of his day. He lived from 1126 to 1198 in Cordoba, Spain. He wrote about Islam, maths, medicine and learning.

Averroes (Ibn Rushd)

quickfire

1.18 What were the four forms of jihad that Averroes defined?

The discipline involved in living daily according to Muslim principles is in itself the greater struggle (jihad).

Key quote

The Qur'an 5:48

If Allah had so willed, He would have made you a single people, but His plan is to test you in what He hath given you: so strive as in a race in all virtues. The goal of you all is to Allah. It is He that will show you the truth of the matters in which ye dispute. **(Yusuf Ali)**

The medieval Islamic scholar Al-Ghazali wrote a book called *The Revival of the Religious Sciences*. This was very influential amongst Sunni Muslims. In it, he quotes Prophet Muhammad as having said: 'The fighter against unbelief is he who fights against his ego in obeying God'. Al-Ghazali went on to describe some of the weapons the soldier of this type of jihad could use. These included the weapons of knowledge, wisdom and reflection.

The practices of Islam can be very demanding upon Muslims. To carry out the five daily prayers requires time and effort. It involves getting up before dawn for the fajr prayer. In the summer this can mean getting up before 5am in the UK. Fasting in Ramadan can involve many tempting situations. In non-Muslim countries, a Muslim is supposed to carry on with their daily routine as normal, passing cafes and shopping centres as they go to work watching others eat. A Muslim may think thoughts like: no one will see me, or a little bit won't matter. These inner thoughts are what Muslims struggle against in the greater jihad. They try to put Islam first and avoid being tempted to break their fast. A Muslim might go out with their friends and be tempted to join in with gossip about their classmates. Jihad can be the struggle not to backbite or say wrong things about another person, whether you like them or not.

Al-Ghazali and other Sunni scholars saw the inner jihad as the greatest and most important struggle. Shi'a scholars have also referred to the greater jihad as a personal struggle to do the right thing and avoid sin. Some Muslims see the greater jihad as more than keeping to the basics of Islam. Sufis develop their inner soul, the **nafs**, to form a deeper relationship with Allah. They practise **zikr**, remembrance of Allah, to take them away from worldly desires in their struggle to feel closer to their creator.

Not all Muslims accept the idea of an inner jihad. Some argue that in the early days of Islam, and as the Islamic Empire expanded, jihad was used to mean war. Then, as the expansion stopped, the meaning changed to mean an inner struggle. The historian Bernard Lewis argues that most early Muslim scholars saw jihad as a holy war, but this changed over time.

Lesser jihad

The jihad that is often referred to in the news as holy war, is **lesser jihad**. In fact, there are two types of lesser jihad. Both are about an outward struggle to improve matters for Muslims. But the first can be done without violence, through preaching, negotiation and getting involved in community projects, charities and so on.

In places, the Qur'an refers to war and violence; in other places, it refers to peace. This requires care to understand and interpret it within the context of the time. Muhammad did engage in battles and raids against other tribes at the time, which should be understood within the context of tribalism of seventh-century Arabia. He introduced some standards that the other tribes had not followed beforehand. He ordered that women and children, trees and crops, should not be hurt or damaged. Abu Bakr further developed the rules of warfare as defensive and not to exploit others to gain booty.

The lesser jihad could mean organising a protest to demand equal rights for Muslims in a country where they are oppressed. It could mean struggling to get

Key terms

Lesser jihad: the outward struggle for Islamic life that may be done without violence or through war

Nafs: the soul or inner self; the soul is in our deepest thoughts and lives beyond death

Zikr: worship by remembering the names of Allah in Sufism

rights and fair treatment for poor Muslims in a country where they are being treated unfairly. The Pakistani Imam **Fazlur Rehman** argues that jihad is a struggle for justice for the poor in society. The South African researcher, **Farid Esack**, saw jihad as a form of social action. When the state of apartheid ended in South Africa, he became commissioner for gender equality, tackling prejudice against women.

Shi'a Muslims teach that lesser jihad can only be called by an Imam in the line of the Prophet's family. The Hidden Imam will return to the world to bring justice and liberate people from oppression in the future. Any Imam calling jihad in this world acts in place of the Hidden Imam.

AO1 Activity

Create a thought shower of all the different types of jihad, with examples, that you have come across in this chapter so far.

The importance and significance of greater jihad as a personal spiritual struggle for every Muslim

Key quotes

The mujahid is the person who makes jihad against himself for the sake of Allah. (Hadith of Prophet Muhammad)

'Shall I tell you what is better for you than spending gold and silver, and better than fighting your enemy?' They said: 'Of course.' He said, 'The remembrance of Allah'. (Hadith of Prophet Muhammad)

Sufi Muslims have particularly stressed the importance of fighting the jihad against selfishness. Sufi holy people struggled against their desires to own luxuries and preferred to live a simple life of prayer. Some even went out of their homes and spent periods of time in the deserts, caves and mountains. They contemplated the world and thought that in their solitude they could get closer to Allah.

Rabia of Basra was a Sufi woman who lived in the Middle East. She wrote many poems about love for Allah. She spent her life fighting against selfish thoughts, preferring to develop selfless love of Allah. The people of Basra saw her running through the streets with a bucket of water and burning torch. They asked Rabia what on earth she was doing. Rabia replied that she was fighting against the fires of hell with the bucket of water. The burning torch she carried to burn down the rewards of Heaven. What she meant was that people should not think of getting to Paradise in a selfish way, to live somewhere nice, like they might own a nice house. She said that true Muslims own nothing other than love for Allah.

Rabia of Basra

The jihad of the nafs

Some Sufis call their journey through life a jihad of the nafs. They struggle against their own self to develop a deeper relationship with Allah. This is sometimes defined in terms of seven stages of the self. As the Sufi rises through the stages, she reaches higher stages of self-awareness, and distances herself from the world around her. The Sufi fights against his ego to find modesty, compassion and through this, freedom. He fights against selfishness, hypocrisy and self-pity.

Key people

Farid Esack: South African lecturer who led the Commission for Gender Equalities after the fall of apartheid.

Fazlur Rehman: Pakistani religious politician who argues jihad includes struggle against inequality in society.

Specification content

The importance and significance of greater jihad as a personal spiritual struggle for every Muslim.

Key term

Mujahid: a Muslim who takes part in jihad

Key person

Rabia of Basra: a Sufi mystic who lived in Basra, present day Iraq, c715–801. She wrote poetry about leaving behind the world in favour of love for Allah.

Some Sufi orders have defined the stages of fighting against the self in order to get closer to Allah.

Nafs
The Self

Struggle against	Nafs al-Kamila **Pure**	Struggle for **Freedom**
Imbalance	Nafs al-Mardiyyah **Pleased**	**God consciousness**
Self-pity	Nafs ar-Radiyyah **Contented**	**Endurance**
Ambition	Nafs al-Mutmainnah **Relaxed**	**Compassion**
Weakness	Nafs al-Mulhimah **Disciplined**	**Modesty**
Hypocrisy	Nafs al-Lawwamah **Critical**	**Self-awareness**
Selfishness	An-Nafs al-Ammara **Wicked**	**Routine**

Simplified version of the Sufi spiritual inner struggle with the nafs

The Sufi struggle against the nafs

Some Muslims reject Sufi practices. They see them as later innovations which detract from Islam. Sufis say that Muhammad went into the desert and meditated in Cave Hira for days on end, and this sets an example for Sufis to follow. Others say that the organisation of the stages of nafs and the Sufi orders is a later **bid'ah**, an innovation, which was not authorised in the word of Allah.

All Muslims go through periods when they may find it a struggle to practise Islam. Some may go through periods of doubt about their faith. Young Muslims, in particular, living in Western countries like the UK, may struggle to understand and practise their faith. Traditional Muslims may shun relationships before marriage, since they feel that marriages should be arranged marriages. Yet temptation may affect many young Muslims as they mix freely with other students at college and university. Social pressure to fit in, join a party, drink alcohol and leave aside prayer times, may create a struggle in the minds of many Muslims as they try to balance modern living with the requirements of their faith.

Islamic traditions include choosing the right friends, so a Muslim is not led astray from their faith. That can be hard to do. Another tradition is to always respect parents. Jihad does not mean that Muslims should shy away from others, so that they can maintain their faith. In fact, it means the opposite in that Muslims should interact and tell others about their religion and make friends with people of different religious backgrounds. This requires confidence and some Muslims may be nervous to do it. It can be regarded as a struggle. That in itself is a form of non-violent jihad.

Key term

Bid'ah: an innovation or something new introduced into religion after the time of the Prophet. Some Muslims reject later practices, such as Sufism, as bid'ah

quickfire

1.19 What is a mujahid?

AO1 Activity

Give examples of everyday things a Muslim might struggle against, and other things they might struggle for, in the greater jihad. Try to think of one example for each stage on the nafs diagram. For example, starting off a Muslim might struggle to get up early to pray, as part of their struggle to keep the routine of the five daily prayers.

The historical context and the specific conditions of lesser jihad

Specification content

The historical context and the specific conditions of lesser jihad.

Many holy books contain passages about war and violence. This is as much true about the Old Testament in the Bible as it is about the Qur'an and hadith. There are some verses that appear to refer to war, and need careful interpretation to be understood. The Qur'an is written in a form of Arabic, and was revealed in the context of tribal Arabia in the early seventh century. A literal translation of the Qur'an, out of context, can give a very different meaning from what may have originally been intended.

Some verses in the Qur'an appear to support jihad as war. The Qur'an 2:190–193 is an example. There are many elements to this section. Muslims are called to fight a war, but only whilst others are fighting against them. It is a call for a defensive war against oppression.

Muhammad faced local tribal enemies, just as others did, in seventh-century Arabia. Attacks on traders and their riches carried by camel caravans from oasis to trading centre across the desert were common. At the Battle of Badr in 624, Muhammad and the Muslims attacked a trading caravan of their enemies and despite being a smaller force, were successful. This victory was seen as a gift from God.

Key quote

The Qur'an 2:190–193

Fight in the cause of Allah those who fight you, but do not transgress limits; for Allah loveth not transgressors. And slay them wherever ye catch them, and turn them out from where they have turned you out; for tumult and oppression are worse than slaughter; but fight them not at the Sacred Mosque, unless they (first) fight you there; but if they fight you, slay them. Such is the reward of those who suppress faith. But if they cease, Allah is Oft-forgiving, Most Merciful. And fight them on until there is no more tumult or oppression, and there prevail justice and faith in Allah. But if they cease, let there be no hostility except to those who practise oppression. (Yusuf Ali)

The Jewish tribes of Madinah

In some places, the Qur'an refers to Jewish tribes negatively. Muhammad gave the Jewish tribes of Banu Qaynuqa and Banu Nadir amnesty, but when they broke the terms and assisted Muhammad's enemies, he forced the Jewish tribes to leave the region. Such references could be interpreted in different ways. If the verses are understood within the context of tribal rivalries, treachery and alliances at the time, then commands to banish and attack could mean that the Muslims were simply behaving in the same way as other tribes would expect them to. The days of early Arabia were violent and cruel and raiding between different tribes was common, just as it was between the Saxons and the Vikings in England at the time. If such verses are taken out of context, they could be interpreted in an anti-Semitic way, to mean persecute Jews. Some Muslims have recognised that there is a problem with anti-Semitism amongst some Muslims, partly due to misinterpretation of these verses.

Muhammad's companion and first Caliph, according to Sunni Muslims, was Abu Bakr. He gave the opinion that on the battlefield women, children and the elderly should not be harmed. Trees, crops and livestock should not be destroyed. Muslims should not double cross others and should remain firm in faith. Religious people, such as monks, should not be harmed. Abu Bakr's opinions added to Muhammad's guidance that war should be defensive. It should not be used to convert others to Islam or to gain property or wealth for oneself.

quickfire

1.20 Describe a feature of the tribal context in which Muhammad lived.

quickfire

1.21 List Abu Bakr's rules for jihad.

Key terms

Anti-Semitism: prejudice against people of the Jewish faith

Banu Nadir: a Jewish tribe exiled by Muhammad after breaching terms of an amnesty

Banu Qaynuqa: a Jewish tribe exiled by Muhammad after breaching terms of an amnesty

Battle of Badr: a raid on trading caravans by Muhammad and the Muslims in 624

The early Muslim Caliphs greatly expanded the Muslim Empire. Within little more than a hundred years it stretched from Baghdad to North Africa. The historian William Montgomery Watt argued that this was probably a period of general warfare to gain wealth and booty, rather than religious warfare for jihad.

The problems in applying lesser jihad today with specific reference to modern warfare

In the modern world, some Muslims reacted against colonial rule and suggested that jihad as an armed struggle could be fought. **Hasan al-Banna**, who led the Muslim Brotherhood in Egypt, called for Muslims to struggle against British rule in that country. In the 1980s, the Soviet Union ruled over the Muslim country of Afghanistan with military force. The Muslim Brotherhood preacher Abdullah Azzam issued a fatwah calling for Muslims to fight jihad against the Soviets. Some Muslims including Osama bin Laden joined this jihad. Militant ideas spread from there to other parts of the world, and Muslim jihadists were responsible for the attacks on the Twin Towers in New York in 2001. In these attacks, the Muslim jihadists committed suicide in their act of flying planes into the World Trade Centre, in so doing killed thousands of innocent people.

Muslims who have joined the modern jihad movement often say they are doing so for the sake of religion, and can find verses from the Qur'an which they feel justified their actions. Other Muslims denounce what they do as un-Islamic. The modern jihadists tend to see the world as Muslim against non-Muslim, and they also oppose other Muslims, such as Shi'a and Sufis, who disagree with them. Mainstream Muslims say that the Qur'an condemns the killing of innocent people and regards it as a serious crime. They also say that it does not justify suicide, as in suicide bombings or any other form of suicide. To use suicide in jihad is a bid'ah. In other words, the jihadists have strayed away from the true teachings of Islam. One of the problems in the modern, information-rich, Internet-accessible world is that people can go onto the Internet and find out all sorts of different Islamic sites. Some of them are written by Muslims who are not scholars and take an extremist view. It can be difficult and confusing for young Muslims to understand the issue of jihad, and small numbers have become involved in terrorism. The vast majority of Muslims condemn such actions.

Suicide as a tactic in lesser jihad has a recent history. Japanese kamikaze pilots flew suicide missions against American naval bases towards the end of World War Two, but there was no tradition of suicide in Islam at the time. The creation of modern bombs has made suicide bombing possible at the pull of a chord; which is too easy for someone who has been brainwashed to carry out in a rash moment. The Qur'an teaches that human life is sacred and is created by Allah; to kill yourself is to take away from Allah the moment of your death that is rightly Allah's choosing. This means that suicide bombing is forbidden. The Qur'an equates the loss of a single innocent life as equivalent to the loss of all of humanity: a serious crime. Some Muslims have condemned suicide bombing but failed to rule it out completely in areas of the world such as Israel, where they feel Muslims are being persecuted in the Israel–Palestine conflict. Others, including the scholar **Muhammad Tahir-ul-Qadri**, have ruled it out everywhere in principle, saying that an injustice does not justify using forbidden tactics in response.

Jihad should not be associated with any one particular group or sect. Sometimes the impression is given that violent jihad originated in Saudi Arabia. Some proponents of jihad came from the Salafi school of thought from Saudi Arabia; others from the Egyptian base of the Muslim Brotherhood. However, some of the strongest opponents of jihad have also been Salafi. Saudi Arabia operates a deradicalisation programme which seeks to re-educate Muslims who have become involved in violent jihad, or are sympathetic to it, by teaching them conservative Islamic beliefs. There are jihad movements amongst the Sufis of Kashmir and the Shi'a militias of Iraq, as well as Salafi Muslims operating in parts of Syria and Yemen.

Specification content

The problems in applying lesser jihad today with specific reference to modern warfare.

Key term

Muslim Brotherhood: a group founded in Egypt in the nineteenth century in opposition to British colonial rule

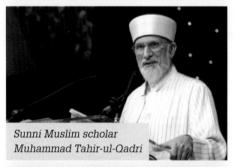

Sunni Muslim scholar Muhammad Tahir-ul-Qadri

Siavosh Derakhti, a Swedish Muslim

Key people

Hasan al-Banna: founder of the Egyptian radical Muslim Brotherhood.

Muhammad Tahir-ul-Qadri: a Pakistani Sunni scholar who produced a detailed fatwa against terrorism and suicide bombing.

Siavosh Derakhti, a young Swedish Muslim, began campaigning against prejudice whilst he was at school. He got his class mates interested in going to visit the remains of Auschwitz concentration camp, where over a million Jews were murdered by the Nazis during World War Two. This inspired him to tackle prejudice. He set up the organisation Young People Against Anti-Semitism and Xenophobia. His peaceful campaign against prejudice is another version of lesser jihad.

Key quotes

The Qur'an 5:32
Whoever kills a person unjustly… it is as though he has killed all mankind. And whoever saves a life, it is as though he had saved all mankind. (Yusuf Ali)

They [terrorists] can't claim that their suicide bombings are martyrdom operations and that they become the heroes of the Muslim ummah. No, they become heroes of hellfire, and they are leading towards hellfire. (Muhammad Tahir-ul-Qadri)

The Qur'an 5:28
If thou dost stretch thy hand against me, to slay me, it is not for me to stretch my hand against thee to slay thee: for I do fear Allah, the cherisher of the worlds. (Yusuf Ali)

Amina Wadud, an American professor of Islam and Imam over men and women at progressive mosques, has called for a gender jihad for women's rights. This is a new way of looking at jihad. She considers that traditionally Muslim men have oppressed women, and now women need to stand up and demand equal treatment. As part of her gender jihad, Amina has led Jummah prayers and preached Friday sermons at mosques where men and women pray together. Her progressive view of Islam is certainly a struggle against the practice of most mosques, which are led by male Imams and in which men and women normally pray with a degree of separation.

Pacifism

There is no tradition of pacifism within Islamic Law schools. However, the Qur'an tells part of the story of Cain and Abel, two brothers who fall out, a story that can also be found in the Old Testament of the Bible. Abel does not fight back against Cain, justifying turning the other cheek rather than fighting back with violence. It can be argued that this justifies non-violence in the face of aggression.

There are a few examples of Muslims who became pacifists. The Pathan Muslim Abdul Ghaffar Khan, from the frontier of Pakistan and Afghanistan, was a good friend of the Hindu Mahatma Gandhi. Both believed in peaceful struggle against the British rule of India in the first half of the twentieth century.

AO1 Activity

You are a radio reporter interviewing a Muslim scholar about why they are opposed to the modern jihadist movement. Write down what they said in the interview in question and answer format. Give clear reasons to justify why they oppose modern, violent jihad.

In the latter twentieth century, Pakistan and India developed nuclear weapons in an arms race against each other. Both wanted control over the disputed territory of Kashmir. Some Muslims argued that nuclear weapons brought prestige and power to Pakistan, and deterred India from invading. Others argued that nuclear weapons should not be allowed, because the bombs would kill many innocent people if used, and the Qur'an forbids the killing of innocent life. The Campaign for Nuclear Disarmament (CND) is an international campaign of people from all faiths and none to remove all nuclear weapons, and has some members who are Muslim.

Key person

Amina Wadud: feminist Professor of Islam from the USA who argues in favour of a gender jihad for women's rights and has led Friday prayers over men and women.

quickfire

1.22 Name two Muslims who influenced the modern jihad movement.

quickfire

1.23 What is Muhammad Tahir-ul-Qadri's opinion on suicide attacks?

Key terms

Pacifism: the idea that violence should never be used, not even in self-defence. Protest and other non-violent means can be used in struggle

Xenophobia: extreme prejudice against another who is perceived as different

Pacifist Muslim Abdul Ghaffar Khan with Mahatma Gandhi

Key quote

I am going to give you such a weapon that the police and the army will not be able to stand against it. It is the weapon of the Prophet, but you are not aware of it. That weapon is patience and righteousness. No power on earth can stand against it. (Abdul Ghaffar Khan)

Key skills

Knowledge involves:

Selection of a range of (thorough) accurate and relevant information that is directly related to the specific demands of the question.

This means:

- Selecting relevant material for the question set

- Being focused in explaining and examining the material selected.

Understanding involves:

Explanation that is extensive, demonstrating depth and/or breadth with excellent use of evidence and examples including (where appropriate) thorough and accurate supporting use of sacred texts, sources of wisdom and specialist language.

This means:

- Effective use of examples and supporting evidence to establish the quality of your understanding

- Ownership of your explanation that expresses personal knowledge and understanding and NOT just reproducing a chunk of text from a book that you have rehearsed and memorised.

AO1 Developing skills

It is now important to consider the information that has been covered in this section; however, the information in its raw form is too extensive and so has to be processed in order to meet the requirements of the examination. This can be done by practising more advanced skills associated with AO1. For assessment objective 1 (AO1), which involves demonstrating 'knowledge' and 'understanding' skills, we are going to focus on different ways in which the skills can be demonstrated effectively, and also refer to how the performance of these skills is measured (see generic band descriptors for A2 [WJEC] AO1 or A Level [Eduqas] AO1).

▶ **Your next task is this:** Below is **a brief summary of the significance of greater jihad as a personal struggle for every Muslim**. You want to explain this in an essay but as it stands at present it is too brief. In order that you demonstrate more depth of understanding, develop this summary by providing examples that will help you explain it further. Aim for 200 words in total.

All Muslims struggle against temptation. It is hard to keep the five daily prayers on time, or donate money to charity when luxuries are available to buy. The greater jihad helps Muslims struggle against their own nafs. This helps them to strengthen faith and think about what is more important in life. Some Muslims take heart from the writings of Rabia of Basra and other Sufis to help them develop inner, spiritual strength. Others follow a deeper jihad of the nafs through several stages of purification in thought and deed, leaving a believer to focus on nothing but the reality of Allah.

When you have completed the task, refer to the band descriptors for A2 (WJEC) or A Level (Eduqas) and, in particular, have a look at the demands described in the higher band descriptors towards which you should be aspiring. Ask yourself:

- Does my work demonstrate thorough, accurate and relevant knowledge and understanding of religion and belief?

- Is my work coherent (consistent or make logical sense), clear and well organised?

- Will my work, when developed, be an extensive and relevant response which is specific to the focus of the task?

- Does my work have extensive depth and/or suitable breadth and have excellent use of evidence and examples?

- If appropriate to the task, does my response have thorough and accurate reference to sacred texts and sources of wisdom?

- Are there any insightful connections to be made with other elements of my course?

- Will my answer, when developed and extended to match what is expected in an examination answer, have an extensive range of views of scholars/schools of thought?

- When used, is specialist language and vocabulary both thorough and accurate?

Issues for analysis and evaluation

Misunderstandings of the term jihad

This section covers AO2 content and skills

Specification content

Misunderstandings of the term jihad.

The term jihad is used in the Qur'an and hadith, the primary sources of shari'a for Muslims. Islamic scholars over the years have given different interpretations about what jihad means. It is therefore not surprising that misunderstandings have grown up. One person's incorrect understanding might be the true meaning to another. Some regard jihad as an inner struggle against temptation to do the right thing. Some encourage jihad as a struggle for morality and to teach and spread Islam peacefully. Others interpret jihad as a holy war. In the media, the term is usually used to mean a holy war waged by Muslims against others, including barbaric acts of terrorism.

Key quote

My mother would have been horrified if she had known that in the West the word jihad has become a code word for holy war … jihad, for my mother, as it does for most Muslims, means perseverance, endurance, and exertion towards excellence. (Khaled Abou El Fadl)

A minority of Muslims misunderstand Muhammad's jihad as offensive. They think he attacked other tribes, or committed war to gain more followers and forcibly convert others to Islam. A few, incorrectly, believe that because he expelled two Jewish tribes, that this justifies anti-Semitism. Most Muslims point out that tribalism in the time of Muhammad involved all of these things. However, Muhammad tried to be more peaceful than others in using force as a last resort. The Qur'an said that there should be 'no compulsion' in religion and encouraged dialogue with Jews and Christians as fellow believers.

Medieval Sunni Muslims such as Al-Ghazali taught that there was a greater jihad, the struggle to follow Islam against temptation within oneself, and lesser jihad, which was an outward struggle. Some people thought his interpretation was a misunderstanding; others that it was authentic to traditions in the Qur'an and hadith which refer to an inner struggle. Shi'a scholars have also recognised these meanings of jihad and encouraged their followers to follow the inner struggle first and foremost. They put restrictions on lesser jihad, which can only be called by educated Imams in limited circumstances of self-defence.

Sufi Muslims may follow an inner struggle to develop their nafs and reach a higher state of God-consciousness. Some Muslims say this is a misunderstanding of jihad and of Islam as these practices go further than the practices of the Companions of Muhammad and are innovations called bid'ah. Sufis argue that the development of the nafs is the most difficult and most important struggle they can undertake because it brings them closer to Allah. Whilst most Muslims would agree that the greater jihad is an inner struggle, few go on to practise the worship of zikr to the extent of Sufis.

Some people associate the term jihad with modern holy wars and terrorism. Groups such as the Muslim Brotherhood and Muslims such as Abdullah Azzam have encouraged this view and Muslims can sometimes be seen in the news involved with terrorism. However, other Muslims condemn these actions and protest: 'Not in my name!' They condemn extremism as a distortion and say that innocent lives must never be taken. The idea of suicide in modern jihad appears to be very new and not supported by the Qur'an, hadith or traditional scholars. As creations of Allah, Islam teaches that humans are not allowed to harm themselves. Only Allah creates life and only Allah takes it away. Those who commit suicide are both harming themselves and deciding the moment of their death: something prohibited in Islam. Nevertheless, there have been terrorists who have appeared

Study tip

It is vital for AO2 that you actually discuss arguments and not just explain what someone may have stated. Try to ask yourself, 'was this a fair point to make?', 'is the evidence sound enough?', 'is there anything to challenge this argument?', 'is this a strong or weak argument?' Such critical analysis will help you develop your evaluation skills

AO2 Activity

As you read through this section try to do the following:

1. Pick out the different lines of argument that are presented in the text and identify any evidence given in support.

2. For each line of argument try to evaluate whether or not you think this is strong or weak.

3. Think of any questions you may wish to raise in response to the arguments.

This Activity will help you to start thinking critically about what you read and help you to evaluate the effectiveness of different arguments and from this develop your own observations, opinions and points of view that will help with any conclusions that you make in your answers to the AO2 questions that arise.

Key quote

The terrorists can't claim that their suicide bombings are martyrdom operations and that they become the heroes of the Muslim ummah. No, they become heroes of hellfire, and they are leading towards hellfire. (Muhammad Tahir-ul-Qadri)

Key questions

What different meanings of the term jihad are there?

Why would some Muslims consider Sufi interpretations of jihad misunderstandings?

How do the media portray jihad? Does this reflect an accurate understanding?

What are the differences between different scholars on the issue?

AO2 Activity

List some conclusions that could be drawn from the AO2 reasoning from the above text; try to aim for at least three different possible conclusions. Consider each of the conclusions and collect brief evidence to support each conclusion from the AO1 and AO2 material for this topic. Select the conclusion that you think is most convincing and explain why it is so. Try to contrast this with the weakest conclusion in the list, justifying your argument with clear reasoning and evidence.

in news media claiming that they have committed actions in the name of Islam. Islamic scholars such as Tahir-ul-Qadri have denounced their actions, exposing their interpretation of jihad as a false one.

Skaykh bin Baz was a leading Saudi Salafi jurist from 1993 to 1999. Bin Baz issued a fatwa supporting the waging of jihad against non-Muslims if they rejected the message of Islam or refused to pay the Jizya tax levied on non-Muslims in an Islamic state. Al-Azhar University in Cairo issued a rebuttal, accepting that jihad could be interpreted as a struggle to call others to embrace Islam, but said this should be done peacefully. In a book called *The Response*, Al-Azhar challenged many of the fatwas issued by Salafi Imams and supported a traditional Sunni interpretation of Islam. The difference was not just the view of one sect: there are Muslims in each sect who take a different opinion. The divergence shows the diversity of belief about jihad. If scholars disagree, ordinary Muslims can easily get confused.

The news media often give the impression that the meaning of jihad is a violent struggle against Western civilisation. They show images of Muslims who fight what they call jihad, sometimes in Middle Eastern countries in support of Islam as a political movement; and sometimes in the West in support of these political Islamist movements and terrorist atrocities. Most Muslims disagree with this, saying that acts of terrorism are nothing to do with Islam and quoting the tradition that killing one innocent life is like killing humanity, referred to earlier in this chapter. Behind these positions, some Muslims have sympathy with the idea of Islam being involved in politics, but disagree with the tactic of jihad employed as a method of achieving it. Others disagree with both the method and the ideal.

Social reformers say that it is a modern jihad to struggle for equality for women and to resist xenophobia, anti-Semitism and other prejudices. This could be seen as a non-violent form of lesser jihad which can reform Islam and make it relevant to the present day. Traditionalist Muslims might argue that this is a misunderstanding of Islam because it is a new approach arising from the needs of today, rather than from the understanding of jihad in the Qur'an and hadith. In their eyes, the original texts should come first.

Al-Azhar in Cairo

The relevance today of the teachings about lesser jihad

Specification content
The relevance today of the teachings about lesser jihad.

Jihad can be defined as greater jihad, a struggle within oneself to make the right decisions and follow Islam completely, and lesser jihad, the outward struggle for Islam. This can be in terms of giving dawah, preaching Islam peacefully to others so that they embrace Islam. It can take the form of joining with others for social action, to improve the good of people in the community by helping charities. Lesser jihad can also take the form of holy war.

Holy war conjures up images of bloodthirsty armies using swords and lances; something that has been left behind hundreds of years ago. In the days of colonial rule right up to the Second World War, there was very rarely any reference to lesser jihad as a holy war. But since the 1970s there has been an upsurge in lesser jihad in the Muslim world.

The Qur'an tells Muslims they could fight for defence against an oppressive ruler. They could make raids on camel caravans. Abu Bakr narrated ten rules telling Muslims how to wage war, based on the principles laid down by Muhammad in the capture of Makkah, which was largely peaceful. Everything possible should be done to resolve matters before reaching armed conflict. War should be defensive: to protect the Muslim community, their lives and their livelihoods. It should not be to gain wealth, or to force others to convert to Islam. Muslims should stop fighting if the other side stops and not carry on. They should not destroy trees or crops and should not harm women or children.

Key quotes

Wherever an Islamic community exists which is a concrete example of the divinely-ordained system of life, it has a God-given right to step forward and take control of the political authority so that it may establish the divine system on earth. When God restrained Muslims from jihad for a certain period, it was a question of strategy rather than of principle. (Sayyid Qutb)

What should people of religious faith or moral conviction do when many in the world have entered into one of these escalations towards violence? Other than situations involving imminent threats of attack when there is no time or opportunity to ponder, reflect, interact, and understand, any decision to use violence without first fulfilling the moral duty of empathetic knowing is necessarily immoral. (Khaled Abou El Fadl)

Some early Muslims fought jihad for territory, for material gain, and either forced or pressurised people they conquered to convert to Islam; however, such cases are in spite of the teachings of Islam. There are also many cases where Muslims did not convert others and lived together peacefully.

Non-violent jihad in the form of dawah has been increasingly embraced by groups which have grown due to changes in society, the rise of social media, and the Internet. Groups such as Tablighi Jamaat have gained millions of followers to promote the mission to encouraging Muslims to take on more conservative religious practice. You might see in the city centres of Great Britain street preachers who are Muslims speaking about the Qur'an to passing shoppers. The importance of freedom of belief in lesser jihad should be noted here. To promote Islam is a duty of Muslims. To put pressure on others and deny their freedom of belief is not acceptable. A forced conversion or an oppressed believer who is not able to act according to free will, is not something Muhammad wanted. Muslims believe that Allah has planned out all actions in the world. To force the pace of conversion is to try to change Allah's plan: only He decides the moment when a person converts or changes their practice. These teachings are important today because sometimes, in their zeal and passion for faith, there are cases where missionary groups or

Key quote

There is neither place nor justification in Islam for extremism, fanaticism or terrorism. Suicide bombings, which killed and injured innocent people in London, are haram – vehemently prohibited in Islam, and those who committed these barbaric acts in London are criminals not martyrs. Such acts, as perpetrated in London, are crimes against all of humanity and contrary to the teachings of Islam. (Fatwa of British Imams)

AO2 Activity

As you read through this section try to do the following:

1. Pick out the different lines of argument that are presented in the text and identify any evidence given in support.

2. For each line of argument try to evaluate whether or not you think this is strong or weak.

3. Think of any questions you may wish to raise in response to the arguments.

This Activity will help you to start thinking critically about what you read and help you to evaluate the effectiveness of different arguments and from this develop your own observations, opinions and points of view that will help with any conclusions that you make in your answers to the AO2 questions that arise.

Key quote

We stand for universal peace, love and compassion. We reject violent jihad. We believe we must target the ideology of violent Islamist extremism in order to liberate individuals from the scourge of oppression and terrorism both in Muslim-majority societies and the West.
(Muslim Reform Movement)

Key questions

What are the different meanings of lesser jihad?

How might teachings about lesser jihad differ in different circumstances?

What are the differences between the views of Sayyid Qutb, Khaled Abou El Fadl and the Muslim Reform Movement?

Why do some Muslims feel it is urgent nowadays to challenge misunderstandings of lesser jihad?

Violent jihad causes loss of life and damage to civilians.

AO2 Activity

List some conclusions that could be drawn from the AO2 reasoning from the above text; try to aim for at least three different possible conclusions. Consider each of the conclusions and collect brief evidence to support each conclusion from the AO1 and AO2 material for this topic. Select the conclusion that you think is most convincing and explain why it is so. Try to contrast this with the weakest conclusion in the list, justifying your argument with clear reasoning and evidence.

university Islamic societies have put undue pressure on Muslims to take a more conservative view of faith. As the Qur'an states, there should be 'no compulsion' in religion.

The leaders of the Muslim Brotherhood told their followers to wage war against foreign powers as a form of self-defence. Hasan al-Banna and Abdullah Azzam promoted jihad against colonial powers; Sayyid Qutb inspired Muslims to take pride in jihad and see it as a duty. Participation in the superpower conflict between the USA and the Soviet Union in Afghanistan was mandated by some shaykhs. Muhammad Tahir-ul-Qadri, a Pakistani Sunni Muslim scholar, wrote one of the most comprehensive rebuttals of the abuses of violent lesser jihad. He condemns terrorism and suicide attacks. According to the Qur'an, to take away one innocent life is like killing the whole of humanity.

Many Muslim scholars argue that it is essential that both Muslims and non-Muslims understand that Islam does not sanction acts of terrorism. In the present day, some Muslims wrongly think it is their duty to get involved in groups who support extreme acts. Some have even travelled to countries to join violent conflicts, leaving distraught Muslims families at home, unable to change their minds. One of the teachings of the Prophet was that it is a greater jihad to look after parents and this was a duty before going on any jihad campaign, so leaving parents to go on jihad without telling them or gaining their permission is forbidden.

In his book on shari'a, Khaled Abou El Fadl emphasises that violent jihad should always be a very last resort. Pacifism should be prioritised as far as possible, although he accepts there are some situations, such as a surprise attack, when Muslims need to defend themselves with force. Conflicts should be solved through mutual understanding and peaceful negotiation. Some commentators have promoted the idea of a clash of civilisations between the West and Islam. They argue they are reflecting reality; others suspect provocation, and call on Muslims to regain their traditional, peaceful heritage so that they can better defend Islam against criticism.

The Muslim Reform Movement is one of several reformist groups which do not see any place at all for violent jihad. The priority should be for a struggle against racism, anti-Semitism, oppression of women and other abuses which still take place amongst some Muslims. Siavosh Derakhti's campaign against anti-Semitism in Sweden, and Amina Wadud's work for equality for women as an Imam and preacher, are relevant here. If lesser jihad means calling people to true Islamic values, then teaching about human rights is a legitimate alternative interpretation of it.

There are so many different teachings about lesser jihad, so it is no wonder that young Muslims are confused and many non-Muslims are worried, because of what they see in the media. That makes it vitally important to challenge misconceptions about lesser jihad. Whether liberal or traditional, many Muslims abhor violence and want to promote an image of Islam that is tolerant and peaceful, and guard against some Muslims being misled by errant interpretations.

Study tip

It is important for AO2 that you include the views of scholars and/or schools of thought when formulating your response to a particular contention. Any discussion of jihad should refer to the opinions of different scholars, teachers and traditions and include a measure of evaluation of the different opinions given in support of your answer. However, make sure that the views you use are relevant to the point that you are making. Your ability to use such views in an appropriate way would distinguish a high level answer from one that is simply a general response.

AO2 Developing skills

It is now important to consider the information that has been covered in this section; however, the information in its raw form is too extensive and so has to be processed in order to meet the requirements of the examination. This can be done by practising more advanced skills associated with AO2. For assessment objective 2 (AO2), which involves 'critical analysis' and 'evaluation' skills, we are going to focus on different ways in which the skills can be demonstrated effectively, and also refer to how the performance of these skills is measured (see generic band descriptors for A2 [WJEC] AO2 or A Level [Eduqas] AO2).

▶ **Your next task is this:** Below is **an argument concerning Muslims and the use of violence through jihad**. You need to respond to this argument by thinking of three key questions you could ask the writer that would challenge their view and force them to defend their argument.

The history of Islam suggests that Muslims cannot be pacifists. Muhammad lived in a tribal age in which he fought against the Quraysh in the Battle of Badr. Compassionate or not, Muhammad did not eschew violence in self-defence. It was a duty to struggle for Islam peacefully, but also, when it came to it, with the sword; and this was commanded by Allah in the Qur'an. Muhammad's companion and first Caliph Abu Bakr confirmed this with rules of engagement. The spread of Islam in the days of the early Caliphate could not have happened without committed Muslims who were prepared to fight for their faith. In the modern day, pacifist Muslims, such as Abdul Ghaffar Khan, are few and far between. Self-defence is permitted. If Muslims do not stand up for their rights then they are not sticking up for what God has decreed. In Bosnia in the 1990s, Muslims had to fight against the Serbians who were massacring their people because of religious hatred. That is not to support terrorism, which is condemned by a vast majority of Muslims. Injuring innocent people, women, children, crops or property in acts of violence or through weapons of mass destruction is in opposition to Islamic tradition.

When you have completed the task, refer to the band descriptors for A2 (WJEC) or A Level (Eduqas) and, in particular, have a look at the demands described in the higher band descriptors towards which you should be aspiring. Ask yourself:

- Is my answer a confident critical analysis and perceptive evaluation of the issue?
- Is my answer a response that successfully identifies and thoroughly addresses the issues raised by the question set?
- Does my work show an excellent standard of coherence, clarity and organisation?
- Will my work, when developed, contain thorough, sustained and clear views that are supported by extensive, detailed reasoning and/or evidence?
- Are the views of scholars/schools of thought used extensively, appropriately and in context?
- Does my answer convey a confident and perceptive analysis of the nature of any possible connections with other elements of my course?
- When used, is specialist language and vocabulary both thorough and accurate?

Key skills

Analysis involves:

Identifying issues raised by the materials in the AO1, together with those identified in the AO2 section, and presents sustained and clear views, either of scholars or from a personal perspective ready for evaluation.

This means:

- That your answers are able to identify key areas of debate in relation to a particular issue
- That you can identify, and comment upon, the different lines of argument presented by others
- That your response comments on the overall effectiveness of each of these areas or arguments.

Evaluation involves:

Considering the various implications of the issues raised based upon the evidence gleaned from analysis and provides an extensive detailed argument with a clear conclusion.

This means:

- That your answer weighs up the consequences of accepting or rejecting the various and different lines of argument analysed
- That your answer arrives at a conclusion through a clear process of reasoning.

T3

Significant social and historical developments in religious thought

This section covers AO1 content and skills

Specification content

The religious, social, moral and political structure of Madinah.

A: The concept of a state governed according to Islamic principles and the political and social influence of religious institutions as a challenge to secularisation

The religious, social, moral and political structure of Madinah

Madinah, the city of the Prophet, was organised and developed by Muhammad over ten years. Muhammad moved to Madinah in the hijrah in 622 to escape persecution in Makkah. He had already developed a reputation as an exceptional character and a trustworthy person. His effect upon Madinah produced a model city and a model way to organise society in the minds of Muslims.

Political

Muhammad had a reputation as a skilled negotiator and peacemaker. As a businessman in Makkah, he walked in on an argument between leaders about which tribe should place the black stone by the Ka'aba. Muhammad got all the leaders to carry a cloth with the stone on it.

An argument between tribes in Madinah had reached stalemate, so a delegation came to Makkah to invite Muhammad over to negotiate. The Banu Aus and Banu Khazraj tribes had a long-running dispute. Many Jews lived in Madinah in different tribes who joined different sides. The Banu Nadir tribe and the Banu Qurayza were allied with the Aus, while the Banu Qaynuqa sided with the Khazraj.

Muhammad negotiated a treaty or treaties which together became known as the Charter or Constitution of Madinah. The local Jewish and pagan tribes, the Muslims from Makkah who had emigrated to Madinah, and, local converts, collectively known as Ansar, all agreed to form one community and live together under the leadership of Muhammad.

Tribal loyalty was a matter of life and death. A person was identified foremost according to what tribe they were from, rather than their individual characteristics. Arabs fought for the reputation of their clan. Alliances were guarded by tribal honour. The Madinah community crossed tribal lines. People were required to care for each other and support each other in times of conflict.

Tribal loyalties shifted, which affected the politics that Muhammad followed. First, Muhammad and the Muslims carried out a raid on the trade caravan of the Quraysh tribe from Makkah, at the oasis of Badr. Then, the Quraysh took revenge at the Battle of Uhud. The Quraysh attempted to storm Madinah, but were held back by trenches built by the Muslims at a battle which became known as the Battle of Trench.

A member of the Banu Nadir tribe went to Madinah with poems to embarrass them about their defeat in Badr. This provoked the Quraysh to take revenge. Muhammad judged the tribe disloyal and expelled them from Madinah. During the Battle of the Trench, the tribe of Banu Qurayza were suspected of treachery. After the battle, the Muslims then fought and killed many of the Banu Qurayza, expelling them from Madinah.

Key terms

Ansar: people who became Muslim in Madinah

Banu Aus: a tribe of Madinah

Banu Khazraj: an opposing tribe of Madinah

Banu Qurayza: a third Jewish tribe, also eventually exiled

Hijrah: the journey from Makkah to Madinah by Muhammad and the Muslims in the year 622. The Muslim calendar is called the hijri calendar because it begins from this date.

Ka'aba: the black cube in Makkah, a central point in which is the focus of Hajj and prayer

Quraysh: tribal leaders in Makkah; for years they were opponents of Muhammad

The Banu Qurayza and Banu Nadir tribes were Jewish. From a modern perspective, it seems terrible that a group of people of one religion were expelled. At the time, this was normal tribal politics. Muhammad lived in that world and managed the circumstances he faced successfully to create relative peace.

Muhammad didn't dictate to people what to do. At the Battle of Badr, he first listened to opinions. Some thought they should advance and surprise the Quraysh at the wells of Badr, whereas others said they should return to Madinah to defend their houses from the rooftops. After discussion, Muhammad decided to advance to Badr. Muhammad's consultations could never overrule any revelation sent from God. This did not involve elections or democracy. However, he did listen. This shura became important for Muslims in the years to come.

Muhammad's political skills came into play in the Treaty of Hudaybiyyah. During negotiations, it was rumoured that one of the Muslims had been killed. Instead of reacting with anger, Muhammad persuaded the Muslims to promise that they would accept his decision as to what to do next. The Muslims agreed. Muhammad continued negotiating and it was found that the rumour was false. A ten-year peace treaty was then agreed.

There was no blueprint for the structure of a state, because Madinah was not a state. This was not the era of states and countries. It was the time of tribes, in which many unpleasant and barbaric acts took place, not just by enemies but by Muslims too. Muhammad tried to make peace between tribes, consulted and always put God's command first. Muslims think of his example when managing political matters even today.

Social

Madinah gave Muslims a fresh start, away from persecution in Makkah. Muslims who came from Makkah were refugees, seeking asylum in Madinah. They left many of their possessions behind in Makkah. On entering Madinah, Muhammad encouraged the emigrants, called the muhajirun, to pair up with the people of Madinah. In particular, the ansar, who were Muslims who lived in Madinah or converted there, played a special role in sharing what they had with the emigrants. This can be seen as an example relevant to integrating and welcoming asylum seekers today.

Racist attitudes were inbuilt in the Makkans. Bilal, a black slave, was badly treated when he converted to Islam. In Madinah Muhammad made an example by appointing Bilal as the first muezzin to give the call to prayer from the first mosque. This showed to everyone that he valued people whoever they were, regardless of skin colour.

Muhammad urged Muslims to treat women well. There are traditions that he addressed women at Id prayers. Muhammad forbade women to cover their faces when entering the sacred places (such as the Ka'aba in Makkah) and said in his farewell sermon that women should be respected. Most women still adhered to tribal norms of veiling outside their homes, and living a life subservient to men. If today a Muslim wanted to follow life in Madinah literally, they might choose a very traditional role for women. If they chose to interpret Muhammad's teachings relative to the society of the day, they might consider the Madinah model liberal and supportive of women.

Key terms

Hudaybiyyah: treaty signed by Muhammad and the Quraysh guaranteeing a period of peace

Liberal: open-minded views

Muezzin: Muslim who gives out the call to prayer

Muhajirun: Arabic word for emigrants

Shura: consultation with the people

Key quote

Remember that your Lord is One. All humankind comes from Adam and Eve. An Arab has no superiority over a non-Arab nor a non-Arab has any superiority over an Arab; also a white person has no superiority over a black, nor does a black person have any superiority over a white, except by piety and good action. Indeed, the best among you is the one with the best character. (Hadith of Prophet Muhammad)

Key quote

You have certain rights over women, but they also have rights over you. You must treat women well and be kind to them as they are your partners and helpers. (Hadith of Prophet Muhammad)

In tribal culture, hands were cut off thieves. People who committed adultery were killed. Muhammad continued these practices. He insisted that everyone be treated equally. Fatimah was daughter of the Prophet and Khadijah. She went through persecutions with Muhammad and helped clear up the rubbish that was thrown onto him. Muhammad did not send her away to a nanny but brought her up himself. So when Muhammad said that she would get the same punishment as anyone else if she were caught stealing, it showed how he would treat everyone equally, even his closest family.

One day Aisha, Muhammad's wife, could not find her necklace and went out to look for it. Muhammad's caravan left without realising Aisha was not there. She was found by a man and returned the next morning. Rumours of adultery spread but Muhammad received a revelation to ask for proof from four eye witnesses. Four witnesses could not be found. After that, it was required that four witnesses testify for a person be found guilty. These traditions became accepted in shari'a, because they were the practice of Muhammad in Madinah.

Economic and moral

Zakat is one of the five pillars of Islam and had been practised to some degree in Makkah. However, it was in the second year of the hijrah in Madinah that it became more organised by Muhammad. He sent out zakat workers to collect and distribute the zakat tax to those in need. It was collected on profits from trade, wealth and crops. There are few records today, but at the time there appears to have been some organisation of zakat with notes of wealth, properties to be taxed, weights of gold and silver and amounts of crops. This was the beginnings of a tax system to redistribute wealth from the rich to those in need.

Muhammad asked Muslims to be fair and not to cheat in their measurement. He had a reputation as an honest trader. This reputation helped Madinah to grow. The political agreements with tribes established peace, which promoted trade. The more open and accommodating Madinah was, the more people from the trade routes of further afield came, taking business away from Makkah. At his farewell sermon, Muhammad forbade Muslims to charge riba, exploitative rates of interest on loans. Madinah was a model for free trade, but not exploitation. Investment was moderated by morality.

quickfire

3.1 What role did Bilal take in Madinah?

Key term

Zakat: one of the five pillars of Islam; 2.5% tax on profit and various other calculated amounts of wealth to be given to those in need

quickfire

3.2 Who were the muhajirun and the ansar?

Muhammad's Mosque in Madinah

Madinah was an oasis where delicious date palms grew. The Muslims developed the date harvests and Madinah dates became renowned for their taste throughout the Muslim world. The waters from the oasis were also used to grow vegetables and feed the community. Muhammad and the Muslim community in Madinah thought positively and put their energy into developing the community. Peaceful, economic development was another way to promote the moral message of unselfishness, unity and 'brotherhood' within Islam.

Religious

Muhammad set up a mosque in Madinah. There is a story that Muhammad decided to build the mosque where his camel sat down, to avoid any dispute between tribal leaders. Muhammad defined the area around the mosque as a centre for peace and reconciliation. Weapons were not allowed in this area and all members of the community, regardless of faith or tribe, were obliged to defend it.

The art of making peace between tribes, peoples and countries can be difficult. In making a peaceful sanctuary in Madinah, Muhammad showed that he understood that he needed more than a treaty to achieve and promote peace among people.

At Madinah, as we shall see in the section on the Constitution of Madinah, people of different faiths lived together as one community. It did not matter whether you were a Muslim from Madinah, a convert, a Jew, a pagan or a Christian, you were expected to be loyal to Madinah.

The revelations at Madinah developed over time. Muhammad had told his followers in Makkah to leave their friends of other religions as they were about to leave the city. At Madinah, new friendships were made and the Christians and Jews were seen as 'People of the Book' who were fellow believers together with the Muslims. Sometimes the Prophet entered debate with Christians and Jews in a good-natured way, and said that Allah would judge where they differed. There were differences with some Christian and Jewish tribes. These have been interpreted in different ways. Some have used them to say that Muslims should separate from other communities. Others say that tribal differences do not mean that at all, they should be explained by the context of the time.

Muhammad and the Muslims wanted to return to Makkah to carry out the Hajj pilgrimage, but their enemies, the Quraysh, refused. They made a treaty at Hudaybiyyah for peace but this was broken after two years. Muhammad entered Makkah with a huge force and cleared the Ka'aba of its idols. The conquest was largely peaceful.

Rose Wilder Lane, 1886–1968, was an American writer who supported the concept of liberty. She argued that people should be free to choose their own religion, make their own trade, move to different places and countries and so on. She wrote a book *The Discovery of Freedom*. The book contains many references to Muhammad as a person who liberated his community and gave them freedom. It is remarkable that the influence of Muhammad in Madinah reached across the world, and was known to Muslims and non-Muslims alike, a thousand years after his death. Rose Wilder Lane considered Muhammad to be a wonderful example of someone who freed his people from tribalism.

Rose Wilder Lane

Key quote
Medina is a sanctuary. Its trees should not be cut and no heresy should be made up nor any sin committed. (**Hadith of Prophet Muhammad**)

quickfire
3.3 In what ways was Madinah a sanctuary?

Specification content

Madinah as the model or ideal for any state governed according to Islamic principles.

Muhammad's tomb in Madinah

Key terms

Caliphate: the Islamic Empire ruled by a Caliph

Sira: an account of the life of a Prophet

quickfire

3.4 What did Maliki fiqh put extra special importance on?

Specification content

The impact of the Constitution of Madinah.

Key person

Ibn Ishaq: lived from 701 to around 767 in Madinah. He wrote the Sira of Prophet Muhammad which was later copied by another writer, Ibn Hisham, from whom the text comes down to us today.

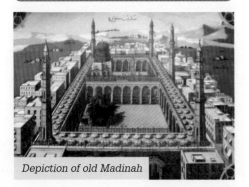

Depiction of old Madinah

Madinah as the model or ideal for any state governed according to Islamic principles

The main practices of Islam as we know them today, through the example of Muhammad, formed whilst he lived in Madinah. The direction of prayer was changed from Jerusalem to Makkah. The five pillars were established as formal practices. Muslims were free to practise their faith. Malik ibn Anas, the founder of an Islamic school of Law called Maliki fiqh, put extra special importance on the practices of the people of Madinah. Whatever they did would have had to have been approved by the Prophet.

In the history of Islam, from the death of the Prophet to the modern day, there have been many different forms of government. Initially the Muslim world was united under a Caliph. It then divided into two Caliphates and became further divided into kingdoms. In the nineteenth century, many Muslim countries were ruled by European colonial powers. During some periods, Muslims felt oppressed by their own kings; at other times they felt they could do better with their own system of government, rather than being ruled by someone else. When it came to their own government, Muhammad's Madinah was seen as the most important model to follow for any state governed according to Islamic principles.

AO1 Activity

Top 10 of the 20s! Madinah in the 20s – not the 2020s, the 620s!

Make a top 10 chart of what happened in the 620s in Madinah. For example, the arrival of the Prophet; the first mosque built. Include two interviews with residents of Madinah looking back over the decade and ask them how their lives changed.

The impact of the Constitution of Madinah

The words state and country are often used together. The modern state developed from around the year 1500 to the present day. If you asked someone in seventh-century Arabia which country they were from they would not have any idea what you were talking about. States and governments, organised by detailed constitutions and codes of law, did not exist. Tribes and treaties were the order of the day. Muhammad left treaties and principles in his example of managing the tribes and peoples of Madinah. These principles could be copied. He did not leave a detailed instrument of government for a modern state.

The Treaty of Madinah, or Charter of Madinah, came about in the early years of Muhammad's time in the city. It may have begun when the Prophet entered the city, and developed through several smaller treaties that were put together. The Treaty is referred to in a book called the Sira of the Prophet by **Ibn Ishaq**, who wrote about Muhammad's life. It is one of the earliest versions of a form of constitution in the world. Where Muslim lands were ruled by colonial powers or corrupt local officials, Muslims who wanted freedom looked to the Treaty of Madinah as a way of making a morally pure form of government.

Constitutions are rules by which a country may be governed. In the UK, the way government runs the country is often referred to as an unwritten constitution. It developed slowly over time, rather than a single document stating how things were to be done. Agreements were made after World War Two which helped Germany to form a modern constitution. These rules can develop and change over time.

Some Muslims interpret the Treaty in a new sense. They want to create a new Islamic country for all Muslims in the world to live in, headed by a Caliph. They look back to the Treaty of Madinah for inspiration. Political Islamist groups include Hizb ut-Tahrir, who say they want to create this new Caliphate and advertise their support for rule by Khalifah. Most Muslims reject their interpretations. Zeyno Baran, a Turkish Muslim, researched Hizb ut-Tahrir and found that the language and concepts they used were much more similar to the Bolsheviks in Russia in the early twentieth century. Their idea of Khalifah was a new concept, very different from the days of early Islam.

From the point of view of a twenty-first-century reader, the Treaty reads as if it is about tribes and feuds. But the tribal references are simply what those living in Madinah would have expected. The treaty accepts tribal identity but brings tribes to live peacefully within the terms of this agreement.

The concept of ummah

The Treaty of Madinah identifies people as members of a community, called the ummah of Madinah. Jews and Muslims together were believers. They would be governed in the same way. You might call them citizens. If they faced war against an enemy tribe, they would support each other regardless of faith. Peoples of the book: Jews, Christians and Muslims; and other tribespeople, all had to follow the same rules. Everyone was free to worship according to their own religion. What was important was that they did not break the tribal alliances.

The word ummah is used by Muslims nowadays to mean the worldwide family of Muslims. Some Muslims have argued that they should set up their own government for Muslims. There are places where non-Muslims have been persecuted and driven out of Muslim lands. The original Constitution of Madinah shows how that was not the way that Muhammad governed. If anything, Muhammad set up a community closer to modern secular governments than a religious state.

The term kuffar was used at the time of Muhammad to mean people who attacked the believers. It was not about whether a person was Muslim or not. Many years after the Prophet's death, Caliphs led a large Muslim Empire. The Arabic language and Islam as a religion became more dominant. It is possible that the distinctions between people based on religion became greater over time.

Ancient Qur'anic manuscript

Key term

Khalifah: the Islamic movement followed by a minority of Muslims who want to recreate the Islamic Empire under a Caliph in the modern world

Kuffar: sometimes interpreted as non-believers or people who had rejected belief

Ummah: originally, the Madinah community of Muslims and others; this terms has evolved to mean the worldwide brotherhood of Muslims

Key quote

Muslims were bound to protect the Jews from their enemies. Likewise, Jews were bound to protect Muslims. Once again manifesting a merciful nature, the Prophet Muhammad extended protection to both combatants and non-combatants so long as they had not engaged in any crimes or atrocities. (Dr John Andrew Morrow)

quickfire

3.5 What did the term ummah originally mean?

Specification content

The role of shari'a law within a state governed according to Islamic principles.

Iran Majlis

The role of shari'a law within a state governed according to Islamic principles

In principle, Muslims believe there is no part of life that is not influenced by God, so God's guidance has a role to play in Islamic countries. If belief in God is the most important thing in your life, then living according to the morals and rules laid out by God in the Qur'an and through the example of hadith should be important in government. Leaders should be morally righteous and pious individuals so that they can be respected by believers. In the Islamic Republic of Iran, that means all representatives should come from the line of the family of the Prophet and be vetted by a Council of religious leaders before standing for office. New laws are scrutinised to ensure they are in keeping with the teachings of the Qur'an and sunna. Any laws that are not will not be put in place. A system of shura consultation is in place: people elect representatives to a Majlis parliament, but the parliament is subject to religious rules. Due to this, Iran is often called a theocracy, where theology and religion are the most important factor in government.

Differences in implementing shari'a between Saudi Arabia, Turkey and Malaysia

In Saudi Arabia, the government wishes to follow the interpretations of the companions of the Prophets. They follow a literal version of Hanbali Fiqh in the application of shari'a law. The difficulty is that this does not define many issues and is rooted in an eighth-century context. This has caused problems in deciding what to do in many cases. Saudi Arabia is known for harsh shari'a sentences, involving corporal and capital punishments. Critics say these are barbaric; however, many Saudi citizens support them because they feel they are literally what God wants. They feel that drug smugglers and terrorists should be executed, and setting that example will deter others from such crimes.

In the nineteenth century, the Ottoman Empire based in Turkey had a Caliph for religious matters. A version of shari'a was applied. The Tanzimat reforms interpreted shari'a in the light of modern reforms. The Tanzimat reforms abolished the death penalty for apostasy. Homosexuality was made legal in 1858, over a hundred years before it was legalised in the UK.

In Malaysia, there is a dual system. Common, secular laws apply to everyone and shari'a laws apply to Muslims. There has been some discussion about increasing the importance of shari'a law courts from dealing with family matters to include other criminal matters. A similar movement is taking place in Pakistan. Some Muslims feel that a shari'a system will be better because it is based on God's laws, which are morally acceptable to them.

Shari'a courts require witnesses to be trustworthy Muslims who believe in God and say their prayers. If witnesses have a sense of God-consciousness, called taqwa in Arabic, then they will be fearful of God's judgement and tell the truth in court. If witnesses do not believe in God's punishment in the afterlife then they might lie. In this way, the principles of shari'a are trusted by some Muslims more than non-religious courts, although shari'a courts pay more weight to Muslim male witnesses than females or non-Muslims. To some this seems very unfair.

Treatment of minorities

Today, we think of everyone as equal before the law. Regardless of religion, you can apply for any job, vote in elections or even stand for parliament. In the Middle Ages, Jews were expelled from England by order of King Edward I. Muslims were expelled from Spain in the sixteenth century. Armenian Christians were persecuted in an attempt to make them leave Turkey in the early twentieth. Religious laws were a source of conflict; however, in Madinah believers of different religions often got on well. Dhimmis were members of different religions who lived under

Key terms

Dhimmi: non-Muslim believer living in Muslim lands

Tanzimat: nineteenth-century reforms of the Ottoman Empire

Taqwa: God consciousness; it is regarded as essential for people to have God in mind to be able to apply shari'a

Muslim rule. They had freedom of religion and were required to pay additional taxes to the Muslim rulers in return.

The United Nations Declaration of Human Rights was an agreement put in place in 1948. Signatory countries promised to uphold people's right to freedom of association, thought, conscience, and religion. Turkey, Pakistan and Iran agreed to sign it but Saudi Arabia abstained, claiming it was against shari'a. In the year 2000 an organisation of Islamic countries agreed a similar document but with reference to shari'a. The Cairo declaration stated that individuals should have a right to: 'freedom and right to a dignified life in accordance with the Islamic shari'a', and they should not be treated differently because of 'race, colour, language, sex, religious belief, political affiliation, social status or other considerations'.

In Pakistan, new blasphemy laws were introduced leaving Christians at risk of accusation. For example, if a group of four Muslim men got together and claimed to witness a Christian abusing the Qur'an, they could demand the death penalty. There have been other cases in different Muslim countries. The Marrakesh Declaration was made in January 2016. Muslim scholars from over 120 countries met because of their concern at how religious minorities were being badly treated by Muslims. They produced a declaration which they said upheld the principles of the Charter of Madinah. They noted that the principles of the Charter of Madinah were upheld by the United Nations Human Rights Declaration, and encouraged all Muslims to uphold mutual tolerance and respect before the law. They called on Muslims to develop inclusive ideas of citizenship, and encourage education so that the rights of minorities could be protected.

AO1 Activity

Make a table with four columns: Saudi Arabia, Iran, Malaysia, Ottoman Turkey.

Add a row below and in it write down how each has interpreted shari'a in their government. Add a further row and write down to what extent do you think each one is in keeping with the Constitution of Madinah.

The challenge of shari'a law within a non-Islamic secular state

In the UK the Monarch is head of state as well as head of the Church of England. The Church is the established religion. In practice, laws work according to secular principles. If you attend a court of law as a witness, you will be asked to take an oath to show you promise to tell the truth. You may do so by swearing with your right hand on your holy book, or make a non-religious declaration. It is your choice which holy book, or none, to use. Members of parliament represent all members of their constituency, regardless of religion, and pledge loyalty to the Monarch. Their religion can influence their experience and view of life, but British values must come first. Many are comfortable with finding a balance between Islam and British institutions. Some feel that secularism is the best way for all Muslims to organise their government.

In a secular state like France, laws are made by people's representatives, without reference to religious text; religious worship, symbols and practices are not part of public life (such as in government, hospitals, schools and state-run institutions). People are free to have their own beliefs but in all government buildings no religion or religious symbols are permitted.

British values are defined by the government as belief in democracy, the rule of law, individual liberty, mutual respect and tolerance of others' faiths and beliefs. These values could include people of different religions or none. Many Muslims are comfortable with following their own faith and British values. They benefit

quickfire

3.6 What were the Tanzimat reforms?

Specification content

The challenge of shari'a law within a non-Islamic secular state.

Key terms

Monarch: King or Queen who is head of state

Secularism: that society should be organised and government run without reference to religion

quickfire

3.7 What was Ali Abd'al Raziq's opinion on secular states?

Key people

Ali Abd'al Raziq: a shari'a judge from Egypt who wrote that secular government was perfectly acceptable for Muslims and in many cases better than rule by Muslim rulers who did not always look after their people.

Akbar Ganji: an Iranian protestor who changed his mind from supporter of religious government to supporter of secular government.

Key quotes

Islam does not advocate a specific form of government. Islam allows us absolute freedom to organise government according to the ideas, social and economic conditions of the times. (Ali Abd-al Raziq)

Religious government is an absurd notion, and if a government is formed under an Islamic banner, it will only serve the interests of a special group of the people, not an entire Islamic society. Thus, if Muslims form a government, it will be a secular, not a religious one. (Akbar Ganji)

from being allowed to wear the headscarf openly if they choose. Many state-run institutions like hospitals and schools are tolerant of Muslims' requests such as a quiet space to pray. A small minority of Muslims want to emphasise difference and disagree with democracy, preferring a Muslim ruler and a shari'a system instead. Most Muslims support elections and some have been elected to parliament and other important positions, for example Sadiq Khan as the Mayor of London.

Ali Abd'al Raziq and Akbar Ganji

Ali Abd'al Raziq, a Sunni shari'a judge from Egypt, wrote a book called *Islam and the Foundations of Governance* in 1925. He wrote that the Qur'an and hadith did not tell Muslims which form of government to follow, so they did not have to follow Caliphs. There was no text that asked Muslims to create a single Muslim government. Furthermore, some Muslim rulers had treated their people badly. Secularism would allow people to criticise and change their governments by voting. This could mean some rulers would be thrown out. Raziq felt this fear was an excuse used by some in the Muslim world to stop secularisation.

Akbar Ganji

Akbar Ganji supported the Iranian revolution in 1979 as a student protestor. The revolution put in place an Islamic government with a form of shari'a law. Akbar changed his mind and protested against it. He decided that secular democracy was good for Muslims. In the days of Muhammad, no such thing as a state existed. There were groups of tribes but there was nothing like a modern country. Muhammad died without leaving a successor or telling Muslims what to do. Therefore, there was no prescribed Muslim state to follow. The early Caliphs were appointed with agreement from the people. Religious laws do not need to be mixed up with laws about running the country. The Prophet was happy to accept many traditions of his time where they helped to manage his city. He did not change everything and label it Islam.

In most of history, Muslim rulers operated separately from their Imams. The Imams dealt with religious and family matters of shari'a and the rulers managed the government, army and provided services for the people.

Muslims must obey the law of the country they live in. Provided they have freedom of worship, all of the other laws should be followed. Some argue that outside of Muslim countries, Muslims may not consider themselves bound by shari'a. Others say that matters of religion include the five pillars of Islam, and to pray five times a day, which should apply anywhere. Some say that if a Muslim lives temporarily in a non-Muslim country, then they may live as a traveller, even if that temporary period is a matter of years.

The five daily prayers can be difficult to achieve in a secular country. What if a Muslim is at school or work at the time of the midday prayer, and cannot get time off? On other hand, to some Muslims, living in a secular country makes life easier. Shi'a Muslims living in Saudi Arabia sometimes complain of poor treatment. In a secular country, it does not matter what sect you belong to. In the UK, many facilities have been put in place such as multi-faith prayer rooms in airports and hospitals to address the needs of Muslims.

Multi-faith prayer room at Heathrow Airport

Issues for analysis and evaluation

The compatibility of Islam with democracy

Democracy is a form of government in which leaders are elected. It originated in the traditions of Ancient Greece and has become the normal way in which leaders are elected in the Western world. Democracy is seen as good because it gives everyone a say in their government. It goes together with freedom of speech and human rights. Throughout much of history, people have struggled against rulers who did not take account of their needs. Men and women have protested to get the vote and in some countries they still do not have it.

In Islam, no one system of government has been defined as the way things need to be done, but there are traditions. The Qur'an and hadith of Muhammad gives Muslims encouragement that everything should be done with the mind-set of belief in God. Muhammad set up the Madinah community and because he was God's final messenger, Muslims follow everything he did. Although it is difficult to interpret what he did because he lived in an age very different from today. Nobody had democratic elections in seventh-century Arabia, because it was an age of tribes not of modern states. Muhammad set up Madinah with a mosque at its centre and with rules set by God. It could be argued that this means Muslims should follow these revelations and not just do what they think in elections. However, how do they know what the revelations mean in the context of the day?

When preparing for battles, Muhammad drew his followers together and listened to different points of view. It could be said this is justification for holding councils, for listening to the people, for the creation of a parliament. After Muhammad, the Caliphs were partly elected by agreement of the companions who held shura consultations. The word shura is still used by Muslims and the creation of a Majlis, a form of parliament, is practised in some Islamic countries. This suggests that elections are entirely compatible with Islam.

Study tip

It is vital for AO2 that you actually discuss arguments and not just explain what someone may have stated. Try to ask yourself, 'was this a fair point to make?', 'is the evidence sound enough?', 'is there anything to challenge this argument?', 'is this a strong or weak argument?' Such critical analysis will help you develop your evaluation skills.

In many modern Western countries, Muslims have engaged with democracy. In the UK, there are Muslim Members of Parliament. Parliament even provides a prayer room for them. Muslims find no difficulty in becoming counsellors and voting in elections in their local areas. By helping everyone in their communities, they are presenting a good image of Muslims and helping Muslims get along well with others. Democratic countries have supported human rights including the freedom of religion, which means that Muslims have benefitted from being freely able to worship and believe what they want. For some Muslims, this is something they have not been able to do in Muslim countries where they have suffered on the grounds of being part of a minority sect or some other reason. In this way, some have found democracy better than any other form of government.

Muslims may prefer their own arrangements for family and personal law but democratic government to determine criminal law. The tribalism of early Arabia can be confused with Islam: many Muslims disagree with some shari'a punishments such as corporal and capital punishments and are happy for criminal laws to be made by modern politicians who are elected. Some Muslims think that they should return to a literal version of the Qur'an and sunna as it was interpreted

This section covers AO2 content and skills

Specification content

The compatibility of Islam with democracy.

Key quotes

We can't equate democracy with Christianity because the largest democracy on earth is India, which is primarily Hindu. The third largest democracy is Indonesia, which is Islamic. Democracy and freedom are not dependent on Christian beliefs. (Jimmy Carter)

It was the first religion that preached and practiced democracy; for, in the mosque, when the call for prayer is sounded and worshippers are gathered together, the democracy of Islam is embodied five times a day when the peasant and king kneel side by side and proclaim: 'God Alone is Great'. (Sarojini Naidu)

AO2 Activity

As you read through this section try to do the following:

1. Pick out the different lines of argument that are presented in the text and identify any evidence given in support.

2. For each line of argument try to evaluate whether or not you think this is strong or weak.

3. Think of any questions you may wish to raise in response to the arguments.

This Activity will help you to start thinking critically about what you read and help you to evaluate the effectiveness of different arguments and from this develop your own observations, opinions and points of view that will help with any conclusions that you make in your answers to the AO2 questions that arise.

Key quotes

It is Allah and not man who rules. Allah is the source of all authority, including legitimate political authority. Virtue, not freedom, is the highest value. Therefore, Allah's law should govern the society; not man's. (Sayyid Qutb)

Every single empire in its official discourse has said that it is not like all the others, that its circumstances are special, that it has a mission to enlighten, civilise, bring order and democracy, and that it uses force only as a last resort. (Edward Said)

The struggle of democratic secularism, religious tolerance, individual freedom and feminism against authoritarian patriarchal religion, culture and morality is going on all over the world – including the Islamic world, where dissidents are regularly jailed, killed, exiled or merely intimidated and silenced. (Ellen Willis)

Key questions

How was consultation exercised in the early days of Islam? Does this mean Islam supports democracy?

Why do some Muslims either oppose or want to put limits on democracy?

Why do you think Edward Said and Ellen Willis disagree? Which approach is best?

AO2 Activity

List some conclusions that could be drawn from the AO2 reasoning from the above text; try to aim for at least three different possible conclusions. Consider each of the conclusions and collect brief evidence to support each conclusion from the AO1 and AO2 material for this topic. Select the conclusion that you think is most convincing and explain why it is so. Try to contrast this with the weakest conclusion in the list, justifying your argument with clear reasoning and evidence.

in the early days of Islam. Some of these Muslims do not agree with democracy as they feel it is guided by people who change their mind according to the time they live in, whereas God's law should not change. These views have been associated with movements which aim to create a new Caliphate after the style of early Arabia. These interpretations are opposed by many Muslim scholars who fear they cultivate extremism.

Sayyid Qutb makes a simple distinction between what he saw as human law and God's law. He put the revelation of God's law above democracy. There can be weaknesses in democracy and it is not a perfect system: if a population becomes angry or faces a stressful situation, it is possible that oppressive democrats could be voted in. Muslims believe that moral standards are set by God and things such as euthanasia are wrong and should not be changed by the will of the people, because it is the will of God that controls all life.

The problem with Sayyid Qutb's argument is that the laws of God are not simple: they are the product of human interpretation. To deny democracy means that a small group of Muslim men, or perhaps one individual, makes interpretations himself and imposes them on others. Most Muslims believe that they are all equal so therefore they should all have a say in decisions. No human being can claim revelation from God since the Last Prophet, so no one is qualified to rule on God's authority. A small number of Muslims have protested against democracy in the UK claiming it was against shari'a law to vote, because God's law should not be dependent on people. However, most Muslims are grateful to exercise their choice, aware that there are still many in Muslim lands who are not given this freedom, shown vividly in the Arab Spring.

The position is slightly different in Shi'a Islam where Imams have authority to guide the people, but there is disagreement between Shi'a Ayatollahs about how far religion should be involved with politics. In Shi'a-controlled Iran, candidates are vetted, as well as the laws they pass, to ensure that they are in compliance with the Qur'an and sunna. Religion has a veto over democracy. By way of contrast, in Iraq the Shi'a leadership support separation of state and religion.

Some Muslims have criticised Western powers for lecturing Muslim countries about democracy and forcing the pace of change. Edward Said, the American academic, criticised his government's policy towards the Middle East. He did not deny that Islam was compatible with democracy but felt that it was not right to talk down to other countries. Ellen Willis, by contrast, felt democracy has a role to play as a liberating force to champion individual Muslims, including women and dissidents, who are regularly oppressed in regimes controlled by Muslim men.

There are a variety of different views held by different Muslims about democracy. It is possible that because it was not defined by Muhammad, Muslims are free to choose what works best for them in the environment and times they live in. Reformist Muslims believe in secular democracy and reinterpreting Islam to address what they see as a need to champion women's rights and the rights of minorities, which may not have been helped by shari'a in some places in the past. Some other Muslims see this as going too far and want to return to the rules of the early Muslims which they feel no one can vote to change.

The extent to which shari'a is an adequate guide for all aspects of a society

Shari'a is seen by Muslims as God's law made in heaven, which is an ideal way of life for them to live. However, there are sometimes difficulties in finding out areas of shari'a not clearly covered by its main sources of the Qur'an and sunna of Muhammad. Society is about the way we live: how people of different backgrounds live together, men and women, rich and poor, black and white, gay and straight, old and young, religious and atheist and a whole variety of different variations of these categories. How society is managed by rules and laws, criminal punishments, rules of trade, politics and elections is a matter of debate.

Key quote

Each individual who personally chooses to obey him directly confronts the divine will expressed in the shari'a and strives to conduct his or her life according to that imperative. This is without the aid of either an intermediary or some manner of collective responsibility. The essence of the obligation to Allah is to act as his vicegerent on earth, ordering the good and forbidding wrong. In other words, it is a duty to accept responsibility for the establishment of proper public order. The law, as the concrete expression of Allah's will and guidance, is therefore central to the individual and collective Muslim identity. (David Waines)

The early Muslims lived in an age when everyone was religious in one way or another. Religious thoughts were in their minds all the time; so it was natural that religious laws could influence all aspects of society. Shari'a was a step forward in that rights of inheritance were awarded to women, and ordinary people had some way to get a kind of justice, which they might not have been able to get before. Nevertheless, shari'a left many questions unanswered which scholars through the ages tried to interpret. As society changed, more questions arose, which meant shari'a was less of a guide. Muslim rulers often managed society and left shari'a law judges to manage family matters.

David Waines explains how shari'a is both personal and communal. Every Muslim believer must make their personal commitment of faith in the **shahadah**. In their everyday life, they must make moral decisions based on what they believe is right and wrong. Muslims make their commitment to make those decisions based on shari'a because they believe God is watching them and will judge them in the afterlife according to the decisions they make. In considering moral issues, inevitably Muslims need to consider the best laws to establish good order in the community at large.

Family life is important to Muslims. They marry according to Islamic tradition with a Nikkah contract. This ceremony is sometimes recognised in shari'a law and upheld by shari'a family courts. If problems occur in the marriage, the Muslim husband and wife can choose to take their differences to a shari'a court who will interpret the Nikkah contract and attempt to agree a resolution, or authorise a divorce. Due to the personal and family nature of such matters, some Muslims prefer to use shari'a courts and these are available in countries such as Pakistan and Malaysia. Some Muslims disagree and feel that shari'a is unhelpful in these situations, because it might not give women an equal hearing due to the pressure of religion.

H. G. Wells pays respect to Islam with his description of the liberating social values of Muhammad's community. They provided a lift to the people who had suffered years of oppression, according to Wells. He suggests these common human values are of good standing. That suggests they are an adequate guide for society. However, it is hard to teach morality to the whole of society through the religious

AO2 Activity

As you read through this section try to do the following:

1. Pick out the different lines of argument that are presented in the text and identify any evidence given in support.

2. For each line of argument try to evaluate whether or not you think this is strong or weak.

3. Think of any questions you may wish to raise in response to the arguments.

This Activity will help you to start thinking critically about what you read and help you to evaluate the effectiveness of different arguments and from this develop your own observations, opinions and points of view that will help with any conclusions that you make in your answers to the AO2 questions that arise.

Key quote

The Islamic teachings have left great traditions for equitable and gentle dealings and behaviour, and inspire people with nobility and tolerance. These are human teachings of the highest order and at the same time practicable. These teachings brought into existence a society in which hard-heartedness and collective oppression and injustice were the least as compared with all other societies preceding it … Islam is replete with gentleness, courtesy, and fraternity. (H. G. Wells)

Key term

Pluralism: different ideas and communities living alongside each other

Key questions

What are the different aspects that make up society?

Why might some people reject shari'a within a multi-faith environment?

Why might some Muslims criticise Tariq Ramadan's position on shari'a in society?

AO2 Activity

List some conclusions that could be drawn from the AO2 reasoning from the above text; try to aim for at least three different possible conclusions. Consider each of the conclusions and collect brief evidence to support each conclusion from the AO1 and AO2 material for this topic. Select the conclusion that you think is most convincing and explain why it is so. Try to contrast this with the weakest conclusion in the list, justifying your argument with clear reasoning and evidence.

belief of one religion. If you do not believe in that religion, or that sect, or even in God at all, then your trust in the values taught will be limited. Countries such as France are completely secular and champion equality of all without the division religion brings. Although to some Muslims, Allah's way is right so they believe that they should use their morals and manners to form laws of state.

Minor rulings from the fatwas of some Imams cause much discussion amongst young Muslims. Is it Islamic to wear a thobe or shalwar kemise (for men) or a veil over the hair or even the face for women? Many Muslim families migrated from areas such as South Asia to the UK bringing with them local cultural heritage. This should not be confused with Islamic shari'a. Tariq Ramadan believes that the general principle of modesty can be applied with local, British dress, as can other aspects of British culture. Shari'a does not need to encroach upon local customs in society.

Key quote

The universality of Islam is shown by the way you can integrate into the local culture. Our young people need to be told, you can dress in European clothes – so long as you respect the principle of modesty. Democracy and pluralism aren't against your Islamic principles. Anything in Western culture that does not contradict the message of Islam can be accepted and integrated … We need a deep faith, but a critical mind. Being British by culture and Muslim by religion is no contradiction. We need to get out of intellectual and social ghettos, and be freed from our narrow understanding. To do that is not easy. The easy way is to become an extremist. (Tariq Ramadan)

Study tip

It is important for AO2 that you include the views of scholars and/or schools of thought when formulating your response to a particular contention. Any discussion of the shari'a would benefit from the views of reformists as well as traditional and Islamist scholars. However, make sure that the views you use are relevant to the point that you are making. Your ability to use such views in an appropriate way would distinguish a high-level answer from one that is simply a general response.

In the modern world, there are many issues that sometimes appear to be in conflict with shari'a. The right to freedom or belief conflicts with the shari'a penalty for apostasy. Equality for women and right to equal treatment and value for gay and alternative relationships appear to contradict traditional versions of shari'a, which give less importance to the word of a woman in court, and impose a penalty for homosexuality. A literal interpretation of some of these traditional rules from shari'a therefore does not provide an adequate guide for all people. However, it depends on the view of shari'a taken. It could be argued that shari'a should be reinterpreted for the modern world and that some of the original teachings were tribal and not religious. Apostasy might have been associated with being a traitor to a tribe as much as with religion. In Ottoman Turkey, an attempt was made to modernise laws to make them more appropriate for the modern day. Homosexuality was legalised and the death penalty for apostasy abolished.

Some Muslims want to return to a position where their idea of shari'a is used as a guide for all aspects of life. They see the early days of Islam as a model and want to put Allah in the centre of all the laws and guidance that they use in life: from family matters to laws of state. Others see the Madinah model as a move towards secularism, where Muslims and non-Muslims lived together as equals in one community. It did not really matter if one was Muslim or not; so, it should not matter about following shari'a now, as long as people live peacefully and in harmony after the example of Muhammad.

AO2 Developing skills

It is now important to consider the information that has been covered in this section; however, the information in its raw form is too extensive and so has to be processed in order to meet the requirements of the examination. This can be achieved by practising more advanced skills associated with AO2. The exercises that run throughout this book will help you to do this and prepare you for the examination. For assessment objective 2 (AO2), which involves 'critical analysis' and 'evaluation' skills, we are going to focus on different ways in which the skills can be demonstrated effectively, and also refer to how the performance of these skills is measured (see generic band descriptors for A2 [WJEC] AO2 or A Level [Eduqas] AO2).

▶ **Your next task is this:** Below is **an evaluation of whether shari'a should form part of state law**. At present, it has no quotations at all to support the argument presented. Underneath the evaluation are two quotations that could be used in the outline in order to improve it. Your task is to rewrite the outline but make use of the quotations. Such phrases as 'according to ...', 'the scholar ... argues', or, 'it has been suggested by ...' may help.

Should shari'a form part of the laws of state? Many believe the body of tradition which forms shari'a is what God has ordered for Muslims to put in place in the world. Muhammad founded the Charter of Madinah which guided people in that city and gave them rights: a moral and Islamic form of government. Muslims copy his example so should try to emulate what he did and the work of his companions who formed the early Islamic Caliphate. The form shari'a takes could be different in different states, but there is an emotional longing by Muslims to have something that appeals to them, free from the corruption of colonialism and post-colonial oppressors, and valid because of its origin with God.

Other Muslims are equally passionate about separating state law from religious command. Muhammad set up a community, not a state. Medieval kingdoms often separated family and civil cases from criminal law. Shari'a does not provide a fair basis for women and minorities whose testimonies are regarded as less than men. Shari'a could be used in family courts as it is in some countries, provided these are voluntary and quite separate from the courts set up by government. Only by separating shari'a from state can all citizens be treated equally regardless of religion.

Key quotes

A body of laws alone is not sufficient for a society to be reformed. In order for law to ensure the reform and happiness of man, there must be an executive power and an executor. For this reason, God Almighty, in addition to revealing a body of shari'a law, has laid down a particular form of government together with executive and administrative institutions. (Ayatollah al-Khomeini)

Religious government is an absurd notion, and if a government is formed under Islamic banner, it will only serve the interests of a special group of the people, not an entire Islamic society. Thus, if Muslims form a government, it will be a secular, not a religious one. (Akbar Ganji)

Key skills Theme 3: ABC

This theme has tasks that concentrate on a particular aspect of AO2 in terms of using quotations from sources of authority and in the use of references in supporting arguments and evaluations.

Key skills

Analysis involves:

Identifying issues raised by the materials in the AO1, together with those identified in the AO2 section, and presents sustained and clear views, either of scholars or from a personal perspective ready for evaluation.

This means:

- That your answers are able to identify key areas of debate in relation to a particular issue
- That you can identify, and comment upon, the different lines of argument presented by others
- That your response comments on the overall effectiveness of each of these areas or arguments.

Evaluation involves:

Considering the various implications of the issues raised based upon the evidence gleaned from analysis and provides an extensive detailed argument with a clear conclusion.

This means:

- That your answer weighs up the consequences of accepting or rejecting the various and different lines of argument analysed
- That your answer arrives at a conclusion through a clear process of reasoning.

Specification content

The challenges to Islam from scientific views about the origins of the universe.

B: The challenges to Islam from scientific views about the origins of the universe

Islam and science

Islam is about belief in God, the unseen, by reading His revelation which Muslims accept without question. Science is about explaining the world by finding out natural laws through observation. It seems that religion and science are poles apart but that would be too simple. Science and Islam were once very closely related, so much so that Islam contributed much to science over the centuries. In the ancient world, the Greeks developed books of mathematics and medicine, and the Romans were known for their engineering achievements. With the fall of Rome, much knowledge became lost to the Western world.

The Islamic Golden Age

The Abbasid Caliphate led the Islamic world in most of the Middle East from 750 to 1258. The first two hundred years of their rule became known as the Islamic Golden Age. At that time Baghdad was the centre of the world, the largest and richest city on earth, and a centre of learning. The House of Wisdom, a library in Baghdad, was said to have a collection of over one million books. Many of the books were translations from different parts of the world. Muslims wanted to find out about knowledge and collected different works written by Ancient Greek philosophers and scientists and translated them into Arabic. **Vizier** Yahya Ibn Khalid, the Prime Minister of the **Caliph**, came from a line of Buddhist priests at the New **Vihara** Buddhist Monastery in Balkh in the mountains of central Asia. He paid for Hindu and Indian medical books to be translated into Arabic, adding to the House of Wisdom. The Caliph Harun al-Rashid encouraged the development of learning in Baghdad which was an open and cosmopolitan centre. His son, Caliph Al-Amin, continued this tradition. It seems a world away from the vision you sometimes get of a primitive and violent tribal centre in the middle of the Dark Ages.

Scientific approach

In science, Muslims were not only interested in reading books, but in developing understanding. The Scientist **Ibn al-Haytham** did more than read classical books. According to Jim al-Khalili, a lecturer at the University of Surrey, he developed what was known as scientific method. He questioned everything, and did not accept it until he found proof. Other religious thinkers at the time questioned whether the Qur'an was written by God at all. Known as the Mutazilah, they were the Caliph's preferred religious teachers for many years. The cafes of Baghdad were places where learned scholars came and could debate with others about religion and science.

Not everyone agrees with the above account. Some historians argue that Muslims added little to science and that the true developments came in Europe with the renaissance. Some Muslims would be horrified at this image of society which is completely at odds with their vision of a conservative religious Caliphate in which everyone became pious Muslims. Today, some people may think that belief in religion is at odds with understanding scientific method. However, Muslims in the Abbasid era didn't think so.

Key terms

Caliph: ruler of the Islamic Empire, seen as both a spiritual and political leader

Vihara: Buddhist temple

Vizier: Prime Minister to the Caliph

Key person

Ibn al-Haytham: Muslim scientist who lived from 965 to 1040 in Baghdad suggested that every effort should be made to enquire, question and be sceptical; not just accept what is seen. This is referred to as scientific method.

Key quote

This, for me, is the moment that Science, itself is summoned into existence and becomes a discipline in its own right. **(Jim al-Khalili)**

One huge difference separates Muslims from many modern scientists. That is belief in God. Think of famous modern scientists and who comes to mind? Perhaps Richard Dawkins or Stephen Hawking? Many modern scientists take the opinion that God does not exist. Science is based on observing what can be seen and making sense of it through reasoning. An example is that different animals seem to have similarities with other animals. Charles Darwin looked at this closely and came up with the theory of evolution: that one species evolved into the next. Take creation. Science tries to understand natural laws in the universe: how

Library in Baghdad in the Islamic Golden Age

gravity works; how atoms form together to make things; the creation of matter. There is no reason why an unseen creator called God should have anything to do with it. After all, you cannot see God. Why on earth would you want to believe in something you cannot see?

Muslims believe in the Qur'an as the word of Allah that is without error. If it says something, it should not be questioned. Yet as we have seen above, some people did question. Some Muslims in the Middle Ages saw the laws of nature as the same thing as God's laws in the Qur'an. The written down holy book was called the Qur'an al-Tadwini and the natural laws of the universe seen in the world as the Qur'an al-Takwini. To investigate science was a way of finding out about Allah's creation, something Muslims in the Golden Age heartily engaged in. The theory of Natural Law developed in the West. It states that there are some things that are naturally right and do not change according to time. These can be morals of human behaviour. Natural laws are also things in nature that can be observed as patterns which repeat. In many ways, the theory of Natural Law and Islamic beliefs are similar. The difference is the all-powerful position of Allah in Islam, who can over-ride natural law if He wants to, in Islam.

Muslims at other times and in other places have sometimes rejected the scientific approach, or been much more cautious. Some have seen science as a threat. Too much logical reasoning could lead a person to reject faith in Allah. The Muslim scholar Al-Ghazali got very frustrated with talking about philosophy and went through a crisis of faith. He then wrote a book against reasoning and in favour of traditional religion. In learning about the creation of the universe, many religious believers feel challenged to come to terms with how belief in Allah can go together with science. Some are comfortable with both their faith and scientific learning. To others, this is a difficult problem to resolve. We shall look at the Islamic and scientific theories of creation below, and see how different Muslims have responded to them.

Professor Stephen Hawking

Key quote

We are each free to believe what we want and it is my view that the simplest explanation is there is no God. No one created the universe and no one directs our fate. This leads me to a profound realisation. There is probably no heaven, and no afterlife either. We have this one life to appreciate the grand design of the universe, and for that, I am extremely grateful. (Stephen Hawking)

Key terms

Qur'an al-Tadwini: the revealed Qur'an, the book

Qur'an al-Takwini: the Qur'an as seen in the natural world

Key quote

In Islam the inseparable link between man and nature, and also between the sciences of nature and religion, is to be found in the Quran itself, the Divine Book which is the Logos or the Word of God. It is both the recorded Quran and the Quran of creation. (Seyyed Hossain Nasr)

quickfire

3.8 What did Ibn al-Haytham develop?

quickfire

3.9 What are the two different sorts of Qur'an?

Specification content

Islamic teachings about creation.

Islamic teachings about creation

Muslims look to the Qur'an and hadith to find out information about how the world was made. There are several references in the Qur'an that are similar to the story of creation in the Old Testament in the bible. Allah, the One, is beyond time and beyond form. Allah is not a created thing and cannot be seen. The essence of the Qur'an, without written form, is with Allah as the source of knowledge. The universe is seen as created by Allah. Nothing happens except for Allah's will; Allah says be and it is. Therefore, Allah is the first cause of creation. If Allah did not decide to start the creation of the universe, then it would not have come into being.

The Qur'an states that the heavens and the earth were together as one, then they were split apart. They then took on their present form. The earth was created in stages: mountains, the heavens, the stars. This happened in periods of time which can be translated as eras, days or unspecified long periods. The Qur'an does not necessarily put the events in an order we would recognise, but says that Allah created all living things that could walk, swim in the sea, crawl on the land and fly in the air and that these came from the water. Allah made beings called angels and jinn, before He made humans. He made the sun, moon and stars, the rain, the vegetables and crops and the fruit trees and grass.

Adam and Hawa

The creation of the first human beings in Islam is described in the Qur'an. This is the story of Adam and Hawa, or Adam and Eve as they are referred to in English. Allah gathered together some clay and moulded it into the shape of the first man, Adam. He breathed life into the clay. Prophet Adam came to life. Hawa was made from the rib of Adam, according to Sunni tradition. Adam and Eve lived in a garden of paradise. Allah ordered all the angels to bow down to Adam. All did so. However, Iblis, referred to by some as an angel or a jinn, was too arrogant to bow down, as he thought he was better.

Adam and Hawa lived in the garden of paradise and Adam was given knowledge of everything, the names of all the creatures. They were allowed to enjoy the fruits and flowers except the one fruit of the forbidden tree. However, Iblis came and tempted Adam and Hawa to eat the forbidden fruit. They both ate the forbidden fruit and in so doing disobeyed Allah. They realised that they had disobeyed and lost their feeling of peace. They covered themselves in shame. As punishment, Allah sent them to live in the world. Allah forgave Adam and Hawa and they lived on earth and gave rise to all human beings. Their family lived on earth, always at risk of temptation by Iblis, the shaytan (Satan).

Islamic tradition speaks of Adam as a giant. On Adam's peak in Sri Lanka, a giant footprint, nearly two metres in length, can be found on the top of the mountain. Muslims in Sri Lanka visit the mountain to see the footprint, which they believe was made when Adam was thrown out of paradise down to earth. The site is also special to Hindus, Buddhists and Christians.

Another explanation for creation is provided in the story Hayy ibn Yaqzan by the Muslim philosopher Ibn Tufayl. He lived in Spain and Morocco when the area was under Muslim rule. In the story, a boy called Hayy becomes isolated on a desert island where there are no human beings. He is brought up by a gazelle. Hayy thinks deeply about the natural world around him. Hayy notices birth and death, new shoots and leaf fall. He begins to think about the meaning of life and where it all came from. He decides that there must be a first cause to the universe that he cannot see, something that is not an object. The universe must have a beginning and end. Hayy looks at the stars and observes that they move in spheres. He worked out the main beliefs of creation without ever reading the Qur'an, a revealed text. He did it by looking at the world around him and thinking rationally

Key quote

First of all, there was nothing but Allah, and then He created His Throne. His Throne was over the water, and He wrote everything in the Book in Heaven and created the Heavens and the Earth. (Hadith of Prophet Muhammad)

quickfire

3.10 How did Hayy ibn Yaqzan find out about creation?

Sri Pada, or Adam's Peak, Sri Lanka

about nature. Eventually Hayy is rescued and returns to civilisation. Despite meeting people who have knowledge of religion through learning and texts revealed by Allah, he finds them materialistic and distracted from true knowledge by their wealth.

It is possible to interpret the story of the forbidden fruit as a parable. Good, humble words are what is required by Allah; evil temptations and thoughts of arrogance are temptations from the devil.

The most important part of the Islamic creation story is that the first cause is Allah. The creation of Hawa, Eve, out of Adam's rib is sometimes interpreted to mean that women came from part of man and are therefore inferior. However, there is no agreement about this. Unlike the Christian creation story, both Adam and Hawa were guilty of eating the forbidden fruit when tempted by Iblis. Hawa was not responsible for tempting Adam. The Qur'an repeatedly refers to the universe as a place where there are signs for people who believe and reflect on them. This would seem to support the idea of a Qur'an revealed through nature; of beliefs worked out by observing the world around as did Hayy Ibn Yaqzan.

The Alhambra in Granada, Spain

Key quote

The Qur'an 22:18

Seest thou not that to Allah bow down in worship all things that are in the heavens and on earth, the sun, the moon, the stars; the hills, the trees, the animals; and a great number among mankind? But a great number are (also) such as are fit for Punishment: and such as Allah shall disgrace. None can raise to honour: for Allah carries out all that He wills. (Yusuf Ali)

Key quote

The Qur'an 14:24–26

Seest thou not how Allah sets forth a parable? – A goodly word like a goodly tree, whose root is firmly fixed, and its branches (reach) to the heavens, – of its Lord. So Allah sets forth parables for men, in order that they may receive admonition. It brings forth its fruit at all times, by the leave of its Lord. So Allah sets forth parables for men, in order that they may receive admonition. And the parable of an evil Word is that of an evil tree: It is torn up by the root from the surface of the earth: it has no stability. (Yusuf Ali)

AO1 Activity

Sort the following list out into two categories: reason and revelation. You may need to look up the meaning of the terms and make a definition of each first. Are there any items from the list that you found difficult to put in one category or the other? Explain your answer.

- Working things out step by step
- Allah's words in the Qur'an
- The way Muslims find knowledge
- A scientific approach
- The approach of Hayy ibn Yaqzan
- The story of Adam and Eve
- Views of Stephen Hawking
- Approach followed by the Abbasids
- Teachings of Al-Ghazali
- Qur'an al-Takwini

The theory of the Big Bang

If you ask scientists about how the universe was made, most would say from a Big Bang. No one was around when the world was made, but many scientific theories suggest that it started with an explosion. Scientists have measured the universe and made calculations about its movement. From that it can be traced back to a single point, around 13 800 000 000 years ago. A very hot, dense mass exploded scattering the universe far and wide. As the heat slowly cooled, particles formed then grouped together atoms, clouds and stars. The Big Bang theory predicted that background radiation would be present in the universe from the Big Bang. As space exploration and measurements were made in the twentieth century, background radiation was picked up and this has been used to support the theory.

However, it is a theory. Some people are sceptical because there are other theories of how the universe was created. There is debate over what was the first cause of the Big Bang. Why did the hot, dense mass form in the first place? What created

Specification content

Modern scientific theories: the Big Bang theory.

quickfire

3.11 What is a first cause?

Specification content

Modern scientific theories: the Steady State theory.

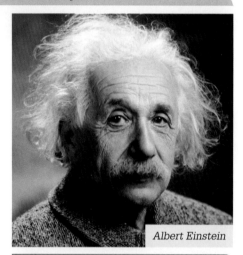

Albert Einstein

Key people

Albert Einstein: early twentieth-century scientist who came up with the theory of general relativity: that time and space are not absolute but relative, i.e. changing.

Al-Biruni: Muslim thinker, geographer and writer who worked out the size of the earth by careful observation and thought that the universe must be created in time by an external creator. Biruni also travelled to India where he was fascinated to learn from Hinduism and study comparative religion.

Avicenna: also called **Ibn Sina** in Arabic, Muslim scholar who wrote many books including a Canon of Medicine. He thought that the universe had to be created by a first cause so it was necessary that a power – God – was there outside time to create it.

it? Once created, a mass can be so dense that natural forces cause it to explode and spread outwards. It could be argued that the mass was spontaneously created. But from what and why? It is possible for religious believers to accept a modified version of the Big Bang theory that incorporates theology. The most important difference is that believers consider Allah as the first cause. Once the universe is created, it is possible for Allah to work through natural forces. Just as Muslims cannot see Allah, nor can scientists go back in time to prove that the Big Bang really happened.

The universe

The Steady State theory

The Steady State theory suggests that the universe did not originate from a Big Bang, but was always there and always much the same. New particles or new matter keeps on being made somewhere in the universe all the time: it did not start at one point in one explosion. The Steady State theory suggests the universe will go on forever. This theory was popular with some scientists in the mid twentieth century.

Albert Einstein earlier introduced his Theory of Relativity. Space and time were not fixed, they were part of the universe and could change as the universe changed. Einstein did not agree that the universe was in a steady state, but he did think that as the universe changed, space and time changed, so there was no use looking for a time when the universe started.

To Muslims, there must be a first cause, and that is Allah. Allah exists beyond the universe. To suggest the universe was always there puts it equal to God. In other words, the creation equal to the creator. To believers that does not make sense. The creator must come first. However, cycles within creation are compatible with the belief that Allah can work through various ways.

A Muslim thinker in the Middle Ages, **Al-Biruni**, spent much time studying and discussing the universe around him. He concluded that time was relative, to some degree like Einstein. Time had different qualities and cycles: it did not fit a linear pattern. Al-Biruni wrote letters to another Muslim thinker of his day, **Avicenna**, to discuss and debate aspects of the creation of the universe, the planets, the stars and their movements.

Al-Biruni worked out through careful observation that the planets were moving in a sphere like pattern. He also concluded that the earth was round. By calculating how far he could see to the horizon from the top of a hill, Al-Biruni worked out that the radius of the earth to an accuracy of 99.7%, incredible for an age before satellites and modern measuring technology. Al-Biruni made his measurement on a hill next to the river valley by the salt mines of Alexander

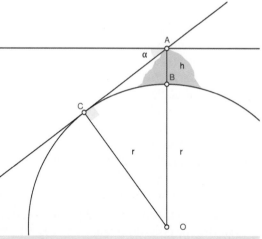

Al-Biruni's calculation of the radius of the earth

the Great in modern-day Pakistan. He was on his way to India to study the Hindu religion, which he had great interest in as he felt Muslims had much to learn from observing what they could from every people.

Expanding/Oscillating Universe theories

The Expanding and Oscillating Universe theories suggest that the universe has a series of cycles. One leads to the next which helps the universe to keep on going forever. Big Bangs might form part of this, but instead of a single Big Bang creating the whole universe, a Big Bang would start off a new phase in the universe and be followed by another Big Bang in the next cycle. The universe would expand for a time, then contract and collapse, then expand again.

Similarly to the other theories, there is no first cause. Muslims do not believe that the universe just happens and is self-sustaining: only God can sustain the worlds. Only God can give a reason or purpose for the creation. God can work through cycles in creation, as a background cause that has ultimate control over all things.

The movements of the planets in the universe and the meaning behind it is called cosmology. It can be studied from the point of view of modern science. Islamic thinkers in the Middle Ages were also interested in it. Al-Biruni wrote a series of letters to Avicenna, one of the most famous Muslim intellectuals from Uzbekistan, in a long-running argument about cosmology.

Avicenna, known in Arabic as Ibn Sina

Avicenna argued that God must exist because there had to be something that existed to cause everything in the first place. The unity in the universe suggested the thing that existed was God. God was the 'necessary existent', the thing that had to be there. One cause led to the next, to the next and so on in a chain that carried on but everything was dependent on that first cause. Avicenna said that the world could carry on being created forever.

Al-Biruni used different reasoning to explain how the world came into being. He felt that the world had a sense of newness and unity. It had to be created by a being and that being was unified. The universe was a sign of God's power and creation. Its newness meant that the universe had to be created by God at a point in time, it could not be beyond time or have always existed. It could be part of an infinite chain of events that carried on forever.

The medieval Spanish Sufi master Ibn Arabi took a different perspective. He said that the universe was a reflection of the qualities of Allah, signs for people who believe. Therefore, if Allah is eternal, then His reflection, the Creation, is not in the same dimension as time. It may go through cycles of birth, death and rebirth, a continuous creation. Allah was a necessary existent for the created world to appear, not a cause. Ibn Arabi's perspective might be taken to support the expanding/oscillating theories.

quickfire

3.12 What reasons did Al-Biruni give for believing the universe was created?

Specification content

Modern scientific theories: Expanding/Oscillating Universe theories.

Key quote

Avicenna's cosmology centralised God as the Creator—the First Cause, the necessary Being from whom emanated the 10 intelligences and whose immutable essence and existence reigned over those intelligences. The First Intelligence descended on down to the Active Intelligence, which communicated to humans through its divine light, a symbolic attribute deriving authority from the Qur'an.
(Michael Flannery)

AO1 Activity

TOPs: Theory – Opinion – Posts

For each scientific theory, write a summary in your own words in no more than two sentences. Explain why a Muslim might or might not be able to agree with it. See if you can find a quote posted in this chapter, from anywhere, which supports that theory; write it out and explain why you think that quote is supportive.

Next, imagine you are carrying out an Internet discussion about how the world was made. Post a series of comments about it, including your own point of view. Make sure you also include other points of view in the discussion. Each post should be short and to the point and on the topic of creation.

Key quotes

The Qur'an 3:26–27

Say: 'O Allah. Lord of Power (And Rule), Thou givest power to whom Thou pleasest, and Thou strippest off power from whom Thou pleasest: Thou enduest with honour whom Thou pleasest, and Thou bringest low whom Thou pleasest: In Thy hand is all good. Verily, over all things Thou hast power. 'Thou causest the night to gain on the day, and thou causest the day to gain on the night; Thou bringest the Living out of the dead, and Thou bringest the dead out of the Living; and Thou givest sustenance to whom Thou pleasest, without measure.' **(Yusuf Ali)**

The Qur'an 24:45

Allah has created every animal from water: of them there are some that creep on their bellies; some that walk on two legs; and some that walk on four. Allah creates what He wills for verily Allah has power over all things. **(Yusuf Ali)**

Key term

Qadr: fate. The idea in Islam that Allah controls all actions and decides a person's journey through life. Muslims sometimes refer to whatever is written for them, meaning whatever God has decided for their life

Sura 3:26–27

To Muslims, Allah has the power to do anything. In terms of the creation, God has power over night and day. It was God who made them in the first place. God is not just the first cause in the universe, but is actively present in day-to-day happenings. There are different beliefs amongst Muslims about how far Allah controls all actions. **Qadr** is the belief in fate or predestination: that Allah has

A Muslim reading the Qur'an

already decided a person's fate before they are born and nothing happens outside of God's plan. On the other hand, life is a test and human beings are free to choose what to do. They have the intelligence to understand right and wrong and are being tested by God to do the right things and obey his commands. Sunni Muslims put more emphasis on Qadr whereas Shi'a may put more emphasis on a person's duty to choose what to do. For both groups, Allah remains at work in creation. It is not a matter of chance or natural forces that events happen.

In the Qur'an Sura 24 the emphasis on God as creator of everything is given, but put in a rather interesting way. The suggestion that everything is made out of water sounds rather like a sequence of creatures, in the same way as the theory of evolution suggests first came fish, then gradually creatures that could walk on land developed. The theory of evolution did not exist at the time the Qur'an was revealed. There is a danger of reading too much into a translation of words given in a different context. It is, nonetheless, interesting to see the similarity.

Sura 23:12–14

Key quotes

The Qur'an 23:12–14

Man We did create from a quintessence (of clay); then We placed him as (a drop of) sperm in a place of rest, firmly fixed; then We made the sperm into a clot of congealed blood; then of that clot We made a (foetus) lump; then we made out of that lump bones and clothed the bones with flesh; then we developed out of it another creature. So blessed be Allah, the best to create! **(Yusuf Ali)**

The Qur'an 15:26

We created man from sounding clay, from mud moulded into shape. **(Yusuf Ali)**

The Qur'an 22:5

O mankind! If ye have a doubt about the Resurrection, (consider) that We created you out of dust, then out of sperm, then out of a leech-like clot, then out of a morsel of flesh, partly formed and partly unformed, in order that We may manifest (our power) to you; and We cause whom We will to rest in the wombs for an appointed term, then do We bring you out as babes, then (foster you) that ye may reach your age of full strength; and some of you are called to die, and some are sent back to the feeblest old age, so that they know nothing after having known (much), and (further), thou seest the earth barren and lifeless, but when We pour down rain on it, it is stirred (to life), it swells, and it puts forth every kind of beautiful growth (in pairs). **(Yusuf Ali)**

The above verses of the Qur'an suggest that human life came out of clay. They also detail the process of human reproduction, from sperm to egg to foetus. A 'clot' is one translation of the Arabic word alaq, which could mean foetus.

Life does not come about through physical means only, but with the permission of God. A distinction can be drawn between the creation of a physical embryo, and an embryo that has a soul. Sura 23 ayat 14 is sometimes taken to mean that 'another creature' refers to the baby and that the soul enters the foetus during pregnancy when life is breathed into the physical being. In science, an embryo is formed in the early stages of pregnancy in the womb after an egg has been fertilised by sperm and is beginning to grow. Later in the pregnancy, the embryo develops into a foetus, which has more identifiable human features.

To Muslims, humans are not just flesh and blood as described by science. They are creations of God and have a soul. The scientific understanding of reproduction can help Muslims discuss and interpret their texts. To a committed believer, the text of the Qur'an and hadith will always come first. In understanding them, modern science can help.

Sura 51:47

Key quote

The Qur'an 51:47

With power and skill did We construct the Firmament: for it is We Who create the vastness of space. And We have spread out the (spacious) earth: How excellently We do spread out! And of everything We have created pairs: That ye may receive instruction. (Yusuf Ali)

As the Qur'an is seen by Muslims as the word of Allah, the 'We' who constructed the universe is God. Power and skill refers to the belief that the universe was made by design, according to God's plan, not by accident. The universe has been made and then spread out. The translation and meaning of this is debateable. At the time, listeners would have no understanding of modern science and the theory of the Big Bang. Some Muslims say that God knew everything and every theory, so could have referred to the process of the Big Bang in these verses. The spreading out of the universe is not unlike the process of the Big Bang.

Key quote

The Qur'an 21:30

Do not the Unbelievers see that the heavens and the earth were joined together (as one unit of creation), before we clove them asunder? We made from water every living thing. Will they not then believe? (Yusuf Ali)

Other verses of the Qur'an refer to the universe as beginning as one unit, then bursting forth and expanding, in a similar way to the Big Bang. Sura 21 ayat 30 also refers to every living thing being made from water. In the theory of evolution, life in the water predates life on land. Slowly creatures in the sea developed small legs and the ability to walk on land. Whether or not this verse refers to this stage of evolution is debated.

Key quote

The Qur'an 71:14–17

Seeing that it is He that has created you in diverse stages? See ye not how Allah has created the seven heavens one above another, and made the moon a light in their midst, and made the sun as a glorious lamp? And Allah has produced you from the earth growing gradually. (Yusuf Ali)

Key terms

Alaq: Arabic word in the Qur'an meaning clot of blood; it can also be translated as embryo

Ayat: verse in the Qur'an

Key quote

Truly the creation of every one of you is brought together in his mother's womb for forty days in the form of a nutfah (a drop of sperm), then he becomes an alaqah (an embryo) for a like period, then a mudghah (human flesh) for a like period, then an angel is sent who blows his soul into him. (Hadith of Prophet Muhammad)

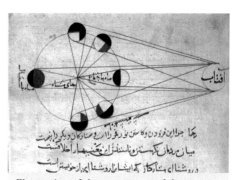

Illustration of the movement of the moon by Biruni

Key quote

The Qur'an 21:104

The Day that We roll up the
heavens like a scroll rolled up for
books (completed), – even as We
produced the first creation, so shall
We produce a new one: a promise
We have undertaken: truly shall
We fulfil it. (Yusuf Ali)

Specification content

Islamic teachings about creation
and their compatibility with modern
scientific theories.

quickfire

3.13 Name three Muslims who might
agree with the concept of evolution.

Key quote

It started out from the minerals and
progressed, in an ingenious, gradual
manner, to plants and animals. The
last stage of minerals is connected
with the first stage of plants, such as
herbs and seedless plants. The last
stage of plants, such as palms and
vines, is connected with the first
stage of animals, such as snails and
shellfish. (Ibn Khaldun)

The gradual nature of the creation is referred to in the Qur'an Sura 71, ayats 14 to
17. Another ayat of the Qur'an refers to a day as lasting fifty thousand years. The
meaning of day in the context of the creation story probably meant an undefined
period of time, which could refer to long periods which science suggests were
needed in the process of creation.

The Qur'an 21.104 suggests that the creation is like a scroll which can be rolled
up and unravelled, followed by a new one. This is similar to the idea of a stable
universe which continues with stages of expansion but never ends, like the
scientific Steady State theory. It could also fit the theory of an expanding and
oscillating creation. However, that does not fit with the clear Islamic belief that
Allah is beyond time and created the universe. So if the universe was created in
time, it cannot have existed forever.

It is easy to read too much in to these verses from the Qur'an. We do not know
what the listeners of early Arabia thought when they heard the Prophet recite
these verses. They certainly did not have the scientific understanding that we have
in the modern world. Nevertheless, some Muslims consider it a miracle that 1400
years ago the Qur'an had such understanding of the nature of the universe.

Compatibility with modern scientific theories

Muslims believe that Allah created the universe as part of his divine master plan.
That is the key difference between Islam and science. Scientific theories of the
creation of the universe suggest theories about how matter could come together
and split apart without the need to refer to a first cause. Be it the Big Bang or one of
the other theories, Muslims believe that God is at work in the creation. It is possible
that God creates the forces to control the universe, and in that way the events
described by modern scientists in their version of creation can be accepted. The
Qur'an seems to agree that change happened gradually; that planets moved apart;
that life then came into being. The difference is that there is a power behind it all
which Muslims call Allah.

The nature and beauty in the world can be observed by Muslims and by scientists
to look for evidence of what happened in creation. Muslim thinkers like Al-Biruni
saw a newness in the world which he thought pointed to God as a creator, a first
cause, and that the universe was created within time. The ideas of the medieval
philosophers tried to make sense of creation by what they saw and what they
could work out by reason, in much the same way as a scientist might do today.
This scientific method can be used to show that there is beauty and meaning in the
universe and a power behind it all.

One of the most controversial scientific theories for Muslims is the theory
of evolution. Many Muslims reject this theory. They believe that if Allah says
something will happen, it can be made there and then. The Qur'an says that Allah
created humans from dust, so we did not evolve from other species. Some Muslims
think that God can work through evolution. One species evolves into another as
part of God's master plan.

Ibn Khaldun was an Islamic thinker who lived in Granada, Spain and in North
Africa, in the Middle Ages. His ideas seem remarkably similar to the theory of
evolution. Ibn Khaldun wrote a book about the gradual process of creation. He
suggested that animals gradually changed from one species to another. Finally,
human kind is reached from the stage of monkeys. Humans are above all the
others because of their ability to think and reflect.

The theory of evolution has become more unpopular with Muslims in recent
times. This has been identified as a concern by some Muslim scientists. The Muslim
science lecturer Nidhal Guessoum, who teaches in the United Arab Emirates, said
that he felt it was his duty to teach Muslims about creation and evolution so they
obtained a better understanding of science.

Key quote

Not teaching evolution would be like going to my students and telling them the planets are not related to the stars, there is no relationship between them and gravitational pull or radiation, and they were all created on one day. We would not dream of describing the cosmos in such a ridiculous manner … We cannot allow people to go into the 21st century with no understanding of science. (Nidhal Guessoum)

Dr Usama Hasan, an Imam and Muslim scientist in East London, caused controversy when he suggested to people in his local mosque that evolution was not at odds with belief in God's creation. It was an intellectual position, but many in his congregation were upset and asked him to step down as a prayer leader. They felt that it was an attack on their beliefs. The episode shows just how strongly some Muslims feel about the topic of evolution.

Some aspects of the Islamic creation story cannot be accepted by modern scientists. The Qur'an refers to miracles, to beings of light called angels who can appear and give Prophets messages, and to unknown supernatural beings called jinn. To many Muslims it is a matter of faith to accept these things. The Pakistani writer Ghulam Ahmed Pervez tried to make sense of them by understanding them as metaphors rather than actual physical beings. To other Muslims, the Qur'an is the literal word of God which should be taken without interpretation to weaken its message.

The history of Islam has a proud heritage of study of science and translation of important works. The scientific method of observation, which enabled modern science to discover the theories of Big Bang and evolution, was created in part by the work of Muslims. Despite all this, there are some who reject the scientific approach today. Believers who have a strong faith in Allah sometimes feel that putting their trust in science is a distraction from greater sources of knowledge in the revealed text of the Qur'an. To them the literal word of God will always come first.

AO1 Activity

Imagine you are a professor of science and you have received a letter of complaint. The complaint is from a Muslim student of science. The complaint is that your college has been teaching evolution whereas the person complaining believes this is against Islam. Write a letter of response. In your letter show that you have understood the student's views and reply using information from Muslim sources in this chapter.

Key skills

Knowledge involves:

Selection of a range of (thorough) accurate and relevant information that is directly related to the specific demands of the question.

This means:

- Selecting relevant material for the question set

- Being focused in explaining and examining the material selected.

Understanding involves:

Explanation that is extensive, demonstrating depth and/or breadth with excellent use of evidence and examples including (where appropriate) thorough and accurate supporting use of sacred texts, sources of wisdom and specialist language.

This means:

- Effective use of examples and supporting evidence to establish the quality of your understanding

- Ownership of your explanation that expresses personal knowledge and understanding and NOT just reproducing a chunk of text from a book that you have rehearsed and memorised.

Key quote

The Qur'an 51:47

With power and skill did We construct the Firmament: for it is We Who create the vastness of space. And We have spread out the (spacious) earth: How excellently We do spread out! And of everything We have created pairs: That ye may receive instruction. **(Yusuf Ali)**

AO1 Developing skills

It is now important to consider the information that has been covered in this section; however, the information in its raw form is too extensive and so has to be processed in order to meet the requirements of the examination. This can be achieved by practising more advanced skills associated with AO1. For assessment objective 1 (AO1), which involves demonstrating 'knowledge' and 'understanding' skills, we are going to focus on different ways in which the skills can be demonstrated effectively, and also refer to how the performance of these skills is measured (see generic band descriptors for A2 [WJEC] AO1 or A Level [Eduqas] AO1).

▶ **Your next task is this:** Below is **a summary of Muslim views of the creation of the world**. At present, it has no references at all to support the points made. Underneath the summary are two references to the works of scholars, and/or religious writings, that could be used in the outline in order to improve the summary. Your task is to rewrite the summary but make use of the references. Such phrases as 'according to ...', 'the scholar ... argues', or, 'it has been suggested by ...' may help. Usually a reference included a footnote but for an answer in an A Level essay under examination conditions this is not expected, although an awareness of which book your evidence refers to is useful (although not always necessary).

The world was made in 7 days or stages, in which God made night and day, the waters and the land, all the living creatures, the day and the night. Allah continues to create all actions in the world because he controls the fate of everyone. The universe came together then split apart in a process controlled by Allah at the beginning of creation. When Allah said be, it became! Some Muslims believe this means there was no scientific process like the Big Bang. The literal words of Allah found in the Qur'an explain the creation. Others believe that the Qur'an seems to agree with the explosion of the universe at the beginning of everything, and God works through scientific theories as the first cause. The beauty in the created world shows that it was made by a creator in the first place, and that creator must have been One. Creation may be explained by observing life and making rational deductions, as the Qur'an can be found in the natural world.

Key quote

Seeing the whole universe as in reality one great being, and uniting all its many parts in his mind by the same sort of reasoning which had led him to see the oneness of all bodies in the world of generation and decay, Hayy wondered whether all this had come to be from nothing, or in no respect emerged from nothingness but always existed ... Hayy had learned that his ultimate happiness and triumph over misery would be won only if he could make his awareness of the Necessarily Existent, so continuous that nothing could distract him from it for an instant ... attainment of the pure beatific experience, submersion, concentration on Him alone whose experience is necessary. In this experience the self vanishes; it is extinguished, obliterated – and so are all other subjectivities. **(Ibn Tufayl)**

When you have completed the task, try to write another reference that you could use and further extend your answer.

Issues for analysis and evaluation

The effectiveness of Islamic responses to the challenges of scientific views about the origins of the universe

This is a complex topic which needs to be defined in order to be understood. Scientific views about the origins of the universe are usually thought to refer to the Big Bang theory. The Big Bang suggests that the universe started with an explosion from a dense mass, and as the universe expanded particles formed and then collected together to make planets. The expansion slowed down to create the universe as we know it today. The Big Bang is a theory which is suggested by scientific measurements of the movements of the planets, background radiation and other theories.

There are other scientific theories about the origins of the universe. The Steady State theory suggests it had no origin because it was always there in more or less the same state as it is now. The Expanding and Oscillating theories suggest that the universe went in cycles, perhaps a series of Big Bangs. At the moment, the Big Bang theory is accepted by most scientists, but these other theories have been suggested by others.

Muslims often comment that these are theories and not proven. The existence of many theories means that scientists cannot be sure. The theory that God made the world could just as equally be true. There are some verses in the Qur'an which could go together with these theories, such as the Qur'an 21:30: 'Do not the Unbelievers see that the heavens and the earth were joined together (as one unit of creation), before we clove them asunder? We made from water every living thing. Will they not then believe?' Joining together and splitting apart could support the Big Bang or the Expanding and Oscillating theory. At the time it was revealed the listeners may not have any concept of modern science, but explanations by modern Muslim scientists help believers to reconcile these theories with their faith. Harun Yahya, the popular rhetorical Muslim who gives dawah about Islam, claims that the Qur'an predicted the 'Big Bang' all along.

Key quote

Could anyone in 7th-century Arabia have known that our atmosphere is made up of seven layers? Could anyone in 7th-century Arabia have known in detail the various stages of development from which an embryo grows into a baby and then enters the world from inside his mother? Could anyone in 7th-century Arabia have known that the universe is 'steadily expanding,' as the Qur'an puts it, when modern scientists have only in recent decades put forward the idea of the 'Big Bang'? (Harun Yahya)

There is one big difference. Muslims insist that there must be a creator God who started the process. They also believe that Allah is at work in the world today by controlling what happens: everything is part of his plan. During the Middle Ages, Muslim thinkers tried to make sense of the origins of the universe. Avicenna thought that there must have been a 'necessary existent' or first cause to start off creation. Al-Biruni thought that the evidence of the newness in creation showed that the world must have been made, and did not always exist. Its beauty was evidence that it was made by a single unity, which he identified with Allah.

Avicenna and Al-Biruni were using reasoning to explain their beliefs, and interacting with each other in discussion. Scientists today also discuss theories using reasoning. Although the modern theories of the creation of the universe were not around in the days of Avicenna, his works continue to inspire Muslims to

This section covers AO2 content and skills

Specification content

The effectiveness of Islamic responses to the challenges of scientific views about the origins of the universe.

Key term

Dawah: Islamic mission to invite others to Islam or set a good example to portray Islam in a good light

AO2 Activity

As you read through this section try to do the following:

1. Pick out the different lines of argument that are presented in the text and identify any evidence given in support.

2. For each line of argument try to evaluate whether or not you think this is strong or weak.

3. Think of any questions you may wish to raise in response to the arguments.

This Activity will help you to start thinking critically about what you read and help you to evaluate the effectiveness of different arguments and from this develop your own observations, opinions and points of view that will help with any conclusions that you make in your answers to the AO2 questions that arise.

think about the cosmos around them. He left intellectual works that Muslims can use to respond to science.

Study tip

It is vital for AO2 that you actually discuss arguments and not just explain what someone may have stated. Try to ask yourself, 'was this a fair point to make?', 'is the evidence sound enough?', 'is there anything to challenge this argument?', 'is this a strong or weak argument?' Such critical analysis will help you develop your evaluation skills.

Some Muslims have responded to the challenge of science by rejecting it. They believe that they should take the Qur'an literally at face value and always regard its words more highly than any other book. Scientists who do not accept God are a threat because they do not accept the word of God. Muslims may gain strength by reading their holy book and putting aside any scientific work that questions their beliefs. But is this effective in challenging scientific theory? Some Muslims retain their traditional views but engage in debate about the creation of the cosmos and the existence of the first cause, Allah. Such debates can be popular and engaging for young Muslims. Today, we live in an age of information and knowledge, in which people want to work things out for themselves. The more Muslims engage in the debate, the more effective their response to scientific theories of creation will be.

Key quote

Our study shows that modern scientific findings do indeed influence modern Muslims' understanding of the Quran's cosmogonical terms, concepts and narratives by modifying the older Tafsir sources, even deviating from them altogether and offering fresh ideas. (Haslin Hasan and Hafiz Mat Tuah)

Some Muslims have reinterpreted the Qur'an in the light of modern science. They believe that it predated modern scientific theories in pointing to the origins of the earth. They largely accept modern science and have used it to make fresh interpretations of the Qur'an. Their work to some extent reflects the belief that the Qur'an can be seen in nature, and observation can be used with rational deduction to work out scientific theory. This can be seen in the work of Ibn Tufayl and his story about Hayy ibn Yaqzan, who worked out theory about the origin of the universe whilst observing things around him, without the help of any divine revelation. Other Muslims have been more wary, particularly of evolution and some aspects of medical science.

If the universe was created by God then an Islamic response is to look after it. Science increasingly recognises the dangers to the planet by global warming and overpopulation. However, there is a difference of approach. In science, rational thinking champions all: it is the duty of humanity to act, otherwise the consequences will be according to natural forces. Muslims agree that they must act for the good of the planet as stewards appointed vicegerents by God, but believe that not everything happens according to logical reasoning. Allah may intervene with miracles or it may be part of His plan to end the world at a certain time. These differences go to the heart of the different approaches of science and religion: rational thought against faith in the unseen. Awe and wonder in the origins of the universe provoke both.

Key term

Tafsir: an interpretation and guide to the Qur'an

Key questions

What does Islam have in common with, and where does it differ from, the Big Bang theory?

What are the different responses of Muslims to scientific theories of the origin of the universe?

Should Muslims update their interpretations of the origin of the universe as a result of scientific theory?

AO2 Activity

List some conclusions that could be drawn from the AO2 reasoning from the above text; try to aim for at least three different possible conclusions. Consider each of the conclusions and collect brief evidence to support each conclusion from the AO1 and AO2 material for this topic. Select the conclusion that you think is most convincing and explain why it is so. Try to contrast this with the weakest conclusion in the list, justifying your argument with clear reasoning and evidence.

Whether or not Islam is compatible with science

To answer this question we need to establish both what we understand by science and what it means to be compatible. Science is the study of the natural world to find patterns, laws and processes that can be proven through experiment, reasoning and deduction. There is no revelation as such. Processes are worked out by enquiry. If something cannot be proved by reasoning, evidence and theory, then it is not accepted.

Compatible means they can go together. This does not have to mean they are exactly the same; however, they can live together, complement and help each other understand the world and how it works. Islam and science involve not only theory but also real people who want to understand things and make sense of their lives, using the tools available to them.

How the world was made can be approached differently, because science suggests a Big Bang or similar theory, but Islam requires belief in Allah as the first cause. It is possible that God was at work in the world during a Big Bang, and existed before it. Some Muslims take the creation story from the Qur'an literally, which is incompatible with science. Others try to explain the two as compatible, with only small differences. Some Muslims have worked out creation using natural observation, like Hayy ibn Yaqzan. This is similar to a scientific approach.

Evolution is rejected by many Muslims who believe that Adam was made out of clay on God's command. The Muslim preacher Harun Yahya rejects evolution out of hand. The scientist Charles Darwin suggested that species evolved in their natural environments into other species, over millions of years. Some Muslims, like the scientist Dr Usama Hasan, think that God could have worked through evolution. This is a point of disagreement amongst different Muslims. Others interpret verses in the Qur'an literally: Allah said 'be' and Adam was born out of clay, not evolved from the animal kingdom.

Key quotes

Evolutionists have been digging fossil strata for about 140 years looking for these hypothetical forms. They have found millions of invertebrate fossils and millions of fish fossils; yet nobody has ever found even one that is midway between them. (Harun Yahya)

Every piece of information the Qur'an contains reveals the secret miracles of this divine book. The human being is meant to hold fast to this Divine Book revealed by Allah and to receive it with an open heart as his one and only guide in life. Islam is a religion based on belief in one God, Allah, who revealed a source of guidance in the Qur'an, the holy book of Islam. Revelation is the ultimate source of knowledge, which gives Muslims understanding of the created world around them and how to live in it. (Harun Yahya)

Harun Yahya goes further and labels the scientific approach inferior to that of reading the Qur'an. He sees simple answers for everything in the Qur'an and where science adds a discovery, it is either already predicted or in accordance with the revealed text. Similar attitudes in the past have proved a stumbling block to progress. Where Muslim scientists could have enquired further they did not, because the results appeared at odds with Ancient Greek thinking which they had translated. This failure to enquire came after some centuries of progress. Rodney Stark argues that this was limited to particular pieces of knowledge, and the failure to progress further was due to the lack of openness to developing scientific theory. He argues that to do so there needed to be some separation of science and religion, so that scientists could enquire and do their experiments without religious pressure

Specification content
Whether or not Islam is compatible with science.

Muslim scientist Jim al-Khalili

AO2 Activity

As you read through this section try to do the following:

1. Pick out the different lines of argument that are presented in the text and identify any evidence given in support.

2. For each line of argument try to evaluate whether or not you think this is strong or weak.

3. Think of any questions you may wish to raise in response to the arguments.

This Activity will help you to start thinking critically about what you read and help you to evaluate the effectiveness of different arguments and from this develop your own observations, opinions and points of view that will help with any conclusions that you make in your answers to the AO2 questions that arise.

Key quote

Averroes and his followers became intransigent and doctrinaire Aristotelians – proclaiming that his physics was complete and infallible and that if an observation were inconsistent with one of Aristotle's views, the observation was certainly incorrect or an illusion. As a result of all this, Islamic scholars achieved significant progress only in terms of specific knowledge, such as certain aspects of astronomy and medicine, which did not require any general theoretical basis. And as time passed, even this sort of progress ceased. (Rodney Stark)

Key questions

Does acceptance of revelation restrict getting involved in rational enquiry in science?

Does belief in miracles mean Muslims reject science?

Is the view that Islam was at the heart of science in the past justified?

AO2 Activity

List some conclusions that could be drawn from the AO2 reasoning from the above text; try to aim for at least three different possible conclusions. Consider each of the conclusions and collect brief evidence to support each conclusion from the AO1 and AO2 material for this topic. Select the conclusion that you think is most convincing and explain why it is so. Try to contrast this with the weakest conclusion in the list, justifying your argument with clear reasoning and evidence.

confining what they could say. This openness and freedom was found only in Europe in the Renaissance and Age of Enlightenment, from the sixteenth century onwards.

Study tip

It is important for AO2 that you include the views of scholars and/or schools of thought when formulating your response to a particular contention. Any discussion of Islam and science would benefit from the opinions of medieval as well as modern scholars. However, make sure that the views you use are relevant to the point that you are making. Your ability to use such views in an appropriate way would distinguish a high-level answer from one that is simply a general response.

Some Muslims disagree and say that Islam not only translated Ancient Greek and Sanskrit manuscripts, but developed scientific thinking further during the Islamic Golden Age. Ibn al-Haytham encouraged people to question, observe and be sceptical. Some people think he was the father of scientific method. Muslims built hospitals for the people and had surgeons who developed eye cataract operations. The medical knowledge of Avicenna advanced herbal medicine, some of which is being researched today for its potential to yield new medicines for recovery from cancer and other ailments. Even in the sixteenth century, the Ottoman Turk Taqi al Din set up a laboratory to experiment with new inventions and created a simple steam engine to turn a whole lamb roasting on top of a fire. Muslims argue their heritage contains so much science that the faith and scientific progress are complementary.

The Istanbul laboratory of Taqi al Din c1575

The position of miracles in religion can be problematic in science, which rejects miracles in favour of rational explanation. Some Muslims say that miracles are the exception, that Allah can intervene in the form of miracles but the true miracle was the revelation of the Qur'an and the beauty of God's creation. To over-rule the natural laws of creation which God made does not make sense. To understand those natural God-given laws through scientific enquiry helps to better understand God's world. Other Muslims disagree and believe in superstition and the miraculous. Some see miracles in the shape of Arabic letters in fruits or cloud forms, as signs that Allah is at work in the world. Sometimes the perception of miracle depends upon our viewpoint: what one person sees as a miracle can have a perfectly rational explanation.

Muslims can get along with science, even if their starting point is different. Some modern scientists come from the point of view that there is no God, which is obviously different. Nevertheless, they can get along with Muslims in their approach to questioning and learning. It depends on your view of religion, there is no single viewpoint that represents all Muslims. Some embrace science and are proud of the contribution of Muslims to science. Others feel that science has departed from the revelations of the Qur'an, and Muslims should therefore withdraw and not become too involved.

Key quote

Al-Afghani preached a common theme to all the reformers, that Muslims could restore the vitality of their societies by reclaiming from the West the rational sciences, including philosophy, which the West had largely borrowed from Muslim culture while it still encouraged a spirit of inquiry. Therefore, in learning science and technology afresh from the West, Muslims would be recovering their own past achievements and fulfilling the in junctions of the Qur'an to explore all manner of knowledge within Allah's creation. (David Waines)

AO2 Developing skills

It is now important to consider the information that has been covered in this section; however, the information in its raw form is too extensive and so has to be processed in order to meet the requirements of the examination. This can be achieved by practising more advanced skills associated with AO2. For assessment objective 2 (AO2), which involves 'critical analysis' and 'evaluation' skills, we are going to focus on different ways in which the skills can be demonstrated effectively, and also refer to how the performance of these skills is measured (see generic band descriptors for A2 [WJEC] AO2 or A Level [Eduqas] AO2).

▶ **Your next task is this:** Below is **an evaluation of whether Islam supports scientific theories about the origins of the universe**. At present, it has no references at all to support the arguments presented. Underneath the evaluation are two references made to the works of scholars, and/or religious writings, that could be used in the evaluation in order to improve it. Your task is to rewrite the evaluation but make use of the references. Such phrases as 'in his/her book ... (scholar) argues that ...', 'an interesting argument in support of this is made by ... who suggests that ...', or, 'the work of (scholar) has made a major contribution to the debate by pointing out ... ' may help. Usually a reference included a footnote but for an answer in an A Level essay under examination conditions this is not expected, although an awareness of which book your evidence refers to is useful (although not always necessary).

Other Muslims believe that the creation story is one of many allegorical, and not literal, sections of the Qur'an. Allah Himself states that some verses in the Qur'an are literal and others allegorical. He also states that the world was made in stages, and the idea of days of creation might just as accurately be translated as billions of years. Islamic scholars in the past have observed similarities between species and speculated that one led to another. Today, many Muslims see God at work through evolution, thereby reconciling it with religious belief in creation.

Does Islam support the theory of evolution? Some Muslims are avid that it does not. They believe that God made the world and everything in it literally in seven days. They also believe that humankind is superior to all other species and separate from them, having been given the right by God to rule over the earth as a steward of God's creation. To suggest that humans are a result of gradual evolution from one species into another reduces the importance of humans and denies the story that Allah breathed life into Adam.

Key quotes

It started out from the minerals and progressed, in an ingenious, gradual manner, to plants and animals. The last stage of minerals is connected with the first stage of plants, such as herbs and seedless plants. The last stage of plants, such as palms and vines, is connected with the first stage of animals, such as snails and shellfish. (Ibn Khaldun)

In the West appeared what is called 'the theory of evolution' which was derived by the Englishman Charles Darwin, who denied Allah's creation of humanity, saying that all living things and humans are from a single origin. We do not need to pursue such a theory because we have in the Book of Allah the final say regarding the origin of life, that all living things are Allah's creation. (Saudi Arabian School text book)

When you have completed the task, try to write another reference that you could use and further extend your evaluation.

Key skills

Analysis involves:

Identifying issues raised by the materials in the AO1, together with those identified in the AO2 section, and presents sustained and clear views, either of scholars or from a personal perspective ready for evaluation.

This means:

- That your answers are able to identify key areas of debate in relation to a particular issue

- That you can identify, and comment upon, the different lines of argument presented by others

- That your response comments on the overall effectiveness of each of these areas or arguments.

Evaluation involves:

Considering the various implications of the issues raised based upon the evidence gleaned from analysis and provides an extensive detailed argument with a clear conclusion.

This means:

- That your answer weighs up the consequences of accepting or rejecting the various and different lines of argument analysed

- That your answer arrives at a conclusion through a clear process of reasoning.

Specification content

Islamic attitudes towards pluralism.

Key terms

Sect: religious sub-group within a
religion

Tawhid: belief in the Oneness of Allah

C: Islamic attitudes towards pluralism

Muslims and pluralism

Modern Britain is a multi-faith society. Most people believe in Christianity, of various different churches. The second most popular position is people who are non-religious, atheist or agnostic. A survey of Wales found that in 2011 57% of people defined themselves as Christian and 32% not religious. Cardiff is a city with significant numbers of followers of other religions, including Muslims, Jews, Hindus, Sikhs, Buddhists and others. Of the Muslims, people originate from different **sects** and ethnic backgrounds. The question is how do Muslims relate to others in a plural society?

The question of pluralism is partly one of theology and partly community. Do followers of other religions go to heaven? How should Muslims relate to them in matters of worship? In their everyday lives, how should Muslims interact with those of other faiths? Charity work can be an area where

Swansea Mosque, located within a renovated church

Muslims work with others. Social events can be an arena of difference. Muslims who do not wish to mix with others in the presence of alcohol, in mixed gender settings, may find themselves apart from the mainstream of society.

Some Muslims are keen to interact with others; some prefer to keep within their own communities. Muslim scholars have defined those of other faiths as infidel, and as fellow believers. It is this diversity of viewpoints that we shall now explore.

Specification content

The diversity in Muslim attitudes towards other religions, including People of the Book.

The diversity in Muslim attitudes towards other religions, including People of the Book

Even before he realised his Prophethood, a monk named Bahira saw the young Muhammad and predicted that he would be a future holy man. After Muhammad received the first revelation on the Night of Power, his wife Khadijah spoke to a Christian called Waraqh who thought it was a genuine message from God.

Muhammad struggled against the idol worshippers and eventually cleared the Ka'aba of idols. The Qur'an repeatedly called on people to believe in **tawhid**, the one-ness of God, and reject worship of others besides God. Against this, Muslims believe that the creation is all part of a divine plan, and all actions are according to qadr, fate. If God made the world and everything in it, then He made the idol worshippers too. This is referred to in Sura 6, ayats 107–108. Muslims are encouraged to be kind to idol worshippers, and not to interfere with them. They should not speak harshly to them because this might put them off Islam.

Key quote

The Qur'an 6:107–108

Revile not ye those whom they call upon besides Allah, lest they out of spite revile Allah in their ignorance. Thus have We made alluring to each people its own doings. In the end will they return to their Lord, and We shall then tell them the truth of all that they did. (Yusuf Ali)

Textual references supporting good interfaith relations

Muhammad promised to protect Jews and Christians in his Charter of Madinah. In the Qur'an Sura 5 ayat 82 it refers to the Christians as 'nearest in love' to the Muslims. Muhammed went to visit a Jewish boy who had helped him when the boy became unwell. He went to see how he was and wish him a good recovery. There are other passages in the Qur'an and traditions from the hadith that are less tolerant of Christians and others. Muhammad recognised that individuals and tribes were not all the same. He acknowledged that some were pious and well meaning; others betrayed his confidence to the enemies of Madinah.

quicKfire

3.14 What was predicted of Muhammad before he became a Prophet?

Muslim men were allowed to marry women who believed in one God. Muslims could also eat meat prepared by Christians and Jews. It follows that Muslims may become the closest of friends with others who are not Muslim. If a Muslim decided to abandon the needs of other Muslims and join a conspiracy against them, then that would be wrong. References in the Qur'an and hadith to disassociating with non-Muslims refer to leaving their alliances at times of tribal conflict.

Different interpretations

The Qur'an states in Sura 5, ayat 51: 'O ye who believe! Take not the Jews and the Christians for your friends and protectors' (Yusuf Ali). This is open to interpretation. It may mean do not enter a formal pact of guardianship with those of Jewish and Christian tribes, as they have their own alliances. A minority of Muslims have given it a new meaning and used the verse as justification to withdraw from mainstream society.

The Qur'an 9.5 asks Muslims to 'slay the pagans wherever ye find them' (Yusuf Ali). The pagans it is referring to are the ones who broke an alliance with the Muslims. The verse goes on to say that if they repent, then help them. Such verses in the Qur'an can be misunderstood. Traditionally, Muslims believe that there are no translations of the Qur'an since Allah revealed it in the classical Arabic as the word of God. All translations are in fact interpretations, since each word is open to different meanings. It is important to understand the context and variety of meanings of each revelation and not jump to the conclusion that a simple translation should be given a literal meaning. Not long after this verse was revealed, Muhammad entered Makkah victoriously and cleared the Ka'aba of idols. He then forgave people who had worshipped idols, abused him and even some who murdered Muslims in the past.

The Islamic University of Al-Azhar is seen as the most important seat of learning in the world for Sunni Muslims, who make up the largest sect within Islam. They became so concerned that some Salafi Muslims were misinterpreting Islam that they issued a book called *The Response*. The book included fatwas from their respected and senior scholars in response to teachings that they felt were wrong.

Al-Azhar ruled that Muslims must not force or put pressure on others to become Muslims. Telling others about the good things with Islam can be done peacefully and properly. It noted with 'dismay' that some Muslims had been charged with blasphemy due to some comments made. People should be allowed freedom and persuaded, not pressured.

Key quote

Prophet (upon him be peace) dealt with Jews; he ate their food, and called them to become Muslims. Yet, he did not put pressure on them to convert, and left them free to make up their own minds. (*The Response*)

Some Muslims think that they should not wish Christians 'happy Christmas' or 'happy Easter'. Al-Azhar ruled that it was perfectly right and proper for Muslims to congratulate others on their festivals, provided they do not declare the Christian faith in Christ, since that would compromise Islamic beliefs. It is quite acceptable to sit with people of other faiths, shake hands and smile, since that will encourage them to think good of Islam.

Some Muslims fear that life in modern Britain can lead young people to become confused about their religion. They feel that it is better for them to keep their distance from those of other faiths so that they can concentrate on learning about Islam. They fear intermarriage may lead to family arguments and confusion for children. By mixing in liberal social circles, students fear breaking key teachings of

Key quotes

The Qur'an 3:113–115

Not all of them are alike: Of the People of the Book are a portion that stand (for the right): They rehearse the Signs of Allah all night long, and they prostrate themselves in adoration. They believe in Allah and the Last Day; they enjoin what is right, and forbid what is wrong; and they hasten (in emulation) in (all) good works: They are in the ranks of the righteous. Of the good that they do, nothing will be rejected of them; for Allah knoweth well those that do right. (Yusuf Ali)

The Qur'an 5:5

This day are all things good and pure made lawful unto you. The food of the People of the Book is lawful unto you and yours is lawful unto them. Lawful unto you in marriage are not only chaste women who are believers, but chaste women among the People of the Book, revealed before your time, – when ye give them their due dowers, and desire chastity, not lewdness, nor secret intrigues if any one rejects faith, fruitless is his work, and in the Hereafter he will be in the ranks of those who have lost all spiritual good. (Yusuf Ali)

Key term

Al-Azhar: Islamic University thought of as the highest source of authority in the world for Sunni Muslims

Islam by drinking alcohol or having affairs before marriage. Others say that Islam is a personal commitment and should not be dependent on what others around are doing. If someone is strong in their beliefs they can cope wherever they are. By interacting with others they are promoting a good image of Islam.

The early Islamic Empire

In the early days of Islam, Muslim conquerors spread quickly over the Middle East and North Africa. It is thought that people converted to Islam in the following two hundred years or so. Khaled Ibn al-Walid led an army to conquer Damascus. He guaranteed the security of its churches. He promised that the Caliph would keep the people safe. The Christians were required to pay a special tax called Jizya, in return for their security. Inhabitants who were accepted as believers but not Muslims were known as dhimmis. Caliph Umar instructed his governors to help the poor people who were dhimmis in the areas they ruled. Umar saw a blind Jewish man in need and allocated to him a sum of money from his treasury for his assistance. When the Abbasids expanded the rule of the Islamic Empire over central Asia they accepted Buddhists as dhimmis too. Buddhists were allowed to continue their meditations as places such as the New Vihara near Balkh. Its high priests accepted Islam and became Viziers, Prime Ministers, for the Abbasid Caliph.

You should not think that the early days of Islam were full of enlightened free choice. There are some nasty episodes hidden in the history of the period, in which people were forced to convert or else killed or tortured. Some people did convert to benefit from the riches of conquest. Muslims argue these things were in spite of Islam. Rulers did not always have Muhammad's example in mind when exercising their power. However, compared to what went before, many accepted Islam because it was that bit more tolerant.

Salvation in heaven

So far we have considered the early history of Islam, but what about the theology of who could go to heaven? Al-Ghazali was a traditional Muslim scholar who taught that most non-Muslims will enter heaven. He thought that Muhammad's way was the best way to God but that many people did not hear it. Others heard it from people who did not give a good impression. Only those people who had heard many times, understood and felt the reality of the good in it, but then rejected that good, would not enter heaven.

Some Muslims believe that only Muslims go to heaven. There are passages in the Qur'an which say that hypocrites who say their prayers but cheat others behind their backs will be denied paradise, but others despite sinful lives will be forgiven by God. The point is that God decides. No one can know until the Day of Judgement.

La Convivencia

Medieval Spain was known as Al-Anadalus and ruled by Muslims for over three hundred years. At times there was strife between communities, but in the main this period was known as a period of relative peace and acceptance of different faiths. The proportion of Jews and Christians who held senior positions, were academic writers, or even held the position of Vizier (Prime Minister) under the Muslim rulers was much higher than the proportion of Muslims who hold senior positions in Western Europe today. Some argue this means Muslim Spain was an open and tolerant place. Muslims passed on the knowledge they had preserved from the Ancient Greeks and this led to the European Renaissance, without which modern Europe might have been very different. The period of Muslim Spain is known as La Convivencia, a period of cultural mixing. Jewish scholarship flourished at this time, whilst Edward I of England taxed English Jews to fund his

Key terms

Jizya: a tax on non-Muslims living in the Islamic Caliphate

La Convivencia: a period of coexistence between Muslims, Christians and Jews during which culture flourished and many academic works were translated, leading to the European Renaissance

quickfire

3.15 What did Al-Ghazali teach about who could enter heaven?

military campaigns and when they could no longer pay sent them to the Tower of London. La Convivencia is a point of contention between some Western writers, who do not accept it was a period of tolerance, and some Muslims, who exaggerate the tolerance as greater than that seen today.

Al-Biruni

As Islam expanded into South Asia, travellers encountered Hinduism. The geographer and scholar Al-Biruni was one of the first to study comparative religion. He thought that all cultures were related to each other as they were all made by people. He did not judge others as right or wrong. He wanted to learn more about them. Al-Biruni saw that some Hindus worshipped idols. He saw others he thought understood the idea of One God, who was eternal and present everywhere. These Hindus Al-Biruni accepted as fellow believers. Al-Biruni tried to write down details about what he saw as facts and not dismiss people of other religions just because they were different. He saw that some Muslims behaved badly by making raids into South Asia, which gave them a bad name. To get over the stigma Al-Biruni studied alongside Hindus and became fluent in their ancient Sanskrit language, so that he could read their religious and scientific texts. The Arabic world benefitted from his translations.

The Mughals of India

Mughal Emperor Akbar lived at the same time as Elizabeth I of England. He built a new capital at Fatehpur Sikri, and included features of different religions in the decoration. The pillars of the mosque had Christian crosses carved in; a saint's tomb was shielded with marble lattice work after the style of Indian Jains. Akbar built a special room called the Ibadat Khana, where he invited Imams to come and discuss Islam. Different Muslims soon started arguing and cursing each other. Akbar was disgusted by their behaviour. He invited Christians, Jews, Hindus, Buddhists and even atheists to come and talk instead.

Akbar concluded that all religions had good in them. He thought that being jealous of others and boasting about yourself were sinful, whereas piety and keeping away from excess were praiseworthy in all faiths. Akbar liked vegetarianism but disliked Priests and holy books. Some Imams accused Akbar of creating a new religion; others said that he was trying to follow Islam without the bad influence of Imams. Akbar made friends with Hindus and celebrated Divali. He allowed people to convert from Islam to Hinduism if they had previously been Hindu but had been forced to convert.

Mughal emperor Aurangzeb imposed shari'a. He banned alcohol and drugs. He ordered his officials to close down around 15 Hindu temples and tried to force people to convert to Islam. He built mosques in their place. Nevertheless, he employed more Hindu administrators to help him win over the central Indian plain, called the Deccan. Aurangzeb was unsuccessful and the Mughal Empire lost ground. The tolerance of his forebear Akbar helped to keep communities together whereas Aurangzeb divided Muslim and Hindu, weakening the Empire. Not everyone sees it this way. Some see Akbar as a heretic, Aurangzeb a pious, orthodox Muslim. The views are reflected in the division of India and Pakistan. In general, Indians prefer Akbar, Pakistanis Aurangzeb.

Islam and Confucianism

Islam spread further east into China, where Muslims encountered different religious traditions altogether, including Confucianism. Confucianism is about searching for unity of the self and the Tian. The Tian may be thought of as heaven, or the one high God, nature, awe, or the way of things. Originally it was a form of pantheism. There are various meanings, often not God. Meditation of the order

quickfire

3.16 How did Al-Biruni approach studying other religions?

Key terms

Confucianism: ancient Chinese philosophical and ethical teachings

Heretic: a person defined as holding views outside what is acceptable in a religion

Ibadat Khana: house to debate religion in Akbar's capital, Fatehpur Sikri

Jain: ancient Indian religion, similar to Buddhism

Mughal: dynasty who ruled most of South Asia in the early modern period

Sanskrit: ancient Indian language in which many Hindu texts are written

Tian: heaven, or the one high God, nature, awe, or the way of things; a form of pantheism

A Chinese mosque

Key terms

Dao: the way, as defined by early Chinese philosophy such as Confucianism

Fa: true ethical law in Confucianism

Han Kitab: texts written by Liu Zhi about Islam and Confucianism

Haqiqa: experience of the reality of truth

Jiao: teachings in Chinese philosophy

Ma'rifa: mystical experience of God

Sheng: sages or holy people who help Confucianists experience deeper mysticism

Tariqa: the way of Sufi orders

of creation helps people to become one with heaven. This leads to transformation of character and community. Compassion brings unity with heaven or return to heaven.

Muslims sometimes think of Eastern religions as completely different from monotheistic religions which believe in one God, but in some ways, it can be argued that Islam fits well with Eastern religions. In Islam, Allah is not a person and has no personal characteristics. There are references in the Qur'an to the 'hand' and 'face' of Allah, but Muslims regard these as no more than metaphors. Allah is described as a set of characteristics like truth, oneness and compassion. Allah is all around and nearer to a believer's heart than their jugular vein. This is not so different from the Confucianist belief in truth and their meditation of the beauty and order in nature.

Liu Zhi was born in the old imperial city of Nanjing, where he lived from 1670 to 1739. He was a Chinese Muslim of the Han culture. He went to Nanjing religious school where he read Chinese classics as well as Arabic and Islamic books, Buddhist and Western texts. After leaving school, Liu Zhi moved to a retreat house in the woods at the foot of the mountain, just outside Nanjing. He translated many Islamic books into Chinese and wrote about Islam in the Chinese language. Liu Zhi saw common ground in Han culture, Sufism and Confucianism. His books became known as the **Han Kitab**.

Liu Zhi wrote that the teachings of the ancient Chinese philosopher Confucius were similar to those of Muhammad and they both testified to the same one truth. He explained that Islam's prohibition on alcohol was similar to the Chinese medical teaching that alcohol can harm the body and damage friendships. Liu Zhi looked deeper into Sufism and found the Sufi path could also be found in Confucianism. In Sufism, Muslims follow the straightway of shari'a. They go on to follow the guidance of a **tariqa**. They develop a deeper understanding of the reality of truth, the **haqiqa**. Finally, they experience the mystical knowledge of God in **ma'rifa**. Confucianists follow the way called **dao**. Then they go on to learn teachings, the **jiao** and develop knowledge of true ethical law, called **fa**. Here they experience deeper mystical knowledge through sages or holy people, **sheng**.

Key quote

What is recorded in the books of Islam is no different from what is in the Confucian canon. Observing and practising the proprieties of Islam is like observing and practising the teachings of the ancient sages and kings.
(Liu Zhi)

Lui Zhi ultimately saw that Islam was best understood through Confucianism. On the one hand, he was an orthodox Muslim who read the Qur'an and hadith. On the other, he was a thinker who saw Islam at one with Chinese philosophy. Many Muslims disagree. They see Eastern religions and philosophy as completely different from Islam. However, in China, local people who

Entrance to the tomb of Liu Zhi

were not Muslim were impressed. Lui Zhi came to be regarded as a **wali**, a saint, by Chinese Muslims who still visit his tomb in Nanjing.

Muslims in the modern world have very different views about other faiths. Some believe that personal faith should not prohibit anyone from marrying who they like, be they Muslim, Hindu or atheist. Some experience different faiths and practices before reaching their own conclusion. Other Muslims want to protect their faith from change and ensure it is passed on to the next generation. For some, living in mostly Muslim communities is the answer.

In some areas of the world, Islam has come into conflict with other religions. In Burma, Muslims complain that some of their mosques have been closed down by Buddhist authorities. In Saudi Arabia, non-Muslims are restricted from entering the sacred sites in Makkah. Some Muslims argue that it doesn't matter what they believe about other faiths as long as they work together for social action. By showing non-Muslims that Muslims care and help them when they are in need, Muslims give a good impression of their religion. Some call this a form of dawah, to bring more people to convert to Islam.

One winter, Storm Desmond left a trail of flooding and destruction across the North of England and Wales. A team from **Al-Imdaad** charity in Blackburn were first on the scene in the Lake District. They helped flooded villagers in a rural area where hardly any Muslims lived. They worked together with charities of other faiths to give out sandbags and bring in emergency supplies. By doing so, they were giving a good impression of their faith.

AO1 Activity

Choose three of the following and explain how they helped develop relations between Muslims and non-Muslims: Muhammad, Akbar, Liu Zhi, Al-Biruni, Al-Ghazali, Caliph Umar.

The teachings found in Sura 42:13, Sura 2:136 and Sura 2:256

Key quotes

The Qur'an 2:136

Say ye: 'We believe in Allah, and the revelation given to us, and to Abraham, Isma'il, Isaac, Jacob, and the Tribes, and that given to Moses and Jesus, and that given to all prophets from their Lord: We make no difference between one and another of them: And we bow to Allah (in Islam). (Yusuf Ali)

The Qur'an 2:256

Let there be no compulsion in religion: Truth stands out clear from Error: whoever rejects evil and believes in Allah hath grasped the most trustworthy hand-hold, that never breaks. And Allah heareth and knoweth all things. (Yusuf Ali)

The Qur'an 42:13

The same religion has He established for you as that which He enjoined on Noah – that which We have sent by inspiration to thee – and that which We enjoined on Abraham, Moses, and Jesus: Namely, that ye should remain steadfast in religion, and make no divisions therein: to those who worship other things than Allah, hard is the (way) to which thou callest them. Allah chooses to Himself those whom He pleases, and guides to Himself those who turn (to Him). (Yusuf Ali)

Key terms

Al-Imdaad: Islamic charity based in Blackburn

Wali: a saint in Islam

Specification content

The teachings found in Sura 42:13, Sura 2:136 and Sura 2:256.

Key terms

Asbab al-nuzul: the circumstances in which a part of the Qur'an was revealed

Psalms: holy book revealed to Prophet Dawud/ David

Sabians: another religious group associated with worship of the stars

Key quotes

The Qur'an 2:62

Those who believe (in the Qur'an), and those who follow the Jewish (scriptures), and the Christians and the Sabians, – any who believe in Allah and the Last Day, and work righteousness, shall have their reward with their Lord; on them shall be no fear, nor shall they grieve. (Yusuf Ali)

The Qur'an 2:113

The Jews say: 'The Christians have naught (to stand) upon; and the Christians say: 'The Jews have naught (To stand) upon'. Yet they (Profess to) study the (same) Book. Like unto their word is what those say who know not; but Allah will judge between them in their quarrel on the Day of Judgment. (Yusuf Ali)

Key person

Abraham: Ibrahim in Arabic, first to clear the Ka'aba of idols, respected as a Prophet.

The Qur'an was revealed in the Arabic of seventh-century Arabia, in a very different context from today. The companions of the Prophet thought it important to understand the context of the revelations, the asbab al-nuzul. This was not always clear. The early Islamic scholar Al-Wahidi wrote a commentary of the Qur'an about the context of the revelations. He drew together various sayings about what was known about the context of different verses in the Qur'an, and who had passed on the information, rather like the hadith collectors wrote down who passed on the hadith. His work helps to explain what was known about the context of some verses of the Qur'an.

No compulsion in religion

Referring to Sura 2 ayat 256, no compulsion in religion, Al-Wahidi notes several traditions about the context. One was about the sons of some of the Muslims of Madinah who had been wet nursed by Jewish women. They were upset that the Jewish tribes were being expelled from Madinah and they said they would become Jewish and leave Madinah too. Their families tried to stop them and wanted to pressurise them to become Muslims. Then the verse of the Qur'an was revealed to the Prophet: 'Let there be no compulsion in religion.'

On another occasion, Christian Syrian traders were selling cooking oil in the market. Two sons of Abu'l Husayn converted to Christianity with the traders. The Prophet told them to leave the city with the traders, and banished them. In a third tradition, a Muslim father from amongst the ansar of Madinah tried to convert his two Christian sons to Islam. They had previously converted to Christianity. The father refused to leave them, so they all went to Muhammad to settle their dispute. The Prophet said to them: 'Let there be no compulsion in religion.'

As in Sura 2 ayat 136, the Qur'an appears to recognise the validity of Christian and Jewish scriptures, which are regarded by Muslims as earlier revelations of the same message of Islam. The Ka'aba was originally cleansed by **Abraham**, known to Muslims as Prophet Ibrahim. Over time, people forgot and started worshipping idols again. Muslims recognise the Torah sent to Abraham, the Psalms of David and the Gospels about Jesus as messages from God. They think the core messages are the same as the Qur'an, but they are incomplete or altered from the original. The Gospels are known as the Injeel in Islam, given to Isa, the name for Jesus in Islam. Isa is referred to as a Prophet, son from a virgin birth, who brought miracles as signs to his people. In Islam, he is not a Son of God. His death and resurrection are referred to in different accounts in Islam. Allah saves him from the people and raises him to himself, to avoid the suffering imposed by the authorities. This is different from the Christian account in which the suffering is all important.

At the time of Muhammad there were discussions between peoples of different religions. That in itself is a model for Muslims to get involved in interfaith dialogue. If Allah judges between people at the Day of Judgement, then we should not be judgemental in this life. It does not mean that all Muslims accept other faiths as equally valid. Most claim that Islam is the ideal and that all people should be encouraged to submit to Allah by following the Islamic faith, but they should not assume that they know best.

'A Common Word' was set up by Muslims and Christians to share their understanding of faith. Over 500 Muslim and Christian intellectuals and leaders signed the document. They shared their common understanding of the Bible and the Qur'an, focusing on love for God and love for thy neighbour. In the UK, Muslim leaders have joined together with Christians and others at major events, such as at Remembrance services and the Royal wedding. After major terrorist incidents, leaders of Muslims and other faith communities gathered to condemn terrorism, to promote peace and to show support to each other at times when Muslims feel under pressure by others angry at events.

The importance of religious freedom in the history of the Islamic religion

Muslims say the shahadah as a statement of belief. The shahadah is simple: it is belief that Allah is the one and only God and Muhammad is His messenger. Beyond that there are considerable variations in belief and practice. Some Muslims say that if God is One, then all Muslims ought to create a single set of beliefs and practices, and leave behind their differences. Several groups have created their own aqidah, which are more detailed statements of belief. All believe in one God, and Prophet Muhammad as His last and final messenger. All aim to try and interpret the original texts of Islam and claim to be accurate.

Are Muslims free to say what they personally think? Many young Muslims in Britain today grow up in traditional households which value respect for parents. They may not say anything to disagree with their traditions. Muslims have great respect for Allah and believe they should speak with humility towards Him, after the model of the Prophet. However, when they go to the mosque, they usually accept the beliefs of that sect. For some Muslims in Shi'a and Sufi groups, they are required to follow the teachings of their Imam or shaykh out of loyalty to him as the interpreter of God's word. What freedom do Muslims have when it comes to individual opinions about faith?

The Qur'an Sura 10 ayats 99–100 provide an interesting explanation for the diversity of belief in the world. If God wanted everyone to he could have made them believe, but he did not. So do not force people to believe. In the Qur'an, it also states that God made people different so that they can learn from one another. This suggests that Muslims should accept people's freedom to be different. Muslims can speak different languages, have different cultural habits, even differences of sect. That should not matter.

Key quote

The Qur'an 49:13

O mankind! We created you from a single pair of a male and a female, and made you into nations and tribes, that ye may know each other not that ye may despise each other. Verily the most honoured of you in the sight of Allah is he who is the most righteous of you. And Allah has full knowledge and is well acquainted with all things. (Yusuf Ali)

Responding to abuse

Muhammad put up with more than his fair share of abuse. The Quraysh of Makkah constantly shouted bad names at him because they disagreed with his beliefs, but Muhammad did not answer back. An old woman used to throw garbage at Muhammad's door in Makkah every morning. One day she did not come. Muhammad went to see where she was and asked if she was all right. From this well-known sunna, Muslims learn not to become angry if they face abuse. They should not respond with violence. Instead, they should win friends with care and compassion.

A Muslim once attacked a Jew who had criticised Muhammad. A Jewish man said Muhammad was less of a person than Moses. When Muhammad heard of this he told the Muslim off: the Muslim should not have reacted by attacking the Jew. The examples of Muhammad are followed by Muslims but in recent years a small number have carried out acts of violence, and sometimes atrocities, in reaction to others.

Specification content
The importance of religious freedom in the history of the Islamic religion.

Key terms

Aqidah: Islamic beliefs. There are various different versions of aqidah according to Islamic sect

Shaykh: Head of a Sufi order or simply respected person

Key quote

The Qur'an 10:99–100

If it had been thy Lord's will, they would all have believed, – all who are on earth! wilt thou then compel mankind, against their will, to believe! No soul can believe, except by the will of Allah, and He will place doubt (or obscurity) on those who will not understand. (Yusuf Ali)

quickfire

3.17 What did Muhammad do when the old woman put garbage by his door?

quickfire

3.18 What happened in the Mihna?

Key person

Moses: Musa in Arabic, regarded as a Prophet in Islam who received the Torah.

French magazine publishers Charlie Hebdo printed cartoons of Muhammad showing drawings of him in a derogatory way. The French media had a tradition of printing whatever they wished out of belief in freedom. Many Muslims felt offended that their holy figure was being portrayed in a disrespectful way. Some reacted with a terrorist attack. Yet the example of Muhammad shows that they should not have reacted with anger at all. If anything, they should have visited the cartoon makers and befriended them, as Muhammad did the old woman who abused him.

The Abbasid Caliph **Al-Mamun** tried to enforce the belief that the Qur'an was written by people, not revealed from Allah. Ahmad ibn Hanbal stood up for his right to say freely what he thought. He was imprisoned and flogged because he said that the Qur'an was made by God, not created by humans. In the end, he was released due to protests by the people. Ahmad ibn Hanbal went on to found the Hanbali School of fiqh, one of the four main madhabs in Sunni Islam. The different schools of law in Sunni Islam developed at this time. They were different because they were allowed the freedom to be different: their rulings were not controlled by the Caliph.

Freedom of expression

In modern society freedom of belief is often associated with freedom of expression. It is common for young people to choose an identity and display it. For example, sports fans may wear their team shirt. Muslims increasingly display symbols of faith such as growing a beard, wearing a prayer cap or wearing a veil. Some fear symbols, particularly for women, are used to put pressure on them not to integrate into Western society. Al-Azhar University in Cairo, Egypt, known as the highest authority for Sunni Muslims, raised a concern about the face veil being worn in women's classes. The head of Al-Azhar said it was not right. Hijab was supposed to be a concept of humility, but the veil was being used as a symbol of outward expression. On the other hand, some Muslims from Salafi and Deobandi backgrounds have encouraged women to wear a face veil. They believe it was a literal command from Allah to cover their faces in public, and that it is a symbol that women are special as well as protected.

Some Muslims investigate different groups and beliefs within Islam and make their own choice. A Muslim might be brought up and attend a mosque which has allegiance to the brewlvi sect, then go to university and change their allegiance to Salafism. There is a great variety of different sects and groups within the UK which can be quite confusing for young Muslims who are trying to decide what to think and believe.

Reformist Muslims

Modern reformist Muslims can take quite different positions on some issues. The imaan.org organisation helps gay Muslims, and provides an analysis of the Qur'an in which it suggests there is nothing wrong with being both gay and Muslim. They also point to the legalisation of homosexuality by the Ottoman Caliph. Other Muslims condemn gay people and say that their actions mean they have left Islam. They think that Islam does not allow people freedom to change what they think are eternal laws made by God. Mawaan Rizwan, a gay Muslim of Pakistani heritage, investigated attitudes to homosexuality within the Muslim community in the UK and in Pakistan, and found that most gay Muslims kept their sexuality secret. Nevertheless, an increasing number of gay Muslims are speaking out. The Big Gay Iftaar was arranged in London during Ramadan for gay Muslims and friends, who were proud of both their faith and their sexuality.

Key person

Al-Mamun: Caliph who launched the Islamic inquisition, the Mihna.

Key terms

Brewlvi: Islamic sect based in South Asia which agrees with the practice of visiting the tombs of Saints and remembering the names of Allah in worship

Charlie Hebdo: French satirical newspaper that published cartoons of Muhammad

Deobandi: South Asian Islamic sect which promotes strict adherence to orthodox Islam

Hijab: humility, or a head or face veil for women

Iftaar: meal to open the fast at the end of the day in Ramadan

Apostasy

Are Muslims free to choose a different religion? Leaving Islam is called apostasy and some Muslim countries have made this illegal and punishable. An apostate is to be encouraged to return to Islam and if they refuse they may face death in Saudi Arabia or Iran. There are passages from the Qur'an and traditions from the hadith which suggest Muslims should not leave Islam, but they have a context mixed up with the tribal alliances of the day. Someone leaving the tribe might also be leaving the religion and going to support an enemy tribe.

Sura 2 ayats 108–109 of the Qur'an are clear that Islam is the way and Allah does not want people to turn away from it. But for those who do, it asks Muslims to 'forgive and overlook'. A Bedouin once converted to Islam then changed his mind. The Prophet did not want him to leave the faith but when he insisted Muhammad allowed him to leave Madinah.

Muhammad suggested that the death penalty could only be applied for adultery, murder and one who leaves and abandons the Muslims. In context, this meant abandoning the loyalty of the tribe, not just leaving the faith. Some Muslims have interpreted it otherwise, but for most, leaving Islam is a matter of personal belief. Muslims do not want people to leave their religion, but ultimately it is a matter of a person's own convictions.

Mina Ahadi, an ex-Muslim

Mina Ahadi is one of the founders of the Council for Ex-Muslims. As a Muslim girl, she felt that her freedoms were restricted. Her interpretation of the Qur'an was that it permitted violence and oppression, particularly of women. Maryam Namazie started a branch of the group in the UK. She was particularly concerned that human rights were being abused within Islam.

The Guardian Newspaper published an article about ex-Muslims with examples of people who had changed their beliefs. Nasreen, another ex-Muslim, was not particularly religious but became involved in the political movement **Hizb ut-Tahrir** as a teenager. Most Muslims regard groups such as Hizb ut-Tahrir as unacceptable and forbid them from meeting in mosques. However, Nasreen wanted to explore different ideas about her faith. She demanded to wear a long black gown at school. 'I said if you don't let me, you're breaching my freedom of expression as a Muslim, and they accepted it', said Nasreen. It felt fun to be a rebel, although slowly Nasreen questioned her beliefs. She felt that showing you were wearing a veil had become more important than what you believed. At university, Nasreen became concerned about the social pressure from other Muslims. She recalled being told off when she ordered some non-Halal food. Eventually, Nasreen decided that religion was not for her and chose to leave.

Committed Muslims draw a distinction between Islam and Muslims. They say that some Muslims do the wrong thing by forcing others to do things they do not wish to do. Parents who force their children to get married to someone they don't want to are doing the wrong thing. Such experiences can put people off religion for life. Islam should not be about force. If someone genuinely experiences love and care from the Muslim community and from their family, they will naturally respond with commitment to Islam.

Key quotes

The Qur'an 2:108–109

Would ye question your Messenger as Moses was questioned of old? But whoever changes from Faith to unbelief, has strayed without doubt from the even way. Quite a number of the People of the Book wish they could turn you people back to infidelity after ye have believed, from selfish envy, after the Truth hath become Manifest unto them: But forgive and overlook. Till Allah accomplish His purpose; for Allah Hath power over all things. (Yusuf Ali)

The blood of a Muslim who bears witness that there is no god but God and that I am his Messenger is not lawful except in one of three cases: a married person who commits adultery; a person who murders another; and a person who leaves his religion and abandons the community of Muslim. (Hadith of Prophet Muhammad)

Key term

Hizb ut-Tahrir: Islamic political group which promotes the idea of forming a worldwide Caliphate to replace modern Muslim countries

Key terms

Convert: someone who has changed religion

Quilliam: a nineteenth-century Muslim convert; also the name of a counter-extremism foundation

Revert: often used when referring to Islamic converts as people who have returned to their natural state of being, i.e. Muslim

Conversion in Islam

Islam is a missionary faith. Muhammad encouraged others to convert to Islam. Inviting others to Islam is called dawah, which can also mean preaching to Muslims to become more religious or even creating a good impression of Islam by being caring and compassionate to others. Many decide to become Muslim because they want to marry a Muslim, and their family ask them to convert. Others describe a special, emotional moment when they converted. Some describe the experience as a period of intellectual discussion when they became convinced.

Allah made the world and made all children, in their natural state, creatures of belief, even if they do not know it. So people are born Muslim and then grow up in another faith because of the family or area in which they were born. When a person converts, they are said to be reverting to their natural, God-given state. They say they are a revert. Others use neither convert nor revert to describe themselves. They say they embraced Islam, because it is something that is warm and emotional, like an embrace.

To become a Muslim, a person should recite the statement of faith, the shahadah, in front of two witnesses. They must do so freely, without threat, and believe it in their heart. After taking on Islam a person then learns more detail about their faith, such as how to perform the five daily prayers. Just like a baby is given a special ceremony in Islam, the same ceremony may be performed on a convert. It is like being born again. Their head is shaved to symbolise making a fresh start and sweets given out to people to celebrate the conversion. Many converts take on a new, Muslim name, often from one of the companions of the Prophet. Others retain their name as a symbol that Muslims can be from any cultural background, and do not need to change.

Some of the staunchest enemies of Muhammad eventually converted to Islam. Abu Sufyan was leader of the Quraysh tribe in Makkah. He opposed Muhammad and had fought the Muslims who were damaging his trade at Makkah. When Muhammad gathered a large force to enter Makkah, Abu Sufyan decided to embrace Islam peacefully. The Islamic Empire spread far and wide over the Middle East, but that did not mean everyone converted. Many non-Muslims accepted the authority of the Caliphs and were slowly converted.

Over hundreds of years, most people were converted to Islam by travelling Sufis. In South Asia, Moinuddin Chisti established a Sufi order which preached Islam. They collected and gave out food to the poor and taught them that regardless of wealth, they were equal in the sight of God. Shrines of Sufi saints were set up which Muslims and those of any religion could visit, and songs in local languages told the stories of Islam in a way that local people could understand. The tomb of Moinuddin Chisti is venerated by Muslims at Ajmer in India to this day.

Quilliam, Cobbold and Yusuf

William Quilliam was a Victorian solicitor who became fascinated by Islam and studied it when he travelled to Morocco to spend time convalescing after an illness. He converted to Islam and set up one of the first mosques in the UK at Liverpool. The Quilliam foundation was set up in 2007 as a counter-extremism foundation, named after William Quilliam. Another famous Victorian convert was Marmaduke Pickthall who travelled India, learned Arabic and wrote a translation of the Qur'an in English.

Lady Evelyn Cobbold was a Scottish aristocrat who converted to Islam. She had grown up in North Africa and had Muslim friends. Later in her life, she suddenly announced that she was Muslim in a most surprising way. Lady Cobbold was the first British Muslim to make the Hajj pilgrimage in 1933. She died aged 96 back in Scotland and was buried on the hillside of her Highland hunting estate. She asked for a simple grave inscribed with words from the Qur'an: 'Allah is the light of the heavens and the earth'.

Key quote

Some years went by, and I happened to be in Rome staying with some Italian friends when my host asked if I would like to visit the Pope. Of course, I was thrilled. When His Holiness suddenly addressed me, asking if I was a Catholic, I was taken aback for a moment and then replied that I was a Muslim. What possessed me I don't pretend to know, as I had not given a thought to Islam for many years. A match was lit, and I then and there determined to read up and study the faith. (Lady Evelyn Cobbold)

Hamza Yusuf is an American convert to Islam. He travelled across North Africa, where he learned about Islam from people who were not well off, but were sincere and practised their faith. This impressed him so much that he became Muslim and went on to make lectures about Islam which inspired many Muslims.

Some Muslim converts went through a difficult period in their life and converted to Islam to make a fresh start. It is not uncommon to find people in prison who convert to Islam whilst still inside. For many, Islam gives them fresh hope and a structure to live their lives. A small minority misunderstand Islam and have become known for inappropriate, even violent or extreme acts. Muslims condemn these and say these are in spite of Islam, not because of their conversion.

The Tablighi Jamaat missionary movement focuses on Muslims who are Muslim of South Asian origin by birth, but do not practise the five daily prayers at their local mosque regularly. They send out preachers to go to homes and convert people to follow a more conservative version of Islam. A small number of Muslims even 'convert' from one group of Muslims to another.

> ## Key term
> Tablighi Jamaat: Islamic missionary group promoting an austere version of orthodox Islam

AO1 Activity

Explain both the process of conversion to Islam, and the experiences people have which bring them to leave Islam. Give an example for each and explain why you think the person may have changed.

Key skills

Knowledge involves:

Selection of a range of (thorough) accurate and relevant information that is directly related to the specific demands of the question.

This means:

- Selecting relevant material for the question set

- Being focused in explaining and examining the material selected.

Understanding involves:

Explanation that is extensive, demonstrating depth and/or breadth with excellent use of evidence and examples including (where appropriate) thorough and accurate supporting use of sacred texts, sources of wisdom and specialist language.

This means:

- Effective use of examples and supporting evidence to establish the quality of your understanding

- Ownership of your explanation that expresses personal knowledge and understanding and NOT just reproducing a chunk of text from a book that you have rehearsed and memorised.

AO1 Developing skills

It is now important to consider the information that has been covered in this section; however, the information in its raw form is too extensive and so has to be processed in order to meet the requirements of the examination. This can be achieved by practising more advanced skills associated with AO1. For assessment objective 1 (AO1), which involves demonstrating 'knowledge' and 'understanding' skills, we are going to focus on different ways in which the skills can be demonstrated effectively, and also refer to how the performance of these skills is measured (see generic band descriptors for A2 [WJEC] AO1 or A Level [Eduqas] AO1).

▶ **Your final task for this theme is:** Below is **a summary of Muslim attitudes towards those of other religions**. You want to use this in an essay but as it stands it is undeveloped and has no quotations or references in it at all. This time you have to find your own quotations (about 3) and use your own references (about 3) to develop the answer. Sometimes a quotation can follow from a reference but they can also be used individually as separate points.

Muslims believe theirs is the last, final and perfect religion so they preach to others to encourage them to embrace Islam. Some Muslims believe everyone will achieve heaven, including those of other religions and those who have not heard the word, but not those who heard, understand and reject. Some Muslims recognise the validity of the Jewish and Christian revelations, although they think these have been corrupted. Muslims lived peacefully and intermarried with Christians and Jews at times, in the early days of Madinah and in Muslim Spain. However, at times non-Muslims were treated less well than Muslims and charged an additional tax for living in a Muslim land. Some Muslims such as the traveller Al-Biruni and Mughal emperor Akbar valued the contribution of Hinduism, Buddhism and other religions. Today, some Muslims aim to forge common ground with those of other faiths in upholding human rights and social action. Others want to preserve their traditions by living somewhat separate lives in largely or exclusively Muslim communities.

The result will be a fairly lengthy answer and so you could then check it against the band descriptors for A2 (WJEC) or A Level (Eduqas) and in particular have a look at the demands described in the higher band descriptors towards which you should be aspiring. Ask yourself:

- Does my work demonstrate thorough, accurate and relevant knowledge and understanding of religion and belief?

- Is my work coherent (consistent or make logical sense), clear and well organised?

- Will my work, when developed, be an extensive and relevant response which is specific to the focus of the task?

- Does my work have extensive depth and/or suitable breadth and have excellent use of evidence and examples?

- If appropriate to the task, does my response have thorough and accurate reference to sacred texts and sources of wisdom?

- Are there any insightful connections to be made with other elements of my course?

- Will my answer, when developed and extended to match what is expected in an examination answer, have an extensive range of views of scholars/schools of thought?

- When used, is specialist language and vocabulary both thorough and accurate?

Issues for analysis and evaluation

The effectiveness of Islamic responses to pluralism

Specification content

The effectiveness of Islamic responses to pluralism.

The modern Western world has developed into a society in which there are many different faiths. People are used to going out to work and study alongside colleagues of other religions. Intellectual freedom gives people the chance to make their own minds up about issues. Within faiths, there are many different groups holding different positions on ethical issues. Yet Islam originated as the faith of extreme monotheism. In other words, there is only one God and God can have no partners, no symbols or images, nothing can stand alongside God. Many Muslims think that means there should be one way to God, through a faith that has one set of beliefs.

In Madinah, Muhammad lived alongside Christians and Jews for many years. However, tribal conflict led to the expulsion of Jewish tribes. It is important to distinguish between tribal intolerance and acceptance of those of other faiths on grounds of religion. This is difficult to do, and literal translations, out of context, can lead to versions of the text being written that promote separation from people of other religions. When Muslims were advised not to take Christians and Jews as friends and guardians, it may have meant a particular group from a particular tribe in one form of formal guardianship. During the same period, Muhammad promoted peace and reconciliation in Makkah. He visited a neighbour's Jewish son especially to see how he was when he fell ill. He commented that Christians were 'nearest in love to the Muslims'. In the early days of Islam as the Empire grew, Islam was at its height when travellers from other regions came to Baghdad and shared their knowledge with others. This required tolerance and open-mindedness from the Muslims.

The period of La Convivencia in Spain was seen by some as the most enlightened and pluralistic in the history of Europe. At the time, non-Muslims occasionally held the office of Vizier, whereas Muslim minorities have never held that office in modern Europe. The proportion of academics of Jewish and Christian heritage who discussed together at Cordoba was reflective of a society where non-Muslims could study freely. There was a flowering of Jewish literature at the time. It has been suggested that we have not yet reached this period of tolerance in modern Europe. Others say that despite relative tolerance, there were bloodthirsty expulsions of whole communities of Jews on occasion, hardly reflective of a society which had embedded pluralism. Nevertheless, the thought of a period of tolerance is looked upon fondly by Muslims today as something to look back on and aim to return to in response to pluralism in the future.

To traditional Muslims who have migrated from a country where they lived in a single faith community, pluralism is a shock to the system. For some, it is a step too far. Socialising with others in the presence of alcohol and with free mixing with the opposite sex is challenging. Some take a literal view of Qur'anic passages which suggest that Muslims should not be guardians and friends with others, and choose not to inter-marry. Some react by withdrawing from society and living mostly in groups of other Muslims. This has advantages. It is easy to organise halal food and not to be tempted during Ramadan by seeing others eat, because all around are fasting. However, to many, this is a failure to respond to pluralism. It can feel frightening to some who have grown up in a Muslim home and do not have experience of living alongside others, if they have to go out and mix. Some have experienced racism or Islamophobia, making them more apprehensive about mixing with those of other backgrounds. Nevertheless, mixing may help to overcome those fears. It is unhealthy not to integrate in the wider community, who may become suspicious of Muslims as a result. Mixing gives Muslims an opportunity to challenge the prejudices of others and promote a good image of their faith.

Key quote

As Peoples of the Book the Christian and Jewish dhimmi communities were not rigidly marked off from the majority Muslim society in the same way that Jews, for example, experienced marginalisation in Christian societies of Europe. (David Waines)

AO2 Activity

As you read through this section try to do the following:

1. Pick out the different lines of argument that are presented in the text and identify any evidence given in support.

2. For each line of argument try to evaluate whether or not you think this is strong or weak.

3. Think of any questions you may wish to raise in response to the arguments.

This Activity will help you to start thinking critically about what you read and help you to evaluate the effectiveness of different arguments and from this develop your own observations, opinions and points of view that will help with any conclusions that you make in your answers to the AO2 questions that arise.

Study tip

It is vital for AO2 that you actually discuss arguments and not just explain what someone may have stated. Try to ask yourself, 'was this a fair point to make?', 'is the evidence sound enough?', 'is there anything to challenge this argument?', 'is this a strong or weak argument?' Such critical analysis will help you develop your evaluation skills

Key questions

What are the different Islamic responses to pluralism?

What can Muslims learn from Muhammad and from La Convivencia?

Why might some people be sceptical of these times?

Why do you think some Muslims react against pluralism and withdraw from mixed occasions?

What is the difference between pluralism in terms of salvation and pluralism in social action?

AO2 Activity

List some conclusions that could be drawn from the AO2 reasoning from the above text; try to aim for at least three different possible conclusions. Consider each of the conclusions and collect brief evidence to support each conclusion from the AO1 and AO2 material for this topic. Select the conclusion that you think is most convincing and explain why it is so. Try to contrast this with the weakest conclusion in the list, justifying your argument with clear reasoning and evidence.

Specification content

Whether or not there is a coherent approach to conversion in Islam.

Other Muslims retain their traditional beliefs and display them when mixing with others. They are happy to pray wherever they are, even with others around them, and feel this helps others to get a good image of Islam. The same is true for charity work, when they help non-Muslims. They believe that Islam is the only way to God and that by showing them good manners and speaking about Islam, others will join them. They are mixing socially, but they do not believe in a plurality of beliefs: Islam is still seen as the only way.

Reformist Muslims take a very different approach. They believe that Muslims should be free to integrate fully in society and adapt their beliefs for modern times. Inter-marriage, friendships with others and alternative relationships such as gay and transgender should all be accepted. To some this is a brave new way of responding to pluralism and much more suited to the times. To others this is an abandonment of the traditions of the times of the Prophet as laid down in the hadith and the Qur'an.

Farid Esack, a University researcher in South Africa, took a leading role in the emergence of the country after apartheid. He became commissioner for gender equality and promoted women's rights, as well as the rights of people of all different faith backgrounds. Farid Esack believed that the true meaning of the Qur'an promotes liberation from oppression and acceptance of pluralism. He also believed that people of different sexuality should be treated equally within the South African state.

The Islamic scholar Al-Ghazali said that everyone had a chance of heaven, including those of other religions, unless they turned away and rejected the message of Islam. The question of who can get into heaven is left to God alone to judge. Some Muslims regard those of other faiths with an ounce of goodness in their hearts as worthy of heaven; or those of whichever religion having a concept of spiritual unity, which Muslims call Allah, as being eligible for salvation. Others reject this pluralism as going too far: if that was true then why reach out to others to convert? They feel that Allah demands people publicly profess their faith as a Muslim, even if it is a last-minute conversion on their death bed, in order to stand a chance of reaching eternal life in paradise.

Some Muslims have taken this theme further and developed links with Christians, producing a guide to the 'Common Word', in which themes shared in the Bible and the Qur'an are a focus for dialogue between faiths. Some Muslims reject this and believe that Allah has given them the final message in the Qur'an, not to be confused with early revelations which have been corrupted over time. In schools and colleges inter-faith events sometimes take place and there may be opportunities set up by youth groups for young people of different faiths to come together and meet. Some mosques have begun opening their doors for visitors of all backgrounds on certain occasions to break down barriers with their local communities.

The diversity of opinion across the world has created a situation in which there is not one, but several different Muslim viewpoints about pluralism. In many ways Muslims are still coming to terms with modernity. Some think that nothing short of an Islamic reformation is an effective response; others that a return to the literal teachings of their faith is needed to keep their religion pure.

Whether or not there is a coherent approach to conversion in Islam

Conversion to Islam means reciting the statement of faith, the shahadah, in front of two witnesses and believing it in the heart. The statement means that there is only one God, and that Muhammad is His last and final messenger. Conversion is sometimes called reversion to the natural state of being, since it is believed that God made all children in the natural state of Islam.

In Muhammad's time, in the first instance his followers converted to Islam and read the shahadah out loud. Some of his enemies converted over the years. During his time in Makkah, Muhammad's family were unconvinced of his message. Then, his uncle converted to Islam giving him protection to preach out loud without fear of attack. After his uncle died, Muhammad and the Muslims faced persecution. Some converts were physically tortured. Bilal was a black slave who converted to Islam. His slave master made him lie on the hot sand of the Arabian desert with heavy rocks on his body, which became very hot in the heat of the sun, as punishment for his beliefs. Muhammad did not turn to violence but moved to Madinah in order to practise faith freely, where more people converted to Islam. When he triumphantly re-entered Makkah, its Quraysh tribal leader Abu Sufiyan converted to Islam without a fight. After Muhammad's death the Islamic Empire grew, but Christians, Jews and believers were recognised and given freedom to practise their faiths.

Forced conversion happened on occasion despite the initial approach of Muhammad to invite people to follow Islam. Some would argue that this is not consistent.

Why convert? Muslims believe that their faith is the true message and is the way to salvation in heaven. But at the same time Muslim scholars such as Al-Ghazali concluded that everyone, including people of other faiths, goes to heaven.

In addition, some people converted to Islam in the early days to gain favour as the Muslim Caliphate grew and took over more land. Riches and career prospects improved with conversion. However, one could argue that such reasons were not acceptable reasons to convert: Muslims are supposed to believe in the Oneness of God and the validity of His last messenger Muhammad. King John of England in the 1200s was excommunicated by the Pope and went to the Almohad Caliph in Morocco pleading for help. King John offered to convert to Islam and make England into a Muslim kingdom if only Caliph Al-Nasir would help, but he was sent away empty handed. Once again, this was more than an invitation to embrace Islam with a hidden agenda.

Forced conversion continued to occur at times in history, but was not approved of in the Qur'an in which Muslims are asked not to force others or speak to them harshly lest they turn away from Islam. Caliph Al-Hakim forced people in his kingdom to adopt Islam, but he was the exception rather than the rule. People thought he had gone mad at the time for ordering the conversions. Other Caliphs generally protected other religious believers, whilst encouraging them to convert and this is more in line with the original ideal.

What if someone wants to convert and then changes their mind? Are they free to leave Islam? Some Muslims say this constitutes the crime of apostasy and others that the person should be allowed to leave if persuasion fails; their punishment will be in the afterlife. Mughal emperor Akbar recognised that some Hindus had been forcibly converted and permitted them to return to Hinduism.

We should also recognise that belief can be a very personal matter which is different for every individual. Some come to Islam after intellectual debate, and are convinced that there is only one supreme God. Others decide to convert to satisfy family members of someone they want to marry, if the family make conversion a condition of the marriage, as is common in many Muslim families. For others, it is an emotional experience in which they feel a sense of mystical adventure. In South Asia, most people converted after hearing stories, music and drama from travelling Sufi holy men, whereas in the West this is quite uncommon. Conversion, then, has a variety of reasons and ways of accepting the faith.

Throughout South East Asia and East Africa, travelling traders spread Islam. Many of them were also members of Sufi tariqa who told stories to entertain the local people and educate them about Islam. The medieval traveller from Tangiers, Ibn Battuta, wrote a book about his travels through much of the Muslim world at the time. He found much variety amongst the Muslims he met. Many accepted the faith but retained their traditional pre-Islamic dress and culture. He describes, for example,

Key quote

The religious frenzy of the Fatimid Caliph Al-Hakim and his decision to destroy churches and synagogues and to enforce Islamisation throughout his realm, were presented by many of his contemporaries as reflecting his insanity … many converted and subsequently returned to their original faiths after the persecutions ended, but many others have left behind their creed and dropped their religion. (Ira Katznelson and Miri Rubin)

AO2 Activity

As you read through this section try to do the following:

1. Pick out the different lines of argument that are presented in the text and identify any evidence given in support.

2. For each line of argument try to evaluate whether or not you think this is strong or weak.

3. Think of any questions you may wish to raise in response to the arguments.

This Activity will help you to start thinking critically about what you read and help you to evaluate the effectiveness of different arguments and from this develop your own observations, opinions and points of view that will help with any conclusions that you make in your answers to the AO2 questions that arise.

Key quote

In my thirty-nine years on this earth, the Holy City of Mecca had been the first time I had ever stood before the Creator of All and felt like a complete human being. Throngs of people, obviously Muslims from everywhere, bound for the pilgrimage were hugging and embracing. They were of all complexions; the whole atmosphere was of warmth and friendliness. The feeling hit me that there really wasn't any colour problem here. The effect was as though I had just stepped out of a prison. You could be a king or a peasant and no one would know. (Malcolm X)

Key term

Takfir: a Muslim declared a non-believer because of following deviant traditions or doctrines

Key questions

What do people need to do to convert to Islam?

What are the connections between conversion and freedom of belief, and what is Islam's position on these issues?

What different reasons do people give for conversion?

Does the diversity within Islam mean people are not all converting to the same beliefs?

AO2 Activity

List some conclusions that could be drawn from the AO2 reasoning from the above text; try to aim for at least three different possible conclusions. Consider each of the conclusions and collect brief evidence to support each conclusion from the AO1 and AO2 material for this topic. Select the conclusion that you think is most convincing and explain why it is so. Try to contrast this with the weakest conclusion in the list, justifying your argument with clear reasoning and evidence

preaching to topless women Muslim converts working the fields of an equatorial village, informing them of the basics of Islam and the dress requirement of modesty. Conversion and taking on aspects of Islam do not automatically go together. Therefore, the approach to conversion may not be completely uniform and coherent within Islamic history.

In the West, some people convert for marriage, some for reasons of theology and some as a change of lifestyle. Conversion in prison occurs where an inmate learns about Islam whilst serving a punishment, and decides to change their life. Some Muslims describe how conversion to Islam helped give them a strong identity and a supportive community which enabled them to free themselves of a former life of crime and drugs. Once again, these are different ways of approaching conversion to Islam.

Some people convert to be accepted in a marriage, where a family would otherwise reject the person. This is particularly true of men since Islamic tradition dictates that only Muslim men may be married to Muslim women. However, Muslim men can marry others who believe in One God. Usually this is taken to mean Christian and Jewish women. This apparent inequality between men and women's positions, and inequality of different religions, is a complication in the requirements for conversion. Therefore this certainly raises the question of the approach to conversion in Islam being incoherent.

Malcolm X was an American who experienced racism and converted to Islam. After visiting Makkah on the Hajj pilgrimage, he felt a new peace. He initially entered the Nation of Islam which had a political agenda to provide separate government for black people who felt abused by the system in the USA. His conversion experience became most meaningful when he experienced the social mixing of people from many different races and cultures at Makkah. This sense of equality and belonging is what draws some people to embrace Islam. Indeed, one could argue that this was very much in line with Muhammad's approach to conversion.

Conversion is thought of as non-Muslims becoming Muslims but sometimes Muslims convert from one sect to another. Usually this does not require any conversion ceremony, but the differences of belief held by different sects may be considerable. Some Muslims even label others as deviant, in a state of takfir and so not a Muslim at all. Practices such as worship of saints' tombs in the eyes of Salafis might make a Sufi a takfiri and justify preaching to them to convert to a different, purer sect of Islam. This certainly suggests differences within Islam in approaches to conversion.

Majid Nawaz, a leading member of the Quilliam foundation counter-extremism think tank, argues against the takfiri approach, and against forced or pressured conversion. Some converts to Islam enter a new-found fervour and are not always well guided to find a moderate and balanced interpretation of faith. It is something they must find themselves in their journey into faith. Yet the numbers converting to Islam are many and the experiences varied. Many women and men say they find inner peace and a spiritual way of life whether it is to Salafi or Sufi, Sunni or Shi'a traditions. Overall, the variety of historical approaches and differences today are evident within Islam; however, what could be seen as coherent is the approach that wishes to see everyone benefit from being part of the Muslim community.

Study tip

It is important for AO2 that you consider many different points of view so that you can make an extensive and relevant response, with depth and breadth. Insightful connections between different approaches studied will help you to show that you have understood different practices and the connections to the beliefs that lie behind them. Understanding conversion to Islam requires understanding of the position of freedom of belief held by different Muslims and how that might be applied to those who want to convert to Islam.

AO2 Developing skills

It is now important to consider the information that has been covered in this section; however, the information in its raw form is too extensive and so has to be processed in order to meet the requirements of the examination. This can be achieved by practising more advanced skills associated with AO2. For assessment objective 2 (AO2), which involves 'critical analysis' and 'evaluation' skills, we are going to focus on different ways in which the skills can be demonstrated effectively, and also refer to how the performance of these skills is measured (see generic band descriptors for A2 [WJEC] AO2 or A Level [Eduqas] AO2).

▶ **Your final task for this theme is:** Below is **an evaluation of the importance of Muslims tolerating the different beliefs of other religions.** You want to use this in an essay but as it stands it is a weak argument because it has no quotations or references in it at all as support. This time you have to find your own quotations (about 3) and use your own references (about 3) to strengthen the evaluation. Remember, sometimes a quotation can follow from a reference but they can also be used individually as separate points.

The Qur'an tells Muslims that there should be no compulsion in religion. It describes the world made of different peoples because that was the way Allah wanted. The implication is that people should have freedom of belief. No one can know the heart and mind of a person. Allah judges according to intentions: if a person was forced to follow Islam then that would not help at Judgement. Muhammad allowed freedom of belief in Madinah: where there were differences with communities it was due to tribal loyalties. He debated with others and taught them to reject idols, but sought to persuade and not force. Nevertheless, the issue of apostasy is a live one, with some Muslims today calling for a punishment, or even the death penalty, if a Muslim leaves Islam. Reformist Muslims argue in favour of freedom of belief as a fundamental human right, including respect for women's rights and Muslims who are gay. Traditional Muslims call for peaceful coexistence but retain adherence to beliefs defined by conservative Sunni and Shi'a scholars.

The result will be a fairly lengthy answer and so you could then check it against the band descriptors for A2 (WJEC) or A Level (Eduqas) and in particular have a look at the demands described in the higher band descriptors towards which you should be aspiring. Ask yourself:

- Is my answer a confident critical analysis and perceptive evaluation of the issue?
- Is my answer a response that successfully identifies and thoroughly addresses the issues raised by the question set?
- Does my work show an excellent standard of coherence, clarity and organisation?
- Will my work, when developed, contain thorough, sustained and clear views that are supported by extensive, detailed reasoning and/or evidence?
- Are the views of scholars/schools of thought used extensively, appropriately and in context?
- Does my answer convey a confident and perceptive analysis of the nature of any possible connections with other elements of my course?
- When used, is specialist language and vocabulary both thorough and accurate?

Key skills

Analysis involves:

Identifying issues raised by the materials in the AO1, together with those identified in the AO2 section, and presents sustained and clear views, either of scholars or from a personal perspective ready for evaluation.

This means:

- That your answers are able to identify key areas of debate in relation to a particular issue
- That you can identify, and comment upon, the different lines of argument presented by others
- That your response comments on the overall effectiveness of each of these areas or arguments.

Evaluation involves:

Considering the various implications of the issues raised based upon the evidence gleaned from analysis and provides an extensive detailed argument with a clear conclusion.

This means:

- That your answer weighs up the consequences of accepting or rejecting the various and different lines of argument analysed
- That your answer arrives at a conclusion through a clear process of reasoning.

This section covers AO1 content and skills

Specification content

The role of the family and the Muslim home as foundational for Islamic principles.

D: The importance of family life for the Muslim religion

Introduction: the importance of the family in Islam

Most religions have specific religious rites to mark special times in life. In Islam, birth rituals and a naming ceremony are performed, and food shared in the family. As the child grows up, the mother is usually the first to encourage them to learn prayers, and the reading of the Qur'an is taught at home as well as in the mosque. The child learns Muslim traditions about how to eat, how to speak politely and kindly to parents and how to dress modestly.

The Muslim family may suggest or approve a partner and make wedding arrangements. It is not only a love affair between two individuals: it is a contract between two families. Close family contact continues with the **extended family** of grandparents, uncles, aunts and others after marriage. When a Muslim dies, arrangements for funerals are made and all members of the wider family help with the preparations. Afterwards they visit the mourning to provide comfort and support.

The modern **nuclear family** of parents and children living apart as small family units was unheard of in the past. This has presented a challenge for modern Muslims. Traditional communities have adapted as technology has developed, affecting everything from work to family life.

In its broadest sense, all human beings are a family as we are all descended from Adam. The family is the community of believers, the ummah, in which everyone is brother and sister to each other. The ummah originally included Christians and Jews in Madinah, but later became narrowed to mean the worldwide community of Muslims. It is common to find Muslims who call total strangers their Muslim brother, and are happy to share food together with a sense of fraternity.

At a local level, the community in which Muslims lived was an extended family. This was the background of many people who migrated from villages in Pakistan, India and Bangladesh to the UK. This provided protection for the elderly and support for the young. Traditions were preserved and standards of morality upheld by everyone in the family grouping. If a youth considered having an affair or taking another's property, there would be plenty of elders around to see that they didn't. The elderly would not need to go into a care home since everyone shared in their care. As everyone in the family village unit was related, there would be no need for women to wear hijab whilst at home or working in the fields, unless they encountered a stranger.

As Muslims migrated to towns and cities or even abroad, such as to the UK, family roles have changed. The family has become the core unit which preserves the traditions of the past in what may feel like an insecure modern world. At the same time, Muslims are interacting with others, creating challenges for the role of the family in the twenty-first century.

Key terms

Extended family: grandparents, parents, children, uncles, aunts, cousins and wider relatives

Nuclear family: parents and children as a small family unit

quickfire

3.19 What are the differences between nuclear and extended families?

The role of the family and the Muslim home as foundational for Islamic principles

Muslims often describe their religion as a way of life. The family more than anything else prepares Muslim children for the way they will live their lives. When a baby is born, the adhan is recited into the baby's ear, often by their grandfather or an older relative. This signifies that the baby will be raised as a Muslim. Around seven days later, a ceremony called the aqiqah ceremony takes place. The baby's hair is shaved from its head, signifying a new life in Islam. The hair is weighed and its equivalent in gold distributed to the poor as thanksgiving to God for bringing the baby into the world. A lamb is sacrificed and the meat shared in a family celebration. Boys are circumcised according to the tradition of Ibrahim.

The traditional Muslim home

Muhammad's treatment of children

Muhammad cared very much for children. Some Muslims insist that he never used corporal punishment on children, so it is a sunna not to do so. He introduced Islam gradually to the young. Muhammad suggested that children could fast for the afternoon in Ramadan and he gave them toys to play with to take their mind off the fast. He allowed his grandsons Hassan and Hussein to play on his back and crawl under him whilst he bowed in prayer. Once, he was so busy playing that he missed the prayer time, and the next prayer time, and did not break off from playing with the children because it was so important. He used to play tick and chase with Hussein.

As an orphan himself, the Prophet experienced suffering. His own sons died during infancy. He cared for children and and when a Jewish neighbour's son was ill, Muhammad went to visit him. He hugged and kissed his grandchildren and said that it was important to express feelings towards them. One tradition suggests that whilst a child sat on Muhammad's lap he had a little accident and some urine came out. The Father, sitting alongside, told the child off, but Muhammad said that it didn't matter about the clothes, they could be washed. It was more important to be careful not to upset the child's self-esteem since that would be harder to repair.

Muhammad encouraged Muslims to adopt and foster children so that they would be brought up as Muslims. Those who look after widows and children receive blessings. Those who fail in their duty of care towards orphans are criticised. Muhammad also taught Muslims not to favour boys over girls. When giving presents, all children should be treated equally, so that they do not become jealous. Some Muslims say that as children are a gift from God, God will provide and they should not exercise any restriction on the size of their families. Others say that the Prophet required Muslims to plan for the needs of their children, so they must exercise family planning.

Upbringing in the faith

In Islam, children are expected to follow, not to question or to decide their beliefs for themselves. Nevertheless, some families give their children some freedom and feel that stronger faith comes from the freedom to reason and experience as an individual. Children are expected to say their prayers and to learn to read the

Key terms

Adhan: the call to prayer, recited out loud in Arabic before each of the five daily prayers

Aqiqah: Muslim naming ceremony for babies and converts to Islam

Key quotes

Be merciful with the orphan, pat his head and feed him from what you eat. This will soften your heart, and enable you to get your needs fulfilled. (Hadith of Prophet Muhammad)

The person who strives on behalf of the widows and poor is like those who strive in the way of Allah and like those who fast in the day and pray at night. (Hadith of Prophet Muhammad)

The Qur'an 89.15–20

Now, as for man, when his Lord trieth him, giving him honour and gifts, then saith he, puffed up, 'My Lord hath honoured me.' But when He trieth him, restricting his subsistence for him, then saith he in despair, 'My Lord hath humiliated me!' Nay, nay! But ye honour not the orphans! Nor do ye encourage one another to feed the poor! And ye devour inheritance – all with greed, and ye love wealth with inordinate love! (Yusuf Ali)

Key terms

Age of maturity: the age at which the traditional requirements of Islam apply

Alhamdulilah: literally, thanks be to Allah for anything referred to

Bar Mitzvah: Jewish rite of passage of commitment

Bayah: Sufi ceremony of commitment

Bismillah: to begin any action in the name of Allah

Ghusul: ritual purification of the whole body, carried out usually weekly before Friday prayers and when needed

Janazzah: funeral prayers in Islam

Jummah prayers: Friday early afternoon congregational prayers

Key quotes

The best among you are those who have the best manners and character. (Hadith of Prophet Muhammad)

The thing that weighs heaviest at the Day of Judgement is good character. (Hadith of Prophet Muhammad)

The Quran 17:23

Thy Lord hath decreed that ye worship none but Him, and that ye be kind to parents. Whether one or both of them attain old age in thy life, say not to them a word of contempt, nor repel them, but address them in terms of honour. (Yusuf Ali)

Should I tell you what are the worst sins? They are to worship others besides Allah, and to neglect your duty towards your parents. (Hadith of Prophet Muhammad)

quickfire

3.20 When is the age of maturity for Muslims?

Qur'an. They learn the rituals of wudu, and of weekly bathing, **ghusul**, before **Jummah prayers** on Friday. A celebration may occur when the child reads the first few words of the Qur'an. Muslims say **Bismillah** before eating to thank God for the food. They say **Alhamdulilah** for anything good that happens to them to show that they believe it has come from God and God should be thanked for this gift.

Children are brought up to be truthful, speak politely and to help others in need. All of these actions are just as much part of the example of Muhammad as prayer and fasting.

It is seen as sinful to neglect parents. Muslims are asked to be tolerant to their elders in old age, and to put up with their bad moods from time to time. When a person dies the body will be washed and wrapped in a shroud like the one used to go on the Hajj pilgrimage. **Janazzah** funeral prayers are held to dedicate that person to Allah and to pray for Allah's mercy for them in the afterlife. The body is buried, not cremated, as it is believed that it will be physically resurrected again in the afterlife. It is buried facing in the direction of Makkah. Muslims consider others in their local community as members of an extended family. When a person dies, they go to visit the grieving relatives to offer support and comfort, and make an effort to attend the funeral prayers. Qur'an reading may also take place in the wake of a death.

A Muslim funeral

Unlike some religions, there is no specific ceremony to mark commitment in Islam. Many Christian churches have a service of confirmation where people as they approach adulthood confirm the promises made on their behalf at Baptism. The **Bar Mitzvah** is a ceremony of commitment in Judaism. Sufi Muslims have ceremonies of **bayah** in which they give commitment to their shaykh with an oath of loyalty, but this does not apply to all Muslims. Muslims disagree about when they are required to follow the five pillars and particularly to pray and fast. Some are encouraged to pray from an early age of seven. Others say that the requirement applies from the time of puberty, still others from the time of marriage, at whatever age that occurs. Some say that it depends on when the individual can understand and make a personal commitment, an **age of maturity** that differs from person to person. When the Prophet's companion Umar was aged fourteen and wanted to accompany adults to the Uhud campaign, the Prophet told him that he had not yet reached the age of maturity. It might be deduced that the age begins around fifteen years old.

Key quote

The Qur'an 49:10

The Believers are but a single Brotherhood: So make peace and reconciliation between your two brothers; and fear Allah, that ye may receive Mercy. (Yusuf Ali)

Muslims are supposed to settle arguments and family disagreements peacefully. Traditions include making peace before Jummah prayers or at least before Id prayers, so that a fresh start can be made. Sometimes honour crimes are reported: family grudges and acts of revenge, even murders. These are hangovers from pre-Islamic tribal tradition and are not justified by the religion itself.

Jummah prayers

The changing role of men and women in Islam with reference to family life

Key quote

A man came to Muhammad and asked: 'Who should be treated the best by me?' The Prophet said, 'Your mother'. The man said: 'Who is next?' The Prophet said: 'Your mother'. The man asked for a third time: 'Who is next?' The Prophet answered again: 'Your mother'. The man asked for the fourth time, and the Prophet then replied: 'Your father'. (Hadith of Prophet Muhammad)

The Qur'an makes clear in Sura 33 ayat 35 that religious duties should be seen to apply to men and women equally.

Marital relations

Some women are promised in marriage at birth, or forced to marry without their consent. Forced marriage is a crime under British Law. It is also not allowed in Islamic tradition. Islamic marriages are contracts between two people who must freely consent in front of witnesses. The groom must pay a mahr gift to the bride to seal the contract, which is also a form of insurance for her in case of divorce. Similarly, pre-nuptial contracts have recently entered British Law. Once a virgin girl came to the Prophet and told him that her father had forced her to marry a man against her wishes. The Prophet gave her the right of divorce. Whereas women in the past might have gone silent for fear of upsetting their relatives, nowadays more are standing up for their rights. Muslim women can keep their family name, their property and any business they may own.

Polygamy is the practice of one man marrying several wives. This is still practised in some Muslim countries, but prohibited in others. Muhammad taught that this was only allowed where all could be treated equally. Women are increasingly refusing permission for their husbands to take a second wife.

In medieval times, girls were sometimes married off to men. Muhammad was said to have had a contract with Aisha at an early age in a similar way to the Christian King Richard II of England who married one of his wives, Isabella, when she was aged 8. It is important to note that we cannot be sure of the ages since dates of birth were rarely recorded in those days. These marriages may have been a form of social care during childhood as opposed to what we understand as a fully functioning marital relationship that we have today. However, some Muslims have taken a stand against child marriage. The Qur'an Sura 6 is said to refer to the age of Nikkah, the marriage contract, and suggests those who marry should not only be physically mature but also mature of mind and thought. Kaleef Karim's analysis of this verse concludes this means at least 18 years old.

Key quote

The Quran 4:6

Test the orphans until they attain puberty; then if you find in them maturity of intellect, make over to them their property, and do not consume it extravagantly and hastily, lest they attain to full age; and whoever is rich, let him abstain altogether, and whoever is poor, let him eat reasonably; then when you make over to them their property, call witnesses in their presence; and Allah is enough as a Reckoner. (Yusuf Ali)

Key quote

The Qur'an 33:35

For Muslim men and women, for believing men and women, for devout men and women, for true men and women, for men and women who are patient and constant, for men and women who humble themselves, for men and women who give in Charity, for men and women who fast (and deny themselves), for men and women who guard their chastity, and for men and women who engage much in Allah's praise, for them has Allah prepared forgiveness and great reward. (Yusuf Ali)

Key term

Forced marriage: where a person is married without consent, illegal in UK as well as in Islamic Law

quickfire

3.21 What are:
(a) the Nikkah?   (b) the Mahr?

Key quote

The widow and the divorced woman shall not be married until their order is obtained, and the virgin shall not be married until her consent is obtained. (Hadith of Prophet Muhammad)

Offering personal prayers at a Muslim wedding

Career advancement

Education was a duty for parents to provide for boys and girls since the time of Muhammad. In recent times the take up of education by Muslim women has been increasing from a low base. The British government sponsors programmes to help provide schooling for Muslim girls in Pakistan under the Department for Overseas Development in collaboration with various organisations. Malala Yousafzai was attacked in Pakistan for defying threats by Taliban supporters for attending school. She was given refuge in the UK where she is now an activist in support of Muslim women's rights to education.

In Indonesia, the majority of Muslim women now have careers, and in nearby Malaysia the majority of postgraduate researchers are now women. Sayeeda Warsi has become a baroness in the House of Lords; Mishal Hussain a BBC presenter and Imtaz Khaliq one of London's most fashionable tailors according to Cosmopolitan magazine. These are all success stories and markers of how far Muslim women are changing the balance of gender roles in modern society.

Challenging abuse

If the Qur'an 4:34 is taken literally, it could mean that men are allowed to dominate and even beat women, but the Arabic has many different meanings including separate, leave, protest, or even play music. The idea of beating a wife seems to be against other Islamic traditions of empowering women.

Islam does not support rape or adultery in any way, but on occasion Muslim women victims have been blamed for the crimes; or the male aggressor has not been found guilty because it has not been possible to get four witnesses, as traditionally required under shari'a. The process of delivering justice is something which reformists say can be done better through a secular system. To some Muslims though, this compromises what they see as the ideal Islamic system of the shari'a.

Female genital mutilation, FGM, is a crime causing lasting pain and harm to reproductive organs. The Grand Mufti of Egypt, Ali Gomaa, issued a fatwa that the practice should be banned. He argued that no tradition of the Prophet could be used to justify this abuse, and Muslims carrying out the crime should be brought to justice. Nevertheless, it remains a cultural practice to be challenged amongst some Muslims.

It used to be considered a duty to have as many children as possible, as they would bring wealth and prosperity to the family. Such attitudes originated in an age where childbirth carried greater risk and many children died at a young age. Some now recognise that if they accept modern medicine then that includes contraception and family planning. The companions of Muhammad practised contraception. Modern Muslim women see this as liberating, freeing them to make decisions about family life and careers. Other Muslims say contraception is interfering with nature and they should trust in Allah to provide for them, however many children they have.

The role and status of women in Islam with reference to feminism

Feminism is to promote and support women's rights and is built on the belief that men and women are equal. Muhammad and the early Muslims improved rights for women. Arabs had a practice of killing baby daughters, which was outlawed under Islam. Marriage became a Nikkah contract which women could refuse. They were given rights of inheritance. Prophet Muhammad, in his farewell speech, made a point of referring to male and female believers equally and emphasised the importance of treating women well. Women kept their separate identity, their family name, after marriage, and had the right of divorce which until the

Key quote

The Qur'an 4:34

Men are the protectors and maintainers of women, because Allah has given the one more strength than the other, and because they support them from their means. Therefore the righteous women are devoutly obedient, and guard in the husband's absence what Allah would have them guard. As to those women on whose part ye fear disloyalty and ill-conduct, admonish them, then refuse to share their beds, and last beat them (lightly); but if they return to obedience, seek not against them means of annoyance: For Allah is Most High. (Yusuf Ali)

quickfire

3.22 What did Mufti Gomaa teach about female genital mutilation?

Specification content

The role and status of women in Islam with reference to feminism.

Key term

Feminism: to advocate women's rights based on equality of men and women

twentieth century was more commonly exercised in the Islamic world than the Western world.

Muhammad's first wife Khadijah was said to have taken the lead in proposing. She was his employer, a businesswoman, and his elder. Muhammad's wife Aisha was known for her intelligence. She passed on over two thousand hadiths of Muhammad and answered many questions of Islamic Law. Aisha played a role in politics during the era of the four righteous caliphs and opposed the fourth, Ali, for his failure to deal with Uthman's assassins.

In medieval times, women in Islamic societies may even have been more empowered than today. Women studied for degrees, taught in mosques, wrote guides to the hadith, and sponsored charitable foundations for people to learn about Islam. One of the oldest universities in the world, Al-Karaouine in Morocco, was founded by Muslim woman Fatima al-Fihri. Ruth Roded found that many Western historians approached the subject expecting to find few women in positions of authority but in fact found the opposite.

Islamists emphasise the security that traditional gender roles give women and that men have obligations and duties towards them. They claim these roles are less stressful and more fulfilling for women than modern lifestyles, which can put stress on women with the expectation to work, have a career and bring up a family all at the same time.

Feminists argue for a reinterpretation of Islam to promote equality, which they say is more appropriate for the present day. Their approach is to champion human rights first, and find texts to fit, whereas traditional Muslim scholars look at the Qur'an and hadith first, and only interpret within the boundaries of traditional scholarship of these texts. Reformists argue now is time to reopen ijtihad and draw fresh teachings.

Hijab

Many modern Muslim women have found choosing to wear hijab a way of expressing their identity which they find fulfilling. Far from suppressing them, it makes them feel special. It is a statement of pride in religion. Others say that it should be banned because it is a symbol of oppression. In the post-war period, many women protested to have the right not to wear the veil in Algeria. Since 2000 in Turkey, others protested with equal passion that they should have the right to wear it.

Hijab originally may have meant modesty or a barrier, not necessarily a hair covering or facial veil. At the time of the Prophet, the Byzantine and Persian women wore veils as a status symbol, so it is possible the use entered Islam from interaction with these cultures. Muhammad's wives were asked to cover their bodies and to veil in the presence of others. Many Muslims of the Salafi and Deobandi schools of thought promote wearing veils and face covering in public. Men are also asked to dress modestly, sometimes referred to as men's hijab. They should cover their navel to knee with loose clothing that does not fit tightly over the body.

Women as political leaders

Some Islamists argue for the creation of an Islamic political system headed by a Caliph. Like the early Islamic Empire, this would be headed by a man. Most of the rulers in Islamic history were men, but not all. Razia Sultana became Queen of Delhi in 1236. The Sultan Iltutmish did not have confidence in his sons, and found that Razia did a good job governing the capital whilst he was away on a campaign one summer. So Sultan Iltutmish appointed Razia his heir. Razia ruled Delhi, donated money to open libraries and schools and rode on horseback around the city wearing men's clothes. She chose not to wear a veil. Her reign provides inspiration for feminists today.

Key quotes

Compared to the pre-Islamic position of women, Islamic legislation meant an enormous progress; the woman has the right, at least according to the letter of the law, to administer the wealth she has brought into the family or has earned by her own work. (Schimmel)

At the time Islam began, the conditions of women were terrible – they had no right to own property, were supposed to be the property of the man, and if the man died everything went to his sons. Muhammad, however, by instituting rights of property ownership, inheritance, education and divorce, gave women certain basic safeguards. (Montgomery-Watt)

If U.S. and European historians feel a need to reconstruct women's history because women are invisible in the traditional sources, Islamic scholars are faced with a plethora of source material that has only begun to be studied. … In reading the biographies of thousands of Muslim women scholars, one is amazed at the evidence that contradicts the view of Muslim women as marginal, secluded, and restricted. (Roded)

The proportion of female lecturers in many classical Islamic colleges was higher than in modern Western universities. (Lindsay)

Muslim woman in hijab

Some Muslim countries have elected female leaders. These include Sheikh Hasina of Bangladesh, Benazir Bhutto of Pakistan and Megawatti Sukarnoputri of Indonesia. Women achieved equal status to men as voters in Muslim Azerbaijan in 1918, somewhat ahead of the UK who only gave women over 30 the vote in that year. In the present day, some countries such as Iran, Pakistan and Senegal encourage women to vote and to stand for parliament, whereas others such as Saudi Arabia are taking the first steps towards including women in parliamentary representation.

Women as religious leaders

Umm al-Darda was a female Islamic scholar and lawyer in Damascus in the seventh century. She used to debate with male scholars in mosques, taught hadith and fiqh and lectured in the men's section. She even prayed together with men and issued a fatwa that women could do so. Feminists argue that in regaining a role in religious leadership in Islam they are following in the true traditions of the early Islamic community. There is even a tradition which suggested Muhammad appointed a woman, Umm Waraqh, as Imam over men and women in Madinah. However this is a disputed hadith.

Rabia of Basra was a famous Sufi mystic who wrote poems about her experiences, which influenced Muslim thinkers for hundreds of years. Tombs to female Muslim saints can be found in Lahore, Cairo and in other parts of the Muslim world. The tomb of Hala Sultan in Cyprus marks the place where Muhammad's aunt died whilst taking part in the Muslim conquest of the island.

The Oxford Muslim Centre is a reformist mosque which argues that women should be guaranteed equal rights in all areas. Traditionally Muslims do not permit women to lead prayers for men and women, although groups of women may be led by another woman. The Oxford Muslim centre invited female Imam, Amina Wadud, to lead Jummah prayers over mixed lines of male and female worshippers. This was seen as a radical step, criticised by some. The majority of mosques in the UK separate men and women and whilst women may join management committees, the prayers are led by men.

Recent discussion is divided on how to approach Muslim women's issues. Some argue that shari'a courts empower women, because it is a requirement that women are not forced into marriage. Shari'a courts might help Muslim women gain support within their community. Others argue that shari'a courts should be abolished, because they put pressure on women to accept the norms of the male-dominated past. In the same way, some argue that veils should be accepted in public to encourage Muslim women to integrate. Others argue they should be restricted to challenge attitudes which view women as less than men.

Film maker Deeyah Khan set up Sisterhood, an organisation to promote the achievements of Muslim women. Sisterhood list their aims as:

- To promote known and unknown women of Muslim heritage who are working for human rights, gender equality, freedom of expression, peace and social justice.
- To build solidarity, to nurture and connect a global community of women of Muslim heritage who stand for a shared vision of a more peaceful, just and inclusive world.
- To bring together voices of women of Muslim heritage across borders through our platforms: Sisterhood magazine and convening our Sisterhood live events.
- To show young women the feminists from Muslim heritage throughout history and into the present: women who have fought for personal rights and bodily integrity, who extended solidarity to women and other downtrodden people, and who improved their societies as scholars, artists, saints and activists.

Key quote

I've tried to worship Allah in every way, but I've never found a better one than sitting around, debating other scholars. (Umm al-Darda)

These aims neatly summarise the drive behind many Muslim feminists as they encourage Muslim women to take a more active role in all areas of modern society.

Some Muslim feminists have fully engaged in all aspects of modern life, including sport. One tradition suggests Muhammad used to race with his wife Aisha and encouraged children to take up swimming and archery. In the Rio Olympics in 2016, Dalilah Muhammad, age 26 of the USA, won gold in the women's 400m hurdles. Majlinda Kelmendi of Kosovo won gold in judo. Sara Ahmed of Egypt, took the weightlifting bronze medal, and Wahyuni Agustiani of Indonesia the silver. Ines Boubakri of Tunisia took bronze in fencing.

Study tip

When writing about feminism in Islam, remember that it is not as simple as feminists and Islamists: there are various shades of meaning. Make sure that you refer to depth and/or breadth, with lots of use of evidence and examples, to bring these out in your answers (B5 band descriptor AO1).

AO1 Activity

After reading the section on 'The role and status of women in Islam with reference to feminism' create a mind map in order to highlight the main issues. Divide into branches to show the different opinions for each issue, backed up by evidence and examples.

The pioneering work of Professor Aisha Abd Al Rahman 'Bint ash Shati'

Professor Aisha Abd al Rahman lived in Egypt from 1913 to 1998. She used the name Bint ash Shati as a pen name to publish her books. The name means daughter of the riverbank. She wrote a series of books including ones about the life of Muhammad and the meaning of the Qur'an. She also authored about women's rights and was a contributor to Egypt's daily newspaper. When she was a child, her father objected to her education, but her mother's insistence resulted in her gaining a degree from Cairo University. She did not follow a traditional religious education but approached religion with passion and emotion. She became a professor and wrote dramatic historical stories about the lives of important women from the early days of Islam. These books helped to inspire people and gain new interest in religion.

Professor Aisha's life should be seen in the context of the history of twentieth-century Egypt. With British rule overthrown, General Nasr tried to modernise the country. Religious courts and universities, such as Al-Azhar, were brought under the control of the government. There was a move to separate out religion and family affairs from government and law. At the same time the Muslim Brotherhood tried to advance the cause of religion in the country, and the Salafist interpretation was gaining popularity. Professor Aisha was independent of all groups, publishing her own views and interpretations.

Professor Aisha saw women's rights, human rights and freedom of belief as important; however, she did not describe herself as a feminist. She spoke strongly in favour of women's rights of equality to education, inheritance, to own property, to have a career, to be free and equal in terms of social justice. She also said that men have guardianship over women, a legal and natural right defined in the Qur'an. She considered the modern feminist movement a distortion.

quickfire

3.23 State two of the aims of Sisterhood.

Deeyah Khan

Specification content

The pioneering work of Professor Aisha Abd Al Rahman 'Bint ash Shati'.

Key quotes

The Qur'an 4:34

And women shall have rights similar to the rights against them, according to what is equitable; but men have a degree of advantage over them. (Yusuf Ali)

Our understanding of this equality has been liberated with the return to the origin of Islam, for the equal, instinctual woman admits that man has a legal and natural right to guardianship over her. (Al Rahman)

Specification content

The role and status of women in Islam with reference to feminism: the contemporary feminist view of Haleh Afshar.

quickfire

3.24 How does Haleh Afshar interpret the Qur'an 4:34 about husbands beating their wives?

Key quote

Our failure to recognise the true value of the mother's great role was a major stumbling block in the early stages of the movement for which our generation paid a terrible price. Thus I hope that we may spare our daughters from falling into the same trap and enable them to realise their full potential in society as Islam— the religion of the deepest insight and intuition. (Al Rahman)

Professor Aisha argued that the Qur'an promoted human freedom, equality and freedom and encouraged modernist thought in Islam. Her approach to text was similar to Salafism in that she largely left aside Sunni interpretations and accepted ijtihad for the present day. At the time of her writing, the government of Egypt was trying to separate out personal family life and religion from constitution and law. Professor Aisha supported the government and agreed that there should be no discrimination on the basis of sex, origin, language, religion or faith. Her work helped to inspire the people to support secularism at the same time as a renewed excitement about Islam, which she communicated through her stories of Muslim women in the past.

Feminists criticise Professor Aisha as she did not challenge a man's 'guardianship' over women. Traditional scholars criticise her independent approach. They say this can lead to inauthentic interpretations, made to suit the desires of the times. Nevertheless, Professor Aisha inspired many Muslim women to pursue education and join the world of modern Islamic scholarship and debate.

The contemporary feminist view of Haleh Afshar

Haleh Afshar was born in Iran, grew up in Paris and England before returning to Iran as a journalist. Haleh, like her mother and grandmother, chooses not to wear the veil and insists on exercising her right to vote. She has criticised the current Islamic system in Iran as being against women's rights, even un-Islamic. She works as a Professor of Women's Studies at the University of York and advises the UN on women's issues.

Haleh Afshar argues that the contribution of women has been systematically erased from history by men. Modern Islamists are backward looking and deny modern, progressive ideas whilst trying to revive interest in Islam. They might appear attractive to the younger generation as they appear periodically, but they in fact distort the past and deny the reality of a plurality of interpretation, always saying they know best.

Haleh Afsar argues that the verses from the Qur'an are wrongly interpreted. She considers that Sura 2 ayat 282 referring to one man as a witness equal to two women only applies to a particular debt transaction, and should not be extended to the general courtroom. Sura 4 ayat 3 should be interpreted as an instruction to men not to have more than one wife. Many verses of the Qur'an are descriptive, argues Professor Afshar, telling us the practice of the Arabs at the time. She argues that Sura 4 verse 34 about men being permitted to lightly beat their wives was a description of Arab practice at the time and not a command for Muslims to follow today.

Key quotes

The Qur'an 2:282

O ye who believe! When ye deal with each other, in transactions involving future obligations in a fixed period of time, reduce them to writing … and get two witnesses, out of your own men, and if there are not two men, then a man and two women, such as ye choose, for witnesses, so that if one of them errs, the other can remind her. (Yusuf Ali)

The Qur'an 4:3

If ye fear that ye shall not be able to deal justly with the orphans, Marry women of your choice, Two or three or four; but if ye fear that ye shall not be able to deal justly, then only one, or a captive that your right hands possess, that will be more suitable, to prevent you from doing injustice. (Yusuf Ali)

Haleh Afsar argues that the Qur'an and the hadith are flexible enough to come up with new interpretations. She traces modern Muslim women interpreters of the Qur'an, some who see themselves as radical and subversive, such as Fatna al-Sabbah, and others who try to blend traditional approaches with re-interpretations, such as Zin al-Din. Whatever the views of any individual, Haleh Afsar argues that no Muslim has authority to tell another what to believe. Muslims have free will and are accountable only to God.

Haleh Afsar found in her research that in the early days of Islam, women played much more prominent roles than later on. Khadijah, Muhammad's first wife, was his employer and a businesswoman. Women led an army against Ali ibn Abi Talib. After the death of the Prophet, men took over and denied the rights of women to understand and interpret the law. The denial of women's education disempowered them as scholars of religion as well as in other areas. Yet some scholars, such as Al-Ghazali, recognised that women could take on any role, including head of government, just not Caliph.

Traditionalist scholars of Islam might criticise Haleh Afshar for making what they see as new interpretations according to the mood of the day. Haleh Afsar's work is modernising and reformist: different from Professor Aisha Abd al Rahman who remained socially traditional. Haleh Afsar argues that Sura 9 ayat 71 of the Qur'an refers to men and women as equals and means that women have a God-given right to exercise authority equally to men in all spheres of life, including religion.

Key quote

The Qur'an 9:71

The Believers, men and women, are protectors one of another: they enjoin what is just, and forbid what is evil: they observe regular prayers, practise regular charity, and obey Allah and His Messenger. On them will Allah pour His mercy: for Allah is Exalted in power, Wise. (Yusuf Ali)

Study tip

Make sure that you are familiar with all the key terms and their correct definitions. This is especially relevant for this section. This will ensure that you are making 'thorough and accurate use of specialist language and vocabulary in context' (B5 band descriptor AO1).

AO1 Activity

What do the approaches of Haleh Afshar and Professor Aisha Abd Al Rahman have in common and where do they differ? Discuss in pairs and then make a table of similarities and differences. Overall, how significant do you think the differences are?

Key quotes

For far too long the domain of Islamic law had been controlled by men; but gradually women and their male allies are making a bid to change this process. They too have returned to the sources ... to come to rather different conclusions from the traditionalists. The flexibility of the laws has opened the way for Muslim women to use interpretations and analysis of the texts and the contexts to create a new and permissive form of Islamic law. (Afshar)

Women, like men, have the right to choose their own path and if necessary commit their own sins and repent or negotiate with the Almighty without intervention by men, be they learned religious figures or fathers, husbands or brothers. (Afshar)

Key skills Theme 3 DEF

This theme has tasks that deal with the basics of AO1 in terms of prioritising and selecting the key relevant information, presenting this in a personalised way (as in Theme 1 ABC) and then using evidence and examples to support and expand upon this (as in Theme 3 ABC).

Key skills

Knowledge involves:

Selection of a range of (thorough) accurate and relevant information that is directly related to the specific demands of the question.

This means:

- Selecting relevant material for the question set

- Being focused in explaining and examining the material selected.

Understanding involves:

Explanation that is extensive, demonstrating depth and/or breadth with excellent use of evidence and examples including (where appropriate) thorough and accurate supporting use of sacred texts, sources of wisdom and specialist language.

This means:

- Effective use of examples and supporting evidence to establish the quality of your understanding

- Ownership of your explanation that expresses personal knowledge and understanding and NOT just reproducing a chunk of text from a book that you have rehearsed and memorised.

AO1 Developing skills

It is now important to consider the information that has been covered in this section; however, the information in its raw form is too extensive and so has to be processed in order to meet the requirements of the examination. This can be achieved by practising more advanced skills associated with AO1. The exercises that run throughout this book will help you to do this and prepare you for the examination. For assessment objective 1 (AO1), which involves demonstrating 'knowledge' and 'understanding' skills, we are going to focus on different ways in which the skills can be demonstrated effectively, and also refer to how the performance of these skills is measured (see generic band descriptors for A2 [WJEC] AO1 or A Level [Eduqas] AO1).

▶ **Your task is this:** Below is **a summary of Muslim teachings and attitudes towards family life**. It is 150 words long. There are three points highlighted that are key points to learn from this extract. Discuss which further two points you think are the most important to highlight and write up all five points.

Muslims usually live in extended families where they keep close contact with relatives. Family life is at the heart of a child's upbringing in the Muslim faith. They are introduced to Islam at birth, and grow up learning the first words of the Qur'an usually from their mother. The family teach a child Islamic traditions including how to eat, wash and pray and manners like speaking softly to others. Family life is also essential in cultivating respect for the elderly. Caring for older people is a duty of Muslims, as is gently nurturing children following Muhammad's example. It is the family that is the basis of social security in caring for orphans and those in need. As a child grows up, family tradition helps it begin practising prayer, fasting and other obligations when it is considered to have reached the age of maturity. Often the family suggest candidates for marriage, which is seen as a contract between two families.

Now make the five points into your own summary (as in Theme 1 Developing skills) trying to make the summary more personal to your style of writing.

1 ....

2 ....

3 ....

4 ....

5 ....

Issues for analysis and evaluation

The extent to which the Muslim family is central to the Islamic religion

This section covers AO2 content and skills

Specification content

The extent to which the Muslim family is central to the Islamic religion.

Family may be defined at several different levels in Islam. Many Muslims live in extended families, with grandparents, aunts, uncles, cousins, brothers and sisters. The family shares the tasks of raising children, caring for the elderly and promoting an Islamic cultural heritage. Actions such as how to eat properly, wash before praying, and bring Islam into daily life are passed on.

Muhammad kept close to him his wives and children, and his Uncle Abu Talib lived nearby and gave protection. However, as an orphan, Muhammad did not have many members of his own family around. He was prepared to leave relatives behind in Makkah if they did not accept his religion. He left them to move to Madinah. This might suggest that to Muhammad belief in Allah was more important than family. However, Muhammad also narrated many hadiths which emphasised the importance of family duties. Muslims should not leave their parents for military campaign unless they were cared for and gave permission. Muslims should respect parents and overlook their faults.

To Shi'a Muslims, the family of the Prophet is all important. Shi'a Muslims believe that spiritual leadership is rightfully descended from the Prophet through Ali. They form the family of the house of the Prophet, and all Shi'a Imams follow in this lineage. Shi'a believe that the family connection to Muhammad brings with it special authority to interpret the Qur'an and provide righteous leadership to the community. Sunni Muslims believe that Caliphs, shaykhs and leaders can be appointed from any lineage.

Key quote

The family deserve the most to be happy, to be treated with good manners and kindness, and to be protected from harm and provided with what benefits them. So, if the man fits this description, then he is the best of people: and if, on the other hand, he acts contrary to this, then he is in the realms of evil. (Imam Shawkaani)

Muslims believe that Allah judges them and sends them to heaven or hell according to their deeds and intentions. Those actions are not just keeping the five pillars of Islam, but also caring for parents and children within the family. Within that family, men were traditionally seen as the guardians of women, but women are allowed to have their own careers provided they can balance their family commitments. To some it can be restrictive, putting a break on women's careers; to others fulfilling, as to bring up children may bring blessings from Allah. For children, the mother is seen as so important that paradise lies at her feet. Caring for elderly relatives is a duty that many Muslims feel pride in carrying out. Others find it a pressure which strains their work–life balance. The extended family can help to share the responsibility, enabling Muslims to provide for their needs.

As the cities of South Asia grew, many young Muslims left their families to find work there. The Tablighi Jamaat movement grew up to support them. Tablighi Jamaat is a conservative Islamic movement which promotes Dawah, Islamic mission, speeches and conferences. They visit Muslims and encourage them to attend their local mosque as much as possible. They ask women to veil and men to wear traditional Islamic clothes as symbols of their identity. They teach their followers not to get involved in politics. As men moved away from their families for work, Tablighi Jamaat formed new bonds to keep them on the straight and narrow amidst the temptations of cities. Therefore, the Islamic community takes on the role of the family in these circumstances.

AO2 Activity

As you read through this section try to do the following:

1. Pick out the different lines of argument that are presented in the text and identify any evidence given in support.

2. For each line of argument try to evaluate whether or not you think this is strong or weak.

3. Think of any questions you may wish to raise in response to the arguments.

This Activity will help you to start thinking critically about what you read and help you to evaluate the effectiveness of different arguments and from this develop your own observations, opinions and points of view that will help with any conclusions that you make in your answers to the AO2 questions that arise.

Key questions

How do Muslims define the term family? What might they include and what might they exclude as acceptable households?

Which is more important: religion or family?

How should Muslims find a life partner?

Key quote

It's crushing to realise that your parents don't accept who you really are. Coming to terms with your own sexual identity is difficult enough but being rejected for something which is a part of you and that you have no control over is devastating. I wanted to speak out about my experience because I know a lot of other young Muslims will be struggling with the same issue. I still think of myself as a Muslim. I've had relationships with men but never introduced any of them to my family. I'd love to get married one day, but I have to face the fact that my family won't be there. (Parvaiz)

AO2 Activity

List some conclusions that could be drawn from the AO2 reasoning from the above text; try to aim for at least three different possible conclusions. Consider each of the conclusions and collect brief evidence to support each conclusion from the AO1 and AO2 material for this topic. Select the conclusion that you think is most convincing and explain why it is so. Try to contrast this with the weakest conclusion in the list, justifying your argument with clear reasoning and evidence.

Some young Muslims react against parents, preferring to make their own decisions. Some experience different Islamic groups at university or in the community around them, and change allegiance against the guidance of their families. In the UK, many young Muslims leave the Sunni traditions of parents for Salafism. They are often critical of elders who do not speak their language or understand their needs. In some cases they feel that the shaykhs and Imams of South Asia practise shirk by asking followers to bow, or by visiting the tombs of saints.

Study tip

Band 5 answers require thorough and accurate use of specialist language and vocabulary in context. You should clearly define what family means in the context of Muslim households, and provide a thorough analysis of the different meanings of the term as you construct your answer.

Some Muslims face pressure to marry someone in the family. Naman Parvaiz faced pressure to enter an arranged marriage but refused because he was gay. He came out to his parents but they did not accept it. Naman sees his sexuality as part of the way God made him, not a choice. Some Muslims might argue that it is the duty of the family as central to the Islamic faith to support him as he is; others that upholding traditional cultural norms requires breaking the family up, as they cannot accept it.

Muhammad made a strong statement about not discriminating against people on grounds of race. Muslims use this to challenge prejudices within families against inter-racial marriages. There are differences of opinion about how far young Muslims can meet, date and request families to approve their choice of life partner, or how far the family should provide a choice to their sons and daughters and ask them to accept or reject it. All agree forced marriage is wrong.

Muslims are more wary of interfaith marriages. Traditionally a Muslim man could marry any believer in one God. Usually this is interpreted as a Muslim, Christian or Jew. Some Salafis reject this teaching and say that Muslims should marry only Muslims. Reformists argue that Muslims should accept love in whatever form it comes: between different religions or between members of the same sex.

A Muslim family enjoying time together.

Whether or not women are equal to men in Islam

Specification content

Whether or not women are equal to men in Islam.

Does this mean that men and women should both have equal access to the same careers, that they should share family chores equally, such as cooking and cleaning in the home, even changing nappies of their baby? Or does it mean that men and women may have different roles, such as breadwinner and housewife, but these should be valued equally by society?

At the time of Muhammad, society was patriarchal. The Prophet's companions who helped him to lead the Muslim community, and led after his death, were all men. However, Muhammad's wife memorised many of his sayings and gave her opinions to religious questions. Muhammad made a point of referring to 'believing men and believing women'. He emphasised the importance of treating women well during his farewell sermon. He accepted employment from businesswoman Khadijah, his first wife. Within the standards of the time Muhammad was radical in promoting the position of women. He gave them the right to refuse someone in marriage and to seek a divorce if they so wished. Women could demand their right if it was denied through shari'a law.

The movement towards women's rights during the time of Muhammad does not mean that they achieved equality. It was a step along the way. Muhammad's wives usually kept seclusion, a form of barrier, tent or veil, between themselves and strangers, whereas he went out in the open. In shari'a law, the testimony of one man was equal to two women. Muslim men could marry women who believed in one God, be they of other religions, but Muslim women could only marry Muslim men.

Men were appointed to lead prayers with a degree of separation between men and women. The Prophet may have appointed a woman Imam over men and women at Madinah, although the reliability of this tradition cannot be proved. Muhammad said that women should not cover their face on Hajj. Even today you can see lines of pilgrims praying, women interspersed between men, although Saudi authorities have been trying to introduce separation. Umm al-Darda was a female Islamic scholar and lawyer in Damascus in the seventh century. Why did women's status deteriorate? Was it because of male-dominated culture, or because of Islam itself?

A report found that only 16% of women in Pakistan were economically active, in contrast to 52% in Indonesia. The position varies greatly by country. In some, women have achieved in many different fields, providing top surgeons, academics and businesswomen. In others, the fields are restricted often not by law but by the attitudes of men who feel threatened by change. It can be argued that this is in spite of Islam: social attitudes take a long time to change. Much of the progress made in women's liberation in the West coincided with the development of technology, which freed up time for women to gain an education. Countries such as Malaysia and Turkey, which are catching up in embracing science and technology, are also amongst the most open for women to pursue careers.

Could women be regarded as more important than men in Islamic tradition? The Prophet was once asked whom to respect and follow the most, and he replied three times, 'your mother'. Only on the fourth occasion did he reply, 'your father'. Educational foundations were sponsored by women, including the first University at Al-Karaouine in Morocco, and a majority of schools in Damascus. Today, around 60% of researchers for the highest degrees in Malaysia and Iran are women. Despite these advancements, Muslims men still dominate positions of power across the Muslim world.

There were very few female Muslim political leaders in history, but there were some. Razia Sultana of New Delhi ruled as a Queen in the same manner as a man. The Muslim theologian Al-Ghazali stated women could hold any role except that

Key quote

The Qur'an 3:195

The Lord answered them: 'Never will I suffer to be lost the work of any of you, be you male or female: Ye are members, one of another.' (Yusuf Ali)

AO2 Activity

As you read through this section try to do the following:

1. Pick out the different lines of argument that are presented in the text and identify any evidence given in support.

2. For each line of argument try to evaluate whether or not you think this is strong or weak.

3. Think of any questions you may wish to raise in response to the arguments.

This Activity will help you to start thinking critically about what you read and help you to evaluate the effectiveness of different arguments and from this develop your own observations, opinions and points of view that will help with any conclusions that you make in your answers to the AO2 questions that arise.

Key quotes

Multiculturalism should not mean that we tolerate another culture's intolerance. If we do in fact support diversity, women's rights, and gay rights, then we cannot in good conscience give Islam a free pass on the grounds of multicultural sensitivity. (Hirsi)

To conservative Muslims … in any criticism of Muslim men, they hear the subversive voices of Western feminists. Mislabelling Muslim women in this way not only denies the specifity, autonomy, and creativity of their thought, but also suggests, falsely, that there is no room from within Islam to contest inequality or patriarchy.

To feminists and non-Muslim Westerners … it is inconceivable that Islam has any truths to offer that may be commensurable with Judaism and Christianity, much less with insights claimed by secular feminists. (Barlas)

Key questions

What do you think the Arabs at the time of Muhammad would have thought about his teachings on women?

Do the contributions of Muslim women in the past mean that men and women are equal in Islam?

Why do you think feminists like Asma Barlas and Ayyan Ali Hirsi disagree?

AO2 Activity

List some conclusions that could be drawn from the AO2 reasoning from the above text; try to aim for at least three different possible conclusions. Consider each of the conclusions and collect brief evidence to support each conclusion from the AO1 and AO2 material for this topic. Select the conclusion that you think is most convincing and explain why it is so. Try to contrast this with the weakest conclusion in the list, justifying your argument with clear reasoning and evidence.

of Caliph. In more recent times, Benazir Bhutto became Prime Minister of Pakistan; Sheikh Hasina Prime Minister of Bangladesh and Megawatti Sukarnoputri the head of state of Indonesia. Their election has challenged cultural ideas of male supremacy and shown Muslim women today that even the role of head of state is achievable. They are a minority amongst Muslim and Western leaders: if Muslim women have not yet achieved equality in the political sphere, neither have those in the West.

Ayyan Ali Hirsi

Ayyan Ali Hirsi takes a different point of view. Raised in a conservative Muslim household, she since left Islam and criticised the religion as failing to uphold women's rights. In her book *Heretic*, she argues that a full-scale reformation of Islam is necessary. Ayyan describes her own experience of abuse when she suffered female genital mutilation at the hands of a man when she was aged 5. As a teenager Ayyan was inspired by a charismatic Salafi teacher and wore the hijab. Ayyan moved to the Netherlands where she was impressed with the liberal political debate and the position of women. She was disgusted by the terrorist atrocities of 9/11 and renounced Islam in 2002. Ayyan argues that Muslims need to stop reading text literally and change the way they look at Islam. She says that as it is, Islam is a force for the suppression of women, which is justified by many verses in the Qur'an and hadith. For Ayyan, interpretations which suggest that it was not so bad are apologising for Islam and that is not good enough. Ayyan feels that the unequal status of women needs to be fought head on.

Asma Barlas argues that women are not seen as equal to men in the area of Islamic scholarship, and she is challenging that. She feels that Islam supports equality. Unlike Ayyan Ali Hirsi, she is not arguing for a full-scale reformation. Asma finds many Western writers are too critical of Islam, and they will not credit the work of Muslim women in the past because they are looking to make the case that there cannot be anything good in Islam. This bias means it is hard for women who are committed to Islam to make the case for equality and be heard in the media, unless they adopt a position critical of what they believe in.

Study tip

The best Band 5 answers at AO2 include confident critical analysis and perceptive evaluation of the issue. When you come to your own opinions about this issue, do not forget the many and varying opinions of others, some of which are mentioned here. The best answers will summarise the different views and provide a critique of them. What do you find convincing in a point of view? What does not add up to you? Ensure that you evaluate different viewpoints before reaching a conclusion.

Measuring the sense of how happy and fulfilled Muslim men and women are depends on personal perceptions, yet is another measure by which the sexes could be compared. You might think of others. Precisely how much weight is to be put on each measure is another area to debate. You might consider the average salary of women to be lower than men as important evidence of inequality. Or, it could be argued that what is more important is that women's and men's prayers and devotions are judged equally by God.

It may be that God made people unequal, or that He just made them different, but equally important; or that Islam regards men and women equally, but Muslims have failed to implement this. The many different possible conclusions reflect the diversity of opinion by different Muslims on this issue.

AO2 Developing skills

It is now important to consider the information that has been covered in this section; however, the information in its raw form is too extensive and so has to be processed in order to meet the requirements of the examination. This can be achieved by practising more advanced skills associated with AO2. The exercises that run throughout this book will help you to do this and prepare you for the examination. For assessment objective 2 (AO2), which involves 'critical analysis' and 'evaluation' skills, we are going to focus on different ways in which the skills can be demonstrated effectively, and also refer to how the performance of these skills is measured (see generic band descriptors for A2 [WJEC] AO2 or A Level [Eduqas] AO2).

▶ **Your task is this:** Below is **a one-sided view concerning the changing role of men and women in family life**. It is 150 words long. You need to include this view for an evaluation; however, to just present one side of an argument or one line of reasoning is not really evaluation. Using the paragraph below, add a counter-argument or alternative line of reasoning to make the evaluation more balanced. Allow about 150 words for your counter-argument or alternative line of reasoning.

Islam is based on Qur'anic revelations which are set for all time. The last, unchanging words of Allah, exemplified through His final Messenger Muhammad, cannot be altered because it is the fashion of the time. Women have an important role within the home in raising children, teaching them to follow the traditions of Islam, including the first words of the Qur'an. To some extent they can also go out to work but not if it affects their tradition role. Modern life blurs the boundaries of gender roles which brings stress upon the woman. Many women find committing their lives to a traditional interpretation of Islam, which means accepting the guardianship of men, and wearing a veil, liberating. This does not mean they are accepting lower status: men and women are different, because Allah made them that way. Even feminists such as 'Bint ash Shati argue that modern feminism distorts a woman's role. Women must be valued, but that does not mean gender roles should be changed for modern society.

Next, think of another line of argument or reasoning that may support either argument or it may even be completely different and add this to your answer. Then ask yourself:

- Will my work, when developed, contain thorough, sustained and clear views that are supported by extensive, detailed reasoning and/or evidence?

Key skills Theme 3 DEF
This theme has tasks that deal with specific aspects of AO2 in terms of identifying key elements of an evaluative style piece of writing, specifically counter-arguments and conclusions (both intermediate and final).

Key skills

Analysis involves:

Identifying issues raised by the materials in the AO1, together with those identified in the AO2 section, and presents sustained and clear views, either of scholars or from a personal perspective ready for evaluation.

This means:

- That your answers are able to identify key areas of debate in relation to a particular issue

- That you can identify, and comment upon, the different lines of argument presented by others

- That your response comments on the overall effectiveness of each of these areas or arguments.

Evaluation involves:

Considering the various implications of the issues raised based upon the evidence gleaned from analysis and provides an extensive detailed argument with a clear conclusion.

This means:

- That your answer weighs up the consequences of accepting or rejecting the various and different lines of argument analysed

- That your answer arrives at a conclusion through a clear process of reasoning.

**This section covers AO1
content and skills**

Specification content

An examination of the problems created by segregation for Muslim communities and individuals living in Britain today with a focus on food, dress, practice of religion and education.

King Offa's coin

E: Islam and migration: the challenges of being a Muslim in Britain today

Who are British Muslims?

A recent census revealed 45 000 Muslims living in Wales and around 5% of the UK population overall. Most came from families of migrants or migrated from overseas themselves. Countries of origin include Pakistan, Bangladesh, Somalia, Yemen, Libya, Iraq and Syria. Some of UK heritage have converted to Islam, mostly women, and some Muslims have decided to leave their faith.

Muslim travellers visited Britain during the Middle Ages. There was a story that one of the ancient Celtic kings, Selbach of Dal Riada, converted to Islam in the eighth century. King Offa of England imitated an Arabic coin with the shahadah engraved around the edge. A Muslim cartographer referred to Britain as the 'Blessed Isles', a land of great beauty and riches.

Sailors came to Britain and in Cardiff a community of Yemeni Muslims became established. In 1889 the convert to Islam, Abdullah Quilliam, established one of the first British mosques in Liverpool. Many have arrived in waves of migration since the 1950s, to find jobs and help Britain rebuild after World War Two. Initially men came, but later their families joined them.

Some Muslims set up corner shops and takeaways, and it is not unusual to find them running these businesses in remote corners of the UK. However, the majority of Muslims live in cities such as London, Bradford and Birmingham, and in particular less well-off neighbourhoods of those cities, forming areas of concentrated social deprivation.

Muslims in the UK belong to many different sects. These include many sub-divisions of Sunnis and Shi'as as well as Salafis, reformists, Sufis and Qur'anists. Many mosques have been established: some famous such as London Central Mosque in Hyde Park; others small community facilities in converted houses.

Muslims have excelled in many spheres of life. Successful politicians include the London Mayor Sadiq Khan, Baroness Sayeeda Warsi, news presenter Mishal Hussain and correspondent Faisal Islam. Some Muslims are very well integrated into UK life, others live largely separate lives and hold conservative Islamic values which may be somewhat different from their average British neighbour. Large numbers of Muslims say they have experienced prejudice, and in some cases verbal or physical attack. Others see Britain as a haven of tolerance and a place of escape from countries where they have suffered persecution.

An examination of the problems created by segregation

In South Africa in the days of apartheid there was a large degree of separation of people of the grounds of race. This was called racial segregation. People lived in different neighbourhoods, had different jobs and even sat in different areas of buses. Nothing like that exists in Britain today. However, there are some localities, particularly in big cities, like London, where a very large proportion of Muslims live.

Tower Hamlets in East London

> **Key term**
>
> Segregation: setting a group apart from others

A large percentage of Tower Hamlets in East London is occupied by Bengali Muslims. The majority of young people across East Birmingham, over 60%, are Muslim. People of different faiths and backgrounds still live and work in these areas, but the balance has changed radically. In some streets, Muslims wishing to live as extended families close to parents, grandparents, uncles and aunts, have bought up several houses. In some schools, children come and go every day and meet few other children except other Muslims.

Over time, groups of Irish, Sikhs and Hindus also concentrated in some localities, then became more integrated and spread out. However, there are larger numbers of less well integrated Muslims living in some areas, perceived as a threat by others living there who've seen their communities change. Areas where large concentrations of Muslims live can be perceived as ghettos. As a result fewer people visit, businesses are less busy and the area declines in prosperity.

A census showed that Muslims lived in more cramped housing than other communities, had poorer standards of education and were more likely to fall ill. The average Muslim had fewer qualifications and was more likely to be unemployed. These figures are averages: there are also some rich and successful Muslims. The average family size of Muslims is larger with more children than those of white UK heritage.

The proportion of Muslims with degrees has risen less than the general population, so Muslims are falling behind. In other respects, Muslims are catching up with standards of schooling. Muslim men are more likely to go to university than women. Muslims are underrepresented in Middle Management and overrepresented amongst the unemployed.

Why are these problems occurring? One theory is because Muslims tend to be less wealthy, they live in neighbourhoods where there are fewer job opportunities, and so are falling behind because of economic reasons. A different theory is that Muslims are becoming segregated because of their attitudes to religion, which is causing them not to mix with those of other faiths or none.

A survey of Muslims was carried out in 2016, called *What do British Muslims really think?* Trevor Phillips analysed the results. In some ways, the results were good: 94% of Muslims felt they could practise their faith freely in Britain; 86% felt they belonged to Britain, and the vast majority opposed terrorism, violence and suicide bombings. Nevertheless, that a minority did not is worrying. Most disagreed with homosexuality and took socially conservative attitudes, unacceptable amongst the general population.

Key quote

Liberal opinion in Britain has, for more than two decades, maintained that most Muslims are just like everyone else, but with more modest dress sense and more luxuriant facial hair; any differences would fade with time and contact. But thanks to the most detailed and comprehensive survey of British Muslim opinion yet conducted, we now know that just isn't how it is. (Phillips)

Trevor Phillips previously supported the policy of multiculturalism and with it celebrating difference. This was the received wisdom for many years, but in the light of this survey and other research, Trevor Phillips changed his mind. There is now a need to integrate further, to promote shared British values amongst all communities rather than allowing some sections to hold different views.

Key quote

The underlying message behind Phillips' analysis throughout yesterday's programme was that Muslims must accept British values, and unreservedly aspire to everything and anything deemed 'British' like the 'rest of us'. The

Key quote

The reasons that ethnic and religious groups spread out isn't easily trapped in statistics, but just about every study and analyst agrees that the strongest motivations here are education and employment. Most people who move away from the area where they were raised do so to get qualifications or jobs. The richer and better educated someone is, the more likely they are to move and mingle, and maybe even inter-marry, to integrate. (Kirkuk)

quickfire

3.25 Identify two areas where large numbers of Muslims live.

Key quotes

Britain's becoming more diverse and if we don't think about this and we're not willing to act on it, the danger is that we'll become more separate …. There'll be far too many places which feel like they're just for the well-off and far too many places which feel like they're just for the poor; there'll be far too many schools which feel like they're just for one minority group or just for one social class. (Taylor)

Many Muslim pupils do worse than their peers for reasons including: overcrowded housing, the relative absence of parental English language skills in some Muslim communities, low levels of parental engagement with mainstream schools, low teacher expectations, the curricular removal of Islam from the school learning environment, and racism and anti-Muslim prejudice. (Curriculum Journal)

Key term

Multiculturalism: the idea that different cultures should co-exist in the same society

Key quote

It cannot be right that people can grow up and go to school and hardly ever come into meaningful contact with people from other backgrounds and faiths. That doesn't foster a sense of shared belonging and understanding – it can drive people apart. I know that at times you are grappling with huge issues over your identity, neither feeling a part of the mainstream nor a part of the culture from your parents' background. And I know that for as long as injustice remains … you may feel there is no place for you in Britain. (Cameron)

Channel 4 poll, and more importantly Phillips' conclusion, has to be understood in a particular context; and that context includes the repercussions of the war on terror, draconian anti-terror policies, the alarming rise of Islamophobia in Britain, and the normalisation of demonising Islam and Muslims in the media. **(Hussain)**

Dilly Hussain, a Muslim author, disagreed. The climate of islamophobia was pushing Muslims into a corner from where it was all the harder to integrate. There was a perception that instead of being encouraged, Muslims were being talked down to and ordered to change their ways and mend their practices. This perception was causing some Muslims to react negatively and be even less likely to integrate in the short term.

If Muslims grow up isolated from other communities, they might be more susceptible to radicalisation. In theory, if you have no friends who are different, then you care less for those people, so you will not care so much if they are attacked. If you grow up alongside others then you will want security for all, and report anything that could cause harm to others.

This theory is disputed. Some British born Muslims of the tiny number who have carried out atrocities were actually integrated into mixed communities. Somehow, their sense of anger and grievance developed so far that they searched out extremist influences, through preachers or online, which inspired them to attack. Many Muslims regard such people as mentally deranged and nothing to do with them. But despite this, the extremists themselves often claimed to act for Islam.

Key quote

For a passionate teenager, watching the suffering in Syria and believing that they are barred from contributing because of double standards driven by Islamophobia can create extreme feelings of alienation. And for those who are converted to extremism, there are usually other factors: contact with a seductive and effective hate preacher, indifference towards or a desire for violence, a sense of purposelessness – in some cases the same factors that attract young people to criminal gangs. **(Hirsch)**

Muslims feel criticised for the actions of individuals whom they disagree with, and never seem to be able to say enough to condemn. Yet at the same time there are many issues in the Muslim community which Muslims have been slow to wake up to. Youngsters who disappear overnight to join an extreme cause leave devastated parents wondering what on earth went wrong. The growing consensus is that much more needs to be done to integrate into mainstream society, to address the psychological needs of the young for identity and belonging firmly rooted in Britain, and then begin to tackle issues of poverty, exclusion and extremism.

Assimilation for Muslim communities and individuals living in Britain today

Key quote

I do not regard integration as meaning the loss, by immigrants, of their own national characteristics and culture …. I define integration, therefore, not as a flattening process of assimilation but as equal opportunity, accompanied by cultural diversity, in an atmosphere of mutual tolerance. **(Jenkins)**

Roy Jenkins, Home Sectary in 1966, defined the consensus for around 30 years. People who migrated to the UK were encouraged to integrate by working, gaining jobs and contributing to the economy. In their home lives, the languages they spoke, clothes they wore and religious practices they followed, difference was not

Specification content

An examination of the problems created by assimilation for Muslim communities and individuals living in Britain today with a focus on food, dress, practice of religion and education.

only tolerated: it was seen as a benefit. This has changed markedly in the past few years. Ian Buruma describes the swing from integration to assimilation. Muslims are now encouraged to assimilate: to learn English, join in with others around them, share common values and accept similarity.

Cultural assimilation might mean items of clothing, social life and friendships. To some, mixing with others is invigorating and an opportunity to promote their faith through their character and actions. To others, mixing freely with members of the opposite sex and in the presence of alcohol is something they could not accept.

Shared British values are defined as belief in democracy, the rule of law, individual liberty, mutual respect and tolerance of those of other faiths and beliefs. The vast majority of Muslims and non-Muslims in British society agree with these values. A small minority of Muslims have, on occasion, claimed democracy is against shari'a. Mutual respect and tolerance means that Muslims should tolerate others where they disagree with them. They do not have to agree with gay lifestyles, but they do have to show tolerance, behave in a polite manner, and treat people who are different equally and with respect. Muslims are still free to take their own views on matters of faith, but are expected to share common British values in the way they interact with others. So Muslims can believe in assisted marriage, but should oppose forced marriage, because it is against individual liberty. Women should be treated equally, under the rule of British law, and not seen as lesser than men in any way.

Key quote

The religious practices and values of Muslims are dissected with a magnifying glass, whilst the conservative and 'illiberal' beliefs of other faith groups are ignored. If the British government insists on continuing its ideological crusade to force Muslims to assimilate to secular liberalism by linking religious orthodoxy to terrorism, then more Muslims will become disenfranchised, grievances will build up, and the widespread dissemination of negative stereotypes within wider society will be a recipe for disaster. (Hussain)

Dilly Hussain believes the government is going too far. He believes that Muslims are being seen negatively in the media and that the moves to British values are a way of targeting Muslims. Dilly believes that Muslims have a proud record of integrating over many years.

Study tip

Whilst learning about assimilation, consider carefully the links between beliefs and practice. The views of scholars may be used in context: show that you understand what those scholars meant in the context of their writing, and how their ideas have been applied in practice. Making connections between the various elements studied in a confident way will help demonstrate that you understand the implications of beliefs and teachings.

Kenan Malik makes a more positive case for assimilation. He criticises multiculturalism for restricting people through the regulations of government policy. Assimilation is more exciting and brings with it opportunities for new cultural experiences. Muslims in Britain should not jump to conclusions that assimilation is something negative; they should see it as a welcoming opportunity and embrace it with open arms.

Key term

Assimilation: acquiring the characteristics of mainstream society

Key quote

Multiculturalism held sway in certain academic and political circles as an ideology: immigrants, and even their offspring, were supposed to stick to the ways of their ancestors; any other choice was seen as a surrender to neo-colonial oppression. But recently, prompted by Islamist violence, the conventional view, especially among 'progressives' who might once have been great champions of cultural authenticity, has begun to swing the other way. Assimilationism has again become the vogue. Muslims in particular are expected to share 'our Western values', whatever they may be — Christian, or sometimes Judeo-Christian, or a rationalist version of the Enlightenment but, in any case, not Islamic. (Buruma)

quickfire

3.26 What is multiculturalism?

Key quote

Muslims have lived in this country for the best part of 70 years, and they continue to contribute positively in numerous professional fields, academic institutions and economic industries. Muslims are the most charitable people in the UK, and do not hesitate to come to the aid of their fellow non-Muslim citizens, as witnessed during last December's flood relief work in the north. Numerous Muslim organisations frequently hold open days at mosques, and engage in community projects hand-in-hand with people of all faiths and persuasions. (Hussain)

Key quotes

Qur'an 5:5

This day are (all) things good and pure made lawful unto you. The food of the People of the Book is lawful unto you and yours is lawful unto them. (Yusuf Ali)

Qur'an 5:3

Forbidden to you (for food) are: dead meat, blood, the flesh of swine, and that on which hath been invoked the name of other than Allah, that which hath been killed by strangling, or by a violent blow, or by a headlong fall, or by being gored to death; that which hath been (partly) eaten by a wild animal; unless ye are able to slaughter it (in due form); that which is sacrificed on stone (altars); (forbidden) also is the division (of meat) by raffling with arrows: that is impiety. (Yusuf Ali)

We know that imported meats, such as chicken and canned beef, originating with the People of the Book are halal for us, even though the animal may have been killed by means of electric shock or the like. As long as they consider it lawful in their religion, it is halal for us. This is the application of the above verse from Sura al-Maidah. (Shaykh Qaradawi)

Key person

Shaykh Yusuf Qaradawi: Egyptian theologian and TV host who has spoken in favour of democracy, having good relations with non-Muslims and the permissibility of eating meat from Christians and Jews. His connections with the Muslim Brotherhood have caused controversy in the past.

Key quote

The experience of living in a society that is less insular, more vibrant and more cosmopolitan is something to welcome and cherish. … As a political process, however, multiculturalism means something very different. It describes a set of policies, the aim of which is to manage and institutionalise diversity by putting people into ethnic and cultural boxes, defining individual needs and rights by virtue of the boxes into which people are put, and using those boxes to shape public policy. It is a case, not for open borders and minds, but for the policing of borders, whether physical, cultural or imaginative. (Malik)

Food

Tradition calls on Muslims to eat halal meat. According to the practice of Muhammad, not all meat could be slaughtered: the pig and birds of prey were forbidden. Meat to be slaughtered should be raised in a natural way, free range, unaffected by unnatural things such as antibiotic injections. The animal should be slaughtered with a sharp knife cutting the throat as the head of the animal faces Makkah, and the Muslim doing the act says the word Bismillah, in the name of God. When the throat is cut blood drains from the animal until it dies.

Halal food store

There are a variety of Muslim practices in the UK regarding halal. Few Muslims insist on organic, free range. Most meat is slaughtered overseen by a Sunni Muslim body called HFA which allows pre-stunning, so the animal does not feel the pain whilst its throat is cut. Some meat is slaughtered according to the HMC body, which insist on the literal interpretation of the practice of the Prophet. Since stunning was not around in his day, they do not allow it. Many Salafi Muslims and some Sunnis insist on this.

The British Veterinary Association submitted a petition to government against non-pre-stunned meat. When an abattoir in Caernarfon expanded in order to supply more non pre-stunned halal, many complained. It is claimed that animals feel pain and stress.

Whilst Muslims prefer halal meat, there are differences of opinion on what else can be eaten. Some Muslims are very strict and check ingredients carefully on packets of crisps, in case they contain meat flavouring. They believe eating it would be haram. Others say that eating food of the 'People of the Book', which includes Christians and Jews and all meat supplied in the UK except pork, as Britain is a Christian country, is acceptable.

The Qur'an can sometimes be confusing on food laws. Sura 5 ayat 3 suggests that any meat slaughtered with the name of anyone other than Allah is haram. Sura 5 ayat 5 suggests that meat of the People of the Book is halal. In the early days of the Prophet in Madinah, the Jews and Christians were regarded as fellow believers in Allah and members of the ummah, whereas later they came to be regarded as separate. This causes confusion amongst Muslims today over whether the Qur'an allows them to eat meat from the local supermarket, or whether it must come from the halal butcher. Most Muslims in the UK insist on checking it is slaughtered according to a halal method. **Shaykh Yusuf Qaradawi**, however, takes a different view.

Many school canteens offer a halal option. Some branches of popular chain cafes offer halal. Even the Royal Navy offers halal food to Muslim sailors, despite the considerable difficulty of supplying it on their ships that travel all round the world. These measures have been taken to help Muslims integrate into society and provide for their needs.

Alcohol is commonly supplied in restaurants and at social occasions in the UK. Muslims believe alcohol is haram, forbidden. Most Muslims avoid drinking alcohol or eating food products containing alcohol. This can be problematic in the UK. Networking, company socials and career advancement can all be harmed by not taking part. Some Muslims will not even attend the room where drinking is taking place, whereas others have no objection and some even are happy to sell and serve alcohol in their shops.

Dress

The Qur'an calls for Muslims to dress modestly. This is for men, just as much as for women. It does not describe what that modest dress should look like. Some Muslims claim it means that women's faces or hair should be covered. Generally, Muslims agree that Prophet Muhammad asked Muslims to cover their bodies modestly, and be humble in their appearance. Muslims may also take pride in new clothes and thank Allah for the gift of nice things to wear.

Muslim men sometimes dress in cultural dress, wearing white baggy **shalwar kemise** from Pakistan or **thobe** from Saudi Arabia. Some men find this a mark of their identity. Others choose to take on Western dress. Traditionally men do not wear gold or silk and wear clothes that are loose enough not to show the shape of the body. Some Muslim men choose to wear a prayer cap.

Key quote

The Qur'an 33:59

O Prophet! Tell thy wives and daughters, and the believing women, that they should cast their outer garments over their persons (when abroad): that is most convenient, that they should be known (as such) and not molested. And Allah is Oft-Forgiving, Most Merciful. (Yusuf Ali)

Hijab can mean a state of humility for women and for men; a place screened off by a curtain; a covering over part or all of a woman's hair; a veil over the face leaving only a slit for the eyes, called **niqab**, or a total covering of the face. The position of the veil for women is hotly debated. Some people believe it is a symbol of oppression that keeps women submissive to men. Others say it gives them a feeling of liberation as a mark of their faith. It can provide a barrier which makes it harder to make non-Muslim friends. Others say that the face veil can hinder communication and potentially endanger security.

The niqab

Key quote

The Qur'an 24:30–31

Say to the believing men that they should lower their gaze and guard their modesty: that will make for greater purity for them: And Allah is well acquainted with all that they do. And say to the believing women that they should lower their gaze and guard their modesty; that they should not display their beauty and ornaments except what (must ordinarily) appear thereof; that they should draw their veils over their bosoms and not display their beauty except to their husbands, their fathers, their husband's fathers, their sons, their husbands' sons, their brothers or their brothers' sons, or their sisters' sons, or their women, or the slaves whom their right hands possess, or male servants free of physical needs, or small children who have no sense of the shame of sex. (Yusuf Ali)

Key terms

Niqab: a full veil for women, also covering their face except for a slit for their eyes

Shalwar kemise: South Asian traditional dress for Muslims, consisting of two loose fitting cotton clothes

Thobe: a single white long dress worn by men in Arabia

quickfire

3.27 What is men's dress code in Islam?

Key quotes

I was raised as an observant Muslim in a British family. Women, I was taught, determine their own conduct – including their 'veiling'. We'd cover our hair only if we freely chose to do so. ... Not until recent years has the idea taken root that Muslim women are obliged by their faith to wear a veil. It's a sign, I think, not of assertive Islam, but of what happens when Islamists are tolerated by a Western culture that's absurdly anxious to avoid offence. (Ahmed)

From the eighth to the early twentieth century, Muslims strove for a broad education (as commanded in the Qur'an), questioned doctrines, and were passionate about scientific advancements, political and social ideals and art. Not even humiliating colonial rule deterred them from the march forward. Now the marchers are walking backwards. The hijab, jilbab, burqa and niqab are visible signs of this retreat from progressive values. (Alibhai-Brown)

The National Secular Society lists three justifications for supporting a ban on the face veil: it will support women's rights by making women feel more equal to men; it may address security fears; and, it may help Muslim women integrate. As the veil causes offence to most people, banning it is in accordance with their wishes. However, banning a form of dress is against individual liberty, a core British value. It may be seen as discriminatory against Muslims.

It might be expected that as Muslim women become established and integrated into Western society, fewer will wear the veil. Recent trends suggest the opposite. More women are wearing the headscarf and more are choosing to cover their faces. This may coincide with the growth of Salafism which supports this dress, or it may be an outward symbol of religion which helps women feel they are recognised for their religion.

AO1 Activity

Make a definition of the terms integration and assimilation. What are the differences between the two? Try to find five examples for each from what you have studied in this chapter so far.

Practice of religion

Muslims in Britain originated from many different backgrounds and brought with them their sects and groups. Some were closely linked to country of origin which provided Imams to preach in the language of the older generation. However, most young people do not understand this language very well and culture and want to mix with other local Muslims of different ethnic heritage.

Shi'a Muslims form a small minority. Deobandi and Brewlvi are the two largest Sunni groups in the UK. The Deobandi group was founded in India in the nineteenth century at a time of colonial rule. Deobandis focus on worship and avoid politics. Their missionary group, the Tablighi Jamaat, provides fellowship and brotherhood to Muslims, organises lectures at mosques and visits Muslims at their houses to encourage them to keep a conservative and puritanical version of Islam.

Brewlvi Muslims are mostly from Pakistan and Kashmir. They follow some Sufi traditions including reciting the name of God after prayer and celebrating the Prophet's birthday, **Milaud an Nabi**, which Brewlvis consider a compulsory Id festival. Street processions take place and food is shared. Coloured lights adorn homes and special festival meals are made. Many other Muslims oppose this as they think it elevates the position of the Prophet and borders on **shirk**, worshipping something besides Allah.

Key quote

The Islamic dress had a thrill to it, a sensuous feeling. It made me feel empowered ... I was unique ... it made me feel like an individual. It sent out a message of superiority. (Hirsi Ali)

Key terms

Milaud an Nabi: a celebration of the Prophet's birthday, regarded as an essential act by Brewlvi Muslims but forbidden by Salafis

Shirk: associating another besides Allah in worship

A mosque in Leeds

The Salafis have been the fastest growing Islamic movement in the UK for the past two decades. Inspired by Saudi Arabia, they attract the young with their clear and simple routines and their belief in the freedom to practise ijtihad or reinterpretation in the light of the companions of the Prophet, without the need to follow the tradition of centuries of learning. Salafis have slightly different prayer rituals from Sunni Muslims.

A number of Sufi tariqas are present in the UK. One of the largest is Jamiat Islami. Their distinctive green turbans and zikr gatherings are a source of strength for Muslims who wish to join a more intense form of mystical worship. There can be tension between Sufis and Salafis, who denounce Sufi activities as invalid.

Within each group there are differences between those who are modern and those traditional; members of their own choice and those who follow by family tradition. Young Muslims enjoy the freedom to go and try out different groups until they find one that feels right for them. For some, an Islamic identity is important especially whilst they are growing up questioning their place in society. Many are not committed to their parents' homeland but also do not feel accepted as Muslims in British society. For them, Islam is their point of stability.

The practice of Islam in the UK has changed and developed. Islam was rooted in equatorial countries where the climate is hot and the hours of daylight and darkness are roughly equal. In mid-summer in the whole of the UK, absolute darkness is not present, which means the conditions for the night prayer and the early morning meal in Ramadan need adjustment. Different sects have come up with differing answers, some several hours apart. A widely agreed fatwa ruled that in such circumstances Muslims should use the timings from roughly a line at the position of the South of France, or Makkah time, but few Muslims follow this.

Do Muslims need to pray and fast at all in a non-Muslim country? One argument is that shari'a does not apply in a non-Muslim state; another that Muslims may adjust their prayers and make up later if need be due to circumstances. Most try to attend the communal Friday prayers, though some will miss them due to work. Prayer rooms have been introduced in most universities and some railway stations, hospitals and airports, making the UK very well resourced for Muslims who wish to pray on the go.

The Oxford Muslim Centre is a liberal mosque which hosted female Imam Amina Wadud to lead Jummah prayers and preach a Khutbah to a mixed gender congregation. They also agree with modern reforms of Islam and the banning of the face veil. At the other end of the spectrum, political Islamist groups are present in the UK including Hizb-ut-Tahrir. There have been concerns about extremist preachers, particularly on university campuses at Islamic societies, who can influence young minds with radical or separatist ideas.

Study tip

Accurate and relevant knowledge showing extensive breadth or depth means that you should acknowledge in your answer the variety of Muslim practice in the UK when writing about this topic. Use evidence to show that you have detailed knowledge in sufficient depth for a range of different examples. Wherever you make a point in your writing, back it up by explaining it and giving an example.

The government has chosen to restrict the entry of some preachers into the UK and suggest home-grown Imams rather than overseas preachers to Muslim leaders. The Quilliam foundation was set up to counter extremist propaganda through the Internet and social media and online. The Prevent strategy aims to educate people who might be thinking about radical actions and it is a statutory duty for teachers and public workers to report any concerns, however small, to the Police. Some

Key term

Jamiat Islami: a Sufi tariqa

quickfire

3.28 What did Amina Wadud do at Oxford?

Key quotes

The policy response to the threat of radicalisation has focused on law, security and intelligence. As the problem spirals out of control, this one-dimensional response, which includes the government's Prevent policy in schools, seems merely to be repeated more aggressively. Applying security and surveillance policy across society not only risks limiting civil liberties, but also isolating mainstream Muslims. This does not counter the manipulative interpretation of Islam being used by extremists to play upon grievances held by some Muslims. (Sahin)

We have to recognise that Muslim faith schools seem to be much more monocultural than Catholic faith schools or Church of England faith schools. It's a very difficult policy because if you have Catholic and Church of England faith schools you can't really deny the need for Muslim faith schools, but there is a different character, they tend to be much less diverse. You can't deny people's desire for faith schools if you support faith schools. What you can do is to really demand that those schools demonstrate that they are actively working to connect with other schools of other faiths and no faith. (Taylor)

Key term

Tauheedul: a successful group of academy schools sponsored by a Muslim foundation

Muslims criticise Prevent and say that more should be done to encourage Muslims to take ownership of counter-extremism programmes.

Education

Muslim children usually go to mainstream schools during the day and madrassah in the evening. At madrassah they learn Arabic, how to say their prayers and the traditions of their faith. The day can be long and hard, making it difficult to balance the demands of school and mosque. Some madrassahs have adopted a Western style curriculum and included Maths and other subjects, in keeping with the original madrassah education.

At some madrassahs there have been reports of inappropriate teachings and corporal punishment. Mosques are encouraged to work with the government to help solve these issues. Some mosques are keen to do so, but with so many mosques in the UK and some led by Imams who do not speak English, there is much work still to do.

Learning the Qur'an at madrassah

Some Muslims attend state-funded Islamic schools, Christian foundation schools and some private Islamic schools. Christian schools are popular with Muslim parents who respect the environment where faith is respected. Not all private schools have been officially approved and there have been issues with some state-funded schools where Muslims have not received a broad and balanced education.

Where many Muslims live close by each other and attend local schools, they may not meet many pupils from different backgrounds. This was part of the problem in Birmingham where the 'Trojan Horse' affair found that governors wanted mainstream non-religious schools to provide an education in keeping with conservative Islamic views. Matthew Taylor, the parliamentarian, recommended mixing schools as far as possible. In Oldham several secondary schools were mixed together so that students of different religious and cultural backgrounds could mix and grow up together.

The Tauheedul academy group, a Deobandi foundation, opened a series of schools which have excelled at examination results and gained OFSTED inspection reports which were outstanding. Abdullah Sahin sees hope in religious studies as a subject for complementing students' prior learning in the mosque and broadening it.

Key quote

The kind of inclusive religious education provided in many community schools would complement such an approach by enabling students, including young Muslims, to develop a contextual understanding of Islam and its contemporary expressions. Instead of surveillance, schools need to encourage collaboration between RE teachers and Muslim educators. This would help pupils to be better informed about Islam and build competence among Muslim students to challenge rigid interpretations of their own religion. (Sahin)

Unlike France where all religious symbols and activities are banned in schools, British Schools are more tolerant and sometimes provide prayer spaces and halal food. Inspectors OFSTED made it clear that face covering, the niqab, is not acceptable as facial communication is needed for learning. Some Muslims frown on learning music and dance, and sex education, whereas others see them as important. Muslims and schoolteachers agree on the common aim of keeping their children well informed so that they can stay safe.

The Muslim College in London was set up by Imam **Zaki Badawi** for training Imams. Malaysia requires Imams to graduate from university with another degree in the social sciences before ministering as an Imam so that they can better address the social needs of their people.

AO1 Activity

Make a spider diagram / thought shower to show all the different ways in which Muslims can improve education. Make sure you include different aspects of education: from schools to madrassahs; university degrees to Imam training.

The role of the Muslim Council of Britain

The MCB describes itself on its website as:

'An independent body, established to promote consultation, cooperation and coordination on Muslim affairs in the United Kingdom.

The Muslim Council of Britain is a non-sectarian body working for the common good without interfering in, displacing or isolating any existing Muslim work in the community.

It is a broad-based, representative organisation of Muslims in Britain, accommodating and reflecting the variety of social and cultural backgrounds and outlook of the community.

The Muslim Council of Britain is pledged to work for the common good of society as a whole; encouraging individual Muslims and Muslim organisations to play a full and participatory role in public life.

The Muslim Council of Britain is a democratic body, built on consultation, co-operation and co-ordination among Muslim institutions and concerned Muslims throughout Britain.'

There are many Muslims in the UK but no agreement on who speaks for them. The Muslim Council of Britain was set up in 1997 as an umbrella body for many mosques and Muslim organisations. It remains the largest group in the UK and has affiliates from most different sects. Its leaders are not elected and do not proportionally represent Muslims in the country, so it has been criticised as an unrepresentative group.

Key quote

British Muslims from a diverse range of faith traditions came together today to affirm their commitment to Muslim unity and pluralism. A historic document was signed by leaders and representatives of a number of organisations from a cross-section of Britain's Muslim community … and ward off any threat to cross-sectarian unity in the United Kingdom. With Britain possessing one of the most diverse Muslim communities on earth, this document is intended to provide an initial framework for respect, dialogue and cooperation amongst Britain's Muslims. (Muslim Council of Britain)

Shaykh Ibrahim Mogra of the MCB became a patron of interfaith educational charity, The Feast. Sir **Iqbal Sacranie** was knighted by the Queen for his services to the country through the MCB. The group has held a lukewarm relationship with government. Whilst representing British Muslims and their issues, in 2003 the MCB strayed into international politics by siding against the UK government's invasion of Iraq. Whilst many Muslims also opposed the Iraq War, the intervention of a faith body into a national matter was a mistake according to some who felt the MCB strayed from its core purpose.

Specification content

The role of the Muslim Council of Britain.

Key term

Sectarian: concerning division between sects or religious groups

quickfire

3.29 Identify two objectives of the Muslim Council of Britain.

Key people

Zaki Badawi: an Imam who set up the London Muslim College to train Imams in the UK. The curriculum includes subjects other than Islam and encourages interfaith dialogue.

Iqbal Sacranie: one of the founding members of the Muslim Council of Britain, knighted by the Queen for his services to the nation.

The MCB takes a socially conservative position on issues such as homosexuality. Peter Clark criticised the MCB's stance on education in his report on Birmingham Schools involved in the Trojan Horse affair. More recently the MCB played a leading role in setting up the means to report incidents of Islamophobia, prejudice and attacks against Muslims, which have been growing in number.

Key quotes

The Muslim community should not be treated as a problematic community, but treated as a community that is willing to play its role in the mainstream. (Sacranie)

As Muslims it is our duty to condemn the killings and our duty to ensure that those on the fringe do not shame our community by justifying the killing of innocent people. (Sacranie)

Faith leaders join together

In 2015 following the Charlie Hebdo attacks in Paris, where extremists attacked hundreds of people in reaction to cartoons about Muhammad, Erik Pickles wrote to Muslim leaders to ask for their help. As Minister in the government in charge of local communities, he asked Imams and Muslim representatives to work with him in doing more to tackle extremism. But the MCB's reaction was initially quite critical. Some spokespeople have given the impression at times that they have supported certain foreign causes without being absolutely clear to condemn violence everywhere.

Nevertheless, the MCB has done much work in organising British Muslims who previously had no voice. MCB representatives attend major public events along with members of other faiths. They meet Christian, Jewish and other faith leaders to agree positions on issues that arise and communicate the importance of the faith and practice of Muslims in their lives today to those in power.

Key quotes

We are proud of the reaction of British communities to this attack. Muslims from across the country have spoken out to say: not in our name. But there is more work to do. We must show our young people, who may be targeted, that extremists have nothing to offer them. We must show them that there are other ways to express disagreement: that their right to do so is dependent on the very freedoms that extremists seek to destroy. We must show them the multitude of statements of condemnation from British Muslims; show them these men of hate have no place in our mosques or any place of worship, and that they do not speak for Muslims in Britain or anywhere in the world. (Pickles)

The MCB brought together a diverse set of British imams to call for peace and calm ahead of the publication of the English version of Charlie Hebdo. ... We hosted a solidarity meeting with Jewish and Christian faith leaders and leaders from civil society in Manchester and London. We have done this not out of apology, but because it was the right thing to do. These are positive acts that bring harmony between our communities. We have spoken out strongly against Islamophobia and anti-Semitism on numerous occasions. (Shafi)

AO1 Developing skills

It is now important to consider the information that has been covered in this section; however, the information in its raw form is too extensive and so has to be processed in order to meet the requirements of the examination. This can be achieved by practising more advanced skills associated with AO1. For assessment objective 1 (AO1), which involves demonstrating 'knowledge' and 'understanding' skills, we are going to focus on different ways in which the skills can be demonstrated effectively, and also refer to how the performance of these skills is measured (see generic band descriptors for A2 [WJEC] AO1 or A Level [Eduqas] AO1).

▶ **Your next task is this:** Below is **a summary of the problems caused by segregation**. It is 150 words long. This time there are no highlighted points to indicate the key points to learn from this extract. Discuss which five points you think are the most important to highlight and write them down in a list.

Segregation creates areas of poverty, where there are fewer opportunities for Muslims to progress. Living in a community together with other Muslims gives strength of identity but means that children have less experience of the wider world, and lack confidence to go out and make the most of opportunities when they grow up. Segregation can mean lower standards in schools due to less mixing, and difficulty in attracting people into the area. As well as these social problems, segregation can leave Muslims confused and lacking a sense of shared Britishness. This can leave them vulnerable to radicalisation, though this is disputed. If Muslims do not share friendships and experiences with others then they may care less about them as people. Muslim women may be more vulnerable to suffering a lack of opportunities within a male-dominated enclave. It can also mean the mainstream of British society gains the idea of Muslims as others, rather than part of the community, which can lead to poor community relations.

Now make the five points into your own summary (as in Theme 1 Developing skills) trying to make the summary more personal to your style of writing. This may also involve re-ordering the points if you wish to do so.

1 ....

2 ....

3 ....

4 ....

5 ....

Key skills

Knowledge involves:

Selection of a range of (thorough) accurate and relevant information that is directly related to the specific demands of the question.

This means:

- Selecting relevant material for the question set

- Being focused in explaining and examining the material selected.

Understanding involves:

Explanation that is extensive, demonstrating depth and/or breadth with excellent use of evidence and examples including (where appropriate) thorough and accurate supporting use of sacred texts, sources of wisdom and specialist language.

This means:

- Effective use of examples and supporting evidence to establish the quality of your understanding

- Ownership of your explanation that expresses personal knowledge and understanding and NOT just reproducing a chunk of text from a book that you have rehearsed and memorised.

Specification content

The possibility of assimilation into a secular society for Muslims in Britain.

Key quote

Under the doctrine of state multiculturalism, we have encouraged different cultures to live separate lives, apart from each other and the mainstream … We have even tolerated these segregated communities behaving in ways that run counter to our values. … All this leaves some young Muslims feeling rootless. And the search for something to belong to and believe in can lead them to this extremist ideology. (Cameron)

AO2 Activity

As you read through this section try to do the following:

1. Pick out the different lines of argument that are presented in the text and identify any evidence given in support.

2. For each line of argument try to evaluate whether or not you think this is strong or weak.

3. Think of any questions you may wish to raise in response to the arguments.

This Activity will help you to start thinking critically about what you read and help you to evaluate the effectiveness of different arguments and from this develop your own observations, opinions and points of view that will help with any conclusions that you make in your answers to the AO2 questions that arise.

Issues for analysis and evaluation

The possibility of assimilation into a secular society for Muslims in Britain

In the 1960s multiculturalism became the dominant theory in race relations: celebrate differences and co-exist. It was assumed that, in time, communities would naturally grow together. Instead, Muslims congregated in certain areas and emphasised their differences. Whereas in the 1960s few wore veils, now the veil and even the face veil are growing in popularity. Concerns have been raised about community cohesion. Those who have not integrated are at a disadvantage from the point of view of getting employment, advancing their careers and enjoying the benefits of an open society. Former Prime Minister David Cameron criticised this policy and called for assimilation of Muslims into wider society under common British values.

In a speech after a terrorist attack, David Cameron outlined his fears that separatism created risks and left young Muslims vulnerable to extremist ideas. Wider society has failed to assimilate them so far. Cohesion is a priority and assimilation not just something to be desired, but essential to combat growing risks and create a cohesive society.

Key quote

We should acknowledge that this [terrorist] threat comes overwhelmingly from young men who follow a completely perverse and warped interpretation of Islam and who are prepared to blow themselves up and kill their fellow citizens. … The root lies in the existence of this extremist ideology. (Cameron)

A survey interpreted by Trevor Phillips found two trends: that in some ways Muslims were integrating and felt a sense of Britishness like other groups. On the other hand, many had socially conservative attitudes, such as intolerance of homosexuality. Whilst that might be a private

Wearing hijab in a park

belief, it can spill over into real prejudice and targeting of individuals in majority Muslim areas if not addressed. Trevor Phillips argues for more assertive liberalism: Muslims should not show prejudice even though their own belief is different, since we are a secular state. Leaders must work harder to root out prejudice and discrimination from sections of the Muslim community.

Key quotes

Contrary to what many people seem to believe, Britain is not riven by a large-scale culture clash. Indeed, despite widespread fears about the integration of Muslims into British culture, there is no evidence that Muslims are less likely to think of themselves as British than other groups. (Manning and Roy)

This process of assimilation is faster for some immigrant groups than others, but not in the way that might be expected. For example, Muslims are not less likely to feel British than those from other backgrounds, and immigrants from Pakistan and Bangladesh assimilate into a British identity much faster than the average, while those from Western Europe and the United States do so more slowly, with Italians standing out as the group that assimilates least into a British identity. **(Manning and Roy)**

Not everyone agrees. Dilly Hussain argues that Muslims become disillusioned when they feel they are preached at. The MCB has encouraged interfaith dialogue, but they and others have not always worked with government with urgency to tackle assimilation. Manning and Roy analysed survey findings to show that Muslims feel as British as others, but that there is a problem with perception of difference.

Some Muslims assimilate well: Sadiq Khan became mayor of London; Sayeeda Warsi a Conservative Party peer and Mishal Hussain a newsreader. Others experience Islamophobia. A website, Tell Mama, set up to report and record Islamophobic crimes, reports a large increase in recent years. This makes it harder to encourage Muslims to integrate. The perception of difference fuels hatred, making matters worse. At the same time, demonstrations have taken place against Muslims by extreme groups.

A minority of Muslims oppose Western society. Groups such as Hizb ut Tahriah preach that Muslims should separate. Sayyid Qutb taught that Muslims should aim to live under shari'a for all aspects of their lives. Inevitably, this would lead to separation from non-Muslims. Shari'a for all aspects of law, family and religious affairs and living in a secular state are not compatible. In a secular state, religion and law are separate.

Most Muslims reject them but many prefer to wear modest veils over their hair and say their prayers on time, and eat halal food. They feel more comfortable in areas where there are mosques, halal meat shops and where women do not face abuse because of a piece of cloth. Other Muslims feel that it is not essential to wear the veil, or that if you do, be confident and show Islam in a good light by mixing in wider society. They point out that a lot has been done to provide facilities for Muslims such as prayer rooms in universities and airports and halal meat in hospital and school canteens. Even the Royal Navy provides halal food for their Muslim sailors whilst sailing around the world.

Study tip

It is vital for AO2 that you actually discuss arguments and not just explain what someone may have stated. Try to ask yourself, 'was this a fair point to make?', 'is the evidence sound enough?', 'is there anything to challenge this argument?', 'is this a strong or weak argument?' Such critical analysis will help you develop your evaluation skills.

Some Muslims think that if assimilation means mixing with others in the presence of alcohol, wearing entirely Western clothes or compromising on when or if they are able to pray, then this is unacceptable. Others point out that core British values do not compromise Islam. British values do not require Muslims to agree with homosexuality in principle, but they must treat gay people with mutual respect and tolerance, challenge prejudice against them and ensure that, if deciding on employment, they are given equal opportunities.

Life for young Muslims in Britain can be confusing. Often distant from the traditions of their parents, they experiment with different traditions of Islam until they find what is right for them. Going to college and university is a time that many integrate further into Western society. Others react against it and associate exclusively with their Islamic society and Muslim friends. Muslims are in a state of change and only time will tell which direction they take.

Demonstration against Muslims in Bradford

Key questions

What are the differences between assimilation and integration?

Why do some people see assimilation as a priority?

Are there any limits to the extent that some Muslims feel they can assimilate?

AO2 Activity

List some conclusions that could be drawn from the AO2 reasoning from the above text; try to aim for at least three different possible conclusions. Consider each of the conclusions and collect brief evidence to support each conclusion from the AO1 and AO2 material for this topic. Select the conclusion that you think is most convincing and explain why it is so. Try to contrast this with the weakest conclusion in the list, justifying your argument with clear reasoning and evidence.

Specification content

The effectiveness of the Muslim
Council of Britain.

The effectiveness of the Muslim Council of Britain

Muslim Council of Britain: Aims and Objectives:

- To promote cooperation, consensus and unity on Muslim affairs in the UK.
- To encourage and strengthen all existing efforts being made for the benefit of the Muslim community.
- To work for a more enlightened appreciation of Islam and Muslims in the wider society.
- To establish a position for the Muslim community within British society that is fair and based on due rights.
- To work for the eradication of disadvantages and forms of discrimination faced by Muslims.
- To foster better community relations and work for the good of society as a whole.

Set up in 1997, the MCB is an umbrella group for the many diverse Muslim organisations in the UK. It was an uneasy coalition: Muslim groups sometimes dislike each other's opinions, and come from different ethnic backgrounds. There has never been any tradition of Sunni Muslim groups accepting a single authority in the past few hundred years. The membership to the MCB was through affiliation, but leaders were not elected directly, causing questions to be raised about the MCB's democratic legitimacy.

Key quote

Although there are hundreds of Muslim-run organisations and charities working on a vast array of issues from education to crime prevention and even promoting militant jihad, few of them have the resources and know-how to operate on a national level, and only one is considered to be an 'unofficial' representative of all Muslims in Britain, including Shi'as and Sunnis: the Muslim Council of Britain (MCB). However, Britain's – just like all of Europe's – Muslim populations are diverse and there is no central command in Islam capable of uniting Muslims who are divided by politics, national origin, and theological differences. (Goerzig and Al-Hashimi)

One of the MCB's founders, Sir Iqbal Sacranie, was knighted for his services to the community. He has advised government and interfaith projects. Muslims from the MCB have joined those from other faith groups on special occasions. The MCB has condemned terrorist actions and taken action to help Muslims report growing incidents of Islamophobia. It has sometimes opposed government, such as by strongly condemning the Iraq War. The MCB also opposed the Prevent strategy for a time, arguing that more positive methods of involving the community in celebrating peaceful Islam were a more effective way at getting Muslims on side. The result was that the MCB had less influence overall, as Ministers looked unfavourably on it as an organisation.

Key quotes

You can't argue with one side of your mouth that Muslims are part of Britain, part of our nation, part of this country and then set up a rival counter-extremism plan in isolation from the rest of the country's plan. (Nawaz)

AO2 Activity

As you read through this section try to do the following:

1. Pick out the different lines of argument that are presented in the text and identify any evidence given in support.

2. For each line of argument try to evaluate whether or not you think this is strong or weak.

3. Think of any questions you may wish to raise in response to the arguments.

This Activity will help you to start thinking critically about what you read and help you to evaluate the effectiveness of different arguments and from this develop your own observations, opinions and points of view that will help with any conclusions that you make in your answers to the AO2 questions that arise.

In 2009 a senior member of the council signed (in a personal capacity) a declaration in support of Hamas, the Islamist group that runs Gaza. The group's boycott of Holocaust Memorial Day from 2001 to 2007 was also damaging. Critics began to pay more attention to the conservative Islamist groups in the council, in particular the Muslim Brotherhood and Pakistan's Jamaat-e-Islami. Sir Iqbal Sacranie, the founding secretary-general, acknowledges that the influence – perceived or otherwise – of such groups has been an issue. 'Being linked to any one particular group or school of thought limits the council's effectiveness', he admits. But he says the MCB is dealing with that problem and broadening its reach. (The Economist)

Where the MCB had failed to engage, has any other organisation succeeded? The Quilliam foundation was set up by people aiming to challenge extremism. Majid Nawaz, one of its leading members, was previously a Hizb ut Tahriah activist who changed his views. He criticises the MCB for being too close to people he regards as extremist. Yet very many Muslims reject Quilliam as being a mouthpiece of government. It has little presence in mosques or community groups. A voice to articulate the wishes of these organisations is still helpful to hear, according to former Home Secretary David Blunkett, even if government does not like what it says. Sometimes frank speech is the best way to resolve issues.

The Muslim Council of Britain published a guide to schools in 2007 which articulated a largely conservative Muslim viewpoint on the needs of Muslims in education. Many Muslim parents prefer a religious-based education but with very few state-funded Muslim schools in the UK, they felt they needed to address issues in the state sector. The guide articulated opinions about integration, tolerance of hijab, the need for prayer facilities and certain comments about areas of the curriculum. The guide gave the impression that Muslims could demand different topics or approaches could be taken, in music or sex and relationship education.

Cleric and member of the MCB, Ibrahim Mogra brought together Imams from different sects to his committee. Sometimes there are sharp differences between Shi'a, Sunnis and various other groups. The MCB overcame many of these to speak as one, more influential voice. Ibrahim Mogra has also supported interfaith charity work and is a patron to the Christian interfaith educational charity, The Feast.

Currently some complain of rising Islamophobia, and others stress the need for more assimilation. This would suggest the MCB has failed in its core aims and objectives set in 1997. Others would argue that the MCB can only ever have limited influence over the many diverse Muslim groups within the UK. Unexpected terrorist incidents challenged the MCB to respond and condemn violence. Ministers have asked the MCB to work with them on the Prevent strategy, but the MCB has suggested an alternative rooted in traditional Islam. However, Dominic Grieve MP led a report, 'The Missing Muslims', in which he discussed leadership with some prominent Muslims including many senior members of the MCB, and made recommendations about how Muslims could more effectively take leadership positions. So there are some positive signs of working together.

Key quote

Defenders of the council point to its 'democratic' procedures; its leaders are elected by the group's affiliates every two years. But these days, when Muslim condemnations of terrorism hit the press they are more likely to come from the Quilliam Foundation, an anti-extremism think-tank that in the past has received government funding and has little traction among most British Muslims. Having the MCB as a clear voice, articulating Muslims' views, is still helpful, insists David Blunkett, a former Labour home secretary. (The Economist)

AO2 Activity

List some conclusions that could be drawn from the AO2 reasoning from the above text; try to aim for at least three different possible conclusions. Consider each of the conclusions and collect brief evidence to support each conclusion from the AO1 and AO2 material for this topic. Select the conclusion that you think is most convincing and explain why it is so. Try to contrast this with the weakest conclusion in the list, justifying your argument with clear reasoning and evidence.

Key skills

Analysis involves:

Identifying issues raised by the materials in the AO1, together with those identified in the AO2 section, and presents sustained and clear views, either of scholars or from a personal perspective ready for evaluation.

This means:

- That your answers are able to identify key areas of debate in relation to a particular issue

- That you can identify, and comment upon, the different lines of argument presented by others

- That your response comments on the overall effectiveness of each of these areas or arguments.

Evaluation involves:

Considering the various implications of the issues raised based upon the evidence gleaned from analysis and provides an extensive detailed argument with a clear conclusion.

This means:

- That your answer weighs up the consequences of accepting or rejecting the various and different lines of argument analysed

- That your answer arrives at a conclusion through a clear process of reasoning.

AO2 Developing skills

It is now important to consider the information that has been covered in this section; however, the information in its raw form is too extensive and so has to be processed in order to meet the requirements of the examination. This can be achieved by practising more advanced skills associated with AO2. For assessment objective 2 (AO2), which involves 'critical analysis' and 'evaluation' skills, we are going to focus on different ways in which the skills can be demonstrated effectively, and also refer to how the performance of these skills is measured (see generic band descriptors for A2 [WJEC] AO2 or A Level [Eduqas] AO2).

▶ **Your next task is this:** Below is **an evaluation concerning the issues of education for British Muslims**. It is 150 words long. After the first paragraph there is an intermediate conclusion highlighted for you in yellow. As a group try to identify where you could add more intermediate conclusions to the rest of the passage. Have a go at doing this.

Muslims spend long days in learning at school and then madrassah in the evening. Some madrassahs have embraced broad curricula but there is still work to challenge abuses in a minority. Learning about Islam alongside Maths and other subjects follows the pattern of education in the early schools of Islam. The best madrassahs help children integrate.

The Trojan Horse affair showed how conservative Muslim governors tried to make mainstream schools more Islamic. This may have been to their liking but damaged prospects of integration for their children. However, there are examples of successful secondary schools such as Tauheedul, where standards are catching up.

British Muslims are falling behind their peers in university education, and women are less qualified than men. Some Imams are trained in London but others overseas. There is a need to improve education for Muslim leaders. One solution used in Malaysia is to make Imams graduate in social science, so they better understand the needs of their people.

When you have done this you will see clearly that in AO2 it is helpful to include a brief summary of the arguments presented as you go through an answer and not just leave it until the end to draw a final conclusion. This way you are demonstrating that you are sustaining evaluation throughout an answer and not just repeating information learned.

F: Western perceptions of Islam

Issues of bias and misrepresentation

Bias in the media has long been a complaint of Muslims. Negative stories seem to predominate. John Richardson researched British newspapers and found that 85% of articles referred to Muslims as if they were a single community, not a diverse mixture, and often portrayed them as a threat.

Since the destruction of the Twin Towers in New York on 9/11 by extremist Muslims using hijacked aeroplanes, Muslim treatment in the media has been disputed. Muslims complain that negative media portrayal fuels Islamophobia. To combat negative impressions, the Islamic Society of Britain put in place Islamic Awareness Week annually, but this was hardly covered by the media.

Key quotes

Islamophobia is often posed as the motivation behind acts of mosque vandalism, hate crimes against individuals thought to be Muslim, sensational press coverage of 'the Muslim threat', the selective policing and surveillance of Muslim communities, and electoral smears in which a candidate is linked to Muslim extremists. (Shryock)

Since media coverage of Muslims and Islam is likely to shape the opinions of those who have limited or no contact with this religion and its people, it is important to analyse the potential associations these media portrayals might have with people's attitudes toward Islam in general and Muslims in particular. (Ogan)

Christine Ogan points out that media coverage should be carefully considered because it can influence people who have little contact with Muslims. Bias and misrepresentation in the media spills over into the minds of millions of people, affecting the way they treat Muslims in their daily lives.

Key quote

We reject the 'cultural relativism' which implies an acceptance that men and women of Muslim culture are deprived of the right to equality, freedom and secularism in the name of the respect for certain cultures and traditions. We refuse to renounce our critical spirit out of fear of being accused of 'Islamophobia', a wretched concept that confuses criticism of Islam as a religion and stigmatisation of those who believe in it. (Together facing a new totalitarianism)

A group of people including ex-Muslims and others signed the declaration: Together facing a new totalitarianism. They felt that the media should be more critical of Islam, not less, and should not be frightened of making criticisms of Muslims for fear of being labelled Islamophobic. They feel that there are serious issues with the way Islam is being interpreted to oppress women and minorities and deny freedom of speech, so people should be allowed to point out these things freely.

Medhi Hasan criticises Western media for over reporting terrorist incidents but failing to report other attacks, just as violent, made by non-Muslims. His televised debates with others who take very different views have gained sizeable audiences amongst young Muslims ensuring that his message challenging Islamophobia gets across.

Key term

Islamophobia: fear of Islam and Muslims, sometimes manifested through negative comments or even verbal or physical attack

Key person

Medhi Hasan: an Oxford University educated Shi'a Muslim and specialist in politics. Mehdi Hasan rose to fame through debating at the famous Oxford Union. On his Al-Jazeera TV shows, Medhi challenges Islamophobic attitudes. Some criticise him for his focus on politics and the fact that he is not a specialist in religion.

quickfire

3.30 Who is Mehdi Hasan?

Specification content

Issues of inaccuracy and Islamophobia throughout the Western world with a particular focus on Britain.

Protest against Islamophobia

quicKfire

3.31 What is Islamophobia?

Key quote

Whether it takes the shape of daily forms of racism and discrimination or more violent forms, Islamophobia is a violation of human rights and a threat to social cohesion.

(Ramberg)

Inaccuracy and Islamophobia throughout the Western world

The English Defence League (EDL) was formed to oppose Islamism, shari'a and Islamic extremism. Many consider it an Islamophobic organisation which targets areas where many Muslims live, inciting hatred. Some oppose the tactics of the EDL but sympathise with its views. Social attitudes surveys find that people are accepting of Muslim neighbours but suspicious about Islam.

Definitions of Islamophobia

Islamophobia is a new term in which came to prominence in the Runnymede Trust report 'Islamophobia: A Challenge for us all' in 1997. Runnymede defines it as 'an outlook or world-view involving an unfounded dread and dislike of Muslims, which results in practices of exclusion and discrimination'.

Some academics define Islamophobia as similar to anti-Semitism, racism or prejudice. Others say the term is meaningless. It might be better defined as hostility to Muslims, since some people dislike all religions and might be described as Islamophobic but are equally phobic of other faiths.

The rise in reported Islamophobia might be a response to attacks such as 9/11. Each time a terrorist claims to act in the name of Islam, more people fear the religion the terrorist claims they are working for. Many Muslims denounce these attacks and say it is not in their name, but images in the media are powerful.

Others claim that the source of Islamophobia is migration. Once living in the West, the failure to assimilate in some areas causes a reaction by established communities. Sayyid and Vakil argue that it is not about areas where people live, but a general phenomenon.

Study tip

When asked to explain or give examples of a phenomenon like Islamophobia, it is worth giving your own definition of the term and making your examiner know that you are aware there are other definitions. It is a good thing to recognise if there is disagreement about a term, which can show thorough and accurate knowledge and breath of response in your answers.

Runnymede Trust Report

Runnymede contrasts what it defines as open and closed views about Islam. Open views are open-minded able to criticise Islam from the point of view of respect, whereas closed views are Islamophobic, or tend to lead towards Islamophobia. Eight questions are posed to determine whether views are open or closed:

1. Whether Islam is seen as monolithic and static, or as diverse and dynamic.
2. Whether Islam is seen as other and separate, or as similar and interdependent.
3. Whether Islam is seen as inferior, or as different but equal.
4. Whether Islam is seen as an aggressive enemy or as a cooperative partner.
5. Whether Muslims are seen as manipulative or as sincere.
6. Whether Muslim criticisms of 'the West' are rejected or debated.
7. Whether discriminatory behaviour against Muslims is defended or opposed.
8. Whether anti-Muslim discourse is seen as natural or as problematic.

The Runnymede report concludes that the sense of corrosive Islamophobia needs to be addressed urgently by opinion leaders.

Reporting Islamophobia

The Muslim Council of Britain states on its website that the best way to tackle Islamophobia is through building stronger bonds between communities. It aims to raise the profile of Islamophobia so that it is given greater prominence, and work with others to combat it. The MCB defines eight categories of incident which can be reported by filling in a form online. These are:

- **Online abuse**, e.g. on social media such as Facebook or Twitter
- **Threatening gestures**
- **Verbal abuse** or threats
- **Hate mail** / written abuse or threats, e.g. emails, letters through the post
- **Attack on a property**, e.g. graffiti, stickers on mosques, pig heads being thrown
- **Discrimination**, e.g. job discrimination
- **Anti-Muslim literature**, e.g. posters, stickers seen at supermarkets
- **Assault**, e.g. objects being thrown at someone
- **Violent assault**

Tell Mama is an organisation set up to help Muslims who have suffered incidents of Islamophobia. Shahid Malik, its chairman, reports a rise in incidents. Most attacks are carried out by teenagers on veiled women, particularly women who wear the face veil. Shahid Malik reports that about 11% of attacks take place in schools and colleges and feels that better teacher training is needed to address the problem.

Despite the gloomy situation, Runnymede envisages a bright future when Islamophobia is overcome. It sees British Muslims becoming fully engaged in all aspects of society in an eight point vision:

1. Islamophobic discourse will be recognised as unacceptable and will no longer be tolerated in public. Whenever it occurs people in positions of leadership and influence will speak out and condemn it.

2. Legal sanctions against religious discrimination, violence and incitement to hatred will be on the statute book.

3. British Muslims will participate fully and confidently at all levels in the political, cultural, social and economic life of the country.

4. The voices of British Muslims will be fully heard and held in the same respect as the voices of other communities and groups. Their individual and collective contributions to wider society will be acknowledged and celebrated.

5. The state system of education will include a number of Muslim schools, and all mainstream state schools will provide effectively for the pastoral, religious and cultural needs of their Muslim pupils. The academic attainment of Muslim pupils will be on a par with that of other pupils.

6. The need of young British Muslims to develop their religious and cultural identity in a British context will be accepted and supported.

7. Measures to tackle social and economic deprivation, unemployment and urban decline will be of benefit to Muslims as to all other communities.

8. All employers and service providers will ensure that in addition to compliance with legal requirements on non-discrimination, they demonstrate high value for religious, cultural and ethnic diversity.

(Runnymede Trust)

AO1 Activity

Make a tree diagram with branches that fan out. In the centre write the title Islamophobia. For the main braches, write on each one a different definition or type of Islamophobia. Then, as the branches fan out, fill in examples of Islamophobia as leaves hanging on the branches.

Key quote

We simply cannot have such hatred fester in our communities and in our societies. With a 326% increase in anti-Muslim hatred reported to us in 2015, we have to deal with this issue … Now is the time to redouble our efforts to tackle such hate from all extremist groups. (Mughal)

Shahid Malik

quickfire

3.32 Give two examples of how a Muslim might experience Islamophobia.

Key quote

The statistics paint a profoundly bleak picture of the explosion of anti-Muslim hate both online and on our streets, with visible Muslim women being disproportionately targeted by cowardly hatemongers. This exponential growth is a testament to the fact that despite great efforts to fight anti-Muslim hatred, as a society we are still failing far too many of our citizens. With the backdrop of the Brexit vote and the spike in racist incidents that seems to be emerging, the government should be under no illusions, things could quickly become unpleasant for Britain's minorities. (Malik)

Specification content

Examples may be drawn from:
political views; views from media
sources (television, radio or
newspapers) and/or online media.

Sadiq Khan

quickfire

3.33 What happened to Juhel Miah?

Key quote

We at The Muslim Council
of Wales are deeply troubled
by the reports that a Welsh
Muslim teacher, Mr Juhel Miah
of Llangatwg Comprehensive in
Aberdulais, was denied entry into
the US. It is outright Islamophobic
discrimination that a British citizen
school teacher travelling with his
school party should be denied entry
into the US.
(Muslim Council of Wales)

The Houses of Parliament, Westminster

Political views

Muslims in Britain have joined political parties, become councillors, MPs and Lord
Mayors. Sadiq Khan as Mayor of London is one of the most high-ranking Muslims
to have been successful in politics. In Wales, the Welsh assembly has an outreach
programme to listen to the views of Muslims. A series of workshops were arranged
for local community representatives to meet with Minister for Public Services,
Leighton Andrews, at the Welsh Assembly buildings in Cardiff.

Key quote

Workshops have been established to hear from a broad representation of
religious leaders and community activists, including those who have had a
public profile in speaking out on extremism and Islamophobia. The aim of the
discussion is to develop closer relationships between the Welsh Government and
Muslim communities in Wales. We are taking action to challenge all forms of
extremism and hate crime but none of us can tackle these issues alone. These
workshops are therefore the first step in an ongoing programme to build trust
and resilience within communities. (Welsh Government spokeswoman)

The Muslim Council of Wales represents the views of Welsh Muslims as an affiliate
of the Muslim Council of Britain. They have been vociferous in standing up for
Muslims. In 2017, a school trip to the United States boarded a plane on route in
Iceland. One of the teachers, a British national Juhel Miah, was taken off the plane
by US security officials without explanation. It was rumoured to be part of a so-
called Muslim ban by President Donald Trump. The Muslim Council of Wales and
Juhel Miah's local authority employer protested about his treatment.

The Westminster government

Over the last thirty years representation of Muslims in parliament has increased.
Members of Parliament have their own prayer room. MPs who happen to be
Muslim have been elected for seats in rural areas where there are hardly any
Muslim voters. This is a positive sign that the people are voting for the issues and
do not mind what a person's private religious faith is.

The Prime Minister records a special message for Muslims for their Id (Eid)
festival every year, available on social media. MPs often make a point of including
Muslims, community groups and mosques in their constituency in discussion and
consultation, to ensure that the Muslim community is well represented.

Key quote

A leaked cabinet committee memo in 2010 showed coalition ministers were
advised on coming into government that it was wrong 'to regard radicalisation
in this country as a linear "conveyor belt" moving from grievance, through
radicalisation, to violence … This thesis seems to both misread the
radicalisation process and to give undue weight to ideological factors'. (Travis)

David Cameron, when Prime Minister, set out his aims to better integrate Muslims
and move the country away from the former policy of multiculturalism. He said
this failed because communities had drifted apart. Instead, common British values
were to be fostered.

The Policy Exchange think-tank, favoured by the Conservative Party, criticised
Muslim communities for separatist tendencies. In a report, Policy Exchange claimed
that Muslims lived more separate lives but also wanted to integrate more. Concern
was raised about unusual ideas circulating amongst Muslims, such as conspiracy
theories against Muslims.

Michael Gove has been one of the most outspoken critics of Islamism. In his book,
Celsius 7/7, Gove claims that a sizeable minority of British Muslims hold Islamist

views or have sympathy with them, which he likens to Communism and Nazism. He says that the media have not done enough to criticise this for fear of being called Islamophobic.

Some Muslims say that Gove's approach makes the situation worse. Understanding radicalisation is not agreed upon. Information from the Home Office, which has developed expertise with the Prevent programme, suggests that Muslims do not go from grievance to exclusion to radicalisation, like a conveyor belt. Alan Travis' review of Gove's book challenges this view.

Sayeeda Warsi, a member of the Conservative Party and House of Lords, criticises British politicians for excluding Muslims from debate. When they try to join in and help, they are regarded with suspicion as subversive, but when they don't, they are regarded as a separatist threat.

Charlie Hebdo

Charlie Hebdo is a French satirical magazine which publishes jokes, cartoons and other material which makes fun of people in power. This is a form of satire. Satire has a long history and important purpose in France and Western countries for pointing out using humour, the ways in which politicians and others abuse power. Liberty, free speech, criticism of anyone and anything, are also highly valued in France. Liberty was one of the most important principles in the French Revolution.

The Charlie Hebdo magazine published a series of cartoons making fun of people, including one of Prophet Muhammad as a bomb. This caused controversy because Muslims thought it was disrespecting their Prophet. Death threats were made against the magazine and in 2015 two gunmen fired into the offices of the magazine's headquarters, killing 12 people.

Muslims were upset that cartoons were drawn of their Prophet, but there are many medieval pictures depicting Muhammad painted by Muslims, including his face. It was forbidden to idolise him, but the act of drawing him was not necessarily a crime. Muhammad used to put up with all kinds of abuse, and did not let it bother him or make him angry. A woman used to insult him daily, and throw rubbish at his door, but one day when she did not come he went to her home to see if she was alright. Muslims following the sunna should therefore befriend their critics.

Those publishing the cartoons had a right to publish, but seemed to depart from the genre of satire. An essential element is that the person being satirised is in a position of power where they can take advantage of or abuse others; however, Muhammad has long gone and the Muslim community in France is amongst the poorest and least represented in power.

French politician Manual Valls stood up for Muslims in condemning those who blamed all Muslims for the attack. He also spoke of the French principle of liberty: people must be free to criticise Islam without fear of the charge of Islamophobia.

Key quote

It is very important to make clear to people that Islam has nothing to do with ISIS. There is a prejudice in society about this, but on the other hand, I refuse to use this term 'Islamophobia', because those who use this word are trying to invalidate any criticism at all of Islamist ideology. The charge of 'Islamophobia' is used to silence people. (Valls)

Key quotes

The West faces a challenge to its values, culture and freedom as profound in its way as the threat posed by fascism and communism. But the response to that challenge from many in the West is all too often confused, temporising, weak and compromised. (Gove)

It was Gove's own long-held and repeated warnings as a journalist and politician that a far more robust response was needed to halt what he believes is a 'conveyor belt' linking religious conservatism and terrorism that added the bite to Theresa May's withering response to his charge of Home Office negligence. (Travis)

So we are in a situation where Muslims who engage with politics or any other British institution are to be viewed as suspicious, and Muslims who don't engage and keep themselves to themselves are to be treated as suspicious for being separatist and disengaged from mainstream society. (Warsi)

quickfire

3.34 Why are Muslims who engage vulnerable, according to Sayeeda Warsi?

Specification content

Examples may be drawn from: political views; views from media sources (television, radio or newspapers) and/or online media.

Fox news coverage in the USA

Key quote

The discourse Fox creates with its audience helps to set a foundation for polarised commentary and to legitimise support for a limitless war on the unknown. (Vultee)

quickfire

3.35 In what ways did Pervez Sadia's research find bias?

Key person

Miqdaad Versi: assistant secretary general of the Muslim Council of Britain

Key quote

You get these inaccurate stories about this threat of there are going to be more mosques than churches which is a complete nonsense. (Mason)

We looked at both nouns and adjectives and the way in which British Muslims were described. And we found the highest proportion of nouns used were about things like extremism, suicide bombers, militancy, radicalism – which accounted for over 35% of the adjectives used about British Muslims – fanatic, fundamentalist – those kinds of languages were used. Islam was portrayed or constructed in the language as dangerous or backward or as a threat. (Mason)

Views from media sources (television, radio or newspapers)

In the USA, Pervez Sadia carried out an analysis of how Arabs and Muslims were portrayed on different television channels. The results are shown in the table below. Negative subjects, shown in the top three lines, gained the majority of air time, whereas positive stories were few and far between. This analysis shows bias in the media.

Issue	Fox News	Special Report	Larry King	Late Edition	Total
War on terror	13	10	14	13	50
Politics	6	9	5	12	32
Crisis (Socio-economic)	4	19	3	4	30
Religion	0	3	2	0	5
International relations	0	1	0	0	1
Human rights	0	1	0	0	1
Development	0	0	0	0	0
Arts and culture	0	0	0	0	0
Total	23	43	24	29	119

The media have a duty to show the news as it is. The reality is that there are some horrible acts being carried out in the Middle East and these cannot be hidden away. Where Muslims commit crimes the media are only being truthful in reporting them. However, the bias is that the media are over-reporting the bad and underreporting the peaceful side of Islam, together with good news stories about how Muslims have integrated.

A group called the Centre for American Progress has been taking action against Islamophobia. They published a report exposing groups and individuals who were spreading misinformation and propaganda against Islam. The report traced funding for work that promoted Islamophobia and sought to expose those who were involved.

Newspapers

Paul Mason and a team from Cardiff University researched over 1,000 newspaper articles over the past eight years. They looked at the way Muslims were described in the stories, what the subjects of the articles were, the photographs that were placed alongside Muslims and the way Islam was portrayed. As with the US media, over 60% of the stories portrayed Islam negatively. Articles focused mostly on radicalism and fundamentalism.

Newspapers covered acts of terrorism together with religious motives, failing to point out political factors and motivators. Islam was represented as a threat, dangerous and backward in a quarter of news stories, and only good in a tiny percentage. Muslims were often placed alongside law courts, police stations and seen in a negative light.

Miqdaad Versi of the Muslim Council of Britain argues that the media should treat Muslims better. He cites two newspaper stories which portrayed Muslims negatively: one in *The Times* which read: 'Call for national debate on Muslim sex grooming' and one in the *Mail on Sunday* entitled: 'Muslim gang slashes tyres of immigration-raid van'. In both cases he questioned why the headline included the word Muslim, when Islam is much against these crimes. The actions do not reflect the teachings of Islam.

The consequences of media portrayal are to change attitudes of people so they are more hostile towards Islam. Public attitudes to Islam have shown that about a quarter of children of secondary school age think Islam supports violence and over a third of adults support policies to reduce the number of Muslims living in the UK.

To redress media hostility, Miqdaad Versi suggests that Muslims must build awareness of the peaceful nature of Islam. Diversity should be encouraged, particularly on the boards of newspapers and media editors. Powerful newspaper owners can affect the editorial content of their titles either directly or through their choice of loyal editors who, however much they claim to have editorial freedom, seem to always write articles which their proprietors are happy with. To address this, the media should be more closely regulated.

Portrayal in film

Ziauddin Sardar and Merryl Wyn Davies analysed the portrayal of Muslims in films in their work, 'Freeze Frames'. The way Islam and Muslims are portrayed helps to shape the way people think about the religion and its followers in real life. The Muslim world in usually shown as a barbaric place where desert Arabs fight and commit treachery on each other. In the 1949 film *Baghdad*, the Princess Marjan is described as 'all the fighting fury, all the glamour you ever thrilled to!'

In time little has changed. In 1992 Disney created a storm when its cartoon version of the *Arabian Nights* was released. It began with a song about Arabia that includes the lines

'Where they cut off your ear,
If they don't like your face,
It's barbaric.'

Key quote

What is happening with these cartoons is that a stereotype is being perpetuated that is not just about the physical appearance of Muslims – they are usually assumed to look like Arabs and dress like Arabs – but also a set of characteristics, that is, that the men are violent, the women oppressed, and that the religion itself is prone to extremes of both violence and oppression. This eases the ability of government to justify to the public their case for unwarranted detention of and violent action against Muslims. (Gottschalk)

Film provides the backdrop for people's discussions about contemporary events. Politicians, broadcasters and people in the coffee shops and shopping centres talk about the films and transfer the image of the Muslims they see into their thoughts about what they consider Muslims to be like in reality. There is no easy answer to challenge this depiction.

Key quote

The reality of Muslims and the Muslim World exists beyond the scope of the freeze frames. But, given the potency and hold they have on popular attitudes, how is the wider picture to be made visible and audible? The coded conventions of cinema and the cultural attitudes they represent and shape are set against a global political problematique that today is broadcast as the dominant issue of our times. (Sardar and Davies)

Documentaries

The broadcast media has helped to present a fair and balanced image of Islam and even a good one at times. Documentaries about Islam and its contribution to art and history have helped to dispel Islamophobia. Waldemar Januszczak has made several series about the contribution of Islam to art and architecture over the centuries. Akbar Ahmed, former Pakistani High Commissioner to London, made a series of programmes about 'Living Islam'. The BBC has made several programmes recently about the history of Islam.

Key quote

A woman of a hundred moods, tempting and beguiling, charming and desirable, imperious and vengeful pitting her beauty and courage against the desert's savage warriors. What is your pleasure? Dancing girls, perhaps, or desert raiders? It's all yours, all the fighting fury, all the glamour you ever thrilled to! (*Baghdad* film 1949)

Key person

Ziauddin Sardar: originally from Pakistan, Ziauddin is now a London-based award-winning intellectual writer. He is a reformist who believes that every generation should reinterpret the Qur'an and hadith for their needs. Ziauddin has been a strong supporter of multiculturalism.

Key quote

Oh I come from a land, From a faraway place, Where the caravan camels roam. Where they cut off your ear, If they don't like your face, It's barbaric, but hey, its home. (*Arabian Nights* film, 1992)

Cartoon depiction of Arabs

quickfire

3.36 Describe how Arabs and Muslims are usually portrayed in films and cartoons.

Specification content

Examples may be drawn from: political views; views from media sources (television, radio or newspapers) and/or online media.

Muslims using online media

Key quote

I have spent months and months criss-crossing the Islamic world, and everywhere I've been I've seen fascinating and beautiful things, some of the most fascinating and beautiful things I've ever seen, made by fascinating and beautiful people who had never shown me anything but kindness, friendship and hospitality. (Januszczak)

Online media

Anton and Peter Tornberg made a thorough study of social media, chat, forums and discussion sites in Sweden. They found posts which showed a degree of Islamophobia. One claimed Muslims were 1000 years behind, another that they had come to take 'our' jobs. Several Muslims posted questions about the basis of Islam with a focus on shari'a, Islamism and whether Islam is compatible with democracy. There was some open-minded genuine discussion about Islam as a religion compared to others. Popular topics were mosques and minarets, cultural aspects of Islam, halal meat, extreme-right parties, freedom of expression and international conflicts, the media, politics and hate statements on the Internet.

Examples of posts which reveal Islamophobia:

- It will never be possible ... to integrate Muslims. Take their perception of women, for example. If a Muslim marries a Swedish woman, he can seem fine and willing to adapt to Swedish rules in the beginning, but when he has more power over her, for example when they've had kids, his deep-rooted perception of women will come out and he'll turn completely.

- Wherever you look there are bomb attacks and other terror activity. The common denominator is Islamic fundamentalism. Why are almost only Muslims committing these acts today?

- Just because Abdullah, Ahmed and Mohammed are marginalised they don't have the right to gang rape Swedish women. I'm so fed up with people blaming sexual assaults on defects of the system. Shouldn't at least a little personal responsibility be demanded from our 'cultural enrichers'?

The position of Muslim women is much discussed, with most online posts assuming men are aggressors and women victims. Islam is often represented as a violent religion by nature: fundamentalist, terrorist, sexist and undemocratic. Most online discussion material was driven by current topics in the mainstream TV radio and newspaper media. The Internet did not seem to divert discussion into anything new.

Key quote

Ultimately, this essentialist depiction of Muslims and Islam that permeates through most predominant topics and over time contributes to constructing them as the 'other': an immature and even backward ethnic group that exists in tension – or even incompatibility – with what is depicted as Western culture. (Anton Tornberg, Petter Tornberg)

iMuslims

Gary Bunt of the University of Wales researched Muslim use of the Internet. In his work, iMuslims, Gary identifies ways in which Muslims have changed the way they find out about faith. Whereas in the past they might consider an issue for weeks and then discuss with respected members of the community, now they are able to look it up on the Internet. 'Shaykh Google' has become one of the most popular Imams in the world! Online experts are available to look up fatwas and give answers very quickly. The problem is that there is no way of knowing how authentic the writer is.

Key term

iMuslims: Internet and ICT use by Muslims which has affected the way they find out about and develop their faith

Many discussions start with conventional knowledge and put Muslims in touch with vast banks of information. If a Muslim wants to find out all the hadith traditions about when and how to give Zakat, it is easy for them to do so. For Muslims considering a particular practice of Islam, such as Sufism, they will be able to join online communities and get in touch with people they might not be able to find locally. Legal rulings of fiqh are discussed. In interpreting anew, fast decisions are made which might have taken a lifetime's deliberation in the past. Conclusions suitable for a local area are no longer the focus: the whole world can join the discussion. This knowledge exchange is developing into a whole 'rewiring' of Islam, according to Gary Bunt.

Key quotes

In some contexts, the application of the Internet is having an overarching transformational effect on how Muslims practise Islam, how forms of Islam are represented to the wider world, and how Muslim societies perceive themselves and their peers. On one level, this may be in terms of practical performance of Islamic duties and rituals, or on the interpretation and understanding of the Qur'an. On another level, this has exposed Muslims to radical and new influences outside of traditional spheres of knowledge and authority, causing paradigmatic shifts at a grassroots level within societies. (Bunt)

As we are primed to react instantly – thanks to social media and 24-hour global television – we can easily set off new patterns of chain reactions. Even apparently trivial actions can rapidly lead to global consequences. … A vegetable vendor can start a freedom and democracy movement that can escalate rapidly – the 'Arab Spring'. (Sardar)

How do people know if a site is mainstream or not? Jihadi groups also use the Internet to upload propaganda, hide their contacts and recruit vulnerable young people. There have been cases of young Muslims becoming radicalised online without their parents knowing. 24-hour news can spark reactions which might have been considered with more reflection in the past.

The Internet is also a tool for challenging unacceptable versions of Islam. Young Muslims can make friends with people of other faiths and none, even if they do not live nearby. It is a means of dating, finding someone to meet to arrange a marriage, out of a Muslim's own choice rather than their families' suggestion. Women who stay at home regularly can make friends, complete online studies, and find out information about their rights. This makes the Internet a positive force for assimilation and integration.

Study tip

Just as the media may be biased in its representation of Islam and Muslims, so commentators quoted in this unit all have their own views, some of which may show a strong bias. It is worth making a note of the background of each commentator, so you understand where they fit into the spectrum of opinion. For example, Ziauddin Sardar takes a reformist Muslim approach.

AO1 Activity

Imagine you are interviewing three young Muslims about their use of the media and the Internet to find out information about Islam. Ask them about the way they find out answers to questions and give examples of the sorts of things they might ask and find out. How does their use of the Internet differ from the way their parents might find out about Islam and the way they think about religion as a result?

quickfire

3.37 How does 24-hour news media affect people?

Key quote

An innovative knowledge and proselytising economy has emerged, causing a challenge to traditional 'top-down' authority models. A collaborative, horizontal knowledge economy, reliant on peer-to-peer networking, has enveloped areas of Islamic cyberspace. Much of the content is also given away for free, and users are invited to make comments, amend information, and provide contributions in some areas. (Bunt)

Key skills

Knowledge involves:

Selection of a range of (thorough) accurate and relevant information that is directly related to the specific demands of the question.

This means:

- Selecting relevant material for the question set

- Being focused in explaining and examining the material selected.

Understanding involves:

Explanation that is extensive, demonstrating depth and/or breadth with excellent use of evidence and examples including (where appropriate) thorough and accurate supporting use of sacred texts, sources of wisdom and specialist language.

This means:

- Effective use of examples and supporting evidence to establish the quality of your understanding

- Ownership of your explanation that expresses personal knowledge and understanding and NOT just reproducing a chunk of text from a book that you have rehearsed and memorised.

AO1 Developing skills

It is now important to consider the information that has been covered in this section; however, the information in its raw form is too extensive and so has to be processed in order to meet the requirements of the examination. This can be achieved by practising more advanced skills associated with AO1. For assessment objective 1 (AO1), which involves demonstrating 'knowledge' and 'understanding' skills, we are going to focus on different ways in which the skills can be demonstrated effectively, and also refer to how the performance of these skills is measured (see generic band descriptors for A2 [WJEC] AO1 or A Level [Eduqas] AO1).

▶ **Your final task for this theme is:** Below is **a summary of what Islamophobia is**. It is 150 words long. This time there are no highlighted points to indicate the key points to learn from this extract. Discuss which five points you think are the most important to highlight and write them down in a list.

Islamophobia is a fear of Muslims and Islam. The Runnymede Trust defined it in their report as a state of mind in which Islam is seen as monolithic, not diverse; separate not integrated; inferior, aggressive and manipulative.

People who demonstrate Islamophobia may tolerate prejudice against Muslims, see anti-Muslim hostility as the norm and fail to reject criticisms. Islamophobia may be shown by prejudicial statements, failure to regard Muslim candidates for jobs equally and even physical attack.

There are various causes for Islamophobia. Some think it is a reaction against Muslims following acts of terrorism. Others feel it is fear of the other due to the build-up of many separate communities of migrants. Some think it is a phenomenon wider than that.

A few people, including some Muslims, reject the concept entirely believing that Islam has many faults and that these need to be exposed and challenged. Islamophobia suggests fear of the religion; a better title might be anti-Muslimism, to reflect that the concept is about how Muslims face prejudice in their lives.

Now make the five points into your own summary (as in Theme 1 Developing skills) trying to make the summary more personal to your style of writing. This may also involve re-ordering the points if you wish to do so. In addition to this, try to add some quotations and references to develop your summary (as in Theme 2 Developing skills).

The result will be a fairly lengthy answer and so you could then check it against the band descriptors for A2 (WJEC) or A Level (Eduqas) and in particular have a look at the demands described in the higher band descriptors towards which you should be aspiring. Ask yourself:

- Does my work demonstrate thorough, accurate and relevant knowledge and understanding of religion and belief?

- Is my work coherent (consistent or make logical sense), clear and well organised?

- Will my work, when developed, be an extensive and relevant response which is specific to the focus of the task?

- Does my work have extensive depth and/or suitable breadth and have excellent use of evidence and examples?

- If appropriate to the task, does my response have thorough and accurate reference to sacred texts and sources of wisdom?

- Are there any insightful connections to be made with other elements of my course?

- Will my answer, when developed and extended to match what is expected in an examination answer, have an extensive range of views of scholars/schools of thought?

- When used, is specialist language and vocabulary both thorough and accurate?

Issues for analysis and evaluation

The extent to which the media influences Western perceptions of Islam

We live in an age of mass, 24-hour media. The Internet is readily available by computer, tablet and mobile phone, providing access to news, history, Islamic literature, chat and discussion sites and online fatwas. To the open minded, this is a brilliant research tool. In countries such as Iran and Saudi Arabia, the media and Internet are censored.

Specification content

The extent to which the media influences Western perceptions of Islam.

Key quote

In the mass media of the world, the 'Muslim' is stereotyped as aggressive, lawless, terrorist, uncivilised, fanatic, fundamentalist, archaic and anachronistic. He is the object of hatred and contempt. (Sardar)

Having said that, there has been much criticism of Western portrayals of Islam in the news media. Television often shows Muslims in a negative light. Muslims are implicated as terrorists, extremists, connected with war zones, crimes, separatism and fundamentalism. There are far fewer good news stories on the news. Surveys have shown that the public, whilst largely accepting the Britishness of Muslims, are also fearful at times of what Islam is about. Some of these social attitudes may be generated by the mass media.

Some argue that the media are only reflecting reality and unacceptable attitudes must be challenged. A group of reformist Muslims, ex-Muslims and others signed the declaration: *Together facing a new totalitarianism*, in which they demand that people speak out where they find unfairness, so that Islam can be opened to criticism and reform. People should not be shy because of their fear for being criticised for Islamophobia. The British politician Michael Gove said that he thought the media were far too reticent in not criticising intolerant versions of Islam enough.

Key quote

After having overcome fascism, Nazism, and Stalinism, the world now faces a new global totalitarian threat: Islamism. We, writers, journalists, intellectuals, call for resistance to religious totalitarianism and for the promotion of freedom, equal opportunity and secular values for all. (Together facing a new totalitarianism)

Others, such as the reformist Muslim, Ziauddin Sardar, criticise the stereotyping of Muslims in the media. Note that there are reformists on opposite sides of the argument when it comes to media influence. He argues that the media approach is counter-productive, causing Muslims to further retreat into their own world, living in outdated versions of their faith. Ziauddin argues that Muslims need to modernise but the media is not helping.

Key quote

I am often dumbfounded by what some of our prominent newspaper columnists have to say about Islam and Muslims. But not too surprised. Stereotyping is an old and, dare I say it, almost respectable institution in Britain. Muslims have been pigeonholed as violent, inferior fanatics for centuries; it provided a good excuse for colonising their lands. (Sardar)

The BBC and Channel 4 have produced documentaries about the heritage of Islam. Art critic Waldemar Januszczak has made programmes in which he is in awe of the contribution of Islamic societies, and thankful to his warm Muslim hosts. In the

AO2 Activity

As you read through this section try to do the following:

1. Pick out the different lines of argument that are presented in the text and identify any evidence given in support.

2. For each line of argument try to evaluate whether or not you think this is strong or weak.

3. Think of any questions you may wish to raise in response to the arguments.

This Activity will help you to start thinking critically about what you read and help you to evaluate the effectiveness of different arguments and from this develop your own observations, opinions and points of view that will help with any conclusions that you make in your answers to the AO2 questions that arise.

Protest against inaccurate media reporting

UK, broadcast regulators monitor news and programming to ensure fairness of approach. People may voice their criticisms but there must be a balance overall.

Journalists and broadcasters such as Mehdi Hasan engage in political debate and claim media bias. Fox News is sometimes accused of bias against Muslims. British newspapers the *Times* and *Sunday Mail* were criticised by Miqdaad Versi of the Muslim Council of Britain for running stories about criminal activity with the title 'Muslim' group commits crime, when Islam is against such activities and critical of individual criminals. These stories can lead people to hate Muslims. The newspapers eventually apologised.

Islamophobia might be a reaction to 9/11, shown graphically in the media. Others think it was due to large communities of Muslim migrants living separate lives. Still others think the media whipped up Islamophobia which has spread in institutions to areas where few Muslims live.

Films often show negative pictures of Muslims. The 1992 cartoon 'Arabian Nights' opened with a song about Arabia: 'Where they cut off your ear, If they don't like your face, It's barbaric, but hey, its home'. Disney changed the lines after a year of complaints. There are a few films which show the opposite. In the film 'Behind enemy lines', the abuse Muslims suffered at the hands of Serbs in Bosnia is exposed through the escape of an American soldier whose plane is shot down.

Study tip

It is vital for AO2 that you actually discuss arguments and not just explain what someone may have stated. Try to ask yourself, 'was this a fair point to make?', 'is the evidence sound enough?', 'is there anything to challenge this argument?', 'is this a strong or weak argument?' Such critical analysis will help you develop your evaluation skills.

The Charlie Hebdo affair caused many Muslims to react angrily to cartoons of Muhammad appearing in a French satirical magazine which had a tradition of freely criticising all religions and politicians. Muslim anger spilled over into a terrorist attack when gunmen shot dead people in the magazine's offices. Islamophobia in France rose in the aftermath. The French tradition of liberty was not an attack on Muslims more than anyone else, and the violent attack on the offices of Charlie Hebdo by terrorists did not represent Muslims. The media had a duty to report the events. The complexity of the situation does not mean the media got it wrong. Nevertheless, many Muslims feel aggrieved that afterwards they were singled out for criticism and wonder if the media could have handled it better.

The Muslim Council of Britain states that the best way to challenge Islamophobia is to build links with other people in local communities. Much good work goes on that is not always reported in the mainstream media. In Wales, the Welsh Assembly met Muslim leaders to talk about the issues of Islamophobia and address them in a series of seminars, covered as reported in an article in the Welsh press. But the vision set by Runnymede in 1997 in their report of a society which has overcome Islamophobia is far from being reached. The media has a part to play in reporting both critically and responsibly to ensure that where criticisms are made, they are balanced and proportionate, so that the public's overall view of Islam is not distorted.

Key questions

What are current Western perceptions of Islam? Are these changing?

In what ways can the media influence people?

What are the views of different Muslims about media influence?

AO2 Activity

List some conclusions that could be drawn from the AO2 reasoning from the above text; try to aim for at least three different possible conclusions. Consider each of the conclusions and collect brief evidence to support each conclusion from the AO1 and AO2 material for this topic. Select the conclusion that you think is most convincing and explain why it is so. Try to contrast this with the weakest conclusion in the list, justifying your argument with clear reasoning and evidence.

Whether or not Islam is accurately represented in Britain today

Islam is represented by MPs in parliament, members of the House of Lords, people in local government, representatives in organisations like the Muslim Council of Britain and Quilliam foundation, images on the media and online; in all kinds of different ways. Islam can be discussed by commentators in political debate and by academics in seminars and discussions. Faith TV shows set up debates between Muslims, atheists and those of other faiths. Books present the findings and personal opinions of researchers as well as those who have experienced a personal journey through faith, which are invariably more popular. Together, they form a body of material which influences people in Britain and the image they gain of Islam.

Sadiq Khan was elected to be Mayor of London. He has been praised as one of the highest ranking Muslim politicians in Britain who has spent time and energy in promoting projects which bring communities together. Baroness Sayeeda Warsi was a member of the Conservative government and House of Lords. Their presence in politics represents Muslims as taking part in the mainstream of British political debate. They present an image of modern, educated Muslims and tolerant Islam. Sayeeda Warsi has also criticised Islamophobia in politics, a concern which many Muslims share.

Key quotes

Consider this example from Polly Toynbee of the *Guardian*, a year and a half ago. British Muslims, she screamed, 'rarely speak out against terror' and 'excuse, rather than refute, the many ferocious verses calling for the blood of infidels in their holy book, verses that justify terror'. This is not simply a statement of monumental ignorance and arrogance, but also one of the finest examples of demonisation. (Sardar)

The link between terrorism and Islam was firm long before September 11, 2001, but it has grown stronger in recent years as high profile enemies in the war on terror have been defined, and have defined themselves, as Muslims. The result, now recognised by journalists, politicians, intellectuals, and other interested parties, is pervasive 'Islamophobia,' a generalised fear of Islam and Muslims. (Shryock)

Media representation of Muslims is more controversial. Ziauddin Sardar criticised many media organisations and commentators for presenting a biased picture of Muslims which does not reflect reality. Scenes of terrorism and crime are regularly shown and not balanced against scenes of success and harmony. Andrew Shryock's research traces this back many years, claiming that media representation of Islam is generally Islamophobic and this has been recognised by many researchers and politicians. Others claim that the media is only reflecting reality and that issues must be exposed and confronted.

Hundreds of different Muslim organisations claim to represent Muslims in Britain today. The Muslim Council of Britain has over 500 affiliates from across the spectrum. There is a degree of internal democracy as officials are elected every two years. However, ordinary Muslims do not have a direct say in this. In surveys, many Muslims feel that the MCB does not speak for them. It has in some ways raised important issues such as Islamophobia. In others ways the MCB has been controversial in opposing the government's Prevent strategy and setting up an alternative. The MCB's guidance for schools represented the views of mostly conservative religious Muslims, and was criticised by reformists such as Yasmin Alibi Brown. Perhaps it is impossible for one group to be representative of over two million Muslims in Britain who hold many and varying opinions.

Specification content

Whether or not Islam is accurately represented in Britain today.

AO2 Activity

As you read through this section try to do the following:

1. Pick out the different lines of argument that are presented in the text and identify any evidence given in support.

2. For each line of argument try to evaluate whether or not you think this is strong or weak.

3. Think of any questions you may wish to raise in response to the arguments.

This Activity will help you to start thinking critically about what you read and help you to evaluate the effectiveness of different arguments and from this develop your own observations, opinions and points of view that will help with any conclusions that you make in your answers to the AO2 questions that arise.

The Quilliam Foundation's Majid Nawaz campaigns against extremism. Quilliam is a research and advisory organisation, not a representative one. High profile political debate host Mehdi Hasan confronts politicians, popular amongst young Muslims tuning in to Al-Jazeera. He expresses his views with passion, but is not representing anyone.

Ayyan Ali Hirsi, an ex-Muslim, wrote about her experiences of practising conservative Islam as a youth and of being abused by male Muslims in her book, *Heretic*. Ziauddin Sardar wrote about his personal experiences of life and grappling with faith from a sceptical, reformist viewpoint in his book, *Desperately seeking Paradise*. These are the views of individuals and do not represent Muslims in general, although they may bring common experiences to light. There are fewer books from committed, conservative Muslims available to represent their thoughts and feelings about life in modern Britain, making it difficult to get an accurate and representative picture.

Hanif Quereshi produced films which have created images in popular imagination. His film, *East is East*, portrayed life in Manchester for a mixed family and their Muslim children facing arranged marriages which they did not want. The film is a comedy but also raises serious issues around arranged marriage and tensions between generations. In *My Son the Fanatic*, Quereshi brings to light how a young Muslim man, Farid, gets involved in political Islam against the wishes of his father, who is increasingly Westernised. Comedy in part, the film exposes how the young can be radicalised by reaction against what they see as sexual immorality and unfairness towards Muslims.

Documentaries about the role of Islam and Science by Jim Khalili; about the history of the Prophet and early Islam by Rageh Omar; and about the Art and Architecture of Islam by Waldemar Januszczak represent an image of the history of Islam which has contributed to the development of civilisation. These programmes challenge the view that Islam is always represented in a negative light.

As Muslims respond to the challenges of the modern world, make new interpretations to address fresh issues, and respond to new technology such as the Internet, the practice of their faith may change. An accurate representation at one time may become inaccurate at another. Reformists argue that Islam must change and that representing problems and issues is a good way to enact it. The more people are aware the more they can be challenged. Media can be used as a campaigning tool, rather than an impartial observer. Others suggest this shows bias and the media should more fairly reflect the lives of Muslims, including those who peacefully practise a conservative version of Islam. Perhaps Islam cannot be accurately represented because Muslims themselves take so many views they cannot agree on what is an accurate representation. It is not just the media to blame.

Key questions

In what ways can Islam be represented in Britain today?

Do Islamic organisations represent the views of Muslims well?

How do newspapers, films and television represent Islam? Is this fair and balanced?

AO2 Activity

List some conclusions that could be drawn from the AO2 reasoning from the above text; try to aim for at least three different possible conclusions. Consider each of the conclusions and collect brief evidence to support each conclusion from the AO1 and AO2 material for this topic. Select the conclusion that you think is most convincing and explain why it is so. Try to contrast this with the weakest conclusion in the list, justifying your argument with clear reasoning and evidence.

Study tip

There are two aspects to this debate: accuracy and representation. Pinpointing definitions of both can be complex but is essential to answer both parts of the question. Confident critical analysis will not be afraid to challenge the terms and offer alternative definitions. Criticism will bring to light different points of view. Do not be afraid to disagree where you find arguments that you think are wrong, provided you also show that you are aware of them and understand them.

AO2 Developing skills

It is now important to consider the information that has been covered in this section; however, the information in its raw form is too extensive and so has to be processed in order to meet the requirements of the examination. This can be achieved by practising more advanced skills associated with AO2. For assessment objective 2 (AO2), which involves 'critical analysis' and 'evaluation' skills, we are going to focus on different ways in which the skills can be demonstrated effectively, and also refer to how the performance of these skills is measured (see generic band descriptors for A2 [WJEC] AO2 or A Level [Eduqas] AO2).

▶ **Your final task for this theme is:** Below are listed **three basic conclusions drawn from an evaluation of how online media affect Muslims today**. Your task is to develop each of these conclusions by identifying briefly the strengths (referring briefly to some reasons underlying it) but also an awareness of challenges made to it (these may be weaknesses depending upon your view).

1. Muslims are able to find out a vast wealth of knowledge on traditional matters previously unavailable or difficult to access. They can look up complete collections of hadith in translation and the rulings of scholars from around the world. They can make links with individuals and groups who may not have a presence locally, such as Sufis.

2. Muslim women can help gain empowerment from the use of online resources. They can study courses, gaining education where going out often might be difficult. They can also research Islam for themselves, rather than learn it from men, and challenge outdated ideas about gender.

3. Muslims can find answers to new questions quickly. What might have taken many years of discussion from scholars can now be debated online, and answers given from scholars as fatwas in minutes. However, Muslims may also suffer from not knowing which are authentically within mainstream Islamic traditions. They may also be vulnerable to radicalisation from groups who deliberately target young Muslims with propaganda online.

The result should be three very competent paragraphs that could form a final conclusion of any evaluation.

When you have completed the task, refer to the band descriptors for A2 (WJEC) or A Level (Eduqas) and in particular have a look at the demands described in the higher band descriptors towards which you should be aspiring. Ask yourself:

- Is my answer a confident critical analysis and perceptive evaluation of the issue?
- Is my answer a response that successfully identifies and thoroughly addresses the issues raised by the question set?

Key skills

Analysis involves:

Identifying issues raised by the materials in the AO1, together with those identified in the AO2 section, and presents sustained and clear views, either of scholars or from a personal perspective ready for evaluation.

This means:

- That your answers are able to identify key areas of debate in relation to a particular issue
- That you can identify, and comment upon, the different lines of argument presented by others
- That your response comments on the overall effectiveness of each of these areas or arguments.

Evaluation involves:

Considering the various implications of the issues raised based upon the evidence gleaned from analysis and provides an extensive detailed argument with a clear conclusion.

This means:

- That your answer weighs up the consequences of accepting or rejecting the various and different lines of argument analysed
- That your answer arrives at a conclusion through a clear process of reasoning.

T4 Religious practices that shape religious identity

Specification content

Beliefs and practices distinctive of Shi'a Islam. Specific Shi'a interpretations of the Five Pillars.

Key terms

Furu al-din: the practices followed by Shi'a Muslims to enact the Usul al-din

Twelvers: the main branch of Shi'a Islam based on the belief of a succession of twelve Imams after the Prophet

Usul al-din: sometimes called the Pillars of Shi'a Islam or beliefs on which the main Shi'a practices are based

Key quote

Protestantism and Catholicism must not be compared to Sunnism and Shi'ism in the Islamic context as has been done by certain scholars. Sunnism and Shi'ism both go back to the origins of Islam and the very beginning of Islamic history whereas Protestantism is a later protest against the existing Catholic Church and came into being some fifteen hundred years after the foundation of Christianity. (Seyyed Hossein Nasr)

D: Diversity within Islam

Beliefs and practices distinctive of Shi'a Islam

The Shi'a, the party of Ali, are known as the largest minority sect in Islam. It is somewhat misleading to think of Muslims today as being made up of two sects: Shi'a and Sunni. In reality, it is far more complicated.

Within Sunni Islam, there are several sects including Brewlvi, Deobandi and followers of different schools of thought (madhabs). Within Shi'a Islam, there are also many sects, including the Twelvers, the Ismailis and Allawis. Sufi Muslims exist within both Shi'a and Sunni Islam. Salafis sometimes reject Sufi and Shi'a practices as incompatible with Islam, whereas some Sunni Muslims reject Salafis as outside the fold, whereas the Shi'a are considered part of traditional Islam. There are many examples across the world where you might find Shi'a Muslims living in harmony with others, on occasion attending each other's mosques and joining their celebrations. In other cases security issues have caused communities to separate, and Muslims themselves have been victims of terrorist atrocities by other Muslims who disagree with their point of view.

In this chapter, the main Shi'a beliefs will be referred to, particularly those of the Twelvers. Contrasts will be made with others, such as the Ismailis, and with Sunni Islam. You should be aware that you will always find those who follow different interpretations and there is a diversity within as well as between groups.

A Muslim woman using prayer beads.

Despite these differences, if you were to visit a typical Shi'a mosque and compare it to a Sunni mosque, you would see pretty much all the same features. The congregation would pray in almost exactly the same way, following the same Arabic Qur'an and focused on the same Allah, the One God, without any partners, idols or statues. All would believe in judgement and life after death, angels, holy books and Prophets.

Shi'a interpretations of the Five Pillars

Shi'a Muslims have different version of the Five Pillars of Islam. The main Pillars from the perspective of the Twelvers are known as the Usul al-din. These can be further classified as beliefs and practices: Usul al-din beliefs and Furu al-din practices.

The main beliefs on which Shi'a practices are based are:

Tawhid – the oneness of Allah

Adl – the concept that Allah is just

Nubuwwah – belief in Prophets (like the Sunni belief in Risalah)

Imamah – belief in the succession of the Prophet's family as leaders of the Shi'a

Mi'ad – belief in the Day of Judgement and Resurrection in the afterlife (similar to the Sunni belief in Akhirah).

The Shahadah or statement of faith of the Shi'a differs slightly from that of Sunni Muslims. To the Sunni Shahadah the Shi'a add these words: Ali is the guidance of God. This reflects the importance they place on Ali who in their eyes was Muhammad's chosen successor.

The main Pillars of Islam for the Shi'a Twelvers can be seen in the table below. They include the Sunni Five Pillars in a slightly different format, and some extra principles which may apply to many actions. Forbidding evil and promoting good could apply to any Muslim, but in Shi'a Islam these are formularised into Pillars which they must follow.

The Ismaili Pillars are somewhat different in that Ismailis follow their Imam's interpretations, which can vary. Ismailis sometimes see the spiritual aspect of the Pillars as the main point, and the physical aspect as less important. Some Ismailis, therefore, practise the greater fast of avoiding backbiting, swearing and being humble towards others, rather than lesser, physical fast of abstaining from eating and drinking. Nevertheless, they are often very strict in the manner of behaviour, which some may find even more difficult than the physical fast! This is not seen as going against any rule of Islam, but rather a different interpretation of it. In this respect you might find much greater difference between an Ismaili Muslim and a Twelver than a Twelver and a Sunni or Salafi Muslim, who strictly adhere to abstinence from eating and drinking.

Twelver Shi'a Furu al-din	Ismaili Pillars of Faith
Twelvers believe in Tawhid, and the other main beliefs of the Usul al-din.	Tawhid: Ismaili belief in the Oneness of God, together with other Muslims.
Imamah: Belief in the succession of Imams in the family of the Prophet and their particular position in the faith. Twelvers follow their Imams who have power to make decisions and rulings for their followers.	Walayah: Ismaili show love and devotion to God, the missionaries, the Imams and the Prophets. The Ismailis are led by the Aga Khan, their Imam, who guides them in the faith.
Salah, five prayers a day read at three times: before sunrise, in the afternoon and after sunset. (Zuhr and Asr; Maghrib and Isha are combined.)	Salah: the current Imam directs Ismaili followers what form of prayer to follow. This varies from other Shi'a and Sunni Muslims.
Sawm, fasting in Ramadan.	Sawm, being humble and avoiding arrogance and backbiting; fasting in Ramadan.

Key terms

Adl: Divine justice – the concept that Allah is just and will carry out justice in balance over this life and the next

Akhirah: life after death

Asr: prayer read in the afternoon once the shadows lengthen

Imamah: belief in the succession of the Prophet's family as leaders of the Shi'a

Isha: the night time prayer

Maghrib: prayer read after the sun sets

Mi'ad: belief in the Day of Judgement and Resurrection in the afterlife

Nubuwwah: belief in Prophets

Risalah: belief in Prophets or messengers from Allah, some of whom bring a holy book

Salah: five prayers a day, read at three times by Shi'a Muslims

Sawm: fasting in Ramadan

Walayah: Ismaili expression of love and devotion to God, the missionaries, the Imams and the Prophets

Zuhr: prayer read just after mid-day

Key terms

Khums: 20% tax paid to the Imams to distribute to the needy

Sajdah: position in prayer when a Muslim places their forehead on the ground

Twelver Shi'a Furu al-din	Ismaili Pillars of Faith
Zakat, alms for the poor.	Most Ismaili have a form of Zakat payment.
Khums, 20% tax paid to the Imams to distribute to the needy.	Most Ismaili also have a form of Khums payment.
Hajj, pilgrimage to Makkah.	Hajj, visiting the Imam. This can mean going to Makkah, practised by some Ismailis. Others say that Hajj means fleeing from oppression anywhere.
Jihad, struggle.	Jihad, the greater and the lesser struggle.
Amr-bil-Maroof: doing the right thing.	
Nahi Anil Munkar: forbidding what is wrong.	
Tawalla: show love for goodness.	
Tabarra: show hatred for evil and disassociate from it.	

Sunni Muslims have traditions that the Prophet Muhammad sometimes combined the prayers of Zuhr and Asr, mid-day and mid-afternoon, by reading one after the other, when the community were busy in some matters of work or gathering the harvest, to make it easier for them so that religion did not become burdensome. Shi'a follow the same traditions, but usually always read these prayers one after the other at one time. Some Muslims believe this amounts to much the same thing. Others emphasise the difference.

When praying, Shi'a Muslims perform **sajdah**, the point during prayer when the forehead touches the ground, with a small clay tablet placed in front of them. This is made of clay from the ground at Karbala, and Shi'a Muslims place their foreheads on this tablet during the most intense moment of prayer, the sajdah. This shows the importance of the historical events that took place in the early days of Islam.

quickfire

4.1 Name two of the main branches of Shi'a Islam.

AO1 Activity

Make a table to show the main beliefs and practices of Shi'a and Sunni Islam. One column should be headed Shi'a and the other Sunni. When you have completed the table, take two highlighters, each of a different colour. Highlight the similarities in one colour and the differences in another. Finally, discuss how far you think the beliefs are similar and different.

The significance of the historical dispute that gave rise to Shi'a Islam

What could be significant about a place in the desert in the Middle East, where a battle occurred over a thousand years ago? The small place known as Karbala was not known widely beforehand, but after a battle which took place there it became one of the most well-known places in the Islamic world particularly for the side which lost the battle.

It was not the battle itself, of course, that made it so famous, but the theological importance which created Islam's biggest division between the Shi'a and the Sunnis. The two different sides of the Prophet's character: his spiritual meditative side which was emphasised by his companion Ali, and his practical compassionate leadership emphasised by Abu Bakr, symbolise the two different traditions which he left behind when he died.

Specification content

The significance of the historical dispute that gave rise to Shi'a Islam with reference to: the succession of Ali; the death of Hussein and martyrdom.

Karbala

There is disagreement over whether Muhammad appointed anyone as his successor. How the community responded led to a situation in which Muslims became divided. What started with supporters of Ali as opposed to supporters of rival leader Mu'awiyah, became a division about truth and righteous leadership as ordained by God.

The succession of Ali

Ali was one of the Prophet Muhammad's closest companions. Shi'a Muslims believe that Allah inspired Muhammad to appoint Ali as his successor, and that Ali was infallible, that is he did not make mistakes or sin. In the Hadith of the Cloak, Muhammad, Ali and Fatimah were together protected by the Prophet's cloth, which might be interpreted to mean that the Prophet meant for his successors to be his family, since Fatimah was the Prophet's daughter and wife of Ali. Shi'a Muslims associate this with a verse from the Qur'an which refers to the 'family' of the Prophet as those who will continue his mission.

A significant amount of debate originates from an event after the Prophet's last sermon. Muslims gathered at a place called Ghadir Khumm, an oasis in the desert, on around 10 March 632. It was here that Muhammad allegedly said words which meant that he appointed Ali as his successor. These are disputed between Shi'a and Sunni Muslims. Muhammad is supposed to have referred to Ali as 'mawla' or master, in succession to him. Some interpreters say 'mawla' means a relative, supporter, ally, freed slave who converted, or client. Shi'a Muslims claim Muhammad appointed Ali specifically as leader and guardian of the Muslims.

Key quotes

Oh people! Reflect on the Quran and comprehend its verses. Look into its clear verses and do not follow its ambiguous parts, for by Allah, none shall be able to explain to you its warnings and its mysteries, nor shall anyone clarify its interpretation, other than the one that I have grasped his hand, brought up beside myself, and lifted his arm, the one about whom I inform you that whomever I am his master, then Ali is his master; and he is Ali Ibn Abi Talib, my brother, the executor of my will, whose appointment as your guardian and leader has been sent down to me from Allah, the mighty and the majestic. (Saying of Muhammad from the Final Sermon)

Mawla may refer to a client, a patron, an agnate, an affined kinsman, a friend, a supporter, a follower, a drinking companion, a partner, a newly converted Muslim attached to a Muslim and last but not least an ally. Most of these categories have legal implications. In Islamic times, the term mawla mostly referred to Muslim freedmen and freed non-Arabs who attached themselves to Arabs upon their conversion to Islam. (Bernards and Nawas)

Sunnis agree that Ali was a Caliph and leader of the Muslims, a rightly guided person and legitimate leader, but the fourth and not the first Caliph. There is dispute over the appointment of Abu Bakr, another of the companions of Muhammad, as the first leader after his death. At the time of his appointment, Muslims met and agreed it, but Ali was tending to the arrangements for the Prophet's funeral at the time. Nevertheless, Ali accepted Abu Bakr's leadership to avoid splitting the community.

Uthman, third Caliph, was murdered, after which Ali was appointed. This caused disputes because some people felt Ali did not actively chase down Uthman's murderers. This ended in the Battle of Siffin, after arbitration failed. The period is known as the period of the first Fitnah or Islamic civil war, a period which set Muslim against Muslim. Despite winning the Battle of Siffin, many of Ali's supporters were, on the whole, ineffective. Eventually Ali was murdered with a

Key quotes

God's Apostle went out one morning wearing a striped cloak of the black camel's hair that there came Hasan bin Ali. He wrapped him under it, then came Hussein and he wrapped him under it along with the other one Hasan. Then came Fatimah and he took her under it, then came Ali and he also took him under it and then said: God desires to take away any uncleanliness from you, O people of the household, and purify you. (Hadith of Prophet Muhammad)

The Qur'an 33:33

Stay quietly in your houses, and make not a dazzling display, like that of the former Times of Ignorance; and establish regular Prayer, and give regular Charity; and obey Allah and His Messenger. And Allah only wishes to remove all abomination from you, ye members of the Family, and to make you pure and spotless. (Yusuf Ali)

quickfire

4.2 According to the tradition, who came under the cloak?

quickfire

4.3 At which event do Shi'a Muslims regard Muhammad as having appointed Ali as his successor?

Key quote

For centuries, Muslim philosophers considered Ali's sayings – such as 'I have never seen a thing except to have seen God before it' and 'If the veils were to be removed from the mysteries of the world, it would not add to my certitude' – to be proof of his supreme metaphysical understanding. His widely known saying 'Look at what is said and not at who has said it' summarises a main characteristic of Islamic thought. (Seyyed Hossein Nasr)

Key term

Metaphysical: abstract thought about the principles of being

quickfire

4.4 What happened at Karbala?

poisoned sword by one of his Muslim opponents, whilst saying his prayers during Ramadan in the mosque at Kufa. The poison took two days to kill him.

Shi'a believe that regardless of the turn of events, Ali was the rightful leader and his death was wrong. They believe that if they accept what happened then this is like accepting wrongfulness and going against God's will. Regardless of time and changes since, Shi'a look back on this as injustice and believe they should always promote what is right, and forbid evil, which therefore has a special place in the Pillars of Shi'a Islam. Many Sunnis also hold Ali in very high regard and many Sufis see him as narrator of many of the most beautiful and spiritual hadith traditions, but they do not go as far as the Shi'a in upholding his claim to be the rightful successor to the Prophet.

Whilst the historical dispute is the best known difference over Ali, his sayings and importance as a Saint in Shi'a Islam and as an inspiration to many in different branches of the faith remain to be told. The Shi'a scholar and philosopher Seyyed Hossein Nasr emphasises the importance of Ali's sayings to all Muslims, regardless of sect, as spiritual inspiration.

The death of Hussein

Hussein was the son of Ali and his wife Fatimah, Muhammad's daughter. Together with his brother Hasan, he used to play with their grandfather Muhammad during childhood. One tradition reports how Muhammad thought play was so important that he continued playing with his grandchildren throughout the afternoon and missed one prayer and the even the next, because he did not want to disturb the children's enjoyment. He even let Hasan and Hussein climb on his back whilst he performed Sajdah.

When Ali became Caliph, not everyone accepted him. His biggest opponent was Mu'awiyah who was governor of Syria. Mu'awiyah and Hasan faced off in various skirmishes as well as making temporary truces. Mu'awiyah's son Yazid succeeded him as Caliph. Yazid demanded Hussein give allegiance to him. Many supporters urged Hussein to oppose Yazid and provide guidance as an Imam. Hussein and Yazi's troops under commander Ubaydullah ibn Ziyad faced off at Karbala. Ubaydullah ordered Hussein to declare allegiance to Yazid, and when he did not he cut off access to the water supply. Battle erupted at Karbala on the 10th of the Islamic month of Muharram 680. In the fighting, men, women and children alongside Hussein were massacred and their bodies mutilated.

A brutal civil war followed which culminated in the establishment of the Umayyad Caliph and the suppression of the supporters of Hussein. However, the events at Karbala were not forgotten. This date is known as Ashura which is marked by special commemorations by Shi'a Muslims. Some Shi'a visit Hussein's grave as a place of pilgrimage.

Passion plays are enacted to show the events of Karbala. Shi'as worldwide make processions and listen to speeches. Some practise self-flagellation to experience some of the pain and suffering that Hussein went through. The events at Karbala are seen as important because no matter how small the group and impossible the situation, the Shi'a did not compromise their position. They regard Hussein as standing up for the right and the true and they too will stand up for the same in today's world, no matter how hard that is.

Ashura mourning for the martyrdom of Imam Hussein.

Key quote

The concept of martyrdom is deeply rooted in the theology of the Shi'a sect. There is a long-standing belief that giving one's life for a just cause is a noble act that is rewarded in heaven. But martyrdom and heroism in the early days of Islam were not the exclusive domain of men. Almost all the descendants of the Prophet – men as well as women, and children – took to the front in the Battle of Karbala to fight against the Caliph Mu'awiyah, whom they accused of usurping power. (Haleh Afshar)

Martyrdom

There are martyrs throughout history and throughout religions. Martyrs are people who have been killed by other people because of their faith. This could be in battle, through murder or some other way. A martyr is killed by another, which is different from the concept of suicide, where a person kills themselves. Suicide is generally regarded as forbidden in Islam. A Shahid is a martyr in Islam, and Muslims who have been killed in battle are commonly referred to as a Shahid or martyr.

Key quote

The Qur'an 3:140

If a wound hath touched you, be sure a similar wound hath touched the others. Such days (of varying fortunes) We give to men and men by turns: that Allah may know those that believe, and that He may take to Himself from your ranks Martyr-witnesses (to Truth). And Allah loveth not those that do wrong. (Yusuf Ali)

Various traditions suggests martyrs are highly regarded in Islam. Some Muslims regard martyrs as having given everything for Islam and will be elevated to heaven automatically, with all their sins overlooked, and granted a place in the highest seventh heaven in paradise. Another tradition is that martyrs are given 72 virgins in paradise. These references are largely metaphorical and give images to rewards in the afterlife which many Muslims believe cannot be fully understood by people in this world. A person may end their life as a martyr and be regarded as such by others, but no one can be sure if they will be regarded as such by the ultimate judge, Allah.

Caliph Ali died when he was assassinated by a poisoned sword during prayer in a mosque in the middle of Ramadan. His death is regarded as a martyrdom. Hussein and his supporters' death at Karbala are regarded as martyrdom which have inspired Shi'a Muslims to this day. In history, Shahid Awwal was known as one of the first Shi'a martyrs. He converted from Sunni to Shi'a Islam but was accused of disrespecting Aisha, wife of the Prophet, and others, as well as drunkenness. He is said to have been imprisoned, beheaded, crucified and stoned as a martyr.

In the Iran–Iraq war martyrdom was encouraged by the Iranian authorities in their war against the Iraqi regime of Saddam Hussain. The graveyard of Behesht-e Zahra holds the graves of many Shi'a martyrs. They are revered and passion plays take place there in a beautified park to commemorate their sacrifice.

Haleh Afshar points out the position of women in the early days of Islam and their participation in fighting and conflict. In the days of the Prophet, Sumayyah bint Khayyat was executed for her conversion to Islam, becoming the first female martyr.

Key term

Shahid: a martyr in Islam. Muslims who have been killed in battle are commonly referred to as a Shahid or martyr

The tomb of Imam Hussein, Karbala

Key quote

Female descendants of the Prophet not only took part in battles but also made history by denouncing Mu'awiyah and publicly declaring the right of the descendants of the Prophet to lead the Ummah, community of Muslims. There was nothing quiet, veiled, absent, or enclosed in the private domain about these women in the golden days of Islam. (Haleh Afshar)

Five are regarded as martyrs: They
are those who die because of plague,
abdominal disease, drowning or a
falling building, and the martyrs
who die whilst they are following
Allah's cause. (Hadith of Prophet
Muhammad)

quickfire

4.5 What does Tahir ul-Qadri teach about
suicide?

Specification content

Beliefs about the Imam.

*Iranian reformist Imam
Mohammad Khatami*

Key term

Ahl al-Bayt: the descendants of the
Prophets who form the Imams of the
Shi'a

Some Muslims argue that the concept of martyrdom has been changed in modern
times and is abused by those who have become involved in modern political
conflict, some of whom have committed suicide bombings in the name of Islam.
There is no denying that such people have claimed to be doing so for Islam and
believed what they were doing very strongly, but at the same time are rejected by
the majority of Muslims. The Internet contains many sayings, supposed fatwas
and other traditions suggesting that Jihad contains so much reward that all sins
may be forgiven, sometimes enticing one or two Muslims into thinking they can
gain a place in paradise by committing such crimes. The Iran–Iraq war worsened
this trend, which some see as starting with the Japanese kamikaze pilots of World
War Two. Some Muslims in Israel continued to use suicide, as did the Taleban
in Afghanistan and Daesh or 'ISIS' in Syria. The Sufi Islamic scholar Muhammad
Tahir-ul-Qadri, denounces all forms of suicide wherever a Muslim may be, because
suicide breaks Allah's sacred command to respect all life and to allow only Allah to
take it away. To take one's own life is seen as eliminating the possibility of paradise
rather than attaining it.

Beliefs about the Imam

An Imam is a prayer leader in Islam. This term means different things to different
Muslims. To some Muslims, it simply means the person at the front who is reciting
the prayers out aloud, when joined by a few others. This could be at home, in a
quiet corner or in a mosque. Any person able to recite, including people who might
have ordinary jobs in other fields, could be an Imam. They might be an Imam just
for that one prayer.

Nevertheless, even for this position, there are some requirements. The leader
should know how to recite the prayers properly, because to recite with errors of
pronunciation means the Qur'an could be recited with a different meaning and the
word of Allah could not be changed. Furthermore, communities gossip and talk:
if the leader was known to cheat or lie or have affairs, then others might say that
their moral qualities fall short of someone who should be setting a good example if
they are going to lead prayers.

Many Sunni Muslims go further. There are training colleges for Imams in different
schools of thought, which teach them how to perform prayers and answer
questions according to the teachings of that sect. The Imam would often give
an oath of loyalty to a Shaykh who is revered for their superior knowledge. Sufi
Muslims in particular take this oath.

Shi'a Muslims go one step further. Following the struggle of Ali and Hussein,
they believe that the righteous leaders of the people are Imams and they must
come from the blood line of the family of the Prophet, not any educated person.
Following the spiritual traditions of Ali, the Shi'a Imams stress the importance of
the right and the true. They are said to be guiding the people and have particular
powers to issue teachings which the Shi'a should follow, and not make up their
own, differing interpretations.

During the time of the Abbasid Caliphate, Imam Jafar al-Sadiq increased the
importance of the Imams. The Shi'a who were at times persecuted banded
together around their Imams who were trusted with authority to make decisions
on all laws. The party of Ali delivered Imams for every age, and these Imams
became known as **Ahl al-Bayt**. Shi'a only accept hadith collections passed on
through the family of Ahl-al-Bayt, which means that some of their hadiths are the
same and some slightly different from the Sunnis.

The Imams are thought not to err in their interpretations. The Imams are not
Prophets and do not have the power to receive revelations, but they do possess the
insight to interpret the hidden, spiritual teachings within the Qur'an and hadith
and make them understandable to the people. The Shi'a believe that they would

not have been left without any guidance at all after the last Prophet. In making interpretations, they may use Aql, reasoning, to a greater degree than Sunni Imams, to interpret the original teachings to match the needs of the people for modern world situations.

Just as Muhammad is known as the last Prophet and was a perfect example, Shi'a believe that Ali was the perfect man. Shi'a Imams do not have any supernatural power, but are thought to be infallible due to their absolute, unquestioning faith in God and their high moral conduct. The people are asked to obey the Imams absolutely so it follows that Shi'a must believe that their Imams are right, otherwise there might be dissent and difference of opinion rather than obedience. The Qur'an 33:33, quoted on page 153, refers to Muhammad and his family, which Shi'a Muslims regard as justification through divine revelation that their Imams, from the family of Muhammad, should be followed in what they tell their people to do.

Mahdi (occultation)

According to various traditions, in the run up to the Day of Judgement, a figure called the Mahdi will appear in earth. Isa will return and join forces with the Mahdi to defeat the Dajjal, the Antichrist. Isa (Jesus) will slay the Dajjal, and unite humankind in a short reign of justice and peace after the great upheaval, just before the end of days. This reign, to Twelvers, will be like a pure Islamic community and society.

Various signs will appear which will show that the Mahdi is about to appear. These include:

- The red death, which means death through spilling blood in war and violence, will kill a third of humanity.
- The white death, which means death by disease and plague, will kill another third.
- Muslims will be false and show their outward identity but neglect their inner faith.
- There will be a great conflict in Syria which will destroy this land.

To the Twelver Shi'a, the Mahdi is the twelfth in the line of their Imams. He was on earth and went into occultation, to return or reappear towards the end of time. Different Shi'a have different opinions on this; some believe he was the seventh Imam and some do not believe in the theory of occultation at all.

Twelver Shi'a claim their Imam, Muhammad al-Hasan al-Askari, is the promised Mahdi. He came from Samarra in central Asia. He went into occultation around 873, but continued to be contacted by deputies for a while. In 939 the major period of occultation began. During the period since, the Shi'a Imams are only really guiding their people because of the absence of the Mahdi; they do not claim equality with him and he will return to earth in the future to bring forth peace and justice on a level that it is not possible for us to reach beforehand.

Key Quote

If there were but one day left until the end of life, God would elongate that day until He sent a man from my household. His name will be the same as my name. He will fill the earth with fairness and justice, replacing the oppression and tyranny that the world is full of. (Hadith of Prophet Muhammad)

quickfire

4.6 What distinguishes the Ahl-al-Bayt?

Specification content
Mahdi (occultation).

Key terms

Dajjal: the Antichrist, a one-eyed monster who will cause terrible suffering on earth before being defeated by the Mahdi and Isa

Mahdi: a saviour type figure who will appear on earth at the time of the second coming of Isa to defeat evil and reunite people in a reign of justice and peace

Key quotes

People will flee from the Mahdi, as sheep flee from the shepherd. Later, people will begin to look for a purifier. But since they can find none to help them but him, they will begin to run to him. (Hadith of Prophet Muhammad)

When matters are entrusted to the Mahdi, Allah will raise the lowest part of the world for him, and lower the highest places. So much that he will see the whole world as if in the palm of his hand. (Hadith of Prophet Muhammad)

Specification content
Pilgrimage.

Kashan Shrine, Iran

quickfire

4.7 List the five most holy places according to Shi'a Imam Jafar al-Sadiq.

Key quote

Peace be on Hussein, who gave his life as a martyr in the way of Allah. He underwent unknown hardships. He was surrounded by a circle of sorrow and grief and killed as a hostage by savage murderers. Peace be on him, a hero and faithful follower of Allah! He faced danger yet was just and fair. (Imam Jafar al-Sadiq)

Key terms

Arba'een: pilgrimage to Imam Hussein's tomb at Karbala, 40 days after the Day of Ashura

Bid'ah: innovations or changes to God's divinely revealed religion

Mawakibs: stalls for pilgrims providing free food and services along the road to Karbala

Pilgrimage

Shi'a Muslims, like their Sunni counterparts, perform the Hajj pilgrimage to Makkah and regard the holy places in Saudi Arabia as sacred pilgrimage destinations. Shi'a also revere the tombs of many of their Imams and visit particular sites which have significance in their history. In this regard Shi'a and Sufi Muslims are quite similar: Sufis also visit the tombs of their holy Shaykhs whom, like Shi'a, they also regard to offer guidance which should be accepted without question. Sufi Muslims respect holy tombs and visit them to respect their faithful departed, remembering their examples which help to guide and inspire them today. Salafi Muslims, by contrast, reject these practices which they claim are acts of Bid'ah, innovations or changes to God's divinely revealed religion.

Imam Ali Mosque, Najaf, Iraq

Ali was regarded as the first legitimate Caliph by Shi'a and was killed whilst praying in a mosque. In the Imam Ali Mosque in Najaf, his tomb together with the tombs of Prophet Adam and Prophet Nuh (Noah) are venerated.

The sixth Shi'a Imam, Jafar al-Sadiq, taught that the Imam Ali Mosque was the third most holy place after Makkah and Madinah. He said that the fourth was the Imam Hussein shrine in Karbala and the fifth the tomb of Fatimah in Qom, Iran. Following the teachings of Imam Jafar, Shi'a pilgrimages to these sites increased over the years till today when over ten million Shi'a visit the mosque in Najaf annually.

Imam Hussein Shrine, Karbala, Iraq

This mosque contains not only Hussein's grave but also those of the others believed by Shi'a Muslims to have been martyred at Karbala. It was said by Imam Jafar al-Sadiq that every night the angels Jibril and Michael visit the grave of Imam Hussein. Karbala is thought to be a sacred land which will form a beautiful valley in paradise. Up to a million Shi'a pilgrims visit the shrine at the time of Ashura, the time of Hussein's death, each year.

Following the Day of Ashura, a 40-day period of mourning is held commemorating the deaths at Karbala. During the 40 days Shi'a Muslims around the world join speeches and events at their local mosques to learn more about these events. At the end of the 40 days, pilgrims walk on foot to Karbala, to visit the tomb of Imam Hussein.

This is known as the Arba'een pilgrimage. Along the way, Mawakibs are set up to provide all the services pilgrims could need including food, water and medicines. These are provided free of charge. The first pilgrims to Hussein's tomb were said to be a Sahaba or companion of Muhammad and his surviving relatives, after which the pilgrimage has been performed each year. The sixth Shi'a Imam, Jafar al-Sadiq, instructed followers to visit the shrine, say special prayers and make their commitment to follow the ideals of the martyr Hussein, who stood up for justice and truth. A translation of part of the Ziyarah prayer can be seen in the key quote by Imam Jafar al-Sadiq.

Holy sites in Makkah and Madinah

The Al-Baqi graveyard in Madinah contains the graves of many Shi'a Imams and those of Fatimah, mother of Ali, and possibly also Fatimah, daughter of Muhammad. The Jannatul Mualla cemetery in Makkah contains the graves of many of Muhammad's relatives, including Khadijah, his first wife.

Visits to graves in Saudi Arabia sometimes bring Shi'a and Sufi Muslims into conflict with the Saudi authorities, who promote Salafi teachings that graves should not be marked. They believe that visiting the graves has become a form of worship, and therefore a form of shirk, association of another thing besides Allah.

Saudi Arabia has even bulldozed some historical remains to prevent them being visited by pilgrims.

Imam Reza Mosque, Mashhad, Iran

The Imam Reza Mosque contains the tomb of Ali ar-Ridha, the eighth in the line of Twelver Shi'a Imams. He became a martyr by being poisoned by followers of rival Caliph Ma'mun. The mosque has been expanded to include a theology college for training Imams, a museum and library. Over twenty million Muslims visit Mashhad each year, making it the most important place of Shi'a pilgrimage. During Ramadan, an outdoor Iftaar is held to share food at the end of the day's fasting, attended by tens of thousands of people as a kind of street party, possibly the largest Iftaar in the world.

Pilgrims visiting the holy tombs perform Ziyarah. This ritual involves making ghusul or wudu beforehand, which means ritual ablution, so that the pilgrim enters the holy site in a state of purity out of respect. A pilgrim should wear clean, new clothes and walk slowly and peacefully towards the shrine with head bowed in humility. During the walk the pilgrim should develop peacefulness in their mind and heart.

In the sanctum of the shrine, arguments, fighting, backbiting and conflict are forbidden. At the entrance, the pilgrim says a personal prayer to ask permission from the holy Imams of the Ahl al-Bayt to enter the enclosure. The pilgrim says blessings to Allah, to Muhammad and to the Ahl al-Bayt Imams under their breadth, again and again. At first sight of the tomb, the pilgrim praises God by saying Allah Akbar, then recites the special Ziyarah prayer which they will have learned off by heart beforehand, in preparation for the pilgrimage. This is read standing, in a soft and quiet voice, facing the tomb. The words of the Ziyarah were compiled by the Shi'a Imams. It ends with a dua prayer, at which point the pilgrim moves to the head of the tomb and turns to face the Qiblah, which is the direction of prayer towards Makkah.

After the Ziyarah prayer has been completed, the pilgrim reads a special prayer of two rakats and asks Allah to give the reward of the prayer to the Saint. After this, any personal requests may be made of Allah, as well as requests from friends and family which they have asked to be passed on to Allah in the vicinity of the saint's tomb. Finally, the pilgrim ends their ritual by asking Allah to bring forward the return of the Mahdi and the reign of justice and peace which he will bring over all the world.

The tomb of Fatimah, Qom, Iran

Not to be confused with the daughter of Muhammad, this tomb is that of the wife of Imam Ali al-Rida who is buried in Mashhad. A beautiful mosque and theology college was built by Shah Abbas in the early seventeenth century. Qom is regarded as a holy city and nothing is allowed to fly overhead, above the mosque, due to its sanctity.

Sacred tombs in Syria

The Ruqayya Mosque in the Syrian capital, Damascus, and nearby cemetery, contains many graves including that of Bilal, the black slave who was tortured when he converted to Islam and became Muhammad's first Muezzin in Madinah. The Zaynab Mosque, also in Damascus, contains the tomb of Zaynab, daughter of Ali and Fatimah.

> ### Key terms
> Dua: personal prayer
>
> Rakat: unit of standing, bowing and prostrating during Islamic prayer
>
> Ziyarah: pilgrimage to a tomb of a holy person

AO1 Activity

Write a tourist leaflet for Shi'a pilgrims to Karbala and Mashhad. In the leaflet explain the rituals they will be participating in and give instructions about what to do. Add details of interest about the history and significance of the cities visited.

Specification content

Muta (temporary marriage) and
taqiyya (concealing belief).

Key terms

Muta: temporary marriage

Taqiyya: concealing belief

Key quotes

The Qur'an 4:24

Also (prohibited are) women already married, except those whom your right hands possess: Thus hath Allah ordained (Prohibitions) against you: Except for these, all others are lawful, provided ye seek (them in marriage) with gifts from your property,- desiring chastity, not lust, seeing that ye derive benefit from them, give them their dowers (at least) as prescribed; but if, after a dower is prescribed, agree Mutually (to vary it), there is no blame on you, and Allah is All-knowing, All-wise. (Yusuf Ali)

The Qur'an 3:28

Let not the believers Take for friends or helpers Unbelievers rather than believers: if any do that, in nothing will there be help from Allah, except by way of precaution, that ye may Guard yourselves from them. But Allah cautions you (To remember) Himself; for the final goal is to Allah. (Yusuf Ali)

Distinct Shi'a beliefs about other issues

Muta (temporary marriage)

Muta is a temporary marriage agreed by contract with a time limit. It is a form of Nikkah, Islamic marriage. However since the time limit could theoretically be very short, a matter of days, and the Nikkah could be arranged with only two witnesses, then this concept could be used by boyfriends and girlfriends at University for sexual affairs without their parents knowing.

There has long been debate over whether Muta is valid or not. The Qur'an 4:24 appears to suggest all other forms of marriage are lawful, other than those mentioned as prohibited, so some take this to mean it is allowed. The Caliph Mu'awiyah had a Muta temporary marriage. On the other hand, Bukhari records a hadith suggesting the Prophet forbade temporary marriage. Mughal Emperor Akbar listened to debates about it in his hall of religions in Fatepur Sikhri, and decided to allow it during his reign.

Shi'a Imams normally require the bride to be unmarried and a believer in God, such as a Muslim, Christian or Jew. She should not be a young, innocent person who is being taken advantage of. When the marriage is over, the bride should wait for some months before remarrying in case she is pregnant – a practice which is also used in the normal Islamic divorce arrangement.

Despite this, some Shi'a Muslims and many Sunnis, as well as reformists, believe Muta is unacceptable. Zeyno Baran criticises Muta as a form of prostitution, which allows men to marry often but which restricts women to periods of waiting after each marriage ends. The spirit of lasting meaningful relationships is not fulfilled through temporary marriages which can last for only three days. On the other hand, some in Iran, where the practice is legal, argue that it is better to allow Muta because it may reduce illegal prostitution, which is widespread in the country.

Taqiyya (concealing belief)

Taqiyya means concealing belief, even lying if need be, which is permitted to Shi'a Muslims under certain circumstances. For much of history, Shi'a Muslims suffered persecution at the hands of Sunnis, sometimes even a matter of life and death. At such times they were advised by their Imams to hide their faith to save themselves. Muhammad's companions were said to have concealed faith at times to avoid persecution. The Qur'an 3:28 recommends believers to guard themselves against others, is sometimes used as justification for taqiyya.

During the Mihna of Caliph Al-Mamun it was demanded that people believe the Qur'an was written by humans, not God. Some Imams agreed not out of belief but to avoid torture. In the sixteenth century, Muslims were persecuted and fled Spain. To avoid torture and death many practised taqiyya and pretended to be Catholic in public whilst practising Islam in private.

Some regard taqiyya as only reasonable given certain situations. Others say it is selling out and you should stand up for what you believe in. There are different traditions within Shi'a Islam: the events at Karbala when Imam Hussein was martyred for refusing the give allegiance to his opponent suggest speaking the truth even when facing persecution and death is a different option to be respected.

AO1 Developing skills

It is now important to consider the information that has been covered in this section; however, the information in its raw form is too extensive and so has to be processed in order to meet the requirements of the examination. This can be achieved by practising more advanced skills associated with AO1. The exercises that run throughout this book will help you to do this and prepare you for the examination. For assessment objective 1 (AO1), which involves demonstrating 'knowledge' and 'understanding' skills, we are going to focus on different ways in which the skills can be demonstrated effectively, and also refer to how the performance of these skills is measured (see generic band descriptors for A2 [WJEC] AO1 or A Level [Eduqas] AO1).

▶ **Your new task is this:** you will have to write a response under timed conditions to a question requiring an examination or explanation of **Shi'a interpretations of the Pillars of Islam**. This exercise is best done as a small group at first.

1. Begin with a list of indicative content, as you may have done in the previous textbook in the series. It does not need to be in any particular order at first, although as you practise this you will see more order in your lists that reflects your understanding.

2. Develop the list by using one or two relevant quotations. Now add some references to scholars and/or religious writings.

3. Then write out your plan, under timed conditions, remembering the principles of explaining with evidence and/or examples.

When you have completed the task, refer to the band descriptors for A2 (WJEC) or A Level (Eduqas) and in particular have a look at the demands described in the higher band descriptors towards which you should be aspiring. Ask yourself:

- Does my work demonstrate thorough, accurate and relevant knowledge and understanding of religion and belief?
- Is my work coherent (consistent or make logical sense), clear and well organised?
- Will my work, when developed, be an extensive and relevant response which is specific to the focus of the task?
- Does my work have extensive depth and/or suitable breadth and have excellent use of evidence and examples?
- If appropriate to the task, does my response have thorough and accurate reference to sacred texts and sources of wisdom?
- Are there any insightful connections to be made with other elements of my course?
- Will my answer, when developed and extended to match what is expected in an examination answer, have an extensive range of views of scholars/schools of thought?
- When used, is specialist language and vocabulary both thorough and accurate?

Key skills

Knowledge involves:

Selection of a range of (thorough) accurate and relevant information that is directly related to the specific demands of the question.

This means:

- Selecting relevant material for the question set
- Being focused in explaining and examining the material selected.

Understanding involves:

Explanation that is extensive, demonstrating depth and/or breadth with excellent use of evidence and examples including (where appropriate) thorough and accurate supporting use of sacred texts, sources of wisdom and specialist language.

This means:

- Effective use of examples and supporting evidence to establish the quality of your understanding
- Ownership of your explanation that expresses personal knowledge and understanding and NOT just reproducing a chunk of text from a book that you have rehearsed and memorised.

Specification content

Islam as a divided or united religion.

The Shah Mosque, Isfahan

Key quote

Protestantism and Catholicism must not be compared to Sunnism and Shi'ism in the Islamic context as has been done by certain scholars. Sunnism and Shi'ism both go back to the origins of Islam and the very beginning of Islamic history whereas Protestantism is a later protest against the existing Catholic Church and came into being some fifteen hundred years after the foundation of Christianity. (Seyyed Hossein Nasr)

AO2 Activity

As you read through this section try to do the following:

1. Pick out the different lines of argument that are presented in the text and identify any evidence given in support.

2. For each line of argument try to evaluate whether or not you think this is strong or weak.

3. Think of any questions you may wish to raise in response to the arguments.

This Activity will help you to start thinking critically about what you read and help you to evaluate the effectiveness of different arguments and from this develop your own observations, opinions and points of view that will help with any conclusions that you make in your answers to the AO2 questions that arise.

Issues for analysis and evaluation

Islam as a divided or united religion

Divisions within Islam are one of the most hotly debated areas amongst young Muslims today. In a religion which focuses so much on the unity of belief in the one God, Allah, it follows that everything should be standardised and Muslims should agree on all the main points of belief and practice. Around the world, all Muslims are taught to read the same original Qur'an in Arabic and say prayers in the same way, facing Makkah, using those Arabic words from the Qur'an and following the same routine. Muslims fast in Ramadan, celebrate Id (Eid) together, and are commonly identifiable by wearing such features as hijab veils and prayer caps.

However, are Muslims really so united? The reality of human experience is that Muslims, who consider themselves brothers and sisters of other Muslims, find that when they visit another country, or another mosque belonging to a different sect, that there are always some differences. The prayer of a Salafi may contain differences of style from that of a Sunni or Shi'a Muslim, for example. Id (Eid) may sometimes be celebrated on different days. The style of clothing varies greatly with culture. Are these differences insignificant? Or should they be removed so that there is only one standard version of Islam? Or are the differences natural, just as God created the world with different peoples, and should be accepted and celebrated as such?

The Sunni and Shi'a split in the days of early Islam created the biggest division in the religion. That said, Sunni and Shi'a agree that it is quite acceptable to join together and pray, and use each other's mosques, and have done so throughout the centuries. In some areas of the world conflict has created division and separation. In some countries the experience of Muslims is that the sects appear to operate independently from each other with their communities divided.

It is possible to analyse the table of the Pillars of Islam, as interpreted by Shi'a Twelvers and Ismailis, but individuals may disagree as to what extent this shows division. It could be argued that the division between Shi'a and Sunni are insignificant. Or it could be said that divisions are not only great between the two major sects, but also within Shi'a Islam since there are many sub groups such as the Ismailis.

Some Shi'a scholars such as Vali Nasr emphasise the differences between the sects. Where the division started with an argument over who should be the leader or Caliph, this developed into a deeper division. Vali Nasr likens this divide to the division between Protestants and Catholics in the Christian Church. The Sunni, supporters of Abu Bakr, focus on the practical down to earth matters and consider individuals to be able to interpret Islamic teachings. The Shi'a, followers of Ali who focused on the devotional side of faith, considered they needed Imams or interpreters to help understand the inner meaning of Islam.

Key quote

Sunnis believe that the Prophet's successor was succeeding only to his role as leader of the Islamic community and not to his special relationship with God or prophetic calling. Underlying these views is the spiritually egalitarian notion – which in the West would be identified with the 'low church' Protestant variant of Christianity – that all believers are capable of understanding religious truth in a way and to a degree that renders special intermediaries between man and God unnecessary. … Shias believe that the Prophet possessed special spiritual qualities, was immaculate from sin, and could penetrate to the hidden meaning of religious teachings. Shias further believe that Ali and his descendants had these special spiritual qualities too … They could understand and interpret the inner meaning of Islam. (Vali Nasr)

Seyyed Hossein Nasr, another respected Shi'a scholar, whilst recognising differences, disagrees. He rejects the comparison to European Christian religious divisions and claims that Sunni and Shi'a traditions are both genuine interpretations from the very early days of Islam, not a later divide. Nasr emphasises that the core beliefs of Tawhid, Risalah and Akhirah: belief in the oneness of God, Prophethood and the afterlife, are common to all Muslims, and the divisions are negligible.

Fuad Khuri argues that sects and divisions come from the times of power and conquest, essentially against the principles of religion. Powerful rulers used religious authority to impose their will and punishments to control society. In modern, secular society, Islamic sects use moral pressure to keep their adherents loyal, suggesting that a person is a bad Muslim if they fail to live up to a detail of identity expression that the sect demands.

Abdul Hakim Murad, the Cambridge University academic, understands these divisions in terms of the less important matters of identity. He explains that if you want to find differences, you can find hundreds of small details that different scholars have made different Fiqh opinions about, but these are not the important aspects of religion: ihsan, realisation of faith in the heart, is what really matters and what few of those who peddle division talk about.

Key quote

Arguments amongst Muslim organisations in the West, for the most part, tend to be on the level of form of religion, a level of Islam with a small, i, as it were. Sometimes of Imaan, almost never does one hear serious discussions of Ihsan. So the religion is imbalanced in favour of the divisive possibilities of its outward forms, because the heart unifies and the law creates, not disunity, diversity. There are thousands upon thousands upon thousands of Fiqh dalils, each of which can be variously interpreted and provide scope for disagreement. But there is only one heart. (Murad)

Nevertheless, it is difficult to ignore the increasingly bitter, sectarian splits within the Islamic world. The Sunni academic Khaled Abou El Fadl criticises the Salafi sect, in its rejection of diversity. Salafis might respond by claiming that they are upholding the true way of Muhammad and the Salaf, who lived around him and who knew best. Critics reject their claim that they understand what was meant best. Some Muslims have been influenced in recent times by the style of modern political movements, some of which demand extreme loyalty and adherence to a single viewpoint, communicated in mass media which did not exist in centuries gone by. The use of rhetoric and slogans is common. Yet these approaches tend to be peddled by people who are not educated in the traditional Sunni and Shi'a theology colleges of Al-Azhar and Qom.

Shi'a teachings such as muta (temporary marriage) and the role and importance of Imams may be seen as differences which further highlight divisions. Yet at the same time the Shi'a contribution to Islam has interwoven with Sunnis through the generations, as different countries and even different theology colleges have changed hands. Al-Azhar, thought of as the highest Sunni seat of learning, was originally a Shi'a foundation; and until roughly five hundred years ago, Iran was largely Sunni.

Study tip

It is vital for AO2 that you actually discuss arguments and not just explain what someone may have stated. Try to ask yourself, 'was this a fair point to make?', 'is the evidence sound enough?', 'is there anything to challenge this argument?', 'is this a strong or weak argument?' Such critical analysis will help you develop your evaluation skills.

Key quote

Ibn 'Abd al-Wahhab was relentlessly hostile to all forms of intellectualism, mysticism, such as Sufism, and any sectarianism, such as Shi'ism, within Islam, considering all of these to be corrupt innovations that had crept into the religion due to un-Islamic influences. In Ibn 'Abd al-Wahhab's view, Islam was fundamentally at odds with the pluralism, diversity, and richness that emerged in the Islamic civilisation because, in his view, the truth was easily attainable. (El Fadl)

Key term

Ihsan: realisation of faith in the heart

Key questions

What areas should be defined as areas of importance within Islam to judge how far different groups are similar or different?

What are the differences between outward identity and inner realisation of faith?

To what extent has recent politics caused division amongst Muslims or merely reflected older divisions?

Are divisions, however many there are, significant in the lives of Muslims?

AO2 Activity

List some conclusions that could be drawn from the AO2 reasoning from the above text; try to aim for at least three different possible conclusions. Consider each of the conclusions and collect brief evidence to support each conclusion from the AO1 and AO2 material for this topic. Select the conclusion that you think is most convincing and explain why it is so. Try to contrast this with the weakest conclusion in the list, justifying your argument with clear reasoning and evidence.

Specification content

The extent to which Shi'a is a unique
form of Islam.

Key quotes

While Sunni jurists tended to emphasise and exhibit deference to the four Caliphs … Shi'i jurists heavily relied on the teachings of the infallible imams, all of whom were the descendants of Ali, the fourth Caliph and the Prophet's cousin, and his wife, Fatimah, the Prophet's daughter. **(El Fadl)**

Setting the Shia apart from the Sunni most emphatically, however, is the great feast of mourning, remembrance, and atonement that is Ashura. From its earliest days, Shiism has been defined by the witness that it bears to the moral principles of Islam – a witness whose greatest public expression takes place in and through the rituals that remind the community of the special status of the imams. **(Vali Nasr)**

AO2 Activity

As you read through this section try to do the following:

1. Pick out the different lines of argument that are presented in the text and identify any evidence given in support.

2. For each line of argument try to evaluate whether or not you think this is strong or weak.

3. Think of any questions you may wish to raise in response to the arguments.

This Activity will help you to start thinking critically about what you read and help you to evaluate the effectiveness of different arguments and from this develop your own observations, opinions and points of view that will help with any conclusions that you make in your answers to the AO2 questions that arise.

The extent to which Shi'a is a unique form of Islam

The word unique means one and only, something that is unparalleled elsewhere. This suggests that the Shi'a sect is different from other Islamic groups, that it is one group and that the differences cannot be found amongst other Muslims.

The party of Ali, the Shi'a, cannot be understood without reference to the early division over who had the right to be Caliph or leader of the Muslims. Whereas Sunnis follow the first three Caliphs, Shi'a emphasise the importance of the Imams. Does this mean that the Shi'a are unique, or simply that there is a difference in emphasis?

Sufi Muslims, many of whom come from a Sunni background, give an oath of loyalty to their Shaykh and follow what he says without question. The Shaykh has been given authority, passed down from Shaykh to Shaykh, which can be traced all the way back to the Prophet. The Shaykh emphasises the mystical side of Islam, which is the focus of Sufi zikr rituals, in remembrance of Allah. Many of the hadith traditions quoted by Sufis come from Ali, the same as used by the Shi'a. There is a difference: Sufi Shaykhs need not be from the bloodline of the Prophet, whereas Shi'a Imams must be from his family. The differences between Sufi and Shi'a might be less in these ways than between Salafi and Sufi.

Shaykh Loftollah Mosque, Isfahan

Nevertheless, the events at Karbala remain central to Shi'a religious practice in the ceremonies held on 10th Muharram and in the subsequent pilgrimage to Karbala, the Arba'een. A few Sunnis, Christians and non-religious people also join Arba'een, which is open to all. But the ritual itself is unparalleled by other Muslims. By contrast, Ziyarah rituals, undertaken by people who visit the tombs of holy people, are undertaken by others, particularly Sunni Muslims in India and Pakistan.

Vali Nasr considers the Ashura commemoration unique to the Shi'a: a remembrance of the tragedy and injustice and Karbala which give Shi'a Muslims their distinct focus on upholding the rights of their cause. Some Shi'a practice self-flagellation to share the feeling of suffering that the early martyrs felt. Fasting is also undertaken. Yet many other Muslims and people of other religions also fast, and many early Christian ascetics lived lives of poverty and devotion, which helped them to focus their mind of purifying thoughts of selfishness and focusing on God. The extent to which Ashura is celebrated could be said to be unique in the religious world, but not all of the practices are.

Certain other aspects of Shi'a belief and practice may be debated. Amr-bil-Maroof: doing the right thing; Nahi Anil Munkar: forbidding what is wrong; Tawalla: showing love for goodness and Tabarra: show hatred for evil and disassociate from it, are all particular to Shi'a Pillars of Islam. However, these are not alien to Sunni Muslims: they would largely agree with them in principle, just they do not have such a formalised version. Khums, the poor tax, is unique to the Shi'a; but poor taxes in general, acts of Sadaqah, and forms of Zakat, are common to both. What might outwardly seem different might actually be quite similar.

Study tip

It is important for AO2 that you include the views of scholars and/or schools of thought when formulating your response to a particular contention, as well as from more current scholars. However, make sure that the views you use are relevant to the point that you are making. Your ability to use such views in an appropriate way would distinguish a high level answer from one that is simply a general response.

There are many beautiful mosques and Islamic complexes in Iran, mostly built in the time of the Safavid dynasty in the sixteenth and seventeenth centuries. Some of these demonstrate almost unparalleled beauty and distinctiveness in the Islamic world. The Blue Mosque in Isfahan, for example, has a most unusual decorated dome representing the universe, perfectly aligned with ever smaller circles rising to the top where a pin hole of sunlight enters the dark space below, symbolising the guidance of Allah, a light in the darkness. However, it may be said that all pieces of art are unique and distinctive: the Chinese Sunni mosque of Xian, built in traditional Chinese style and influenced by carved serpents of the eastern tradition, is equally beautiful in a different way and equally unique.

The answer to the question ultimately depends on what importance is given to the differences between the traditions. If it is felt essential to emphasise a key feature, such as Ashura, which cannot be found in the same way in Sunni Islam, then Shi'a Islam should be regarded as unique. On the other hand, if it is felt that all the key principles are common to all Muslims, then it may be said that the different branches are merely different expressions of the same, common faith.

Key questions

What does the word unique mean when applied to religious sects?

Are there any aspects of Shi'a devotion which cannot be found in any other religious tradition, Muslim or non-Muslim?

To what extent are Shi'a and Sufi Muslims similar and to what extent different?

AO2 Activity

List some conclusions that could be drawn from the AO2 reasoning from the above text; try to aim for at least three different possible conclusions. Consider each of the conclusions and collect brief evidence to support each conclusion from the AO1 and AO2 material for this topic. Select the conclusion that you think is most convincing and explain why it is so. Try to contrast this with the weakest conclusion in the list, justifying your argument with clear reasoning and evidence.

Key skills Theme 4

The fourth theme has tasks that consolidate your AO2 skills and focus these skills for examination preparation.

Key skills

Analysis involves:

Identifying issues raised by the materials in the AO1, together with those identified in the AO2 section, and presents sustained and clear views, either of scholars or from a personal perspective ready for evaluation.

This means:

- That your answers are able to identify key areas of debate in relation to a particular issue

- That you can identify, and comment upon, the different lines of argument presented by others

- That your response comments on the overall effectiveness of each of these areas or arguments.

Evaluation involves:

Considering the various implications of the issues raised based upon the evidence gleaned from analysis and provides an extensive detailed argument with a clear conclusion.

This means:

- That your answer weighs up the consequences of accepting or rejecting the various and different lines of argument analysed

- That your answer arrives at a conclusion through a clear process of reasoning.

AO2 Developing skills

It is now important to consider the information that has been covered in this section; however, the information in its raw form is too extensive and so has to be processed in order to meet the requirements of the examination. This can be achieved by practising more advanced skills associated with AO2. The exercises that run throughout this book will help you to do this and prepare you for the examination. For assessment objective 2 (AO2), which involves 'critical analysis' and 'evaluation' skills, we are going to focus on different ways in which the skills can be demonstrated effectively, and also refer to how the performance of these skills is measured (see generic band descriptors for A2 [WJEC] AO2 or A Level [Eduqas] AO2).

▶ **Your new task is this:** you will have to write a response under timed conditions to a question requiring an evaluation of **Muta (temporary marriage)**. This exercise is best done as a small group at first.

1. Begin with a list of indicative arguments or lines of reasoning, as you may have done in the previous textbook in the series. It does not need to be in any particular order at first, although as you practise this you will see more order in your lists, in particular by way of links and connections between arguments.

2. Develop the list by using one or two relevant quotations. Now add some references to scholars and/or religious writings.

3. Then write out your plan, under timed conditions, remembering the principles of evaluating with support from extensive, detailed reasoning and/or evidence.

When you have completed the task, refer to the band descriptors for A2 (WJEC) or A Level (Eduqas) and in particular have a look at the demands described in the higher band descriptors towards which you should be aspiring. Ask yourself:

- Is my answer a confident critical analysis and perceptive evaluation of the issue?

- Is my answer a response that successfully identifies and thoroughly addresses the issues raised by the question set?

- Does my work show an excellent standard of coherence, clarity and organisation?

- Will my work, when developed, contain thorough, sustained and clear views that are supported by extensive, detailed reasoning and/or evidence?

- Are the views of scholars/schools of thought used extensively, appropriately and in context?

- Does my answer convey a confident and perceptive analysis of the nature of any possible connections with other elements of my course?

- When used, is specialist language and vocabulary both thorough and accurate?

E: Islam and change

This section covers AO1 content and skills

Sufi philosophical thought about the nature of God and religious experience

Sufis are Muslims who may follow a spiritual path to God. The term Sufis can apply to groups of Muslims, organised into tariqa, or it can apply to individuals who regard themselves as Sufi because they take a spiritual approach to their faith. There have been many famous Sufis. Rumi, a Sufi from Turkey, influences many even today with his bestselling books of poetry which have topped the sales charts for books in recent years in the USA.

Ibn Arabi, a medieval Muslim theologian from Spain, wrote exceptionally deep philosophical works. He talked of the concept: the self-realisation of God, in which a Muslim can realise as a product of their experience and meditation, what God is like. This contrasts the basic repeat and recite the Qur'an approach, which does not place such emphasis on thought and reason.

The Sufi Shrine at Ajmer in India is visited by millions annually and is known as a centre for poor relief. Muslims donate and distribute food daily and the Sufi saint who brought Islam to the area taught and converted people through his Sufi practices, strength of character and storytelling. The poor felt valued and the stories of Islam explained through songs and parables in a language that the people could understand. In this way, the Sufi approach brought Islam to most in South and East Asia and sub-Saharan Africa.

Sufis meditate on the person of Muhammad as a perfect example, and express love for him by celebrating his birthday each year. They also visit the tombs of Sufi saints and remember their example. Sufis aim to experience a vision of Muhammad in their dreams.

Sufi orders practise different rituals from mainstream Shi'a and Sunni Muslims. They gather on Thursday evenings for Zikr meditations, singing of Islamic songs called Qasidas. They meditate with dance into a trance in which they experience the loving reality of God. To Sufis, this is what is special about their practice and is part of their spiritual journey upwards on an arc of ascent through spiritual stations towards heaven. To most severe critics, this is an innovation based on cultural practices which puts them outside the fold of Islam.

The Qutb (Sufi spiritual leader)

The Qutb is a spiritual teacher. Some Muslims believe the Qutb is head of a line of saints. Qutb are particularly important because they have a spiritual connection to God who guides their teachings. The perfection and infallibility of the Prophet is manifested and shown through the Qutb teacher. Another meaning of Qutb is another dimension of axis in the universe. The Qutb is at the centre of the worldview for his followers; the axis of their life. Allah and the spiritual life is, in turn, at the centre of their life, thereby creating an example to inspire others.

The famous Sufi, Ibn Arabi, wrote that there was a hierarchy of spiritual people with one Qutb leader at the top. This does not necessarily mean a person present on earth. The Qutb can be an abstract concept of a being to be imagined. He can be earthly, and in this case it is known as the temporal Qutb. All beings except angels, jinn and a few others pledge allegiance to the Qutb to gain guidance.

For Sufis, the head of a religious order may be referred to as a Qutb. They provide spiritual guidance to the order and they must be obeyed. The Mureed gives an oath of allegiance to the teacher. In practice, the Sufi teacher gains respect through loving and gentle guidance; to order a follower to follow commands which

Specification content

Islam and change – the development and influence on religious belief and practice within Islam of: Sufi philosophical thought about the nature of God and religious experience.

The tomb of Rumi, Konya

Key terms

Mureed: person who gives bayah, an oath of loyalty, to join a Sufi order

Qasidas: Sufi songs

Qutb: spiritual, infallible Sufi leader

Specification content

The Qutb (Sufi spiritual leader).

quickfire

4.8 What is the difference between a Qutb and a Mureed?

Specification content

The role of the teacher.

Key quotes

The Qur'an 60:12

O Prophet! When believing women come to thee to take the oath of fealty to thee, that they will not associate in worship any other thing whatever with Allah, that they will not steal, that they will not commit adultery (or fornication), that they will not kill their children, that they will not utter slander, intentionally forging falsehood, and that they will not disobey thee in any just matter, then do thou receive their fealty, and pray to Allah for the forgiveness (of their sins): for Allah is Oft-Forgiving, Most Merciful. (Yusuf Ali)

The Qur'an 48:18

Allah's Good Pleasure was on the Believers when they swore Fealty to thee under the Tree: He knew what was in their hearts, and He sent down Tranquillity to them; and He rewarded them with a speedy Victory. (Yusuf Ali)

suppress or curtail their life is not the style which Sufis take. The leader, most commonly referred to as a Shaykh, provides love and comfort to the followers and in return they reciprocate with devotion.

The Islamic teacher Sayyid Qutb, referred to elsewhere in this book, should not be confused with the Qutb spiritual teacher – in his case it was his surname, not a title.

The role of the teacher

In the year 7 after Hijrah, known as 7 AH in the Muslim calendar, the Prophet took the city of Makkah in a largely peaceful conquest. Some of the people of Makkah decided to convert to Islam and give allegiance to Muhammad with oaths of bayah. Several women were amongst those

A Sufi teacher and disciple

who gave oaths. As a result, the principle of giving allegiance became accepted and is practised today by Sufis as an oath given by the Mureed, the follower, to the Shaykh. Sufi orders, known as tariqa, have particular ceremonies for the giving of bayah (an oath). Commonly, the Mureed kneels before the Shaykh, who places his hands upon the head of the follower and recites words of the Qur'an. The follower is asked if they willingly and of their own accord are giving obedience to the Shaykh, and they are asked to then recite Surah Fatiah. Fellow Sufis will greet, hug and kiss the new Mureed as if they are a new-born baby welcomed into their family, share the news with other brothers and sisters in their Sufi order and celebrate with a meal at the end of the Sufi gathering.

The Sufi teacher guides the follower to the religious knowledge which, they believe, the ordinary person cannot access. This is similar to the concept of the Imam in Shi'a Islam. The relationship is like that of a servant and master. The servant willingly follows the master's guidance in all matters. The servant gives love and devotion to the master, who in turn feels the servants' needs and adjusts his teachings so they are the guidance required for the station of spiritual development that the Mureed is currently experiencing.

Sufis commonly kiss the hands of their Shaykh and ensure they visit him as regularly as possible. Being in his presence gives them blessings and they ask for his prayers. If the Shaykh requires anything the Mureed will jump to supply it, be it food or water, and offer it first to the Shaykh before anyone else. Shaykhs are

A Sufi shrine at Ajmer, India

often humble and shun gifts and luxuries. It is more common for the Shaykh to ask Mureeds for spiritual offerings, such as to read particular extra devotions, or to live a humble life, or to help with poor dues at the Shaykh's spiritual centre.

Some Muslims regard Sura 60:12 as a description of an event around the time of the Treaty of Hudaybiyyah during the life of the Prophet. They argue this is not an instruction for Muslims to follow today, and that it is not acceptable to give oaths to Shaykhs. Their viewpoint is that this elevates the role of Shaykh above that of an ordinary human being who makes mistakes just like anyone else, and that the only being worthy of unquestioning allegiance is Allah.

The use of parables

The Qur'an and hadith contain numerous parables which help Muslims to understand things which might otherwise be unintelligible to human minds. The Qur'an itself states that some verses are literal and others allegorical. One Islamic tradition is that each verse of the Qur'an has seven layers of meaning, and the hearer may reach a different layer of meaning according to their level of spiritual enlightenment. For centuries Sufi teachers used parables as a means of telling others about Islam, a form of Dawah, to make the teaching accessible.

Key quotes

The Qur'an 3:7

He it is Who has sent down to thee the Book: In it are verses basic or fundamental (of established meaning); they are the foundation of the Book: others are allegorical. But those in whose hearts is perversity follow the part thereof that is allegorical, seeking discord, and searching for its hidden meanings, but no one knows its hidden meanings except Allah. And those who are firmly grounded in knowledge say: 'We believe in the Book; the whole of it is from our Lord' and none will grasp the Message except men of understanding. (Yusuf Ali)

Demonstrate the unknown in terms of what is called 'known' by the audience. (Sufi master Ibrahim Khawwas)

One of the most well-known parables from the Qur'an is that of the light: the light representing knowledge and inspiration. Another parable from the Qur'an is that of the spider's web, which is likened to the person who builds their faith on gods other than Allah. Parables may be used to teach Muslims things to follow, or to understand an unfamiliar teaching, or to encourage listeners to change their attitude to life.

The parable of Conference of the Birds, written by Persian poet Farid ud-Din Attar, is one of the most famous. The birds of the world flock together and decide to find the phoenix to be their king. Phoenix is a mythical figure, called Simorgh in the poem.

The wisest bird leads the birds in search of Simorgh. However, each bird represents a different human failing, and drops by the wayside. The birds seek knowledge far and wide across all the world.

The birds fly over seven valleys: the valley of quest, where dogma is left behind; the valley of love, where reasoning is cast aside; the valley of knowledge, where worldly knowledge is forgotten; the valley of detachment, where materialism is disposed of; the valley of unity, where the birds realise everything is interconnected; the valley of wonderment, where the birds experience awe and wonder; and the valley of annihilation, where all ideas of selfishness are left behind and the birds become timeless. Only 30 birds were left when they arrived in China and finally found Simorgh whilst looking at their own reflections in a lake.

The Conference of the Birds is at the centre of the opening ceremony of the annual Fes Festival of World Sacred Music. Sacred music from many cultural traditions is performed, including from Sufi, Christian and Jewish heritage. Talks and speeches are made and tolerance promoted. The goal is to create a global soul.

AO1 Activity

Design a leaflet to explain the use of parables, including a labelled sketch of the symbolism in the Conference of the Birds. Explain how and why symbols are used and how they have helped Muslims understand their faith.

Specification content

The use of parables.

Key quotes

The Qur'an 24:35

Allah is the Light of the heavens and the earth. The Parable of His Light is as if there were a Niche and within it a Lamp: the Lamp enclosed in Glass: the glass as it were a brilliant star: Lit from a blessed Tree, an Olive, neither of the east nor of the west, whose oil is well-nigh luminous, though fire scarce touched it: Light upon Light! Allah doth guide whom He will to His Light: Allah doth set forth Parables for men: and Allah doth know all things. (Yusuf Ali)

The Qur'an 29:41

The parable of those who take protectors other than Allah is that of the spider, who builds (to itself) a house; but truly the flimsiest of houses is the spider's house; if they but knew. (Yusuf Ali)

quickfire

4.9 What is the focus of the annual Fes conference?

A Sufi enacting a parable, Sudan.

Specification content

The direct personal relationship of teacher to pupil.

The direct personal relationship of teacher to pupil

As has been mentioned above, a Mureed gives bayah to a Shaykh to join a Sufi order. Sufi orders are known as tariqas and there are many different ones, with long histories stretching back to the Prophet. The Shaykh is known as a **Murshid**, a spiritual guide for the Sufi.

The Murshid, the spiritual guide, gives inspiration from his heart to his follower.

The pledge made by the Mureed is an agreement to strive in the way of Allah and keep to the rules of faith. Bayah literally means to sell, so the follower sells himself, or rather donates his freedom, to the Shaykh, who also devotes his energies into spiritual care for his disciple.

Sufis claim the Prophet accepted bayah from his companions, the Sahaba, before they joined him for Jihad or for other purposes, or as a general pledge. One hadith tradition records that a companion came to the Prophet and that he was asked to pledge allegiance. The companion asked for what purpose? The Prophet replied: for the worship of Allah.

Ismaili Shias who declare bayah say: 'I declare and accept that the Mowlana Hazar Imam is the Lord of the age, my spiritual master. I promise to be absolutely obedient and loyal to him.' The follower then bows their head and the master touches their hand and forehead, and is sprinkled with holy water over their face.

In many Sunni Sufi tariqas, the Murshid will take the right hand of the Mureed, or else he will hold a cloth and the people becoming Mureeds will hold the other end of the cloth in a line. The follower will first learn about the Sufi path and would be guided by the Murshid, particularly regarding interpreting their meditations and spiritual exercises. They are often given a book of devotions to learn and a robe to wear at the gathering after the bayah ceremony.

quickfire

4.10 What is a Murshid?

Key terms

Murshid: a Sufi Shaykh who guides a Mureed

Zuhd: asceticism in Islam – to live apart from the world to meditate upon God

Specification content

The role of asceticism.

The role of asceticism

Throughout the centuries some Sufis have detached themselves from the world in order to help concentrate on leaving behind material concerns to gain a deeper relationship with Allah. Asceticism means to detach from the world, and may be shown by living alone, in quiet places, sometimes in deserts or caves or simple dwellings far away from civilisation. Ascetics recall the tradition that Muhammad himself used to go to caves and out into the desert to meditate on the meaning of life before he received the first revelation on the Night of Power.

Asceticism, called **zuhd** in Islam, may include fasting, giving up of material wealth, wearing only a single woollen cloak, sleeping on the ground, living by begging or through finding fruits in the wild, and shunning all but necessities. Zuhd involves giving up not only possessions but also thoughts: all thoughts of benefitting yourself are given up too. This means giving up all attachments to this life and thinking all the time about the next life, in heaven. Some ascetics lived a life of celibacy, although there is no enclosed monastic tradition of monks and nuns in Islam, unlike Christianity.

Sufis who have reached higher levels of spiritual consciousness may lose all knowledge of themselves and their surroundings and appear to be lost, distant, unable to communicate with people around them. They gain a deeper consciousness of Allah and put their trust entirely in Him.

Key quote

I detached my heart from the world and lessened my desires so much that for thirty years I have performed every prayer as though it were my last. (Rabia of Basra)

Personal, mystical religious experience as a way of experiencing God

Maqam is a deeper consciousness developed by Sufis. Following strict routines and formal devotions can help a Sufi to achieve this. These start with the five Pillars but then progress to additional morning and evening prayers particular to the Sufi order. Attendance at Sufi gatherings is usually on a Thursday evening, when formal rituals such as chanting the names of Allah over and over again, singing qasida songs and other Sufi devotions take place.

Fana in Sufism means to let the self die: to give up desires for oneself; to lose one's ego, and focus instead on God. **Hal** is a description of a state of being during Sufi spiritual practices. During Sufi zikr, remembrance of Allah, a Sufi may reach a state of ecstasy when they jump up in a trance-like dance, unaware of their surroundings, and temporarily enter a state of hal. As a God-given state, hal can occur at any time and is unpredictable. The Sufi should let go of their attachments to timetable, routine and formal worship, and allow themselves to continue to worship more deeply in formless state of hal. A believer may speak in tongues, that is to say almost meaningless words and sounds, within this state.

The medieval Spanish Muslim Ibn Arabi wrote philosophical works about the self-disclosure of God: the idea that God can be understood and experienced through one's own thoughts and experiences. Ibn Arabi refers to the shari'a as a basic guide to use when needed, but to the veils as the greater knowledge which are lifted to reveal the greater truth. The lifting of the veils may be achieved through understanding the cosmos, the universe, becoming bewildered and asking questions. To become confused due to this is, in Ibn Arabi's eyes, a sign of a high state of understanding.

Key quote

The need of the self for knowledge is greater than the person's need for the food that keeps it wholesome. Knowledge is of two sorts: first knowledge is needed in the same way that food is needed. Hence it is to exercise moderation, to limit oneself to the measure of need. This is the science of the shari'a's rulings.

The second knowledge, which has no limit at which one can come to a halt, is knowledge that pertains to God and of the resurrection. This is because on that day the Real Himself will make demands through the lifting of the veils; that is the day of Differentiation. It is for all intelligent human beings to be upon insight in their affairs and to be prepared to answer for themselves. (Ibn Arabi)

To Ibn Arabi and many Sufis, they are not rejecting the revelation of the Qur'an and the traditional forms of Islamic learning. They are saying that meditation and self-realisation help them to gain a higher spiritual awareness of God. Ibn Arabi refers to a saying of Muhammad which states that to know oneself is to know God. Therefore delving into one's own thoughts and reflecting on ones experiences are not only valid but deep, according to him.

Key quote

The self is an ocean without a shore. Gazing on it has no end in this world or the next. (Ibn Arabi).

In his day Ibn Arabi was opposed by some more traditional Islamic scholars. He argued that Islamic Law was only a temporary means to a higher goal, to which some said he was departing from orthodox traditions. Ibn Arabi claimed that he was not inventing anything different, but rather confirming the same revealed truths which were sent through holy books and prophets, using different means.

Specification content

The role of personal, mystical religious experience as a way of experiencing God.

Key terms

Fana: losing one's ego to focus instead on Allah

Hal: a deep state of spiritual consciousness in which a Sufi loses control and awareness of their surroundings and takes on a trance-like meditative state

Maqam: deeper realisation developed by Sufis by following ritual

quickfire

4.11 How do Sufis reach a state of hal?

Reading personal prayers beside graves

Key quote

How do we come to know what we know? Basically, from three sources: following the authority of knowledge transmitted from others (whoever these others may be – prophets, scientists, teachers, parents, journalists), rational investigation, and direct experience of what is real. Ibn Arabi makes thorough use of all three but he recognises transmission as the most basic. Then come direct experience, then rational investigation. (Chittick)

Key quote

The realisation is all important. Without the realisation, people are simply transmitters or arm-chair theorisers or dreamers. On this issue Ibn Arabi likes to quote the response of the famous Sufi Abu Yazid to unsympathetic critics: 'You take your knowledge dead from the dead, but we take our knowledge from the Living who does not die.' (William Chittick)

> ### AO1 Activity
>
> Imagine you are writing an interview with a new Sufi Mureed for a magazine about Sufism. Ask the Mureed a series of questions about how they developed their interest before agreeing to give an oath of allegiance. Describe the oath ceremony, and ask the Mureed about how they develop a deeper sense of realisation of faith through help from their spiritual master and attendance at dhikr gatherings.

Variety of Sufi devotional practices

Key quote

My servant draws near to Me through nothing I love more than that which I have made obligatory for him. My servant never ceases drawing near to Me through supererogatory works until I love him. Then, when I love him, I am his hearing through which he hears, his sight through which he sees, his hand through which he grasps, and his foot through which he walks. (Hadith qudsi of Prophet Muhammad)

There are many different Sufi traditions which are outlined in this section. Practices vary across the world. A common tradition in South Asia is to visit the tombs of holy people to remember their examples and read personal prayers at the site in the hope that the spiritual blessings of the heart of the true believer buried there will help achieve success for the request.

Sufis in Pakistan celebrate a festival at the tomb of Qalandar Lal Shahbaz in Sindh each year. The Hajj traditions are re-enacted in the village: there are three stone Pillars representing the devil which pilgrims throw stones at and they circumambulate the tomb of the saint. Such 'little Hajj' traditions can be found at several shrines in South Asia and originate from earlier times in history when many poor people converted and, without modern transport, found it impossible to undertake the pilgrimage thousands of miles west to Makkah. The true meaning of Hajj is to visit God's house and according to Sufi tradition, God lives in the heart of the true believer, so a visit to the saint's tomb enables the pilgrim to partake in the true meaning of Hajj, without the less important physical journey.

Sufi Ustadh Mahmoud Shelton blends New Age religious interest and alternative traditions with Sufi practice. Writing from the perspective of a British Muslim, he finds common interest with sacred traditions handed down from ancient British people. One tradition is that there are centres of spiritual energy, one of which is centred on the Welsh mountain, Cadair Idris. Celtic mythology suggests this was the seat of the giant called Idris, itself a name found in both Welsh and Muslim tradition. In Islamic tradition the cosmos is under the care of Prophet Idris. Visits to wild and beautiful places, to meditate on the naturally created world and stargaze at the universe help to increase wonder for the power of the Creator.

The traditions outlined above are some of the more unusual and not without their critics. Many Muslims would eschew them and avoid participation in what they see as local traditions more rooted in ancient customs than in puritanical, Arabian Islam. On the other hand, it is argued that although different, the traditions are just

Specification content

The variety of Sufi devotional practices including dhikr (remembrance), muraqaba (Sufi meditation) and sama (spiritual listening, specifically whirling).

A Muslim woman using prayer beads.

quickfire

4.12 Why might a Sufi visit the Welsh mountain Cadair Idris?

Cadair Idris Mountain, Gwynedd

a means to achieve true religious experience and it is a strength to recognise and develop local forms of Islam since, after all, Allah created human kinds different and this should be celebrated.

Dhikr (remembrance)

Dhikr, also written as zikr, is the remembrance of Allah through particular activities such as chanting the names of Allah over and over again. This is often done whilst counting on the beads of a Tasbih, which is a string of prayer beads used as an aid to the practice.

Muslims remember God by saying his name within the word Bismillah at the start of any task, and Alhamdullilah as thanks to God for providing for them, such as at the end of a meal. Some Muslims also sing the Shahadah at the end of their prayers in mosques of the Sufi-friendly Brewlvi sect. Many Muslims use common Arabic phrases from the Qur'an and hadith to recite as forms of dhikr, and these are also used by Sufis in particular services.

For members of a Sufi tariqa (path), the weekly dhikr service is the focus of spiritual life. The service usually begins after maghrib prayer on Thursday evenings, starting with a short recitation from the Qur'an and then a series of chants of the names of Allah or similar short Arabic phrases. The gathering may then pause with a homily, a short talk by the Murshid, with a spiritual meaning, designed to encourage the humility of the Mureeds. The gathering then becomes more lively as qasidas are sung. It may then develop to the stage where some Sufis jump up into a state of dance and ecstatic energy, in which they enter the state of hal. The service then calms with a shorter meditative recitation and a short recitation of the Qur'an, paralleling the opening, rather like a carefully designed musical symphony. At the end of the evening food is shared.

There are various different cultural traditions and variations on the above service. African dhikr services often include drums and tambourine type instruments. The hadra is another form of dhikr gathering practised across North Africa.

Muraqaba (Sufi meditation)

Sufis have defined various stages of Muraqaba, meditation, which help them develop their spiritual awareness. These have various names and associated practices according to Sufi teachers. The justification for muraqaba can be traced, according to Sufis, to the Qur'an and hadith.

Key quote

My servant continues to draw near to Me with supererogatory works so that I shall love him. When I love him I am his hearing with which he hears, his seeing with which he sees, his hand with which he strikes and his foot with which he walks. (Hadith qudsi of Prophet Muhammad)

Specific stages of meditation bring a Sufi Muslim into heightened awareness of God, rising and then descending from their mental alertness. A diagram of these stages is shown on page 174. Only the most experienced of teachers would be expected to reach the highest levels of meditation. Sufis are cautioned that these practices can be very powerful and that it is essential to choose a spiritual guide to carefully prepare and counsel the follower who is practising the higher levels of meditation.

The poetry of Rumi contains deep, mystical poems representing forms of meditation in which he refers to God as his beloved. Works of Rumi have inspired millions of people, Muslims and non-Muslims, to enter deeper into the realms of spiritual meditation. Some Sufis have gone further and gone beyond what is acceptable in traditional Islam. The poet Mansur Hallaj declared that 'I am God' due to his close meditation with Him. This crossed the line for many Muslims who felt he was declaring shirk.

Key terms

Dhikr: also referred to as zikr, particular practices and services to remember Allah

Muraqaba: Sufi meditation, of which several stages have been defined

Tasbih: prayer beads used as an aid in dhikr and meditation

Key quotes

Muhammad said to his companions, 'Shall I tell you about the best of deeds, the most pure in the Sight of your Lord, about the one that is of the highest order and is far better for you than spending gold and silver, even better for you than meeting your enemies in the battlefield where you strike at their necks and they at yours?' The companions replied, 'Yes, O Messenger of Allah!' He said, 'Remembrance of Allah.' (Hadith of Prophet Muhammad)

The Qur'an 50:16

It was We Who created man, and We know what dark suggestions his soul makes to him: for We are nearer to him than (his) jugular vein. (Yusuf Ali)

Sufis perform dhikr/zikr

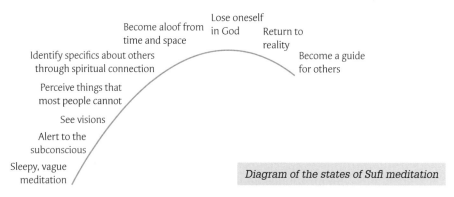

Lose oneself
in God

Become aloof from   Return to
time and space   reality

Identify specifics about others   Become a guide
through spiritual connection   for others

Perceive things that
most people cannot

See visions

Alert to the
subconscious

Sleepy, vague
meditation

Diagram of the states of Sufi meditation

Sama (spiritual listening, specifically whirling)

The Sufi dervishes of the Mevlevi order, followers of the Turkish poet Rumi, perform a particular symbolic whirling dance as part of their devotions. Spinning in circles represents the planets of the solar system. The ritual act of the whirling dervishes is called Sama. The practice started when Rumi was walking in the bazaar and heard the tap tap tapping of the jewellery makers, shaping their gold into jewellery. This reminded him of Sufi chants. Rumi stretched out his arms and started whirling in delight.

The flute accompanies the dance which follows a brief recitation of the Qur'an. The dervishes wear long white robes and a high hat, which represents the gravestone of the ego of the self. They enter wearing a black cloak which is removed for the dance, symbolising spiritual rebirth. Beginning with arms folded, this represents the unity of God, during whirling the right hand is pointed upwards towards God's blessings and the left hand down to earth.

The ritual is said to develop purity and love in the mind of the believer. Rumi thought of the circling of the Ka'aba when performing the dance, making the spiritual connection with the holy city.

Key term

Sama: Sufi whirling dervish ritual

quickfire

4.13 What do the hat and cloak symbolise in the Sama ritual?

Whirling dervishes

AO1 Developing skills

It is now important to consider the information that has been covered in this section; however, the information in its raw form is too extensive and so has to be processed in order to meet the requirements of the examination. This can be achieved by practising more advanced skills associated with AO1. For assessment objective 1 (AO1), which involves demonstrating 'knowledge' and 'understanding' skills, we are going to focus on different ways in which the skills can be demonstrated effectively, and also refer to how the performance of these skills is measured (see generic band descriptors for A2 [WJEC] AO1 or A Level [Eduqas] AO1).

▶ **Your new task is this:** you will have to write a response under timed conditions to a question requiring an examination or explanation of **Sufi beliefs about religious experience**. This exercise can either be done as a group or independently.

1. Begin with a list of indicative content, as you may have done in the previous textbook in the series. This may be discussed as a group or done independently. It does not need to be in any particular order at first, although as you practise this you will see more order in your lists that reflects your understanding.

2. Develop the list by using one or two relevant quotations. Now add some references to scholars and/or religious writings.

3. Then write out your plan, under timed conditions, remembering the principles of explaining with evidence and/or examples. Then ask someone else to read your answer and see if they can then help you improve it in any way.

4. Collaborative marking helps a learner appreciate alternative perspectives and possibly things that may have been missed. It also helps highlight the strengths of another that one can learn from. With this in mind, it is good to swap and compare answers in order to improve your own.

When you have completed the task, refer to the band descriptors for A2 (WJEC) or A Level (Eduqas) and in particular have a look at the demands described in the higher band descriptors towards which you should be aspiring. Ask yourself:

- Does my work demonstrate thorough, accurate and relevant knowledge and understanding of religion and belief?

- Is my work coherent (consistent or make logical sense), clear and well organised?

- Will my work, when developed, be an extensive and relevant response which is specific to the focus of the task?

- Does my work have extensive depth and/or suitable breadth and have excellent use of evidence and examples?

- If appropriate to the task, does my response have thorough and accurate reference to sacred texts and sources of wisdom?

- Are there any insightful connections to be made with other elements of my course?

- Will my answer, when developed and extended to match what is expected in an examination answer, have an extensive range of views of scholars/schools of thought?

- When used, is specialist language and vocabulary both thorough and accurate?

Key skills

Knowledge involves:

Selection of a range of (thorough) accurate and relevant information that is directly related to the specific demands of the question.

This means:

- Selecting relevant material for the question set

- Be focused in explaining and examining the material selected.

Understanding involves:

Explanation that is extensive, demonstrating depth and/or breadth with excellent use of evidence and examples including (where appropriate) thorough and accurate supporting use of sacred texts, sources of wisdom and specialist language.

This means:

- Effective use of examples and supporting evidence to establish the quality of your understanding

- Ownership of your explanation that expresses personal knowledge and understanding and NOT just a chunk of text from a book that you have rehearsed and memorised.

Specification content

The possibility of a personal mystical
union with God in Islam.

Key terms

Amal: application of religious
knowledge

Ilm: knowledge in Islam about the
religion and the sacred

AO2 Activity

As you read through this section try to
do the following:

1. Pick out the different lines of
   argument that are presented in
   the text and identify any evidence
   given in support.

2. For each line of argument try to
   evaluate whether or not you think
   this is strong or weak.

3. Think of any questions you may
   wish to raise in response to the
   arguments.

This Activity will help you to start
thinking critically about what you
read and help you to evaluate the
effectiveness of different arguments
and from this develop your own
observations, opinions and points
of view that will help with any
conclusions that you make in your
answers to the AO2 questions
that arise.

Issues for analysis and evaluation

The possibility of a personal mystical union with God in Islam

Rumi is known as one of the most famous poets in history for Muslims and
non-Muslims alike. His poems focus on the mystical side of experience. In 'Say
I am You', God and the world are indivisible: Rumi
appears to see God in everything, a form of pantheism
common to Eastern religions. Through Sufi techniques
such as meditation, God can be seen in the mist, the
sunshine and in the inner self.

Reading personal prayers

The idea of a mystical union with God inspires many to
delve deeper into religion. Others see it as a departure
from the orthodox traditions of Islam. Ibn Arabi
describes religion as love manifested in all the different
worldly traditions. If that is true, what value had
outward form at all? Does it mean that the outward
traditions of Islam can be dispensed with?

Key quotes

Say I Am You
I am dust particles in sunlight.
I am the round sun.
I am morning mist,
and the breathing of evening.
I am wind in the top of a grove,
and surf on the cliff.
I am all orders of being, the
circling galaxy,
the evolutionary intelligence, the lift
and the falling away.
What is and what is not.
You who know Jelaluddin,
You are the one in all, say who I am.
Say I am you.

(Jelaluddin Rumi)

My heart has become capable of every form: it is a pasture for gazelles and a
convent for Christians, and a temple for idols and the pilgrims Ka'aba and the
tables of the Torah, and the book of the Qu'ran. I follow the religion of Love:
whatever way Love's camels take, that is my religion and faith. (Ibn Arabi)

Nuh Keller, a Sufi Shaykh, provides a response which justifies Sufi knowledge
seeking as within the bounds of Islamic tradition. He refers to the hadith of
Bukhari, in which the Prophet reports Allah as saying that when His servant
draws near to Him He becomes His hearing and sight: in other words, the person
experiencing mysticism sees everything from the perspective of how God might see
it, and upholds God's values of right and wrong.

Key quote

Purifying the heart (like virtually all other traditional Islamic disciplines)
requires that the knowledge be taken from those who possess it. This is why
historically we find that groups of students gathered around particular Shaykhs
to learn the discipline of Sufism.

This is a way of expressing that such a person has realised the consummate
awareness of tawhid or unity of Allah demanded by the shari'a, which entails
total sincerity to Allah in all one's actions. Because of this hadith, and others,
traditional Ulema have long acknowledged that ilm or Sacred Knowledge is not
sufficient in itself, but also entails amal or applying what one knows as well
as the resultant hal or praiseworthy spiritual state mentioned in the hadith.
(Keller)

The Sufi saint Rabia of Basra succinctly describes the importance of mystical union in her poem. She asks Allah to reject her requests if she is making them for the selfish desire to get to heaven or avoid hellfire. Only union with Allah is acceptable. The experience of the Sufi is to achieve this.

Key quote

O God, if I am worshipping you out of fear of Your hellfire, cast me into it. And if I am worshipping you out of desire for Your paradise, prohibit me from entering it. And if I am worshipping You for the sake of Your noble face, do not prohibit me from seeing You. (Rabia of Basra)

Study tip

It is vital for AO2 that you actually discuss arguments and not just explain what someone may have stated. Try to ask yourself, 'was this a fair point to make?', 'is the evidence sound enough?', 'is there anything to challenge this argument?', 'is this a strong or weak argument?' Such critical analysis will help you develop your evaluation skills.

Mystical union with Allah to some emphasises a feminine aspect of Islam which is neglected in other traditions. Laurence Galian describes how the 'Divine Feminine', the compassionate side which is central to Islam, is best experienced through mysticism. Some Sufi tariqas describe their mystical quest as a woman who can touch the most inner heartstrings.

Key quotes

The Divine Feminine has always been present in Islam. This may be surprising to many people who see Islam as a patriarchal religion. Maybe the reason for this misconception is the very nature of the feminine in Islam. The Divine Feminine in Islam manifests metaphysically and in the inner expression of the religion. The Divine Feminine is not so much a secret within Islam as She is the compassionate Heart of Islam that enables us to know Divinity. Her centrality demonstrates her necessary and life-giving role in Islam. (Galian)

In some Sufi orders the goal of the mystical quest is 'personified as a woman, usually named Laila which means "night"… this is the holiest and most secret inwardness of Allah… in this symbolism Laila and haqiqa (Divine Reality) are one'. (Van Doodewaard)

Some Muslims prefer to think of God as separate from such experiences since there is a danger that Sufis could consider themselves too close to God and encroach upon the role assumed by the Prophets. There is no knowing whether the mystical experience is but a made up dream or really from God in origin. The authority of the Qur'an and the hadith is accepted by Muslims, but the inner experiences only by the people who experience them. Instead of a single, unified faith, individual experiences could create an Islam of as many different forms as there are Muslims. Some people regard this as a wonderful thing; others as a departure from the origins of the faith.

Key questions

What forms could mystical union take?

Can mystical experience be justified through traditional Islam?

Why do you think some criticise Islamic mysticism?

How can a feminine version of the Divine be experienced through mysticism?

AO2 Activity

List some conclusions that could be drawn from the AO2 reasoning from the above text; try to aim for at least three different possible conclusions. Consider each of the conclusions and collect brief evidence to support each conclusion from the AO1 and AO2 material for this topic. Select the conclusion that you think is most convincing and explain why it is so. Try to contrast this with the weakest conclusion in the list, justifying your argument with clear reasoning and evidence.

Specification content

The religious validity of Sufi
devotional practices.

Key term

Wird Latif: devotional prayer of a Sufi
Mureed

AO2 Activity

As you read through this section try to
do the following:

1. Pick out the different lines of
   argument that are presented in
   the text and identify any evidence
   given in support.

2. For each line of argument try to
   evaluate whether or not you think
   this is strong or weak.

3. Think of any questions you may
   wish to raise in response to the
   arguments.

This Activity will help you to start
thinking critically about what you
read and help you to evaluate the
effectiveness of different arguments
and from this develop your own
observations, opinions and points
of view that will help with any
conclusions that you make in your
answers to the AO2 questions
that arise.

The religious validity of Sufi devotional practices

A Sunni Muslim might read their five daily prayers, avoid excessive thought leading
to doubt and focus on strengthening their faith in Allah. At Jummah prayers they
would listen to guidance from their Imam, and guard their actions to ensure they
follow the morally upright path in the hope of achieving heaven in the afterlife. A
Sufi would disagree with none of this, but their pattern of life might be different. A
Sufi Mureed might read their own devotional prayer, called the Wird Latif, in the
morning and the evening each day, and attend a Thursday evening dhikr gathering.
They would focus on chanting the names of Allah and singing qasida songs to
achieve a state of heightening meditation and consciousness of Allah. In so doing
they would follow the guidance of a spiritual teacher.

Sufi religious practices are hotly debated. Some see them as the height of
devotion, others as innovations which change the nature of Islam. Salafi scholars,
in particular, criticise Sufism, which is not common in Saudi Arabia and was not
generally a feature of Arabic tribal tradition in the area. The Salafi A.A. Tabari wrote
a refutation of Sufism as a guide and quoted the tradition of Abdullah bin Masood
who forbade Sufi dhikr, or a similar tradition, when he found it being practised in
a mosque in Iraq. Since this tradition was from the early days of Islam, he believes
it was authentic and better guidance for Muslims today than other, later traditions
which may have been influenced by human opinion, or earlier traditions from pre-
Islamic religions.

Key quote

Abdullah bin Masood, governor of al-Koofeh, Iraq, happened to enter the
mosque one day, and saw some people sitting in circles. In the middle of each
circle was a heap of pebbles, and in every circle was a man instructing the
people: 'Say, SubhanAllah (Allah is far removed from every imperfection) a
hundred times. Say, Alhamdulillah (praise be to Allah) a hundred times. Say,
Allahu-Akbar (Allah is the Greatest) a hundred times.'

Whereupon Abdullah bin Masood said to them, 'O people, you are either
following a religion which is better than that of the Messenger of Allah, or you
are entering through a door of deviation without consideration.' They responded,
'By Allah, we intend to do a good thing.' He exclaimed, 'How often one intends
to do good but never attains his purpose.' The above quotation clearly shows
that sincerity and good intentions alone are not sufficient to render acts of
worship acceptable to Allah. The acts must first conform to the Book of Allah
and the Sunnah of His Messenger. (Salafi scholar A.A. Tabari)

The sayings of some Sufis such as Rumi suggest that Sufis are comfortable with
other religious traditions. Hesham Bazaraa addresses the tradition that Sufis need
a teacher, Murshid of Shaykh to guide them. In life we all need experts to help us,
and this does not mean we worship them. Hesham also refers to the tradition that
at Judgement Muslims may appeal to Prophet Muhammad for help. Asking the
blessings of Muhammad, seeing him in visions and celebrating his birthday are all
common Sufi traditions.

Key quotes

Christian, Jew, Muslim, shaman, Zoroastrian, stone, ground, mountain, river,
each has a secret way of being with the mystery, unique and not to be judged.
(Rumi)

Sufism is a blend of various thoughts and philosophies. By intermingling a few
traces of Islamic teachings with it ... Greek philosophy, and in particular the

teachings of Neo-Platonists, have left an indelible mark on many aspects of Sufism. This came about as a result of the translation of Greek philosophical works into Arabic during the third Islamic century. Greek pantheism became an integral part of Sufi doctrine. (Watt)

William Montgomery Watt wrote from the objective standpoint of an outside observer, not a critic, and noticed that many Sufi practices seemed to be similar to earlier practices of other religions. In the eyes of many Muslims, if there is one God and one Truth, it is logical that many different traditions will encounter the Truth in different ways, so there is nothing wrong with emulating others.

The Naqshbandi are a Sufi tariqa order and a Haqqani is a teacher or Murshid within that tradition. They see asking the Prophet as a means to an end, of which there is nothing wrong in practice. Al-Azhar is seen as the highest authority in the Sunni Muslim world, one of the oldest Universities. Abd al-Halim of Al-Azhar was asked for a Sunni Muslim opinion over whether the practices of Sufism were acceptable. He said that they were: that the aims of the Sufi were to find Allah and that this was just a different way of getting to the same end as followed by mainstream Muslims.

The tomb of Rumi, Konya

Key quotes

Seeking help with the Prophet and other prophets and pious persons, is only a means of imploring God for the sake of their dignity and honour. ... The Prophet is but the intermediary means between the one asking for help and the One asked in reality. (Haqqani)

The ascetic is one who turns away from the goods of the world and its pleasant things. The worshipper is one who is careful to observe the acts of worship. The Sufi is both an ascetic and a worshipper. Thus the Sufi abstains from the world, since he is beyond the point where anything can distract him from God. Also, the Sufi is a worshipper because of his constancy with God and his link with God (may He be exalted). He worships God because God is suitable for worshipping, not out of desire or fear. (Imam Abd al-Halim, Al-Azhar)

Some young Muslims visit Sufi gatherings and consider joining Sufi orders. Others refrain on the grounds that they feel it goes beyond orthodox practice. It is a divisive subject: practices which lead to the height of experience and inspiration for some; or practices that detract from the divinely revealed straightforward practice of faith for others.

Study tip

It is important for AO2 that you include the views of scholars and/or schools of thought when formulating your response to a particular contention, as well as from more current scholars. However, make sure that the views you use are relevant to the point that you are making. Your ability to use such views in an appropriate way would distinguish a high level answer from one that is simply a general response.

Key quote

No one can claim that asking other than Allah for help is unconditionally Shirk, because Allah has put some of our needs with His servants, e.g. doctors, mechanics, policemen. This point is often ignored by Salafis who are quick to accuse, 'Shirk!' Regarding whether it is permissible to ask the Prophet for support then remember that the people will ask him for his intercession on the Day of Judgment and Insha'Allah he will give it. Is it permissible to ask him then when we are in judgment before our Creator but not now? (Bazaraa)

Key questions

What are the main Sufi practices and how do they differ from the traditions of mainstream Sunni and Shi'a Muslims?

What is the concept of Bid'ah and do you think is applies in this case?

In what ways can Sufi practices be said to be a different method to achieve the same ends?

AO2 Activity

List some conclusions that could be drawn from the AO2 reasoning from the above text; try to aim for at least three different possible conclusions. Consider each of the conclusions and collect brief evidence to support each conclusion from the AO1 and AO2 material for this topic. Select the conclusion that you think is most convincing and explain why it is so. Try to contrast this with the weakest conclusion in the list, justifying your argument with clear reasoning and evidence.

Key skills

Analysis involves:

Identifying issues raised by the materials in the AO1, together with those identified in the AO2 section, and presents sustained and clear views, either of scholars or from a personal perspective ready for evaluation.

This means:

- That your answers are able to identify key areas of debate in relation to a particular issue

- That you can identify, and comment upon, the different lines of argument presented by others

- That your response comments on the overall effectiveness of each of these areas or arguments.

Evaluation involves:

Considering the various implications of the issues raised based upon the evidence gleaned from analysis and provides an extensive detailed argument with a clear conclusion.

This means:

- That your answer weighs up the consequences of accepting or rejecting the various and different lines of argument analysed

- That your answer arrives at a conclusion through a clear process of reasoning.

AO2 Developing skills

It is now important to consider the information that has been covered in this section; however, the information in its raw form is too extensive and so has to be processed in order to meet the requirements of the examination. This can be achieved by practising more advanced skills associated with AO2. For assessment objective 2 (AO2), which involves 'critical analysis' and 'evaluation' skills, we are going to focus on different ways in which the skills can be demonstrated effectively, and also refer to how the performance of these skills is measured (see generic band descriptors for A2 [WJEC] AO2 or A Level [Eduqas] AO2).

▶ **Your new task is this:** you will have to write a response under timed conditions to a question requiring an evaluation of **whether Sufi rituals are Islamic**. This exercise can either be done as a group or independently.

1. Begin with a list of indicative arguments or lines of reasoning, as you may have done in the previous textbook in the series. It does not need to be in any particular order at first, although as you practise this you will see more order in your lists, in particular by way of links and connections between arguments.

2. Develop the list by using one or two relevant quotations. Now add some references to scholars and/or religious writings.

3. Then write out your plan, under timed conditions, remembering the principles of explaining with evidence and/or examples. Then ask someone else to read your answer and see if they can then help you improve it in any way.

4. Collaborative marking helps a learner appreciate alternative perspectives and possibly things that may have been missed. It also helps highlight the strengths of another that one can learn from. With this in mind, it is good to swap and compare answers in order to improve your own.

When you have completed the task, refer to the band descriptors for A2 (WJEC) or A Level (Eduqas) and in particular have a look at the demands described in the higher band descriptors towards which you should be aspiring. Ask yourself:

- Is my answer a confident critical analysis and perceptive evaluation of the issue?

- Is my answer a response that successfully identifies and thoroughly addresses the issues raised by the question set?

- Does my work show an excellent standard of coherence, clarity and organisation?

- Will my work, when developed, contain thorough, sustained and clear views that are supported by extensive, detailed reasoning and/or evidence?

- Are the views of scholars/schools of thought used extensively, appropriately and in context?

- Does my answer convey a confident and perceptive analysis of the nature of any possible connections with other elements of my course?

- When used, is specialist language and vocabulary both thorough and accurate?

F: Ethical debate about crime and punishment (including arguments posed by scholars from within and outside the Islamic tradition)

Traditional Muslim views about punishment for crime

Crime and punishment is one of the most controversial areas of Islam. The media sometimes present Muslims as proponents of barbaric punishments such as the death penalty, chopping off of hands for theft and so on. In reality, the situation is far more complex and different groups of Muslims interpret teachings in very different ways. Many things that you might see in the media are crimes that have nothing to do with Islam. Tribal societies still exist in many parts of the world and carry out their own punishments for violations of family honour, including honour killings and revenge punishments, done by tribal vigilantes who have no authority in Islam to do so and are very much against the process of shari'a law.

Traditional shari'a law divides crimes into three main categories. **Hudud** crimes transgress God's laws, as defined in the Qur'an and sunna. They are given fixed punishments. **Qisas** crimes are against other individuals who may call for retaliation or compensation. **Tazir** crimes are unspecified exactly in religious texts and are left to be decided by the Qazi judge. The judge follows the interpretations of the schools of Islamic Law in which he is educated, such as Hanafi Sunni or Jafari Shi'a. As discussed in the chapter on shari'a, many countries have historically, and today, operated dual legal systems with most criminal law dealt with by state authorities, whereas shari'a courts have a more limited role for family affairs. At times when Islamic courts have had a greater role in judging criminal matters there have been wide variations in application depending on the rulers of the state at the time.

Despite the focus on this chapter on punishment, it is a topic rarely talked about in day-to-day practice by Muslims. The Qur'an teaches that Allah is All Forgiving and All Merciful, and one Islamic tradition is that Allah's mercy is 99 times greater than His wrath. When punishment is considered it is often referred to in the afterlife in hell, according to the balance of deeds considered on the Day of Judgement. Earthly punishments are less important for Muslims, and they often look the other way or hide a person's misdemeanours out of humility for their own failings rather than criticising their faults and asking for punishment.

Categories of punishment: qisas

One day, the parents of a girl came to the Prophet saying their daughter had been in a fight and another girl slapped her and broke her tooth. They wanted revenge. So the Prophet agreed that she had the right to take the same actions back on her opponent.

Qisas is a form of retribution, revenge or, in simple terms, getting your own back. If a person is murdered, their family may take the murderer to court and ask for a qisas punishment in kind: the death penalty. They have a right to ask for the equivalent of the crime. However, the Qur'an encourages Muslims to accept repentance and compensation as alternatives to death.

This section covers AO1 content and skills

Specification content

Traditional Muslim views about punishment for crime.

Pakistan's secular police force

Key terms

Hudud: crimes against God's commands punished as defined in shari'a

Qisas: crimes against individuals punishable at the request of the victim or their family

Tazir: unspecified lesser crimes which may be sentenced at the discretion of a Qazi

Specification content

Categories of punishment: qisas

Key quote

The Qur'an 2:178

O ye who believe! The law of equality is prescribed to you in cases of murder: the free for the free, the slave for the slave, the woman for the woman. But if any remission is made by the brother of the slain, then grant any reasonable demand, and compensate him with handsome gratitude, this is a concession and a Mercy from your Lord. After this whoever exceeds the limits shall be in grave penalty. (Yusuf Ali)

Key term

Diyya: a monetary payment of compensation in place of the death penalty

quickfire

4.14 What may a victim's family demand in a case of murder?

Specification content

Categories of punishment: hudud.

Key quote

It is only the merciful who are granted mercy by the All-Merciful. Be merciful to those on earth and the Lord of the Heavens will be merciful to you. (Hadith of Prophet Muhammad)

Muhammad's hadith restricts the death penalty to murder, adultery and those who reject the Islamic faith and at the same time turn against the Islamic community. Some Muslims have interpreted this hadith in a different light and said that it only applies to Muslims, so therefore non-Muslims can be given the death penalty for other crimes. Some have interpreted it to mean that anyone leaving the faith can be subject to the death penalty, even if is a personal decision and they do not betray the Muslim community in time of need. This has led some to criticise Islam for not guaranteeing freedom of belief, a universal human right.

Corporal punishment

Key quote

The blood of a Muslim who confesses that none has the right to be worshipped but Allah and that I am His Apostle, cannot be shed except in three cases: In qisas for murder, a married person who commits illegal sexual intercourse and the one who reverts from Islam (apostate) and leaves the Muslims. (Hadith of Prophet Muhammad)

Diyya is a monetary payment of compensation in place of the death penalty. A family may demand compensation or acts of charity to make up for the crime committed. The Qur'an says those who give up retaliating gain the reward of being forgiven for some of their crimes by God. It also warns Muslims to be fair in judgement, since those who do not judge fairly are no better than the criminals.

Key quote

The Qur'an 5:45

We ordained therein for them: 'Life for life, eye for eye, nose or nose, ear for ear, tooth for tooth, and wounds equal for equal.' But if any one remits the retaliation by way of charity, it is an act of atonement for himself. And if any fail to judge by (the light of) what Allah hath revealed, they are (No better than) wrong-doers. (Yusuf Ali)

Categories of punishment: hudud

Hudud crimes are those against God's revealed laws in the shari'a, derived from the Qur'an and sunna. These form the most well-known Islamic punishments and some of the most controversial. Crimes which Muslim scholars have traditionally declared subject to hudud include the following:

- Adultery with a married women
- Becoming intoxicated
- Armed robbery (except for Shafi Fiqh)
- Slander
- Apostasy of belief and against the community
- Rebellion (except for Hanafi Fiqh)

Already in this brief list, you can see that not all scholars from different law schools agree,

A medieval Muslim Qazi

and the differences become wider once circumstances are taken into account. Traditional punishments included the death penalty, corporal punishment in the form of flogging, amputation of limbs and, for much of history, mercy and forgiveness. Indeed, the central principle in the application of the hudud punishments is maximising mercy.

There is some disagreement about the authenticity and meaning of this hadith. There is no denying that some countries have imposed strict punishments, and today hundreds of death penalty sentences and amputations are applied each year in Saudi Arabia and Iran. Human rights organisations, supported by progressive and reformist Muslims, have denounced these punishments as unacceptable and should play no role in the modern world. Reformists say the literal interpretation of Qur'anic punishments should be updated to be more relevant to the modern world.

In what circumstances can the punishment of amputating the hand for theft be carried out? The medieval scholar Kafi al-Subki provided an 83-point checklist of excuses to be completed. If any one of these conditions could not be fulfilled, then the punishment could not be carried out. The made the punishment practically impossible to legitimately impose. The checklist stated that the crime must have been carried out in Makkah, must be admitted by the thief who does not later retract his admission; cannot be any number of types of items and cannot be from a relative; must have been stolen within a month and not returned; and the thief must agree and turn up in court, as must two male witnesses who agree on every point.

The companions of Muhammad often made allowances for people and allowed any ambiguity to exempt someone from the punishment of amputation for theft. They often required them to confess on two or three occasions. A British scholar of Arabic who visited Egypt in the nineteenth century wrote that no one could remember a punishment being applied in their lifetime. Records from five hundred years of Ottoman history show that application of the death penalty was rare.

A story from the time of the Mamluks in Egypt in the twelfth century records how shari'a hudud punishments could only properly be applied in limited circumstances. The transgressions of the Sultan in ordering the death penalty, against the safeguards of shari'a proof required, were punished by God who then took away his empire, according to a popular folk tale.

In the reign of the Mamluk Sultan, two magistrates in Cairo fell out over an affair. A Shafi magistrate noticed that his friend, a Hanafi magistrate, had a gorgeous wife. One day, he noticed that the Hanafi magistrate was out, so the Shafi magistrate managed to enter the house and went to bed with the Hanafi's wife. A neighbour saw them and sent a message to the Shafi who ran home. He found the two in bed together and locked them in the bedroom whilst he called the authorities to come and catch them in the act. The guilty Hanafi magistrate asked for mercy and offered money to be let off, but the Shafi refused and made him sign a confession of guilt there and then.

The ferocious Mamluk Sultan called all the judges together and asked their opinion. One declared that the couple be stoned to death, to which the Sultan agreed. However, they then retracted their confession. The judges agreed that in shari'a, this meant that there was no legal way to punish the couple. Anyone who killed them would themselves be guilty of murder. The Mamluk Sultan became angry and dismissed all the judges, and ordered the killing of the pair. In time, the Mamluk's luck changed and he fell from power in Cairo. The scholars wrote that God had punished the Sultan, because he was a murderer who had transgressed shari'a.

Nevertheless, some Muslims have increased their application of hudud punishments in recent times. Whereas the Ottoman Empire only recorded one case of stoning in five hundred years, there are many in Saudi Arabia today. Some see

quickfire

4.15 Give two crimes for which a hudud punishment may be applied.

Key quotes

Ward off the hudud from the Muslims as much as you all can, and if you find a way out for the person, then let them go. For it is better for the authority to err in mercy than to err in punishment. **(Hadith of Prophet Muhammad)**

The Qur'an 5:33–34

The punishment of those who wage war against Allah and His Messenger, and strive with might and main for mischief through the land is: execution, or crucifixion, or the cutting off of hands and feet from opposite sides, or exile from the land: that is their disgrace in this world, and a heavy punishment is theirs in the Hereafter; Except for those who repent before they fall into your power: in that case, know that Allah is Oft-forgiving, Most Merciful. **(Yusuf Ali)**

The Qur'an 5:38–39

As to the thief, male or female, cut off his or her hands: a punishment by way of example, from Allah, for their crime: and Allah is Exalted in power. But if the thief repents after his crime, and amends his conduct, Allah turneth to him in forgiveness; for Allah is Oft-forgiving, Most Merciful. **(Yusuf Ali)**

hudud punishments as successful because they are deterrents. Others see them as a literal application of God's law. They refer to the Qur'an and hadith which record times when the Prophet was told to apply hudud. If they are applying the literal, others question why new barbaric methods such as shooting are used when this had not been invented in the time of the Prophet. Some say these punishments are described in the Qur'an, but that does not mean Muslims are compelled to copy them, they were simply the practice of the time. Fundamentalists may desire some form of pure, Islamic society, but in their desire to hasten it on earth they may have applied a version of shari'a punishment many people find unacceptable.

Categories of punishment: tazir

Specification content

Categories of punishment: tazir.

Tazir is the third main category of punishment under traditional shari'a, which is carried out for lesser offences. The judge, the Qazi, has leeway of what punishment to apply and often the different law schools do not agree on the same punishments. The standard of proof required may be less but the crimes are seen as important because of their damage to the community.

Key quote

The Qur'an 4:16

If two men among you are guilty of lewdness, punish them both. If they repent and amend, leave them alone; for Allah is Oft-returning, Most Merciful. (Yusuf Ali)

quickfire

4.16 What is a tazir crime?

A drugs offender

The word tazir is not used in the Qur'an; however, there are cases in which the Qur'an suggests there should be flexibility, such as in the case of lewdness. Examples in which a tazir punishment might be applied include cheating when selling goods, such as by measuring out too little; lying as a witness; spying on others such as for an enemy state; and, according to some Muslims such as Hanafi scholars, homosexual acts.

There are various punishments which might be applied including fines, flogging, separation from the community, and seizing stolen goods, property or the like. Pakistan, Brunei and Iran are countries that use tazir in modern times. Brunei imposes a strict interpretation of tazir and punishes adult male Muslims for failing to attend Friday Jummah prayers without good excuse. Iran punishes women who do not wear hijab or who are caught kissing their boyfriends in public.

AO1 Activity

Make a table to summarise the three main types of Islamic punishment, with three columns, one type of punishment in each. Include a definition, justification for the punishment and examples of crimes for which it is valid in each column.

A comparison of different views about the death penalty

Specification content

A comparison of different views about the death penalty.

Capital punishment means administering the death penalty for certain crimes. It has long since been abolished in the UK and western European countries. It is still carried out in some states in the USA, and banned in others. Most Islamic countries carry out the death penalty and some of the highest numbers of executions in the world are carried out by two of the most religious Islamic countries: Saudi Arabia and Iran. There are other Muslim countries, such as Albania and Bosnia in Eastern Europe, who do not use the death penalty.

The Qur'an is used as justification for capital and corporal punishments. Surah 5 suggests that many barbaric punishments may be carried out, unless the criminal repents. The hadiths appear to add the punishment of stoning for sex outside marriage. Nevertheless, it is debated how far these were descriptions of what took place at the time, and how far these were instructions for Muslims to follow afterwards, and in what circumstances, since the punishments were not always applied equally and in all similar circumstances by the Prophet.

Over time the main Islamic schools of Fiqh grew up and with them different interpretations about the death penalty. The death penalty is suggested for someone who converts to another religion and rejects the roles and responsibilities of the Muslim community they live in.

Some schools of thought suggest the death penalty should be carried out for Muslims who carry out homosexual sex in a public place in front of four or more people. The Hanafi Mahdab suggests it is up to a judge to decide what punishment that should be, varying from a verbal reprimand up to the maximum of a hundred lashes. For the crime to be carried out but witnessed by fewer than four people or in private, there is no shari'a punishment: it is between a person's individual conscience and God.

In some Muslim countries the shari'a process has been usurped by popular pressure, or even people taking matters into their own hands and administering punishment as vigilantes. This is against shari'a too, since it has been agreed by the traditional schools of thought that the proper process of making judgement was also given by God through the Islamic traditions. Some countries do not follow traditional rulings or make new punishments according to the ideas of their rulers, as they see fit.

Islamic Law allows for the victims of crime or their families to accept a compensation payment, rather like a large fine, to be paid instead of corporal or capital punishment. These fines can be very large. In the case of murder, a victim's family can demand the death penalty or demand compensation. In this way, shari'a was a means of reducing honour killings in the early days of Islam in a very honour craven tribal society, rather than increasing physical punishments.

Reformist Muslims reject the death penalty in all circumstances. They regard it as relevant to the time but not applicable nowadays. Reformists emphasise the human rights of all and see the death penalty as a form of abuse which is another form of violence, and adds nothing to the good of society. Imadad Dean Ahmad, president of Minaret of Freedom organisation, argues against the death penalty in all but the most serious of crimes.

A modernist scholarly view (Tariq Ramadan)

Tariq Ramadan wrote an article calling for the suspension of the death penalty across the Islamic world whilst a review is carried out. He wanted to bring Muslim scholars into a process of discussion in which the punishment could be debated and reviewed. He stopped short of calling for the complete abolition of the death penalty because he thought this would be ineffective, and those who believed in a literal interpretation of the Qur'an would simply ignore his call. Some criticised him for apologising for those who promoted barbaric punishments, whereas he claimed that he was simply trying to be practical.

Key quote

We launch today a call for an immediate international moratorium on corporal punishment, stoning and the death penalty in all Muslim majority countries. Considering that the opinions of most scholars, regarding the comprehension of the texts and the application of hudud, are neither explicit nor unanimous (indeed there is not even a clear majority), and bearing in mind that political systems and the state of the majority Muslim societies do not guarantee a just

Key quote

I believe that the death penalty should only be applied as a punishment for wilful murder or for widespread criminal activity of a most serious nature, such as terrorism. However, because the criminal system in the United States has been unable to enforce the death penalty in a fair-handed manner, especially as regards the racial and ethnic backgrounds of the perpetrators, and because of the frequency with which people have been convicted of capital crimes and later shown to have been innocent, I believe that there should be a moratorium on the death penalty until such time as these flaws in the system can be fixed. (Imadad Dean Ahmad)

quickfire

4.17 Why do reformist Muslims reject the death penalty?

Specification content

A modernist scholarly view (Tariq Ramadan).

Tariq Ramadan

185

and equal treatment of individuals before the law, it is our moral obligation and religious responsibility to demand for the immediate suspension of the application of the hudud which is inaccurately accepted as an application of Islamic shari'a. (Ramadan)

A traditionalist Islamic scholar (Sheikh Ahmad Ash-Sharabasi)

Key quote

Death penalty is not a recent legislation, so it should not be subject to different views on whether to impose, lift or cancel it. It has been ordained a long time ago. ... All lawmakers legalise self-defence, and they say it is permissible for one to kill a person who attacks him, if there is no other way. So in resisting the attack, man is compared to the society as it fends off aggression. That is, a murderer deserves death penalty because he has trespassed against the whole society by killing one of its members. So, when the society calls for death penalty for such a criminal, it is really in a state of self-defence. (Ash-Sharabasi)

The Egyptian traditionalist Sunni scholar Sheikh Ahmad Ash-Sharabasi argues in favour of the death penalty. He argues that it is a form of self-defence, and that just as an individual may fight back against an attacker, society should fight back against criminals who attack the values of the rule of law. In the case of murder this means applying the death penalty.

Some traditionally minded Western Muslims agree. Dr Shahid Akhtar argues that the death penalty is applicable in some cases of murder, adultery and apostasy against both belief and the Muslim community. However, Muslims should aim to reform the criminal not focus on the punishment: the real punishment is in the afterlife.

Qisas, which means to follow suit, allows victims or their followers to demand the same punishment on the criminal as he or she carried out. However, the Qur'an only appears to allow the death penalty in the case of murder and in crimes against the community. In the second category, traditional Muslims do not agree on a comprehensive list.

> ### AO1 Activity
> Working in pairs, imagine you are two lawyers in a courtroom. One person will be arguing in favour of applying the death penalty as a punishment for murder and one against applying this punishment. List your strongest five arguments on each side.

The response of James Rachels (non-Islamic scholar)

The late James Rachels was an American academic who has carried out in-depth research into crime and punishment and reviewed the purposes, methods and effects of the death penalty.

Rachels identifies different reasons for punishment. One is to exact vengeance for the crime: to take retribution. This restores the balance of justice in the minds of the victims and their families. The Enlightenment thinker **Kant** thought that those who did wrong deserved a good beating in retribution. However, the philosopher **Bentham** thought that this only created more suffering in the world. Another

---

Specification content

A traditionalist Islamic scholar (Sheikh Ahmad Ash-Sharabasi).

A traditionalist Muslim

quickfire

4.18 How can the death penalty protect society, according to Shaykh (Sheikh) Sharabasi?

Key people

Immanuel Kant: a German philosopher who wrote about the relationship between reasoning and human experience.

Jeremy Bentham: English philosopher who founded the modern Utilitarian movement.

Specification content

The response of James Rachels (non-Islamic scholar).

theory is to put in place strict punishments such as the death penalty that will act as a deterrent so severe that no one else will risk doing the crime.

In the past few decades, people have sought to understand the causes of crime and educate and rehabilitate criminals through their punishment. The aim is to make them productive members of society so they will not reoffend. Rachels argues that all of the theories of punishment are utilitarian in that they are for practical use to make society safer. Punishment requires the criminal to feel guilty, to be treated equally to other criminals, to face a punishment proportionate to the crime and for those with particular circumstances to have these understood.

Rachels reviews several arguments against the death penalty. An eye for an eye approach makes the punishers no better than the criminal since they are agreeing with the action they carried out. If a murderer is himself or herself killed in retaliation, both criminal and punisher are in effect doing the same thing.

Key quote

When a rational being decides to treat people in a certain way, he [decides] that this is how people are to be treated. Thus if we treat him the same way in return, we are doing nothing more than treating him as he has decided to be treated. If he treats others badly, and we treat him badly, we are complying with his own decision. (Rachels)

There are a number of cases in which someone has suffered the death penalty but has later been found to have been innocent. Some cases have occurred in the USA in the context of disputed crimes with a racial element. It has been suggested that the death penalty may not be effective in societies where it is carried out. In some countries, including Muslim lands, the death penalty has been carried out on women, children and minorities.

Rachels fundamentally considers practical, utilitarian issues as the cornerstone of his argument. What works for society overall to benefit is what counts. This contrasts with Muslims who choose, at the end of the day, to consider revealed truth from the Qur'an to be the most important consideration. Muslims interpret this in different ways, but all regard it as the most important justification for punishment, regardless of whether it works or not.

Key term

Utilitarianism: practical decision making to benefit the most number of people, justifying decisions according to what works best

quickfire

4.19 What do Utilitarians see as the purpose of punishment?

Key skills

Knowledge involves:

Selection of a range of (thorough) accurate and relevant information that is directly related to the specific demands of the question.

This means:

- Selecting relevant material for the question set

- Be focused in explaining and examining the material selected.

Understanding involves:

Explanation that is extensive, demonstrating depth and/or breadth with excellent use of evidence and examples including (where appropriate) thorough and accurate supporting use of sacred texts, sources of wisdom and specialist language.

This means:

- Effective use of examples and supporting evidence to establish the quality of your understanding

- Ownership of your explanation that expresses personal knowledge and understanding and NOT just a chunk of text from a book that you have rehearsed and memorised.

AO1 Developing skills

It is now important to consider the information that has been covered in this section; however, the information in its raw form is too extensive and so has to be processed in order to meet the requirements of the examination. This can be achieved by practising more advanced skills associated with AO1. For assessment objective 1 (AO1), which involves demonstrating 'knowledge' and 'understanding' skills, we are going to focus on different ways in which the skills can be demonstrated effectively, and also refer to how the performance of these skills is measured (see generic band descriptors for A2 [WJEC] AO1 or A Level [Eduqas] AO1).

▶ **Your new task is this:** It is impossible to cover all essays in the time allowed by the course; however, it is a good exercise to develop detailed plans that can be utilised under timed conditions. As a last exercise:

1. Create some ideal plans by using what we have done so far in the Theme 4 Developing skills sections.

2. This time stop at the planning stage and exchange plans with a study partner.

3. Check each other's plans carefully. Talk through any omissions or extras that could be included, not forgetting to challenge any irrelevant materials.

4. Remember, collaborative learning is very important for revision. It not only helps to consolidate understanding of the work and appreciation of the skills involved, it is also motivational and a means of providing more confidence in one's learning. Although the examination is sat alone, revising as a pair or small group is invaluable.

When you have completed each plan, as a pair or small group refer to the band descriptors for A2 (WJEC) or A Level (Eduqas) and in particular have a look at the demands described in the higher band descriptors towards which you should be aspiring. Ask yourself:

- Does my work demonstrate thorough, accurate and relevant knowledge and understanding of religion and belief?

- Is my work coherent (consistent or make logical sense), clear and well organised?

- Will my work, when developed, be an extensive and relevant response which is specific to the focus of the task?

- Does my work have extensive depth and/or suitable breadth and have excellent use of evidence and examples?

- If appropriate to the task, does my response have thorough and accurate reference to sacred texts and sources of wisdom?

- Are there any insightful connections to be made with other elements of my course?

- Will my answer, when developed and extended to match what is expected in an examination answer, have an extensive range of views of scholars/schools of thought?

- When used, is specialist language and vocabulary both thorough and accurate?

Issues for analysis and evaluation

The effectiveness of Islamic ethical teachings as a guide for living for Muslims today

**This section covers AO2
content and skills**

Specification content

The effectiveness of Islamic ethical
teachings as a guide for living for
Muslims today.

Islamic ethics are based on the revealed truth given in the Qur'an and the example
of Muhammad in his sunna. At first sight, there appears little flexibility in this. If
Allah declares that society be controlled by punishment to enforce adherence to His
will, then that is what should happen. Reality is far more complicated. The Qur'an
covers the story of Cain and Abel, in which punishment is offered as three choices,
but the best in the sight of Allah is forgiveness. This would imply that in principle,
there should be space in Islamic societies for rehabilitating people guilty of crime
so that they can change their ways and contribute to the common good.

Key quote

In the Qur'anic discourse, beyond the story of Cain and Abel, we find that
there are various articulations and pronouncements directed at murder and
punishment, but not necessarily mandating execution or the death penalty as a
recourse … When it comes to talking about the ultimate punishment, capital
punishment, it talks about intentional murder, and it says that in the case of
intentional murder there are three options. One option is that the family of the
victim would demand compensation … a sum of money in compensation … The
second possibility is that the family of the murderer demand exaction, i.e., then
the offender would be killed. And third is to forgive… And it's quite interesting
here, the Qur'an goes on to say, in the same verse in which it endorses the three
part structure, it says, and those who forgive are higher in the sight of God.
(El Fadl)

Islamic ethics are sometimes better understood in terms of public and private. It
is unethical to display sexual conduct in Islamic societies because it offends and is
regarded as impolite and going against the directions of Allah. However, in private,
everything is a matter of personal conscience. In many Islamic societies outward
behaviour appears strictly governed by Islamic codes of morals and manners. In
private, all the vices sometimes associated with the West happen commonly. It is
seen as a virtue, if a Muslim sees a friend doing wrong, to hide their sin. If a college
girl saw her friend going out with a boyfriend, against Islamic tradition, they might
look the other way rather than tell her parents. In this way a traditional society is
maintained. Some see this as based on hypocrisy: people show one thing in public
and another in private. Others see this as respect for Allah's laws for the good of
society, even when individuals don't live up to the highest standards, at least they
don't advertise their shortcomings.

Key quote

If a friend among your friends errs, make seventy excuses for them. If your
hearts are unable to do this, then know that the shortcoming is in your own
selves. (al-Qassar)

In most secular states ethics are formed by democratic governments creating laws
for the good of the people, and enacting what works best. In this way they can be
said to be utilitarian or practical. Islam, on the other hand, does not allow ethics to
overrule revelation. The commands of the Qur'an come first. Yet there is provision
for Shura, consultation or democracy in a form, in Islamic tradition. The Qur'an is
not so clear on many modern ethical issues which need the guidance of scholars,
use of analogy and even reinterpretation to be properly understood.

Traditional Islamic punishments create ethical challenges in terms of human rights.
Is it ethical to put in place punishments which are forms of retribution? This might

AO2 Activity

As you read through this section try to
do the following:

1. Pick out the different lines of
   argument that are presented in
   the text and identify any evidence
   given in support.

2. For each line of argument try to
   evaluate whether or not you think
   this is strong or weak.

3. Think of any questions you may
   wish to raise in response to the
   arguments.

This Activity will help you to start
thinking critically about what you
read and help you to evaluate the
effectiveness of different arguments
and from this develop your own
observations, opinions and points
of view that will help with any
conclusions that you make in your
answers to the AO2 questions
that arise.

An Imam in his office

be seen as continuing tribal codes of the past: an eye for an eye. Some would argue that victims have a need to feel that the people who have wronged them and their family have been punished, so there is value in retribution. Others feel that it is better to enact the death penalty on a few people as a deterrent rather than allow many more people to suffer at the hands of criminals who feel that softer punishments are worth risking.

On the other hand, deterrents create societies based on fear, and drive problems underground. Rehabilitation might be a better interpretation of the Islamic tradition of mercy and forgiveness. As James Rachels argues, rehabilitation can yield more long-term good for everyone in society, including the victims, when the criminals change and reform.

Traditional Islamic punishments include the death penalty, which many today see as immoral. How can people take away another life? Even from the religious perspective, to some it does not make sense that following Allah's mercy should involve taking a life that only He, as creator, should be entitled to take away. Those who agree with the death penalty say that it is a mercy because it is kinder on society as a whole which does not have to suffer more of such crimes. Opponents disagree and say the punishment is sometimes wrongly applied and is not effective. Physical punishments, such as severing a hand for theft, applied by some Middle Eastern regimes today, are argued by some to be effective deterrents to protect society from evils; by others they are said not to work and simply push problems underground.

Serious social problems exist in many communities across the Muslim world. Some of these are the product of high population growth creating stress on resources; others on how to reconcile modern living with traditional moral frameworks. Within the UK, there are issues regarding the high crime rate amongst some Muslims. Is this due to a detachment between faith and the requirements of the law, or other social factors such as life, for many, in deprived communities? Some argue that the divide between the way ethics is understood by most people in society and those Muslims who understand ethics first in terms of God's revealed law, creates a disconnect that makes moral decisions difficult. Others say that many modern Muslims are able to reconcile the two and make educated, rational decisions for themselves.

In some ways Iran is known for harsh shari'a punishments, but its rehabilitation programme for drug addicts has become known as a good example to other countries where rehabilitation has overcome a problem. There is a major drug addiction problem in the country and traditional shari'a punishments have not worked. Progressive policies were started in local communities by compassionate people and backed by charities and non-governmental organisations. The aim has been to get addicts to rehab and to stop them harming themselves. Clean needles have been given out free to those on the streets and in prison, and condoms to sex workers, to reduce rates of infection. Methadone has been made available on prescription to help wean addicts off more dangerous heroin.

Key questions

What should ethics and moral decision making be guided by?

Is it important to apply the same ethical values in private and in public?

Are traditional Islamic punishments such as the death penalty unethical?

In what ways can the spirit of compassion be applied by Muslims on moral and ethical matters?

AO2 Activity

List some conclusions that could be drawn from the AO2 reasoning from the above text; try to aim for at least three different possible conclusions. Consider each of the conclusions and collect brief evidence to support each conclusion from the AO1 and AO2 material for this topic. Select the conclusion that you think is most convincing and explain why it is so. Try to contrast this with the weakest conclusion in the list, justifying your argument with clear reasoning and evidence.

Key quote

[A progressive] approach has been championed by the public – as a bottom-up movement – and by public institutions (or some of them at least) as timely reforms. Today, every Iranian city and even many towns and villages, have methadone clinics, rehabilitation centres and 'detox camps', to which people seeking support or medical treatment can resort. NGOs are also active at the margins of the cities providing clean syringes and limited everyday medical care for street addicts. Iran is a model for many countries in the region and other countries wanting to reform criminalising drug policy look to it. (Ghiabi)

The extent to which Islamic teachings on punishment can be applied today

Specification content
The extent to which Islamic teachings on punishment can be applied today.

There are two opposite modern trends: one is to focus on Islamic aspects of mercy, and modernise punishments in line with the world we live in. The Ottoman Empire in the nineteenth century updated their legal codes along the lines of modern European powers without criticism from Islamic scholars. Reformists argue the death penalty and other physical punishments belong to another age. They deny human rights and in any case, are unlikely to work for the overall benefit of society. Better to study utilitarian punishments that work and focus on rehabilitating criminals so they change their ways and contribute for the good of others.

A second trend is to increase strict punishments. Pakistan, Brunei, Iran and Saudi Arabia, all have hudud ordinances for certain crimes. Partly in reaction against the modern world and what they see as the unfairness of previous colonial rule or unjust rulers, some Muslims look back on a mythical age imagining a pure society in which people followed the revealed shari'a law. Extreme groups have claimed to put in place strict punishments to create such a view of society.

The reality is very different. In many cases early Islamic societies did not apply any one particular version of shari'a punishment: it depended on the opinion of the ruler. Society was not pure and people were often more forgiving than the impression created by some Muslims today. There were corporal and capital punishments recorded in the Qur'an and the days of Muhammad, which if interpreted literally read uncomfortably for reformist Muslims. However, they argue they were descriptions of cultural practice which are nowadays inappropriate as we modernise and improve human rights.

The Shi'a Islamic state of Iran includes qisas punishment in its legal code. Murderers may be taken to court by the victim's family and the life of the murderer demanded in retribution. It is also possible for the victim of a violent attack to request the same physical punishment they have suffered to be carried out on their attacker. An Iranian woman, Ameneh Bahrami, was blinded in an acid attack and demanded her attacker, Majiv Movahedi be blinded in return, but on the morning of the day of punishment she changed her mind and forgave him instead.

Cultural practices may be combined with Islam, in some regions, to create qasis punishments. There are cases of girls being forcibly married to others in Pakistan and Afghanistan, in return for crimes committed by family members within the tribe. This appeases tribal law, but goes against the Islamic teaching that marriage cannot be forced.

In Saudi Arabia, public beheadings and physical punishments are commonplace. They argue that with the rise of drug addiction, for instance, harsh punishments are necessary to provide a deterrent to the people. Opponents argue that the punishments are not only wrong, but they create a society in which everything still happens secretly. This is worse because it is more difficult for victims to get justice, especially if they are weaker members of society such as women, those of other nationalities or faiths or members of the Shi'a sect.

Key quote

It is nearly impossible for a thief or fornicator to be sentenced, unless he wishes to do so and confesses. (Rudolph Peters)

Key quote

An Islamic opposition to the death penalty must begin by acknowledging that the Qur'an may clearly be read as giving special exemption (from the general prohibition on killing) to the taking of a murderer's life. ... The responsibility of a Muslim is justice. Will the killing of a murderer produce justice? There is no justice here. No needs are met, no fear is alleviated. This idea does not work. The hallmark of truth is that it works. It is a far more serious error of Islamic ethics to demand a human death in circumstances when there are doubts about guilt or innocence, where the bereaved are not consulted about their wishes,

AO2 Activity

As you read through this section try to do the following:

1. Pick out the different lines of argument that are presented in the text and identify any evidence given in support.

2. For each line of argument try to evaluate whether or not you think this is strong or weak.

3. Think of any questions you may wish to raise in response to the arguments.

This Activity will help you to start thinking critically about what you read and help you to evaluate the effectiveness of different arguments and from this develop your own observations, opinions and points of view that will help with any conclusions that you make in your answers to the AO2 questions that arise.

and when the penalty is selectively applied based on the pernicious fantasy that some lives have more value than others. (Rabia Terri Harris)

Rabia Terri Harris argues that it is not right to apply the death penalty today. She argues that death does not bring justice, and does not work in practice. There are many cases, particularly in the USA, where alleged criminals who are black have been convicted in dubious cases by all white juries, and sentenced to death.

Medieval Muslim scholars in some cases could find many reasons why punishments should not be applied: so many as to make the punishment almost impossible. Even without these excuses, punishments for adultery requiring four adult, reliable male witnesses to see the act, are very unlikely to be found, making it practically impossible for shari'a to be applied in reality.

Islamic revivalists such as the South Asian Scholar Maududi encouraged the use of shari'a punishment as part of a moral code yearned for by people increasingly turning to Islam as their identity. Strict shari'a punishments deter people from transgressing the commands of Islam. Others, including members of the group Jamiat Islami, argue that it is essential to create a just society based on God consciousness before any punishment can be applied. First, the people must believe in God and take the moral instructions into their hearts before they can apply them in their lives. If this is lacking, to impose Islamic punishments is like putting the cart before the horse.

Human rights groups have reported widespread abuses in some countries due to the interpretation of Islamic punishments by some. Groups of men in Pakistan have been known to allege a woman has committed adultery and all swear witness testimony so that she may be found guilty according to shari'a. If these men took into their hearts the true message of Islam then they might think twice before lying.

The secular state and the changing role of religion in the modern world mean that to many Muslims, crime and punishment is carried out by secular authorities, and Islamic punishment is the realm of God in the afterlife. To secular Muslims, this means that human rights can be championed, abuses challenged, and practical punishments applied for the good of everyone in society. Adultery and affairs might be better dealt with by care and counselling than punishment, and homosexuality would not be defined as wrong at all. Nevertheless, some believe that Muslims in the past were more compassionate at times than we sometimes think, and seldom applied punishments for these matters.

Study tip

It is important for AO2 that you include the views of scholars and/or schools of thought when formulating your response to a particular contention, as well as from more current scholars. However, make sure that the views you use are relevant to the point that you are making. Your ability to use such views in an appropriate way would distinguish a high level answer from one that is simply a general response.

Women protest in Iran against abusive imprisonment.

Key questions

What are the main Islamic punishments and in what cases were they originally applied?

What exceptions might be given where proof may be lacking or circumstances mean that a punishment might not be applied?

How do modern human rights and secular states affect the concept of punishment in Islam?

AO2 Activity

List some conclusions that could be drawn from the AO2 reasoning from the above text; try to aim for at least three different possible conclusions. Consider each of the conclusions and collect brief evidence to support each conclusion from the AO1 and AO2 material for this topic. Select the conclusion that you think is most convincing and explain why it is so. Try to contrast this with the weakest conclusion in the list, justifying your argument with clear reasoning and evidence.

AO2 Developing skills

It is now important to consider the information that has been covered in this section; however, the information in its raw form is too extensive and so has to be processed in order to meet the requirements of the examination. This can be achieved by practising more advanced skills associated with AO2. For assessment objective 2 (AO2), which involves 'critical analysis' and 'evaluation' skills, we are going to focus on different ways in which the skills can be demonstrated effectively, and also refer to how the performance of these skills is measured (see generic band descriptors for A2 [WJEC] AO2 or A Level [Eduqas] AO2).

▶ **Your new task is this:** It is impossible to cover all essays in the time allowed by the course; however, it is a good exercise to develop detailed plans that can be utilised under timed conditions. As a last exercise:

1. Create some ideal plans by using what we have done so far in the Theme 4 Developing skills sections.

2. This time stop at the planning stage and exchange plans with a study partner.

3. Check each other's plans carefully. Talk through any omissions or extras that could be included, not forgetting to challenge any irrelevant materials.

4. Remember, collaborative learning is very important for revision. It not only helps to consolidate understanding of the work and appreciation of the skills involved, it is also motivational and a means of providing more confidence in one's learning. Although the examination is sat alone, revising as a pair or small group is invaluable.

When you have completed the task, refer to the band descriptors for A2 (WJEC) or A Level (Eduqas) and in particular have a look at the demands described in the higher band descriptors towards which you should be aspiring. Ask yourself:

- Is my answer a confident critical analysis and perceptive evaluation of the issue?
- Is my answer a response that successfully identifies and thoroughly addresses the issues raised by the question set?
- Does my work show an excellent standard of coherence, clarity and organisation?
- Will my work, when developed, contain thorough, sustained and clear views that are supported by extensive, detailed reasoning and/or evidence?
- Are the views of scholars/schools of thought used extensively, appropriately and in context?
- Does my answer convey a confident and perceptive analysis of the nature of any possible connections with other elements of my course?
- When used, is specialist language and vocabulary both thorough and accurate?

Key skills
Analysis involves:

Identifying issues raised by the materials in the AO1, together with those identified in the AO2 section, and presents sustained and clear views, either of scholars or from a personal perspective ready for evaluation.

This means:

- That your answers are able to identify key areas of debate in relation to a particular issue
- That you can identify, and comment upon, the different lines of argument presented by others
- That your response comments on the overall effectiveness of each of these areas or arguments.

Evaluation involves:

Considering the various implications of the issues raised based upon the evidence gleaned from analysis and provides an extensive detailed argument with a clear conclusion.

This means:

- That your answer weighs up the consequences of accepting or rejecting the various and different lines of argument analysed
- That your answer arrives at a conclusion through a clear process of reasoning.

Questions and answers

Theme 1 DEF

AO1 answer: *An answer examining the importance of the hadith.*

A weaker answer

The hadith are the actions of Prophet Muhammad. He lived from 570 to 632 in Arabia in the city of Makkah and then Madinah. His actions should be understood in the context of the tribal society at the time. His actions form the hadith. **1**

Bukhari travelled around the Middle East to many countries, asking people what they knew about the Prophet's sayings. He had a brilliant memory and learned them all off by heart. On one occasion people questioned him and tried to catch him out but he recalled exactly who said what to whom about Muhammad's sayings. Bukhari was the most important hadith collector. **2**

Muslims use the hadith in their prayers every day. The Arabic words help them to feel they are in touch with the Prophet, who founded their religion, Islam. They want to follow his every example because he was the perfect model of a person. **3**

Shi'a Muslims regard the hadith as more important through being passed down by Ali, whom they think should have been the first Caliph. **4**

Having said that hadith are important, another point of view is that they are not important because it is that the Qur'an alone that is the word of God. I think that the hadith are important but less important that the Qur'an. **5**

Commentary

1. The introduction has confused hadith with sunna. Muhammad's action formed the sunna, which are largely recorded in his sayings, the hadith. The difference needs to be explained.

2. This paragraph is not specific, and does not directly address the question, which is about the hadith's importance. It could be made relevant by explaining that Bukhari was so accurate that Muslims regarded his hadith as an important and reliable source.

3. This paragraph suddenly jumps to Muhammad's example, which though important, does not follow logically from the paragraph before. The words from the hadith may be thought of in everyday life but it is the Qur'an that is used in prayers.

4. This paragraph is incorrect. Shi'a Muslims put the same importance on hadith and have their own collections, which are similar, but passed down only by members of the Prophet's family.

5. This paragraph contains some important information but needs to be expanded upon and explained. Qur'anists reject the hadith; traditional Muslims see hadith as the second source of information after the Qur'an, but still important.

Summative comment

This is a weak answer with a basic level of understanding and with no substantial explanations or examples. There are some important points which are not properly explained, so their value is missed. There are also a few errors. The answer needs to be improved by being much clearer about the points being made and explaining their significance in terms of the focus of the question, which is the importance of the hadith.

AO2 answer: *An answer that evaluates the place of Ijtihad in the modern world.*

A strong answer

The modern world presents a series of new ethical problems for Muslims not directly answered by the Qur'an and hadith, and others where answers appear not to fit modern lifestyles. Reformists argue there is a place for Ijtihad, reinterpretation, to find new answers. Many traditionalists argue the gates closed in the Middle Ages. Islamists also accept Ijtihad but from a different perspective. **1**

Reformist Muslims recognise that some traditional Islamic teachings appear to treat women unequally from men and condemn alternative lifestyles, such as homosexuality. They argue that the greater principle of human rights, which Prophet Muhammad championed in his time, justifies the use of Ijtihad to reinterpret the teachings of Islam for the present day. Reformists see an important place for modernising Islamic teachings to address abuses which have taken place and create an interpretation of Islam which is cohesive with living in a plural, secular world. **2**

Many traditional Sunni Muslims argue that the gates of Ijtihad were closed in the Middle Ages. Scholars of Fiqh, the law schools, answered all of the main questions and as time went by, Muslims could not be as aware as they were of answers the Prophet would likely have given. Therefore, any interpretations should not be new but should emulate those given by the early scholars. **3**

Shi'a Muslims take a different approach. Their Imams are thought to possess the power to interpret scripture and continued to make Ijtihad through the ages, using a greater degree of reasoning, but still along traditionalist lines. **4**

Muslims who follow modern movements which aim to increase the position of Islam within society, regard Ijtihad as important but in a different way from reformists. Salafi Muslims reject the idea that interpretation is the preserve of scholars through the ages and say that Muslims should directly access the teaching of the Prophet and the Sahaba, his companions, to make new interpretations for today. At the same time, they reject innovation in religion and wish to strictly preserve the original style of worship, and reject accepting modern socially liberal views. [5]

Debate within the Muslim world about a range of issues shows the need Muslims have for guidance that they feel is not answered clearly by traditional teachings. I believe that because the world has changed so much, Muslims should make new interpretations, as long their intention is to do the right thing for Allah. [6]

Commentary

1 A clear introduction which defines the way the essay will proceed in the following paragraphs and sets the scope of the answer.

2 Sets out the reformist case giving reasons why they support Ijtihad, from a modern liberal perspective.

3 Rejects modern Ijtihad from a traditional perspective, justifying this from the point of view that early scholars knew better.

4 Describes the Shia perspective, justifying the use of Ijtihad by the belief in the power of their Imams.

5 Clearly describes an alternative viewpoint and explains why this is different from Ijtihad by reformists.

6 The conclusion takes the essay back to the introduction by referring to modern issues which require a response, then adds a personal view point which raises the importance of personal intention.

Summative comment

A strong answer with a clear structure, this essay makes reference to different points of view and concludes with a personal response. It could be further enhanced by quotations or examples, such as reference to Al-Ghazali and closing the gates of Ijtihad, or quotes from reformist or Salafi scholars to justify why they might use Ijtihad in their different ways.

Theme 3 ABC

AO1 answer: *An answer that examines Islamic beliefs about the creation of the universe.*

A weaker answer

Allah made the world and everything in it in seven days. He made the worlds, the seas, the creatures and then Adam and Eve, the first people. [1]

God made the universe out of nothing. The Qur'an says it spread apart and came together. This proves that the Qur'an was a miracle because it confirmed the details of the Big Bang theory 1400 years ago. God knows everything and the Qur'an is from God so that's why He already knew this theory. [2]

The difference between religion and Science is God. Scientists do not believe in God. They think that the world just happened by chance. Muslims believe in Allah. Nothing happens without His say so. He was the one that planned it all out and controlled the creation of the universe. [3]

When Allah finished making the universe He then went on to create the animals, plants and people. The beauty in the world proves that Allah created it because no one else could have just made such wonderful things. [4]

Since Allah created it, He can also take it away. Allah is outside of the universe and exists before and after it and will take it away one day when it disappears into a giant black hole. That will be our fate in the end of time. [5]

In conclusion, I agree that God made the world and everything in it, as you cannot just have a universe made out of nothing, you need God to start it off. [6]

Commentary

1 The subject of this question is the creation of the universe, not the details of the creation of people in the world, so the short introduction here is only partly relevant.

2 Some Muslims, such as Harun Yahya, agree with this viewpoint, but it is by no means universally agreed. Others might disagree and say the Qur'an is not referring to this or perhaps it could be used to support another theory, the Expanding Oscillating Universe theory. This needs to be made clearer.

3 Simply put, there is some good information here although not all scientists are atheists. This paragraph could be improved with more detail about why there needs to be a first cause, which Muslims see as God, and why some might disagree.

4 Some Muslims say Allah continues to create the universe. Some, such as Al-Biruni, could be quoted here to back up this paragraph.

5 There are some good points here which would be better integrated into earlier paragraphs. However, the black hole idea is from science, not Islam.

6 This is a simplistic conclusion which supports the first cause theory, and would have been better introduced earlier on and backed up with evidence, such as by referring to Avicenna.

Summative comment

Despite referring to many relevant points, such as the First cause, the role of Allah and so on, this essay is confused in parts, lacks detail and references to support it, and does not clearly build up an argument. The points need to be sorted out and reordered. A more detailed and accurate explanation of Islamic and scientific theories should be included, which clearly sorts out Big Bang, black holes and the views of scientists and atheists.

AO2 answer: *An answer that evaluates whether Islam is compatible with pluralism.*

A strong answer

Pluralism means accepting there are different ways which are equally valid. We live in pluralistic societies in which people of different faiths and none work and socialise together. Individuals choose different lifestyles and partners. In religion, pluralists believe people can choose their beliefs and there are many different paths which lead to God and heaven. [1]

The Constitution of Madinah guaranteed rights to minorities and allowed freedom of religion to others such as Christians and Jews, who were also recognised as genuine believers. At times Muhammad fought against those of other faiths, but this might have been because of tribal politics rather than faith. On the other hand, Islam was always seen as the ideal religion, the last revelation, and people were not free in the way that they are today to choose their religion. [2]

Early Muslim leaders such as Caliph Umar paid benefits to poor Christians and insisted that their places of worship were kept safe when Muslims conquered Jerusalem. There are occasions in history when Muslim armies spread across the Middle East and others were treated less favourably and even forced to convert. At other times, such as in Islamic Spain, Muslims lived together with Christians and Jews whose culture was usually respected and flourished. [3]

Some Muslims treat others around them with respect according to the behaviours they feel are recommended by the Qur'an and hadith. They are happy to live together and share community events. But they do not accept that others have a place in heaven. They interpret Islamic teachings to mean that people must convert to Islam to get to heaven in the future, as they believe they will be asked about who they believe in at Judgement. These Muslims consider it their duty to preach dawah to others to encourage them to embrace Islam. [4]

Modern reformist Muslims often celebrate pluralism and the advantages of living in secular societies, enabling Muslims to learn from different people around them. When Islam was it its height, it was open to knowledge translated from other cultures, so therefore Muslims should welcome the opportunities it brings. [5]

I believe that Islam is compatible with pluralism, and that Muslims can respect and learn from others, but in many areas of the world today human rights abuses of minorities show that some Muslims disagree. I think that is in spite of Islamic teachings of mutual respect, not because of them. [6]

Commentary

1. A strong introduction which clearly defines pluralism both in terms of society and in terms of accepting others' beliefs.

2. A well-balanced paragraph which includes points that can be used to support pluralism and those against from the lifetime of Muhammad, which is the main focus here.

3. Another well-balanced paragraph the subject of which is the broad sweep of Islamic history.

4. This paragraph expands upon the different definitions of pluralism mentioned in the introduction. Quotations from Qur'an and hadith would help here. An alternative way of structuring the essay could be to divide this paragraph into two to address the different meanings in more detail.

5. A different angle, which could be expanded by reference to lifestyles. Reformists might accept homosexual relationships as equally valid, for example.

6. A clear personal viewpoint in support of the question is given at the end.

Summative comment

A strong answer, which takes a broad perspective largely from Islamic history and traditions. There are different possible ways of organising this essay: different viewpoints could be taken as the focus of each paragraph, and an argument built up that way. Nevertheless this way is also good and works overall. The essay could further delve into differences of viewpoint around pluralism in terms of whether non-Muslims can get to heaven, by referring to different beliefs, one being that those who have not heard or have not rejected the message can, another being that only those who specifically accept it are admitted to paradise in the afterlife.

Theme 3 DEF

AO1 answer: *An answer that explains the notion of Islamophobia.*

A weaker answer

There is a lot of prejudice against Islam nowadays. Muslims can find it harder than other people to get a job. This is a form of Islamophobia. This answer is asking what Islamophobia is all about which I am going to explain in the next few paragraphs. [1]

Tell Mama is a website and phone line which was set up for Muslims to report incidents of attack and prejudice. There has been an increase in racism recently which has led to more attacks. This is one form of Islamophobia. **2**

Some people in the newspaper criticise Islam. They do not like what Islam teaches and disagree with the Prophet. A French magazine made cartoon images which upset many Muslims and was unfair. **3**

The Runnymede Trust wrote a report about Islamophobia. They said that people who think of Muslims as all the same and don't see people as individuals do it. They said that Muslims should be treated equally just like any other group. **4**

Terrorists give Muslims a bad image and I can understand why others feel frightened of Muslims as a result. However, there is no need to take it out on Muslims in revenge. **5**

The government and the Muslim Council of Britain are working to address Islamophobia so that hopefully, in the future, it disappears and Muslims are allowed to wear hijab and pray openly without fear of attack. **6**

Commentary

1 A simple definition of Islamophobia is made. The last sentence of the introduction is not needed and does not add anything to the answer.

2 Racism and Islamophobia are different: Muslims are not a race. This paragraph needs to be corrected.

3 It is legitimate to criticise Islam, the point is that many in the media are imbalanced in their criticism. The point about cartoons of the Prophet is complex and some would argue it is freedom of speech and satire; others that it hurt Muslim feelings so was unhelpful, but was not necessarily Islamophobia, because the magazine criticised others at least as much.

4 This is a good paragraph which could be better expressed, added to and included at the start of the essay since it better covers the subject.

5 This brief paragraph could be expanded since it is on the right lines.

6 Aspects regarding dress and prayers and the MCB could be expanded on here.

Summative comment

There are many points in this essay which are wrong because the writer has not been clear and precise. It is important to be clear on terms and to explain carefully what is meant. Many points are referred to without being properly explained and the order to the essay does not make best sense.

AO2 answer: *An answer that evaluates the contribution of feminism to Islam.*

A strong answer

Feminism is about promoting women's rights as equal to men. At first sight, Islam might seem like a male-dominated religion, led by male Imams and founded by male Prophets. Women wear veils and appear to be unequal to men. How can feminism have made any contribution? **1**

In the days of the Prophet, women were badly treated and babies who were girls were sometimes killed. The Prophet stood up against such injustices and told Muslims to treat women well. He granted rights of inheritance and said women should be educated. He married one, Khadijah, who was also his boss in business and his senior. This suggests Muhammad promoted feminism. **2**

Medieval schools and universities were founded by women as often as men. There is even a tradition that Muhammad appointed Umm Waraq as a female Imam. Rabia of Basra was one of the most famous Sufis. **3**

In modern times, there have been female heads of state in Muslim countries including Pakistan, Bangladesh and Indonesia. More women than men achieve postgraduate degrees in Iran. Muslim feminists such as Haleh Afshar argue that Islam promotes women's rights. **4**

However, Muhammad valued women, but not as equals of men. Their roles were different, and although women could have careers, they also had duties in the home. During the Middle Ages, male-dominated Islamic society rarely promoted women. **5**

Many Muslim feminists today say Islam is in need of reform. Feminism is a provocative force which contributes questions and debate to Islam so that Muslims can think about what are the main principles of their faith. **6**

Haleh Afshar, and other prominent Muslim feminists, sometimes differ from others in that they still emphasise and value their roles as mothers and leaders in the home, rather than completely equal partners of men. **7**

In today's world, feminist Muslims are calling on Islam to change and reform. Aminah Wadud, a female Imam from the USA, provokes Muslims into considering feminism. I think that the traditional roles for men and women in Islam are different, but this does not mean that women have a lesser status. **8**

Commentary

1 A provocative introduction which addresses the stereotype that Islam is male dominated and gains the attention of the reader.

2 3 4 Build up the case for Islam's contribution to women's rights from the time of the Prophet, through Muslim history to the present day in that order. It is

a logical way of building up points on one side of the argument.

5 6 7 Do the same from the point of view of the limitations of Islam's contribution.

This way of setting out the essay makes sense. A different way of organising the paragraphs could be to put them in order of the strength of argument.

8 The conclusion leads to a personal response at the end which could be developed.

Summative comment

A strong essay which covers different points of view to a provocative question. A broad range of different points are covered. Quotes and references could have been added, particularly from the Qur'an and hadith, both in favour of women's rights and those which do not appear to promote them. Inequality in shari'a is another area which could be covered. Nevertheless, it is not possible to refer to everything in timed conditions and this makes a good attempt.

Theme 4 DEF

AO1 answer: *An answer that examines the main features and purpose of Sufi rituals.*

A strong answer

Sufis are Muslims who follow an inner, spiritual path to God. Their rituals include taking bayah, an oath of allegiance to a Mushid teacher; participating in dhikr services which are ways of remembering Allah; meditation to achieve a higher spiritual awareness; and visiting the tombs of saints and companions of the Prophet. **1**

The bayah ritual involves a Mureed, or seeker, reciting a prayer and stating that they will be obedient to a Shaykh or guide who leads a Sufi order. The guide normally places his hands on the head or hand of the follower, or they are connected with a cloth. The purpose is to publically proclaim commitment which is necessary because Sufis believe they need guiding to understand the deeper mysteries of their faith. **2**

Dikhr services on Thursday evenings are the focus of the week. Arabic chants, qasida songs and entering a trance-like dance are rituals that may be observed. The purpose is to strengthen the experience of Allah, which happens when the Sufi enters hal, a deeper consciousness where they become unaware of the world around them and fully focused on God in preparation for the more important world in the afterlife. **3**

Sufis are guided by their Murshid in their dreams and meditations so that they can achieve a sense of union with God. These rituals vary according to the development of the person. The guide will prescribe what is needed to be

done, because everyone is at different stages and without this a Sufi might go on the wrong track. Some renounce the world and go into asceticism, called zuhd, in which they practise austere rituals of prayer, fasting and individual devotions. **4**

Sufis perform Ziyarah, particularly in South Asia and Iran, in which they visit the tombs of saints. They purify themselves first, recite Arabic prayers and make personal requests in their mind in the presence of the goodness of the Shaykh's tomb. Since Allah lives in the heart of the true believer, some Sufis regard the visit as equivalent to the greater spiritual meaning of Hajj, which is pilgrimage to God's house in Makkah. For those unable to make the journey, the visit to the saint's tomb satisfies this pillar. **5**

The ultimate purpose of Sufi rituals is to develop God consciousness and through that deeper faith. Sufis do not see the rituals as gaining extra reward for heaven, because their purpose is not to do that, but instead to gain a deeper loving relationship with God. To them, this comes above all else. **6**

Commentary

1 A straightforward introduction which concisely defines terms and sets out the structure of the answer.

2 The bayah commitment ceremony, a logical place to start, is clearly explained.

3 The main Sufi ritual is described and the purpose of this, in hal, is explained. The answer is not clouded with too much detail: there is a balance between the amount of description and the amount of explanation.

4 The paragraph follows the same format, referring to meditation.

5 A particular perspective of South Asian Sufis is covered here, which Iranian Shi'as might also agree with. It could be worth pointing out that some Muslims disagree with this practice and not all follow it, as they believe it raises the status of the person buried there above that of an ordinary human and in visiting a person may be performing an act of shirk.

6 A conclusion which adds to the essay by providing an overview of the purposes and clearly rounds off the end.

Summative comment

Overall, this is clearly a strong answer. Each of the main middle paragraphs contains factual details of the rituals followed by explanation of why they are done, i.e. the purpose. The structure follows that clearly indicated by the introduction and goes further in the conclusion by explaining the overall main point. Possibly a quote or reference to the name of a Sufi would help improve this good answer even further.

AO2 answer: *An answer evaluating whether Muslims need a teacher to understand their faith.*

A weaker answer

Islam was founded 1400 years ago. It is difficult to understand the Arabic from those times and what Muslims meant, therefore Muslims need someone to help them understand today. **1**

I agree with this question. Muslims today don't understand ancient Arabic, so they need a teacher to tell them what the words mean, otherwise they might get confused or even think the text means something that it does not. The best person to ask is the Imam because he is qualified to understand what it means. Sufis can also ask their Shaykhs because they guide them to understand what the Qur'an means with their special services and meditations. **2**

I disagree with this question because Muslims should also work it out for themselves. Why should I follow Islamic teachers who have lived hundreds of years ago? They cannot be more accurate than the companions who lived around the Prophet. Islamic bookshops provide guidebooks and leaflets about the saying of the companions which Muslims can buy and then make their own minds up. Besides, there are lots of different Imams and they never agree with each other. If you go to them as a guide you might end up even more confused and not knowing which one is right from which group: Sunni, Shi'a, Salafi or Sufi. **3**

In conclusion, I think the disagree points are stronger. I don't want anyone else telling me what to believe and I would rather look things up myself on the Internet than go to an Imam. **4**

Commentary

1 A simplistic introduction which only addresses one aspect of this question, language. A broader definition of the scope of the question is needed.

2 A long paragraph of agree points which could do with being broken up into shorter paragraphs in which each point is better explained. The point about Imams refers to the Shi'a belief that only their Imams, from the family of the Prophet, have the power to interpret what the unclear verses of the Qur'an mean and that the people should not make up their own interpretations. Sufi Mureeds who give allegiance to a Murshid guide accept what they say absolutely, as they believe it is essential to follow a guide to reach a higher state of God consciousness.

3 Another long paragraph which again could be broken up. It does not follow well from the previous paragraph as it suggests the writer is confused as to whether they agree or disagree. A better way of putting it would be to write that they understand why some people disagree (i.e. even if they don't personally take that view). This paragraph effectively describes the position of Salafis and should be recognised as such. There are others who are not Salafi who also believe that, from a modern reformist viewpoint, no one had a monopoly on the truth and people should be free to work things out for themselves.

4 A personal viewpoint which is poorly expressed and backed up by the writer's feeling rather than justified logically by reasoning.

Summative comment

A teacher could be a Shi'a Imam, a Sufi Murshid, a scholar or some other form of help. This is not clearly identified in this response which misses the point. Reasoning is not built up in the long middle paragraphs. The language is simplistic and conversational rather than academic. A better conclusion would be to give a couple of reasons why the disagree points, in the writer's view, are stronger.

Quickfire answers

Theme 1 DEF

1.1 Literally, the straight path. It has come to mean Islamic Law.

1.2 He went from Uzbekistan to Makkah, Madinah, Baghdad, Jerusalem, Damascus and Egypt.

1.3 If it went against the Qur'an or was biased to any one tribe; if it referred to later events or was extreme in any matter.

1.4 Acceptable narrators were honest, had good memory or were pious; unacceptable narrators were known for not telling the truth on some matter, or spreading rumours, or unsure of who told them the hadith.

1.5 The companions met together and agreed that Abu Bakr should take the role of Caliph.

1.6 Shafi'i, Hanafi, Malaki and Hanbali.

1.7 Al-Shafi had sharp intellect: he was a good archer, a chess strategist and had a photographic memory.

1.8 That the Qur'an was created by people, not revealed by God.

1.9 Qiyas is comparison to find a teaching from a similar example; aql goes further and allows a teaching to be drawn by logical reasoning.

1.10 Caliph Al-Mamun tried to force people to believe that the Qur'an was created by people, not the word of God.

1.11 Particularly cases of adultery, sexual cases and family matters. (At some places and in some times in history other criminal cases have been heard in shari'a courts by agreement with the ruling authority.)

1.12 A person might be found innocent or guilty by the judge; they could be freed; forgiven by the victim's family; asked to pay compensation; or given a punishment by the judge. The punishment might be a compulsory punishment or one which the judge has discretion over.

1.13 Equal opportunities, such as to be treated equally with those of other faiths or none when applying for a job.

1.14 A parliament in Iran or, generally, a Muslim gathering.

1.15 Knowledge and science were valued and Muslims sought out books from the classical world to translate.

1.16 The compilation of the Qur'an by Zayd bin Thabit under Caliph Uthman.

1.17 Mortgages are allowed when necessary for housing and autopsy of a body after death is permissible.

1.18 The jihad of the heart, the word, the hand and the sword.

1.19 A mujahid is someone who carries out jihad.

1.20 Tribal features included: raiding camel trade caravans, deals, treachery, inter-tribal warfare.

1.21 Women, children and the elderly should not be harmed; trees, crops and livestock should not be destroyed; Muslims should not double cross others and should remain firm in faith. Religious people, such as monks, should not be harmed. War should be defensive. It should not be used to convert others to Islam or to gain property or wealth for oneself.

1.22 Hasan al-Banna, Abdullah Azzam.

1.23 They are forbidden and lead not to heaven but to hellfire.

Theme 3 ABC

3.1 Muezzin who gave the call to prayer in the mosque in Madinah.

3.2 The muhajirun were the emigrants who had moved from Makkah and the ansar were the people of Madinah who became Muslim.

3.3 The Prophet said it was a sanctuary and forbade weapons, conflict and so on in a special area in the city.

3.4 The traditions and customs of the people of Madinah.

3.5 Ummah originally meant the Madinah community including believers of different faiths.

3.6 The Tanzimat reforms were carried out by the Ottomans in Turkey in the nineteenth century. They legalised homosexuality and stopped the death penalty for apostasy.

3.7 Ali Abd'al Raziq wrote in favour of secularism. He thought Muhammad did not set any one system of government, so Muslims could choose secularism and that would be better because it would stop some rulers oppressing Muslims.

3.8 Ibn al-Haytham developed scientific method of careful observation, questioning and deduction, according to modern scientist Jim al-Khalili.

3.9 Qur'an al-Tadwini: the revealed Qur'an, the book. Qur'an al-Takwini: the Qur'an as seen in the natural world.

3.10 Hayy ibn Yaqzan was stranded on a desert island without people and learned from the animals and nature around him, together with careful thought and reasoning, about the creation.

3.11 A first cause is the idea there must be something, such as God, to start everything off. It is particularly referred to in the creation of the universe and used to refute the theory of the Big Bang in which matter was created spontaneously in an explosion, without a first cause behind it all.

3.12 Al-Biruni observed nature and saw that it was fresh and new. That newness meant that it was created within time – it didn't always exist. The unity within creation suggested to him that it was created by a single source, which he thought was God.

3.13 Ibn Khaldun, Nidhal Guessoum, Dr Usama Hasan.

3.14 A monk named Bahira saw the young Muhammad and predicted that he would be a future holy man.

3.15 Al-Ghazali taught that most non-Muslims will enter heaven. Only those people who had heard many times, understood and felt the reality of the good in it, but then rejected that good, would not enter heaven.

3.16 Al-Biruni was one of the first to study comparative religion. He thought that all cultures were related to each other as they were all made by people. He did not judge others as right or wrong. He wanted to learn more about them.

3.17 One day she did not come. Muhammad went to see where she was and asked if she was alright.

3.18 Abbasid Caliph Al-Mamun tried to enforce the belief that the Qur'an was written by people, not revealed from Allah. He set up the Mihna, the Islamic inquisition, in which many were arrested and tried because of their beliefs.

Theme 3 DEF

3.19 Nuclear families are small, parents and children; extended are large and include grandparents, aunts, uncles and cousins.

3.20 The age of maturity is debated. Some say around 18 years, when a person is mature enough in body and mind for marriage. Others say 15, because Umar when aged 14 wanted to accompany the Prophet to Uhud but was told he was not yet at the age of maturity. Others say puberty at whatever age it occurs for the individual.

3.21 (a) The Nikkah is the marriage contract

(b) The Mahr is a payment from groom to bride to seal the marriage contract.

3.22 Mufti Gomaa taught that female genital mutilation is prohibited and has no basis in Islamic Law.

3.23 Any two from the following aims of Sisterhood: promote Muslim women's heritage; build solidarity; bring together voices of Muslim women; to show young women feminists the struggle of their history.

3.24 Haleh Afshar states that the Qur'anic reference to husbands beating their wives is a description of Arab practice at the time. It is not an instruction to Muslims today.

3.25 Bradford; East Birmingham; Tower Hamlets, amongst others.

3.26 The ideas that different cultures should co-exist in the same society.

3.27 Men should wear loose clothes that do not show the shape of their body and do not include gold or silk.

3.28 Amina Wadud led Jummah prayers and preached a sermon at Oxford Muslim Centre for a mixed group of male and female Muslims.

3.29 Co-ordinate Muslim affairs; represent Muslims in Britain; work for the common good; co-ordinate Muslim societies.

3.30 Medhi Hasan is an Oxford graduate famous for his political debating at Oxford University and on Al-Jazeera television.

3.31 There are many definitions of Islamophobia including prejudice or negative thoughts about Islam; a form of racism; a fear; or according to some an invalid concept.

3.32 Islamophobia might be experienced through an online message; by threatening gestures; by verbal abuse; in written down threats like hate mail; by an attack on a mosque or property; in discrimination such as in the world of work; in anti-Muslim literature; in objects being thrown; or in physical assault.

3.33 Juhel Miah, a teacher from South Wales, was removed from a plane going to the USA with a school trip.

3.34 Muslims who engage may be treated with suspicion and seen as suspicious, as if they must have a hidden agenda.

3.35 Pervez Sadia found that US television usually showed negative stories about Islam, and rarely showed positive stories.

3.36 Arabs and Muslims are often portrayed as backward, living in the desert, often violent men.

3.37 24-hour news can lead to people reacting without thinking and chain reactions spreading a story, such as Arab Spring, or negative information about Islam.

Theme 4 DEF

4.1 Twelvers and Ismailis.

4.2 Muhammad, Ali, Fatimah, Hasan and Hussein (i.e. the family of the Prophet).

4.3 The gathering at Ghadir Khumm.

4.4 Imam Hussein and his supporters were massacred when they refused to accept the rule of Caliph Yazid.

4.5 Tahir ul-Qadri taught that suicide is haram (forbidden) in all cases, including suicide in jihad in all circumstances, as Allah gives life and only Allah should decide when to take it away. Those committing suicide might find themselves unable to enter paradise.

4.6 The Ahl-al-Bayt are the scholars of the Shi'a, in the family line of the Prophet, who are distinguished by their insight into the meanings of the Qur'an and ability to make authoritative Islamic teachings.

4.7 Shi'a Imam Jafar al-Sadiq lists the five most holy places as: Makkah; Madinah; Imam Ali Mosque in Najaf, Iraq; the Imam Hussein shrine in Karbala; and the tomb of Fatimah in Qom, Iran.

4.8 A Qutb is a spiritual leader, such as the head of a Sufi order, and a Mureed is a follower who gives him allegiance.

4.9 The annual Fes conference is about sacred world music and symbolism, with the Conference of the Birds poem centre stage.

4.10 A Murshid is a spiritual guide who assists a Mureed in their spiritual development.

4.11 Hal is a temporary trance-like state Sufis reach in deep devotion usually during dhikr gatherings after building themselves up with chants and qasida songs.

4.12 A Sufi interested in alternative local traditions might visit Cadair Idris mountain as a centre of spiritual energy and Celtic mythology, the seat of giant Idris who is also thought of as an important Prophet in Islam. They might meditate on the universe and natural beauty and consider the Creator God.

4.13 In the Sama whirling dervish ritual, the hat represents the gravestone of the ego and the cloak the old life which is removed as a symbol of rebirth as part of the routine.

4.14 The victim's family may demand a qisas punishment, the like of the crime, or ask for a diyya payment in compensation.

4.15 Adultery with a married woman; becoming intoxicated; armed robbery (except for Shafi Fiqh); slander; apostasy of belief and against the community; rebellion (except for Hanafi Fiqh).

4.16 Tazir crimes are other minor crimes for which a Qazi judge has discretion over the punishment.

4.17 Reformists see the death penalty as against fundamental human rights and inappropriate for today's world. They think that the Qur'anic injunctions should be reinterpreted and not taken literally.

4.18 Shaykh Sharabasi argues the death penalty is a form of self-defence for society against criminals who take away people's safety.

4.19 Utilitarians regard what is most practical and effective as the right thing, so whatever creates most benefit for most people in society by creating peace and lawfulness is the best form of punishment. Revealed religious texts are not taken into consideration.

Glossary

Abbasid: family who ruled the Islamic Empire during the eighth and ninth centuries when the schools of thought were founded

Adhan: the call to prayer, recited out loud in Arabic before each of the five daily prayers

Adl: Divine justice – the concept that Allah is just and will carry out justice in balance over this life and the next

Age of maturity: the age at which the traditional requirements of Islam apply

Ahl al-Bayt: the descendants of the Prophets who form the Imams of the Shi'a

Ahl dariha: home, or household, or community

Akhirah: life after death

Alaq: Arabic word in the Qur'an meaning clot of blood; it can also be translated as embryo

Al-Azhar: Islamic University thought of as the highest source of authority in the world for Sunni Muslims

Alhamdulilah: literally, thanks be to Allah for anything referred to

Al-Imdaad: Islamic charity based in Blackburn

Allawi: a Shi'a Islamic sect largely in Syria and Turkey

Amal: application of religious knowledge

Ansar: people who became Muslim in Madinah

Anti-Semitism: prejudice against people of the Jewish faith

Apostasy: leaving a faith, seen by some as a crime

Aqidah: Islamic beliefs. There are various different versions of Aqidah according to Islamic sect

Aqiqah: Muslim naming ceremony for babies and converts to Islam

Aql: reasoning used particularly by Shi'a scholars in working out Islamic teachings where the Qur'an and hadith are unclear

Arba'een: pilgrimage to Imam Hussein's tomb at Karbala, 40 days after the Day of Ashura

Asbab al-nuzul: the circumstances in which a part of the Qur'an was revealed

Asr: prayer read in the afternoon once the shadows lengthen

Assimilation: acquiring the characteristics of mainstream society

Ayat: verse in the Qur'an

Banu Aus: a tribe of Madinah

Banu Khazraj: an opposing tribe of Madinah

Banu Nadir: a Jewish tribe exiled by Muhammad after breaching terms of an amnesty

Banu Qaynuqa: a Jewish tribe exiled by Muhammad after breaching terms of an amnesty

Banu Qurayza: a third Jewish tribe, also eventually exiled

Bar Mitzvah: Jewish rite of passage of commitment

Battle of Badr: a raid on trading caravans by Muhammad and the Muslims in 624

Bayah: Sufi ceremony of commitment

Bias: the idea that a person might be unfair or one sided, and reflect this in what they say

Bid'ah: an innovation or something new introduced into religion after the time of the Prophet. Some Muslims reject later practices, such as Sufism, as bid'ah

Bismillah: to begin any action in the name of Allah

Brewlvi: Islamic sect based in South Asia which agrees with the practice of visiting the tombs of Saints and remembering the names of Allah in worship

Bukhari: a collection of hadith named after the most famous collector Bukhari from Uzbekistan, who lived from 810 to 870

Burkini: woman's beach costume covering most of the body and hair

Caliph: ruler of the Islamic Empire, seen as both a spiritual and political leader

Caliphate: the Islamic Empire ruled by a Caliph

Charlie Hebdo: French satirical newspaper that published cartoons of Muhammad

Civil: relating to family life or society; personal matters rather than criminal

Confucianism: ancient Chinese philosophical and ethical teachings

Convert: someone who has changed religion

Daif: a weak hadith, thought of as unreliable because of questions about the chain of transmitters

Dajjal: the Antichrist, a one-eyed monster who will cause terrible suffering on earth before being defeated by the Mahdi and Isa

Dao: the way, as defined by early Chinese philosophy such as Confucianism

Dawah: Islamic mission to invite others to Islam or set a good example to portray Islam in a good light

Deobandi: South Asian Islamic sect which promotes strict adherence to orthodox Islam

Dhikr: also referred to as zikr, particular practices and services to remember Allah

Dhimmi: non-Muslim believer living in Muslim lands

Diyya: a monetary payment of compensation in place of the death penalty

Dua: personal prayer

Extended family: grandparents, parents, children, uncles, aunts, cousins and wider relatives

Fa: true ethical law in Confucianism

Fana: losing one's ego to focus instead on Allah

Fatwa: the opinion of an Islamic scholar on a matter, binding only on themselves and those who pledge allegiance

Feminism: to advocate women's rights based on equality of men and women

Fiqh: interpretation or deeper understanding of Islamic Law

Forced marriage: where a person is married without consent, illegal in UK as well as Islamic Law

Furu al-din: the practices followed by Shi'a Muslims to enact the Usul al-din

Ghusul: ritual purification of the whole body, carried out usually weekly before Friday prayers and when needed

Greater jihad: the inner or inward personal struggle of a Muslim to live the Islamic life

Hadith qudsi: sayings of Muhammad that are thought to have been directly inspired by Allah

Hadith: a saying of the Prophet Muhammad

Hajj: pilgrimage to Makkah, one of the five pillars of Islam

Hal: a deep state of spiritual consciousness in which a Sufi loses control and awareness of their surroundings and takes on a trance-like meditative state

Halal: approved action in Islam, also Halal meat approved for Muslims because it is blessed with the name of Allah

Han Kitab: texts written by Liu Zhi about Islam and Confucianism

Hanbali: Sunni Islamic school of thought originating from the scholar Ahmad ibn Hanbal, 780–855

Hanifi: Sunni Islamic school of thought originating from the scholar Abu Hanifa, 702–772

Haqiqa: experience of the reality of truth

Haram: a forbidden action

Hasan: hadith which have been collected and are thought of as good with the exception of one or two minor questions about their authenticity

Hawza: special schools attended by Shi'a mujtahids

Hayy Ibn Yaqzan: story about a boy called Hayy who grew up amongst the animals and nature on an island without any other people around. Hayy worked out by looking at the natural world that there was a creator

Heretic: a person defined as holding views outside what is acceptable in a religion

Hijab: humility, or a head or face veil for women

Hijrah: the journey from Makkah to Madinah by Muhammad and the Muslims in the year 622. The Muslim calendar is called the hijri calendar because it begins from this date

Historical critical: modern methods of understanding sources by analysing context, bias and cross referencing

Hizb ut-Tahrir: Islamic political group which promotes the idea of forming a worldwide Caliphate to replace modern Muslim countries

Hudaybiyyah: treaty signed by Muhammad and the Quraysh guaranteeing a period of peace

Hudud: crimes against God's commands punished as defined in shari'a

Ibadat Khana: house to debate religion in Akbar's capital, Fatehpur Sikri

Ibadi: an Islamic school of thought which is neither Shi'a nor Sunni but has elements of both

Iblis: not a person but referred to sometimes as a fallen angel or jinn. Iblis refused to follow Allah's command to bow down to Adam because of his arrogance. He tempts people in the world to reject Allah's command and follow their own desires. Also referred to as shaytan or Satan

Iftaar: meal to open the fast at the end of the day in Ramadan

Ihsan: realisation of faith in the heart

Ijma: agreeing a teaching by consensus of scholars or even the whole community

Ijtihad: forming a personal opinion

Ilm: knowledge in Islam about the religion and the sacred

Imaan: literally means faith in Islam; a group which supports gay, lesbian bisexual and transgender Muslims

Imamah: belief in the succession of the Prophet's family as leaders of the Shi'a

iMuslims: Internet and ICT use by Muslims which has affected the way they find out about and develop their faith

Isa: the Arabic word for Jesus, who is regarded as a Prophet in Islam

Isha: the night time prayer

Islamophobia: fear of Islam and Muslims, sometimes manifested through negative comments or even verbal or physical attack

Ismaili: Shi'a Islamic school of thought originating from the scholar Al-Qadi al-Nu'man d.974

Isnad: the chain of transmitters, who passed on the hadith to who, all the way from the first person to hear Muhammad until the time the hadith was written down

Jafari: Shi'a Islamic school of thought originating from Imam Jafar al-Sadiq, c700–765

Jahiliyyah: state of ignorance according to Muslims which pre-dated the coming of Prophet Muhammad

Jain: ancient Indian religion, similar to Buddhism

Jamiat Islami: a Sufi tariqa

Janazzah: funeral prayers in Islam

Jiao: teachings in Chinese philosophy

Jihad: striving and struggle in favour of the way of Allah according to Muslims, which can take various different forms

Jizya: a tax on non-Muslims living in the Islamic Caliphate

Jummah prayers: Friday early afternoon congregational prayers

Ka'aba: the black cube in Makkah, a central point in which is the focus of Hajj and prayer

Khalifah: the Islamic movement followed by a minority of Muslims who want to recreate the Islamic Empire under a Caliph in the modern world

Khums: 20% tax paid to the Imams to distribute to the needy

Kuffar: sometimes interpreted as non-believers or people who had rejected belief

La Convivencia: a period of coexistence between Muslims, Christians and Jews during which culture flourished and many academic works were translated, leading to the European Renaissance

Lesser jihad: the outward struggle for Islamic life that may be done without violence or through war

Liberal: open-minded views

Ma'rifa: mystical experience of God

Madhab: the name for a school of Islamic Law

Maghrib: prayer read after the sun sets

Mahdi: a saviour type figure who will appear on earth at the time of the second coming of Isa to defeat evil and reunite people in a reign of justice and peace

Mahr: a payment from the groom to the bride to seal the contract of marriage

Majlis: parliament in Iran or gathering of Muslims

Makruh: an action that is disapproved of but which is, nevertheless, permitted

Maliki: Sunni Islamic school of thought originating from the scholar Malik ibn Anas, 711–795

Maqam: deeper realisation developed by Sufis by following ritual

Matn: the body of text within a hadith

Mawakibs: stalls for pilgrims providing free food and services along the road to Karbala

Metaphysical: abstract thought about the principles of being

Mi'ad: belief in the Day of Judgement and Resurrection in the afterlife

Mihna: the Islamic inquisition when the Caliph or ruler decided to tell the Muslims what they should believe and set up trials and punishments for those who refused to agree with him

Milaud an Nabi: a celebration of the Prophet's birthday, regarded as an essential act by Brewlvi Muslims but forbidden by Salafis

Monarch: King or Queen who is head of state

Mubah: an everyday action not covered by shari'a, therefore neither approved nor disapproved (also referred to as halal)

Muezzin: Muslim who gives out the call to prayer

Mufti: Islamic teacher who may make interpretations of shari'a

Mughal: dynasty who ruled most of South Asia in the early modern period

Muhajirun: Arabic word for emigrants

Mujahedeen: the plural of Mujahid. Muslims who take part in jihad

Mujahid: a Muslim who takes part in jihad

Mujtahid: an Islamic scholar considered qualified to make authoritative teachings

Multiculturalism: the idea that different cultures should co-exist in the same society

Muraqaba: Sufi meditation, of which several stages have been defined

Mureed: person who gives bayah, an oath of loyalty, to join a Sufi order

Murshid: a Sufi Shaykh who guides a Mureed

Muslim Brotherhood: a group founded in Egypt in the nineteenth century in opposition to British colonial rule

Mustahab: a recommended action

Muta: temporary marriage

Mutazilah: Islamic belief that God is totally separate from creation, so did not make the Qur'an

Nafs: the soul or inner self; the soul is in our deepest thoughts and lives beyond death

Nikkah: Islamic marriage contract

Niqab: a full veil for women, also covering their face except for a slit for their eyes

Nubuwwah: belief in Prophets

Nuclear family: parents and children as a small family unit

Ottoman: rulers of Turkey, Saudi Arabia and much of the Middle East from the sixteenth to the nineteenth centuries

Pacifism: the idea that violence should never be used, not even in self-defence. Protest and other non-violent means can be used in struggle

Pluralism: different ideas and communities living alongside each other

Prophethood: the idea that some people are given a special role as messengers of God

Psalms: holy book revealed to Prophet Dawud/ David

Qadr: fate. The idea in Islam that Allah controls all actions and decides a person's journey through life. Muslims sometimes refer to whatever is written for them, meaning whatever God has decided for their life

Qasidas: Sufi songs

Qat: opinions over which the Imams were certain

Qazi: Islamic judge (sometimes spelled Qadi)

Qisas: crimes against individuals punishable at the request of the victim or their family

Qiyas: comparison to a similar situation to arrive at a teaching

Quilliam: a nineteenth-century Muslim convert; also the name of a counter-extremism foundation

Qur'an al-Tadwini: the revealed Qur'an, the book

Qur'an al-Takwini: the Qur'an as seen in the natural world

Qur'anism: to follow the teachings of the Qur'an but reject the hadith as a source of authority

Quraysh: tribal leaders in Makkah; for years they were opponents of Muhammad

Qutb: spiritual, infallible Sufi leader

Rakat: unit of standing, bowing and prostrating during Islamic prayer

Revert: often used when referring to Islamic converts as people who have returned to their natural state of being, i.e. Muslim

Riba: monetary interest paid in addition to repaying a loan

Risalah: belief in Prophets or messengers from Allah, some of whom bring a holy book

Sabians: another religious group associated with worship of the stars

Sahaba: those who lived around Muhammad and witnessed his actions

Sahih: the best and most reliable hadith, which have been collected with a reliable chain of transmitters

Sajdah: position in prayer when a Muslim places their forehead on the ground

Salafism: belief that Muslims should go back to the literal practices of the companions of Muhammad independently of the schools of thought and the interpretations of their scholars

Salah: five prayers a day, read at three times by Shi'a Muslims

Sama: Sufi whirling dervish ritual

Sanskrit: ancient Indian language in which many Hindu texts are written

Sawm: fasting in Ramadan

Sect: religious sub-group within a religion

Sectarian: concerning division between sects or religious groups

Secular: not religious, without reference to religion or God

Secularism: that society should be organised and government run without reference to religion

Segregation: setting a group apart from others

Shafi'i: Sunni Islamic school of thought originating from the scholar Al-Shafi, 767–820

Shahadah: statement of faith for Muslims

Shahid: a martyr in Islam. Muslims who have been killed in battle are commonly referred to as a Shahid or martyr

Shakk: teachings over which the Imams had doubt

Shalwar kemise: South Asian traditional dress for Muslims, consisting of two loose fitting cotton clothes

Shari'a: literally, the straight path; known as Islamic system of law

Shaykh: Head of a Sufi order or simply respected person

Sheng: sages or holy people who help Confucianists experience deeper mysticism

Shirk: associating another besides Allah in worship

Shura: consultation with the people

Sira: an account of the life of a Prophet

Sufi: someone who follows an inward, spiritual version of Islam

Sunna: the actions of the Prophet Muhammad, an example for Muslims

Tablighi Jamaat: Islamic missionary group promoting an austere version of orthodox Islam

Tafsir: an interpretation and guide to the Qur'an

Takfir: a Muslim declared a non-believer because of following deviant traditions or doctrines

Tanzimat: nineteenth-century reforms of the Ottoman Empire

Taqiyya: concealing belief

Taqlid: imitation, to follow another Muslim teacher's opinions

Taqwa: God consciousness; it is regarded as essential for people to have God in mind to be able to apply shari'a

Tariqa: the way of Sufi orders

Tasbih: prayer beads used as an aid in dhikr and meditation

Tauheedul: a successful group of academy schools sponsored by a Muslim foundation

Tawhid: belief in the Oneness of Allah

Tazir: unspecified lesser crimes which may be sentenced at the discretion of a Qazi

Thobe: a single white long dress worn by men in Arabia

Tian: heaven, or the one high God, nature, awe, or the way of things; a form of pantheism

Twelvers: the main branch of Shi'a Islam based on the belief of a succession of twelve Imams after the Prophet

Ulema: Islamic scholars

Ummah: originally, the Madinah community of Muslims and others; this terms has evolved to mean the worldwide brotherhood of Muslims

Usul al-din: sometimes called the Pillars of Shi'a Islam or beliefs on which the main Shi'a practices are based

Utilitarianism: practical decision making to benefit the most number of people, justifying decisions according to what works best

Vihara: Buddhist temple

Vizier: Prime Minister to the Caliph

Wahm: reasoning which had errors in it

Wahy: revelation, also inspiration to Prophets

Wajib: a compulsory action in shari'a

Walayah: Ismaili expression of love and devotion to God, the missionaries, the Imams and the Prophets

Wali: a saint in Islam

Wird Latif: devotional prayer of a Sufi Mureed

Xenophobia: extreme prejudice against another who is perceived as different

Zaidiyyah: Shi'a Islamic school of thought originating from Zayd ibn Ali, 695–740

Zakat: one of the five pillars of Islam; 2.5% tax on profit and various other calculated amounts of wealth to be given to those in need

Zann: opinions considered true through reasoning

Zikr: worship by remembering the names of Allah in Sufism

Ziyarah: pilgrimage to a tomb of a holy person

Zuhd: asceticism in Islam – to live apart from the world to meditate upon God

Zuhr: prayer read just after mid-day

Index